# POMPEY

# POMPEY
## THE REPUBLICAN PRINCE

### PETER GREENHALGH

WEIDENFELD AND NICOLSON
LONDON

First published in Great Britain by
George Weidenfeld and Nicolson Limited
91 Clapham High Street
London SW4 7TA

ISBN 0 297 77881 1

Printed in Great Britain by
Butler & Tanner Ltd, Frome and London

*To the memory of Sir Frank Adcock*

How great those men whose fortunes through the world
Shone forth, whose fates all heaven observed!
To future years and peoples yet unborn
Their story will come down through fame alone –
Or what my work can profit their great names –
And when their wars are read, all will be moved
With hope and fear and prayers, though far too late,
Spellbound, as if these things were still to come,
Not past; and all will still take Pompey's side.

LUCAN, Pharsalia, 7.205–13

# CONTENTS

# LIST OF MAPS AND ILLUSTRATIONS

MAPS

ILLUSTRATIONS (*between pages 160 and 161*)

# PREFACE

*I have written and compiled a narrative which is worth
the attention of those who wish to observe the measureless
ambition of men, their terrible lust for power, their
unwearying perseverance and the forms of countless ills ...*
Appian, *The Civil Wars*, 1.6

The first volume of *Pompey* ended with the assertion of his political will
through the 'Three-headed Monster', which was Varro's name for Pompey's partnership with Marcus Crassus and Julius Caesar in 59 BC. In
62 he had returned from his great feat of empire-building in the East with
the reputation of a Roman Alexander, the wealth of nations, and a praiseworthy determination to lay the ghost of Sulla's pupil. By disbanding
his army as soon as he landed in Italy he had dispelled all fears that he
might establish a military dictatorship; and when he celebrated the most
magnificent triumph Rome had ever seen in the following September, it
was not as master but as first servant of the Republic. But a Roman Alexander was not easily accommodated by less equal peers and rivals in the
Republic's jealous aristocracy. When Pompey tried to marry into the senatorial establishment by offering himself and his elder son for the nieces
of Marcus Cato, he was rejected. When he pressed for grants of land
for his demobilized veterans and for the ratification of his eastern settlements, he was constantly thwarted by Cato's faction in a Senate largely
motivated by a mixture of personal vendetta, a desire to cut any great
man down to size, and an understandable fear of the immense local and
international patronage which Pompey would enjoy from a devoted army
settled on farms within calling distance of Rome and from a network of
Oriental rulers and republics whose obligations were more to the general
than to the state. He spent a fortune preparing what should have been
a foolproof political strategy for the beginning of 60, but when he was
outmanœuvred yet again, he appeared to acquiesce in the frustration of
his plans.

If men like Cicero had not been so blinded by an exaggerated sense
of their own importance, they might have guessed that the conqueror
of the three parts of the inhabited world was not really a spent force
on the political battlefields of Rome, but they allowed themselves to
be dangerously deceived by appearances. The *éminence grise* was busy

creating a new political coalition which would overwhelm all opposition in the following year: he buried the hatchet with his old rival Marcus Crassus and backed a promising new protégé, Julius Caesar, for the consulship of 59. A lingering hope of winning the Senate's approval was reflected in the mild and unexceptionable nature of the Land Bill which Caesar published to provide for Pompey's veterans, but when Cato still succeeded in opposing it in the House, Caesar was ready to legislate directly through the people. The 'Three-headed Monster' was first revealed to a horrified opposition when Pompey and Crassus appeared at Caesar's side to proclaim their support for the plebiscite: it was a formidable combination of prestige, resources and demagogy, and with backing from the votes and fists of Pompey's veterans and a subtle appeal to the equestrian tax-farming interests, it was unbeatable. The opposition tribunes who had promised to veto the Bill collapsed. Caesar's fellow-consul Bibulus, Cato's son-in-law, tried to suspend all public business by declaring that he was watching the heavens for omens, but this transparent manipulation of religion to party-political ends could not frustrate the popular will, and the Bill became law amid the extraordinary scenes described in the last chapter of *The Roman Alexander*.

Having been rejected by the senatorial establishment and forced to turn their flank by a wholly democratic route, Pompey had no further hesitation about abandoning compromise and getting exactly what he wanted. While Bibulus doggedly maintained his scrutiny of the heavens, further plebiscites not only ratified Pompey's arrangements in the East *en bloc* but included the public land of Campania in the distribution to his veteran soldiers. Ironically this politically sensitive area had been the target of legislation proposed by Crassus' protégé, the tribune Rullus, in 63 when Pompey had been in the East and Cicero had condemned it as being against his interest. Now it was in the gift of Pompey with Crassus' blessing, and as his veterans flocked southwards to receive their new farms, the evicted tenants made ideal recruits for the army which Caesar was preparing to take to Gaul as proconsul the following year. For Pompey was delighted to promote the military as well as the political career of this most effective of his protégés. Indeed he regarded Caesar in much the same light as he himself had been regarded by Sulla in the civil wars of his youth, and with the typically Roman desire to keep a good piece of business in the family, he sealed their political partnership by marrying Caesar's daughter, Julia. For the delighted Caesar it meant a lasting claim on the support of Rome's greatest citizen whose conquests and wealth he so admired and longed to imitate. For Pompey it meant a charming young wife, the securing of a high-yielding political investment, and the prospect of some Gallic conquests which would be a familial extension of his own power of patronage. Patron and protégé were in perfect accord.

But if the Three-headed Monster had been an unstoppable political vehicle and a necessary one, it had been a rough ride, and Pompey had not enjoyed the whole of 59 by any means. He was always reluctant to get his triumphal toga sullied by the mud-slinging of popular politics. Whereas he loved to lead his troops from the front on the battlefields of Empire, he preferred to fight his political battles by remote control, and he would have been happier still if he could have won the Senate's acceptance of his proposals and avoided an ideological confrontation. He had not enjoyed his unaccustomed unpopularity in the summer when democratic enthusiasm had waned, his own veterans had disappeared to claim their farms, and the evicted tenants had flocked to Rome to reinforce a popular reaction against the 'proud kings'. There had been demonstrations against Pompey in the theatres, and there had been conspiracies against his life. But a year is a long time in politics, and by the end of 59 his popularity had been restored and his enemies further discomfited by the skilful manipulation of a professional informer named Vettius, who had exposed a real or pretended assassination plot. It was of course tiresome of Bibulus to have maintained his star-gazing opposition to all the Monster's legislation in 59 and there would doubtless be attempts to have it annulled on this pretext in the following year when Caesar would be out of office, but this had been provided for. Both the consuls-elect for 58 were the Monster's friends. One was Aulus Gabinius, the tribune of 67 who had proposed Pompey's commission against the pirates and had since served with Pompey in the East. The other, Pico, was a member of the family, since Caesar had married his daughter. And there was also the tribune Clodius, the debauched demagogue who had special obligations to Crassus and hated Cicero as well as the Monster's main opponents. With these impressive political watch-dogs to guard his interest Pompey felt pleasantly free of the necessity to do any public biting or even barking himself, and he resumed the posture of magnificent aloofness which he considered appropriate to a Roman Alexander who was prince of citizens in an aristocratic Republic.

In my preface to the first volume of *Pompey* I gratefully acknowledged the help of many people in making this book. I thank them all again, and I add special thanks to my friends Edward and Ilias Iliopoulos who gave me invaluable assistance in my expedition to the battlefield of Pharsalus.

*Athens, December 1979*                                          P.A.L.G.

# 1

# CLODIUS, CICERO AND CORN

Gnaeus Pompeius, a man who never has had, has not now,
and never will have a rival in courage, wisdom and renown,
has given to me, as one private friend to another, what he has
always given to the state as a whole – safety,
security and dignity.
Cicero, *Speech to the Roman People after his Return
from Exile*, 16

As the year 59 drew to a close and the new magistrates of 58 prepared
to enter office, Pompey watched the testing of his political nexus with
interest rather than anxiety. As usual the tribunes had nearly three weeks'
start over the magistrates proper whose year began on 1 January, and
though by no means all ten of the new tribunes entering office on 10
December were Pompey's adherents and one or two were frankly hostile,
the energetic Clodius made such a flying start that he left the rest of them
standing bemused. It was no ordinary tribune who was ready to promul-
gate four provocative Bills on his first day; and when the consuls handed
over to their successors at the end of the month, he was ready with his
veto to stop the outgoing Bibulus from giving his report on his year in
office. It was no secret that Bibulus had prepared some less than flattering
remarks about the domineering colleague who had turned what should
have been the pinnacle of his career into a year that men joked about
as the consulship of 'Julius and Caesar'. Everyone was waiting to hear
him reiterate that all Caesar's legislation was invalid because it had been
enacted while he was watching the heavens, and if he had been allowed
to have his say, it would have been a dangerous confession of the
Monster's vulnerability at a critical time. For while it was true that both
new consuls and the most energetic of the new tribunes were adherents
and beneficiaries of the Pompeian coalition, the new praetors were much
less tractable, and two in particular were sufficiently undismayed
to spearhead the opposition on entering office on 1 January 58.

One of these was the same Domitius who had featured on the revised

list of conspirators denounced by the informer Vettius for supposedly plotting to assassinate Pompey in 59. The name of the other was Memmius,
and Suetonius tells us that these two collaborated 'to try to move an inquiry into the conduct of Caesar as consul'. According to Cicero and
the notes of ancient commentators, they asserted Bibulus' indefatigable
sky-watching as grounds for declaring the whole of Caesar's legislation
invalid, and their attack as sufficiently serious for Caesar to defend himself in three speeches delivered before the Senate on the first three days of
the new year. Only then, when these days of what Suetonius describes
as 'futile wrangling' had left the Senate in an apparently satisfactory state
of internal disagreement, did Caesar leave Rome and take personal command of the army that was waiting to be led to his Gallic provinces. Even
so he had no sooner left the city than charges were laid against the quaestor whom he had left behind to make some final arrangements, and not
long afterwards he was himself impeached by an enemy tribune named
Antistius. And this was an indirect attack on the validity of Caesar's governorship and the underlying legislation, for a proconsul's *imperium* conferred immunity from prosecution. Caesar responded by appealing to the
whole college of tribunes for confirmation that he might not be prosecuted
'when absent on the public service', but though this counter-move was
successful and the impeachment was dropped, it is significant that he did
not immediately march north to his provinces. For the time being his
army was more useful in Italy, and barring any sudden emergencies in his
provinces he intended to keep it there until those who had been chosen
to secure the interests embodied in the legislation of 59 had been given
the chance to demonstrate their loyalty and effectiveness.

Pompey had been well aware of the need to protect himself and his
father-in-law from attempts to rescind the legislation of 59, but he was
as reluctant as ever to take an active part in popular politics. The situation
required a replacement demagogue who was backed by the legislative
and physical power of supporters in the city, for once Caesar's army had
left for Gaul and Pompey's veterans were settled on their new farms they
could be called on only in an emergency. The answer was Clodius, 'this
man of high nobility' whom Velleius describes as 'eloquent and reckless,
recognizing no limits either in speech or action save his own will, energetic
in the execution of his evil schemes, notorious as the debaucher of his own
sister, and accused of defiling the most sacred rites of the Roman People'.

Instead of relying on temporary popularity from would-be farmers
among the urban poor, Clodius had decided to direct his appeal to that
large section of the proletariat whose aspirations went little higher than
bread and circuses, whose existence was irreversibly urbanized, and
whose reaction to the offer of a small-holding in the country would have

been one of horror when there was so much more fun to be had in the imperial city. His programme was designed to urbanize and organize political violence to a degree of specialization never before conceived by even the most extreme of demagogues. His first Bills were measures to abolish the fixed payment for the public distribution of corn and to legal-ize the re-formation of the political clubs and guilds which had been sup-pressed by senatorial decree in 64 'because they were considered to be against the public interest'. According to Cicero the institution of a com-pletely free corn-dole cost the state some seventy million sesterces a year, or one fifth of the total annual income, but what was that to Clodius and the urban poor? As for the legalization of clubs and guilds, these were organizations of free-born citizens, freedmen and slaves of varying degrees of disrespectability and generally much given to riotous excess. They provided a network for political manipulation that was virtually ready-made, and as the senatorial decree of 64 had done little more than drive them underground, their re-emergence was so rapid that they were ready and able to celebrate it on 1 January under the presidency of Clo-dius' henchman Sextus Cloelius, master of one of the more disreputable guilds and reviver of the violent Compitalician Games which had been their annual New Year event.

After he had proposed these Bills which no one dared oppose, Clodius ensured that he would be able to carry future legislation through the ple-beian assembly without the threat of star-gazing opposition by proposing a third Bill prohibiting that particular ritual on days set aside for the trans-action of public business. In future, if the gods disapproved of anything, they must make some effort to show their disapproval by the odd thunder-bolt or some other unmistakable omen, or a magistrate must lie about their having done so at the appropriate time: it would no longer be enough for him to say that he was watching the skies just in case the gods were to send a sign. The Bill was not retrospective in its application, but its passage into law provided another stick with which to beat down the two troublesome praetors and others who were still claiming that a whole year's popular legislation had been invalidated by what was patently a gross abuse of religious practice.

With the benefit of hindsight we can see the year 58 as marking a new chapter in the increasingly bloody history of the degeneration of Roman politics into organized hooliganism and the ultimate anarchy which would make Pompey what he had always longed to be, the champion of the senatorial establishment; and since this would involve him in civil war with Caesar, it is tempting to see Clodius even now as the protégé of a Caesar who did not trust his son-in-law to look after his interests while he was away in Gaul. But there is nothing to suggest that Pompey and Caesar had any conflict of interest or mutual suspicion at this time. They had joined in sponsoring Clodius for the tribunate because the preservation of the legislation of 59 was to their mutual benefit, because Clodius had the demagogic ability to defend it in the rough-and-tumble of the Forum, and because Cicero had to be kept quiet. Their mistake was in supposing that Clodius would remain tied to their apron-strings once he had accumulated sufficient political capital of his own to give him an independence that came quicker than either they or he could have foreseen. But for the time being they watched with high satisfaction as he manipulated his tribunician powers to the discomfiture of their opponents; and when Clodius proceeded to turn his political machine against Cicero, Pompey averted his eyes with more embarrassment than regret as the man to whom he had so often promised his protection was now driven into exile by that implacable but useful foe.

This does not imply that Pompey's promises of protection had been one long exercise in duplicity. When Clodius had been seeking support for the tribunician elections he had been in no position to demand terms from Pompey or Caesar, and while he had no doubt always hoped to be able to ruin Cicero in 58 in revenge for the latter's attempt to secure his conviction in the sacrilege trial of 61, it is extremely unlikely that there was a tacit agreement to this effect between Clodius and his sponsors or that Dio is right in making revenge the sole spring of Clodius' ambition. If Cicero had taken any of the opportunities offered to show active support for the Pompeian interest, Pompey might have carried out his promise, and Clodius would have had to accept it. If the attempt of Domitius and Memmius to undo Caesar's legislation had been countered by a powerful speech from Cicero, it would not have been too late to cement Pompey's obligation to protect him. As it was, he said nothing. By his own account Domitius and Memmius were his friends, and at least one ancient commentator attributed his disaster to a silence that Pompey found far from golden. Nor was it a redeeming feature in Pompey's eyes that Cicero refrained from actively opposing the counter-measures of Clodius, against whose proposals he had initially intended to deploy not only his own oratorical powers but the far more effective veto of a friendly tribune named Ninnius. What caused him to hold back, says Dio, was not a concern for the Pompeian interest but a false promise by Clodius not to take any action against him if he would not oppose the Bills. Too late he learnt that a *quid pro quo* with Clodius meant giving something for nothing, and as soon as the Clodian proposals about corn and clubs had safely passed beyond the threat of veto, their jubilant author felt no scruples whatever about breaking a bargain he had never meant to keep.

It was 4 January when Clodius' first batch of Bills became law by vote of the plebeian assembly, but scarcely a month elapsed before he was promulgating some more, among which was one pronouncing the sentence of exile for anyone guilty of having put to death a Roman citizen uncondemned by the Roman people. Moreover this Bill was to operate retrospectively, and while it named no names and could in a sense be seen as a wholesale condemnation of all the senators who had voted for the execution of the Catilinarian conspirators of 63, it was clearly aimed at Cicero, the consul who had been ultimately responsible. That worthy was now literally terrified out of his toga. Doing everything he could think of to try to arouse sympathy and support he dressed as a knight to dramatize his appeal to the clans whose business interests he had always championed, but though large numbers of equestrians attended a public meeting and sent a deputation to lobby the Senate on Cicero's behalf, Dio tells us that the consuls not only refused them access to the House but formally reprimanded the senators Hortensius and Curio who had accompanied them. The tribune Ninnius then urged all Cicero's friends to demonstrate their support by putting on mourning as for a public calamity, but the consuls forbade this too. Only Cicero himself could not be prevented from changing his clothes yet again, and when Clodius saw him drooping about the streets in deepest mourning he made sure that he had something to weep about by organizing mobs to jeer him at every turn and cover him with filth. Appian says that Cicero even covered himself with filth and made a thorough nuisance of himself by approaching perfect strangers in the streets and reciting his tale of woes at antagonizing length. But these histrionic attempts to arouse public sympathy were as unavailing as the more hopeful approaches which he made to the man who really mattered.

When distinguished friends like Marcus Lucullus went to see Pompey to make representations on Cicero's behalf, they were politely received and just as politely referred to the consuls. Representations to Crassus had the same result, which was all very correct but not at all helpful when the consuls were clearly unsympathetic for a very good reason. Simultaneously with the Bill against Cicero Clodius had promulgated another proposing to bestow the attractive governorships of Syria and Macedonia on Gabinius and Piso when their consulships were over; and if Pompey now promised to take whatever action might be required to save Cicero on condition that the consuls gave him their official sanction, he could appear handsome in his promises without the slightest danger of having to carry them out. Sympathy and advice were plentiful, cheap, and useless. Against the opposition of both consuls and the most popular and powerful of the tribunes no one could do anything for Cicero save by illegal force, and no one cared that much about Cicero except Cicero himself. He may have been unrealistic enough to consider a resort to arms, as Dio says he did, but when he later claimed credit for deciding to go peacefully he was merely making a virtue of inability. His choice was a simple one: to go voluntarily, or to wait to be told to go. His friends, true and false, gave conflicting advice, and when he decided to spare himself the final humiliation, he left Clodius free to carry the Exile Bill unopposed, destroy his house, and prolong the sweetness of revenge by promulgating a second Bill condemning him by name.

While our sources are in basic agreement on these facts, there is some difference of opinion on the role of Pompey and Caesar in the affair. According to Dio they not only failed to prevent Clodius' revenge on Cicero but actually initiated it. It was their idea that Clodius should neutralize Cicero's planned opposition to his first batch of Bills by making a bargain which he had no intention of honouring, and when the bargain had served its purpose they gave different advice to Cicero in order not to appear to have instigated Clodius themselves. Caesar urged him to yield and accept a safe post on his military staff. Pompey told him that Caesar had advised him badly because of secret enmity towards him. Pompey's own advice was to stay and stand his ground against a tribune 'who would be helpless as long as Cicero was present', and when he reinforced this appeal to Cicero's vanity with assurances of his own assistance, the orator no longer hesitated to attach himself to the great man 'of whom he had no suspicions, for Pompey was widely respected and honoured for having saved numerous men from dire perils at the hands of judges and accusers'. At an assembly convened outside the city-walls Caesar declared somewhat ambivalently that he was against retrospective legislation although he was also against the illegality of the executions which Cicero had authorized, as indeed he had made clear at the time. Crassus was similarly unhelpful, 'showing some favour to Cicero through his son but nevertheless taking the side of the people himself'. And Pompey proved remarkably inaccessible. He kept reiterating his assurances, but somehow his affairs at that time seemed to require so many journeys out of town that he was never there when he was needed, and it gradually became clear even to Cicero that he never would be. It was the last straw. From pleading with Pompey Cicero began to abuse him openly, toyed with the idea of a resort to arms, and rapidly despaired to the point where he fled Rome before Clodius' Bill could come to the inevitable vote.

Dio's version of events may be little more than a personal interpretation based on the premise that Pompey and Caesar were able to control their protégés. On the other hand there were contemporaries who made the same allegations, and one was Piso himself when Cicero attacked him in the courts three years later and tried to have him condemned for misgovernment in his ill-gotten province of Macedonia. Unfortunately Piso's speech is not recorded, but Cicero's leaves no doubt that Piso had taunted him with convenient selectivity in blaming the consuls of 58 for his exile while ignoring 'the most influential men who really deserved his resentment'. 'We all know who you mean,' replied Cicero, facing the insinuation squarely.

But let me tell you that Gnaeus Pompeius, in spite of the efforts of so many people to place obstacles in the way of his devoted affection for me, has always held me in the highest esteem, always judged me most worthy of his intimacy, always desired that I should not only be safe but also most distinguished and properly recognized. Yours were the falsehoods, yours the wickedness, yours the evilly fabricated allegations of my treacherous plots against his life, yours the desire for provinces – with you in fact rests all the blame for my being shut out from Pompey's presence and debarred from all intercourse with him even through the mediation of all those who cherished my welfare, his glory and the security of the state. This was what prevented his having the courage of his convictions, since certain persons who could not alienate him from me had nevertheless succeeded in retarding his desire to be of service to me.

And Cicero went on to tell how various distinguished senators had called on Pompey and had been referred by him to the consuls, 'for Pompey was unwilling to oppose an armed tribune of the people unless backed by a public resolution, though he said he was ready to take up arms if the consuls would act upon a decree of the Senate and defend the constitution'. But does such a vigorous public denial of Piso's insinuations by a Cicero then deeply obliged to Pompey for restoring him from exile undermine or confirm them?

The same question must be asked of all the other post-restoration speeches in which the orator took such great pains to exonerate Pompey and his two principal political allies from any responsibility for his exile. Clodius, he maintained, had only pretended to have the approval of Pompey, Caesar and Crassus for the Bill of Exile, and the reason why these three had let this claim go unchallenged was not that they were anything but well disposed to Cicero in their hearts but that they were forced to keep silent 'because all their measures of the previous year were being undermined by the praetors and they were therefore unwilling to alienate the popular tribune who was defending them'. And Cicero constantly reinforces his justification of Pompey's failure to save him by referring to the circulation of rumours that Cicero was conspiring against Pompey's life. But all this smacks of the special pleading which came all too easily to a legal mind. If Cicero had really enjoyed Pompey's confidence, Pompey would hardly have believed such rumours, and the only convincing excuse for inactivity by a genuinely well-disposed Pompey is that 'his own worries touched him more closely than mine'. For while there need be no doubt that Pompey referred Cicero's friends to the consuls to authorize his promised intervention, there is equally no doubt that Pompey knew that the consuls would not do so, and this remains true whether Pompey had control of the consuls or, as Cicero maintained, an independent Clodius had 'bought' them by promising to secure them attractive provincial governorships without reference to Pompey.

It is not then in Cicero's public utterances after his restoration that any flaw can be found in Dio's reconstruction of Pompey's role as *éminence grise* behind the moves to exile the orator whom he had promised to defend. The only writings of Cicero that are likely to reveal his true beliefs are the more private of his private letters, and there are one or two of these which do suggest that he genuinely believed Pompey's sin to be one of omission rather than commission. In a letter which he wrote to his brother in August 58 he gave as his reasons for his flight into exile 'the sudden defection of Pompey, the estrangement of the consuls and praetors, the timidity of the tax-farmers, and the armed gangs of Clodius'. If that represents his real view, he believed that Pompey had not instigated his exile but had abandoned him for reasons unspecified. And the same belief finds expression in a letter which Cicero wrote to Atticus nearly nine years later when he was debating whether or not to go with Pompey if Pompey decided to leave Italy in the Civil War of 49. The very fact that this letter is so scathing of Pompey gives unusual credibility to a word of faint praise, and when it catalogues among many criticisms of a man 'who has not an iota of sense or courage' the fact that 'he was more active in effecting my restoration than preventing my banishment', the likelihood is that Cicero did not believe that Pompey had engineered his exile. Of course it remains possible that Cicero himself never knew the truth, but the fact that Clodius began to turn against Pompey soon after Cicero's exile suggests that Dio's interpretation is wrong, that Pompey was, as Plutarch says, 'neglectful of what was going on in the Forum', and that he saw no reason to exert himself on behalf of a man who had ignored every opportunity to display a firm commitment to his interests. Embarrassment counted little under the law of political expediency which governed Pompey's 'defection'. Moreover exile was not irrevocable, and when Pompey passed by on the other side it may well have crossed his mind that a future restoration would put the chastened orator under a deeper obligation to him than the mere prevention of a fate whose miseries were more keenly appreciated by those who experienced them.

With Cicero out of the way early in March, Marcus Cato became the next target of Clodius' legislation, and as the only obligation felt by Pompey to Cato was to avenge himself for the insult of a rejected marriage alliance in 62 and for persistent political opposition ever since, it would not be surprising if Clodius' Bill to get rid of him had more than merely the blessing of Pompey and his allies. Nor was there any ground on which Cato himself could object, for Clodius was proposing to 'exile' him not as a criminal but as a public servant entrusted with a mission of great importance and requiring a man of the supreme incorruptibility on which Cato had always prided himself. The Bill proposed the deposition of the wealthy King Ptolemy of Cyprus (brother of the Egyptian monarch of the same name), the annexation of his island as part of the Roman Empire, the organization of its administration, and the removal to Rome of all the contents of the royal palaces and treasuries. They were measures which would at one stroke secure a source of wealth that would help to offset the cost of Clodius' free distributions of corn and ensure that a political opponent would be kept out of Rome for a long time, perhaps even forever if the king attempted any sort of resistance to the man who was to be sent without forces to depose him. Cato himself had no illusions about Clodius' ulterior motives in proposing him for this mission, and though this unwelcome gift was wrapped in so many layers of public flattery that it was hard to refuse, he still tried. But Clodius was ready with a sharp retort to the ingratitude of a man who would refuse the favours of the Roman People. ' "Very well," ' he told Cato, ' "if you do not consider it a favour, you shall undertake it as a punishment" '; and that is what Cato had to do, much to the satisfaction of Pompey who doubtless raised a goblet to wish his enemy a long and uncomfortable voyage. But if Pompey also drank to the continuing prosperity of the tribune who seemed a worthy successor to Caesar as a defender of his interests in the Forum, he would soon realize that Clodius was himself becoming dangerously intoxicated by the heady repetition of success.

According to Appian it was the overwhelming success of Clodius' revenge on Cicero that was chiefly responsible for Pompey's rude awakening from a state of magnificent complacency, 'for when Clodius had demolished Cicero's town and country houses he was so elated by the affair that he began to compare himself with Pompey, who was the most powerful man in Rome at that time'. If Pompey saw his failure to protect Cicero as a matter of political expediency, Clodius saw it as a sign of weakness, for Pompey had 'bound Clodius by every kind of guarantee, oath and agreement to do nothing against Cicero during his tribunate'. Cicero had of course done nothing to deserve Pompey's protection, but what weighed with Clodius was the possibility that Pompey had felt unable to keep his promise even if he had wanted to. Although Pompey had irresistible latent power in his own veterans and Caesar's legions, a man who was basically a constitutionalist could not always resort to threats of military action to achieve his ends. And once Caesar had left for Gaul, Clodius began to believe that Pompey was a political paper tiger, magnificently helpless against a tribune who could manipulate the urban democracy with a dexterity unimagined even in the headiest days of Gaius Gracchus.

Moreover there were other powerful men who would be glad to see Pompey humiliated, and it is likely that they included the former supporters of Catiline in general and Marcus Crassus in particular. There is no reason to doubt Cicero's claim that 'Clodius had reconstituted Catiline's veteran bands' in 58: if Clodius had not been a Catilinarian but a member of Cicero's bodyguard in the critical days of 63, he had since been given a reason for personal revenge on his old leader. As for Crassus, he had never forgiven Cicero for foiling his attempts to establish Italian and overseas power-bases against the threat of Pompey's return from the East, and the fact that he had joined Pompey when he had proved unable to beat him does not mean that he loved him any more in 58 than he had done in 63. To Crassus Clodius was the latest and most promising in a succession of protégés whom he had sponsored in order to further his own ambitions against those of greater men, of whom Pompey had always been the greatest. Clodius was the political heir of Rullus, Catiline and Caesar, all of whom Crassus had sponsored at more or less expense but with little to show for it. If Catiline had achieved the consulship in 63, the tribune Rullus might have secured for Crassus not only the free hand in Egypt which Crassus had failed to get for himself as censor in 65 but also the power-base in Italy which Caesar's agrarian legislation of 59 had just secured for Pompey. As it was, the scheme had been thwarted by Cicero's ousting of Catiline at the polls and the check-mating of Rullus in the Forum, and when Catiline had failed again at the consular elections for 62 Crassus had had to write off as a dead loss yet another expensive investment. From Caesar at least he had gained some return through the legislation of the previous year, but Caesar was far from being a wholly owned subsidiary, and most of the dividends which he paid went to Pompey since their marriage-alliance. But Clodius had no such divided loyalties. Pompey and Caesar had sponsored his tribunate, but so far as Clodius acknowledged any obligation for services rendered it was to the financier who had bought his acquittal at the sacrilege trial in 61 when Cicero had been striving to get him convicted and Pompey could not have cared less. And now that a shared satisfaction at the success of Clodius' revenge on Cicero can only have strengthened their community of interest, it will not be surprising if Crassus was hand in glove with Clodius as the latter proceeded to assert his political independence.

It began probably early in May with a tug-o'-war over the custody of Tigranes, the rebellious prince whose father Pompey had conquered and reinstated on the Armenian throne. After featuring in Pompey's triumphal extravaganza the young man had been kept under close arrest at Rome, and it now occurred to Clodius that it might be lucrative as well as politically challenging to attempt to rescue him from the custody of his guardian Lucius Flavius, the former tribune who had proposed a Land Bill for Pompey's veterans in 60 and no doubt owed his elevation to the praetorship of 58 to Pompey's continued support and influence. Dio maintains that Clodius had been bribed to free Tigranes, but while it is reasonable to suppose that he expected some tangible expression of thanks from a rescued prince and his grateful supporters, there is no reason to doubt that his primary motive was to demonstrate Pompey's weakness with total disregard of the possible consequences to the stability of Armenia and the whole of the East. His opportunity came when Flavius invited him to dinner at his house. During the course of the evening the tribune expressed a desire to see the Armenian prince, and the unsuspecting Flavius promptly obliged, anxious to gratify the curiosity of an amiable and powerful guest. The same request had probably been made many times before, and when Clodius playfully invited the prince to join the banquet, Flavius remained entirely unconcerned until his guest took his leave and Tigranes too. And there was nothing that Flavius could do to stop him, for the tribune was sacrosanct.

The next day it was doubtless a rather red-faced Flavius who went to Pompey to explain how it was that Clodius was now keeping the prisoner at his own house and leaving him unchained. At first Pompey was more perplexed than alarmed at what seemed extraordinary behaviour on the part of a tribune whom he had helped to create and had so far found most satisfactory. He sent Clodius an instruction to restore Tigranes to Flavius in full confidence that it would be obeyed. Clodius not only ignored it but took a swaggering and unbound Tigranes for walks about the streets in a show of open defiance which Pompey could hardly mistake. Angrily he appealed to the consul Gabinius to deal with the matter, and Gabinius did so, not only out of obligation to Pompey for his consulship but because he had made his own name and fortune out of Pompey's Eastern campaigns, and an affair of this sort touched his own honour as much as his sponsor's. It also touched his future, for if he was obliged to Clodius for legislation that would send him to govern Syria next year, the last thing he wanted was to arrive in his province and find an Armenian civil war destabilizing the whole region. Gabinius accordingly accompanied Pompey to Clodius' house, in confident expectation that the tribune would be easily overawed into obedience by the appearance of a consul preceded by his twelve lictors, accompanied by the greatest man in Rome, and followed by a retinue of even more than usual magnificence. But it soon became painfully apparent that they had failed to appreciate either the efficiency of Clodius' organized hooliganism or his determination to use it against any number of conquerors or consuls, for instead of meeting an apologetic and humbled tribune they found themselves beset by a gang of thugs who demonstrated their respect for the consul's authority by smashing up its symbols before his eyes and 'roughing up his followers with blows and wounds'.

After this episode Clodius thought it prudent to put Tigranes out of reach of Pompey's agents before they could avenge this insult to his dignity. He tried to get the prince away by sea, but when the ship carrying Tigranes down the west coast of Italy was forced to put in at Anzio, the tribune apparently changed his mind, decided to bring Tigranes back to Rome, and sent his henchman Sextus Cloelius to escort him. Why is not known, but if he hoped to smuggle him back to Rome secretly, he was disappointed. Pompey had told Flavius to stop at nothing to recover his prisoner, and as Flavius was doubtless ready and able to pay anything for information, he soon discovered that Tigranes was being brought back to Rome, and set out to intercept him with enough friends and followers to do more than argue. The two parties met at the fourth milestone from the city, and 'a battle was fought in which many fell on both sides, though many more from Flavius' party. Nor were the casualties limited to hired ruffians. A Roman knight who was an intimate of Pompey lost his life, and even the praetor himself only just made it back to Rome without a single companion.'

Thus the second blood went to Clodius too, and we can well understand that Pompey became more than a little 'indignant' when a tribune whom he had helped to create began 'using against him the tribunician power which he had helped to restore', especially as Plutarch adds that Clodius started interfering more directly with Pompey's greatest achievement 'by attacking some of the arrangements which he had made in the East'. Exactly which these were Plutarch does not say, but we know of at least one other besides the Tigranes affair from Cicero's references to a Clodian plebiscite of 58 which granted the title of king and control of the lucrative little temple-state of Pessinus to Brogitarus. The latter was one of the three tetrarchs to whom Pompey had entrusted the government of the three tribes of Galatia under the senior partnership of Deiotarus, who was Brogitarus' father-in-law and the only tetrarch of the three to have been honoured by Pompey with a royal title. But Brogitarus was no longer satisfied with an equality which made one tetrarch more equal than the other two, and when his agents approached Clodius with their master's request for the title of king and control of Pessinus, it was merely a question of fixing the price. Clodius was no more concerned about the dangers of destabilizing Galatia than Armenia. He was happy to fuel the rivalries of potentates anywhere in return for the means to fuel his own source of power at home, and once the first instalment of Brogitarus' payment on account had been distributed by his agents to Clodius' thugs in the Temple of Castor, the passage of the Bill at the plebeian assembly was a foregone conclusion.

Pompey's first thought for bringing this mad dog to heel was to bite him back, but wiser second thoughts decided him to stifle his anger and bide his time with an outward appearance of magnificent indifference. To have made a further public fuss over Tigranes' escape would only have enhanced Clodius' victory. As it was, Pompey's apparent unconcern was so convincing that it fooled even Cicero, who so often complained that you never knew where you were with him but now rejected the message of encouragement which his friend Atticus had sent after dining with the great man soon after the event. 'If the Tigranes affair has blown over,' replied the gloomy exile, 'my hopes are extinguished with it.' Yet only four days later the tribune Ninnius was proposing Cicero's recall to a crowded Senate and at Pompey's instigation. For Pompey had not needed a dinner-table conversation with the smooth-tongued Atticus to persuade him that the cause of Cicero's restoration would be a useful stick with which to threaten Clodius, and although its actual use was promptly vetoed by a tribune friendly to Clodius, this was only one of several weapons with which Pompey was preparing to counter-attack and one that he was content to flourish rather than wield for the time being. Pompey still regarded Cicero as an uncertain ally whose obligation to his eventual restorer could only ripen with the length of his absence, whereas his premature recall might even jeopardize the legislation of 59 more seriously than Clodius if a triumphant homecoming went to his head. And if Cicero was wrong to believe that the Tigranes affair had done nothing to benefit him, the letters which he wrote throughout the summer were right to doubt the sincerity of Pompey's professed commitment to his restoration.

In the meantime there was a much more literal wielding of sticks against Clodius. Gabinius had been as little amused by Clodius' affront to his consular dignity in the streets of Rome as by his interference in Pompey's settlement of the East, and he had required little prompting from Pompey to rent a mob of his own with which to defend himself in the Forum and thus create the rapid escalation of public violence which was exactly what Pompey desired. For not every Roman citizen enjoyed daily gang-warfare in the streets, and just as Pompey's reputation had been diminished by his heavy descent into the Forum in support of Caesar's demagogy in the previous year, so now a return to his preferred posture of aloofness from direct involvement in popular politics restored his stature in the eyes of any citizen who had anything less valuable than his life to lose. The disturbances also encouraged Cicero's friends to tell him that absence was making the popular heart grow fonder of him too, but Cicero rightly replied that this was reading too much into what was purely the result of '*their* falling out with each other', by whom he meant Clodius and Gabinius. Pompey himself was worrying less about Cicero or Clodius at this time than they were worrying about each other. His overriding concern in the summer of 58 was with the elections for 57, when Clodius would be out of office and as many reliable Pompeians as possible must be in the most powerful positions. And his instigation of an inevitably abortive attempt to recall Cicero at the end of May had indirectly helped his canvass by reobsessing Clodius with a distracting and counter-productive vendetta. It caused Clodius to veto all discussion of Cicero in the Senate, the Senate to react by refusing to transact any public business at all while the veto remained in force, and Quintus Cicero to return from his governorship in Asia to a welcome whose extraordinary warmth was attributed to a reflected enthusiasm for the exiled brother. But that brother's contemporary correspondence shows no trace of the retrospective optimism which he claimed to have derived from all these manifestations of popularity. He knew that his potential usefulness to Pompey was the key to his restoration, and if Pompey achieved what he wanted at the elections, that key might well be lost.

If the proof of a pudding is in the eating, the number of plums which Pompey extracted from his electoral *pièce de résistance* was a formidable tribute to his skill in that particular branch of political cookery. Admittedly the electoral system was such that the better-off clientele had greater power to select from the menu than the indigent rabble who were the best customers of Clodius' legislative soup-kitchens, but all the same it was an organizational and expensive *chef d'œuvre* for Pompey to secure both consulships for the following year for intimate and reliable friends. One was Metellus Nepos, the latest in the line of former legates whom Pompey had supported for the joint-headship of state since his return from the East. Nepos had served under Pompey against the pirates and in the Syrian campaigns, and his loyalty to his powerful patron was as great now as it had been in 62, when as tribune he had made several well-intentioned but ham-handed attempts to promote the absent Pompey's interests in Rome. The other was Lentulus Spinther, an intimate friend both of Pompey and, unlike Nepos, of Cicero too, though Cicero knew well enough that there was nothing to hope for from Spinther's friendship unless and until Pompey decided to assert himself whole-heartedly for his restoration. In early July Atticus wrote encouragingly that Pompey had 'promised to take up his case after the elections', but the elections came and went and Pompey did nothing. He continued to keep Cicero's friends warmed up with expressions of his good intentions, but endless promises without action were cold comfort to the anxious exile until he heard from Atticus in mid-September that Pompey had written to Caesar about the matter and was waiting for his father-in-law's reply. Perhaps it was true. If so, it was not because Pompey dared not act without Caesar's agreement but because he valued the opinion of his closest and shrewdest protégé and wished to keep him abreast of events in Rome. And whether it was true or not, it was a useful excuse for the procrastination on which Pompey had decided for reasons that had nothing to do with his commonly supposed inability to act and every-thing to do with the continuing urban violence which was increasing to his own advantage.

As the summer progressed, riots, stonings and fights were daily occur-rences. The consular *fasces* were broken more than once, and while it was Gabinius who was more active in playing Clodius at his own violent game, even his colleague Piso was wounded on one occasion (much to the delight of Cicero, who never forgave him for doing nothing to help and much to obstruct the attempts of others to secure his recall). On 11 August Pompey himself became the target of an attempted assassination as he entered the Senate. A dagger slipped from under the tunic of one of Clodius' slaves, and when the man was grabbed and hauled before Gabinius to explain what he had been doing approaching Pompey with an offensive weapon, he confessed that he had intended to stick it between the great man's ribs. And that, according to our sources, caused Pompey to return home and stay out of public life completely until the end of Clodius' tribunate. For a time he was actually besieged by armed gangs stationed around his house under the command of one of Clodius' freedmen named Damio, but when the anti-Clodian tribune Novius referred to this 'siege' in the Senate a week after the attempted assassina-tion, he declared on record that no amount of intimidation was going to make *him* dance to Damio's tune now that the latter was calling for tribunician vetoes against the Pompeian praetor Flavius.

Pompey was not short of bodyguards of his own. He never moved with-out a vast retinue, and he was certainly no personal coward. If he used the danger of assassination as an excuse to stay out of the Forum and the Senate, it was because it suited him to let the senatorial establishment see how well it could manage without him. Ever since he had returned from the East Pompey had been suffering from the envy of less equal peers. At first they had been terrified of him as Sulla's pupil, but when he had shown that nothing was further from his mind than *coup d'état*, they had called his moderation weakness and vented their jealous resentment by opposing his desired legislation. They had forced him to ride roughshod over them in support of his agent Caesar whose demagogy had finally managed to turn their flank in the previous year, and now they had their reward as another demagogue was making the strong-arm tactics of 59 look like child's play by comparison. Pompey could afford to bide his time. Clodius was becoming increasingly unlovable outside his intimate circle and the most impecunious of the citizens. Cicero was gaining popularity, less on his own merits than because he was Clodius' principal victim and arch-enemy. And now that Clodius had turned against Pompey too, it was rapidly becoming forgotten that Pompey had been the sponsor of the man who was now trying to assassinate him and was ringing his house with ruffians. It was only a matter of time before his former enemies would be begging Pompey to act. If he were to act prematurely, there would be renewed cries of 'Sulla's pupil' as his veterans swept into the Forum; and if Clodius were to be killed in the inevitable street-battles, the death of a sacrosanct tribune could always be used against him just as Cicero's once popular execution of the Catilinarian conspirators had recoiled against its author five years later. Clodius would be out of office at the end of the year, but there was no danger that the urban violence would then decrease. Pompey could look unhurriedly forward to being needed by those many political enemies who were already so alarmed at the situation that they found little joy in his pretending to have undergone the political emasculation which they had always tried to inflict upon him.

It was also satisfactory that Clodius' constant attacks on the validity of Caesar's legislation served only to invest both the legislation and Pompey's own image with the respectability which derived from Clodius' enmity. There was no real danger to the vital legislation because the benefit to Clodius lay not in destroying it but in attacking it unsuccessfully. His object was to show that if the attacks being made on the validity of his tribunate were successful they would also automatically invalidate Caesar's legislation. It was a subtle application of the principle that attack is the best form of defence, and it worked because the weapons with which Clodius attacked Caesar's legislation were religious objections similar to those which were being aimed against him. The charge against Clodius was that his adoption into a plebeian family had been carried through 'contrary to the rites of religion and the sanctity of the auspices', that he was therefore ineligible for the tribunate, that he was therefore tribune illegally, and that every measure which he had passed as tribune could therefore be declared invalid. The charge which Clodius now pressed against Caesar's laws was that Caesar's acts had been passed equally 'inauspiciously' because his fellow-consul Bibulus had been maintaining a politically paralysing watch on the heavens. With an aplomb that can only have compelled the admiration of a strategist like Pompey, Clodius actually held a mass-meeting to which his brother, the praetor-elect Appius Claudius, brought Bibulus himself and the whole college of augurs to answer his questions. First the augurs were asked to confirm that proceedings in the legislative assembly were sacrilegious when observation of the heavens was in progress, and once they had obliged, it was a jubilant Bibulus who came forward to affirm that he had been watching the heavens during Caesar's legislative activity. But Bibulus was no more enamoured of Clodius' demagogy than of Caesar's, and while he was gratified to be able to make a public attack on Caesar, he made a point of adding that Clodius' tribunate was just as sacrilegious as Caesar's laws. And thus he played right into Clodius' hands. Clodius had succeeded in 'fettering his own tribunate to the very measures of Caesar which he was supposed to be attacking', and when he later declared to the Senate that he would go and 'bring Cicero back on his own shoulders' if they would only invalidate Caesar's laws, he showed himself anything but the 'lunatic' which Cicero found it convenient to label him after he had been restored to Rome by the man whose interest had guaranteed the impregnability of those laws.

In the meantime Cicero continued his anxious letters from exile. In September he wrote to Atticus: 'You said that Pompey was going to take up my case and would appoint an agent to deal with it as soon as he received the letter he was expecting from Caesar. Was there nothing in it? Or was Caesar's letter unfavourable? Or is there still hope? You mentioned that he said something about "after the elections". Please let me know the worst.' In October he wrote to his family with cautious optimism about the new tribunes for 57, 'if only we can rely on Pompey', and he was soon to be proved right in doubting the value of any attempt to restore him without Pompey's active support. On 29 October eight of the existing tribunes, anxious to demonstrate some independence before their year expired, asserted themselves against Clodius by publishing a Bill for Cicero's recall. But it was only in distant retrospect that Cicero made much of this gesture as a show of loyalty to himself. At the time he recognized it for what it was, a futile exercise in political window-dressing, and he wrote as much to Atticus. The eight proposers of the Bill knew from the outset that there was nothing they could do to prevent its being vetoed by Clodius or their other colleague who supported him, and when Atticus urged that it was nevertheless a step in the right direction for even a hopeless Bill to have been formally published in defiance of Clodius' prohibition of any discussion of Cicero's restoration, Cicero wrote back in late November with undisguised contempt for the eight tribunes: they had demonstrated their timidity and impotence more clearly than their independence, not only because as tribunes themselves they had nothing to fear from a colleague's attempt to forbid discussion of any issue but because they had virtually invalidated their own Bill by inserting a clause subjecting it to any existing public legislation, which of course included the prohibition against repeal contained in Clodius' original act of banishment.

Far from being cheered Cicero was realistically depressed by the futility of the eight tribunes' attempt, and he was rightly sceptical of Atticus' assurances that his prospects would be brighter in the following year. It was true that one of the consuls-elect, Lentulus Spinther, had spoken strongly in favour of the eight tribunes' Bill in the Senate, and even the other 'was showing good will towards him' with an apparent change of heart that was clearly Pompey's doing, for Cicero had no reason to suppose that Metellus Nepos would be less hostile as consul for 57 than he had been as tribune in 62. But Cicero knew that he was ultimately dependent on Pompey, and when the friendly tribune-elect Sestius failed to secure Caesar's good offices on his behalf, he began to despair that Pompey could ever be made to do more than toy with the cause of his restoration.

The new year brought a further disappointment to Cicero and a formidable demonstration that Clodius was still as powerful out of office as in it. No doubt with Pompey's blessing the newly installed consul Spinther proposed Cicero's recall in the Senate. No doubt at Pompey's insistence his newly installed colleague Nepos declared that he would support the motion and lay aside his personal enmity towards Cicero if it were in the interest of the state to do so. Then Spinther called upon the senator Lucius Cotta to open the debate, and this eminent jurist not only supported Cicero's recall but argued that a resolution of the Senate would be sufficient to bring him back on the grounds that the Clodian law under which the people had exiled him could be declared unconstitutional as having been drafted *ad hominem*, and therefore there was no need of popular legislation to revoke it. These arguments were clever and cogent and well received by the House, but they evidently did not suit the next speaker who, 'while praising and commending Cotta's opinion, nevertheless thought it best to have a vote of the people on the matter to make absolutely sure of the thing'. It was a very diplomatic way of disguising the fact that the very last thing which that speaker wanted was an attempt to recall Cicero without reference to the popular assembly, where Clodius' mobs could be relied upon to ensure that it did not succeed and thus demonstrate the need to authorize armed intervention. And the speaker was of course Pompey himself.

But Pompey need not have worried. When the Senate's debate was nearly over and successive members had spoken enthusiastically for Cicero's recall, a tribune named Atilius Serranus rose to his feet before the vote was due to be taken. This man was a supporter of Clodius, and though he pretended to be swayed by the gale of protests and pleas which blew up against his threatened veto and asked to be given the opportunity to reconsider his position overnight, the next morning found him adamant in his opposition. Cicero's supporters in the Senate struggled in vain to bring about a vote on the issue over the few days that remained for meetings of the House that month, and once it became clear that the Senate was hamstrung, a tribune named Fabricius assumed leadership of the pro-Cicero lobby and promulgated a Bill of recall which he promised to bring before the plebeian assembly on 23 January.

The result was a shambles. Fabricius took possession of the rostra before daybreak, but he soon found out that Clodius' gangs had been in position all night at strategic points in the Forum, outside the Senate House and at the voting area. Once the Forum had filled and Fabricius was preparing to call upon the people to form up in their tribes and vote on his proposal, Clodius gave the signal to start the famous riot which 'filled the Tiber with bodies, choked the capital's sewers, and spilt so much blood in the Forum that it had to be mopped up with sponges'. Clodius himself had borrowed a band of gladiators for the occasion from his brother Appius Claudius, who had been collecting large numbers of these gruesome entertainers to perform at the funeral of a recently deceased member of that great patrician family. When Clodius swept into the Forum at the head of these professional killers, Fabricius and his friends had no chance, despite the efforts of another tribune named Cispius who came along to help and was beaten off by superior force. As for Cicero's brother Quintus, who found himself in the thick of things, he saved himself only by lying doggo among some corpses as Clodius' mobs hunted everywhere for him with dripping swords. But that was Clodius' only disappointment from what was otherwise a most satisfactory day – a triumph for his mastery of urban violence and a clear indication that he was never likely to be beaten by constitutional means.

Nothing could have suited Pompey better. Needless to say, he was not in the Forum on 23 January, nor – to judge from Cicero's silence – were either of the consuls or indeed many of those tribunes who would later be most vigorous in support of Cicero's recall when Pompey judged that the time was right. And if he smiled his approval to the tribunes Milo and Sestius as they now began to recruit their own gangs of gladiators, it was a smile of pleasurable anticipation at fuelling the political conflagration which Cicero described on his restoration with rhetorical colour but not necessarily exaggeration.

The Forum had been virtually captured. The temple of Castor was garrisoned by runaway slaves as though it were a fortress. All business was carried on amid the uproar, gangsterism, violence and brute force of men made desperate by poverty and recklessness. Magistrates were driven from our temples, though most were kept from getting near them in the first place or even from entering the Forum. Gladiators belonging to the praetor's retinue were arrested, brought into the Senate, made to confess, put in chains by Milo, released by Serranus. The Forum was littered with bodies of Roman citizens murdered by night, yet not only was no special commission appointed to investigate but even the existing courts were suppressed. You saw a tribune lying on the ground, bleeding to death from more than twenty wounds. The house of another was attacked with fire and sword by the army of Clodius – a man who knew that he could never win the political game by keeping to the established rules and thus resorted to arms, firebrands, daily assassination, arson and pillage with his army. He proceeded to attack that tribune's house, lie in wait for him on the streets, assault and terrorize him. But that resolute man could not be disconcerted. He prosecuted Clodius in court. But what happened? A consul, a praetor and another tribune published new edicts of a novel kind: 'Let not the accused appear, let him not be summoned, let there be no inquiry, let no one be permitted even to make mention of judges or judicial proceedings.'

The tribune whose house was attacked was Milo, and when he proceeded to bring Clodius to court it is significant that 'a consul' as well as 'a praetor and a tribune' took action to prevent any judicial proceedings. The tribune was Clodius' friend Serranus, and the praetor was Appius Claudius, Clodius' brother; but the consul was Pompey's particular protégé, Nepos. If Nepos had been persuaded to express support for the recall of Cicero at the beginning of the year, he was afterwards allowed a free rein not only to resume his personal vendetta but to give more general support to his cousin Clodius until Pompey decided that it was time to bring his head round again some four months later.

In late June or early July 57 we find Cicero writing to Nepos to thank him for a 'kind address in the Senate' and for 'laying aside his enmity' as obligingly now as at the beginning of the year, and it is hard not to see Nepos' volte-face as the action of a weighted political weathercock swinging against its natural bias when the breath of Pompey's pleasure blew hard enough in the opposite direction. The situation had now deteriorated to the point where Pompey felt confident that his intervention would enjoy the almost universal backing of the Senate and propertied classes. Under the leadership of the consul Spinther, supported now by his colleague, the Senate passed a series of pro-Ciceronian resolutions which culminated in a vote of 416 to 1 in favour of his recall, the sole dissentient, needless to say, being Clodius himself. The rest of the senators, including all the magistrates, voted the way that Pompey now wanted them to vote, not because they had all turned against Clodius but because they no longer dared to be seen opposing an issue which had become synonymous with the cause of restoration of order in the capital. And Spinther's famous proclamation, ' "Let all who seek the safety of the Republic come together" ', was Pompey's authorization to summon his veterans from their farms in Campania and elsewhere in Italy.

The pretence that fear of Clodius' mobs had kept Pompey out of politics in the latter part of 58 is now shown to be little more than Cicero's attempt to sweeten the unpalatable truth that Pompey had not left the pleasures of private life for Cicero's sake because he had not wanted to do so. Clodius' mobs were still formidable. Indeed, the new Bill for Cicero's recall was to be brought not before the usual legislative assembly which voted by tribes but before the centuriate assembly in which the ballot was biased in favour of the propertied classes, and the use of this usually elective assembly for a piece of legislation indicates how great a control Clodius still exercised over the urban poor. And Pompey was taking no chances once he had staked his reputation on the passage of this Bill. He went in person to the new colony of his veterans at Capua to summon them to Rome for the vote. He repeatedly declared his support for the Bill both to the Senate and people, and he personally escorted Quintus Cicero into the Forum 'with a large force'. But it was not in the Forum that the Bill was passed. The centuriate assembly met in the Campus Martius, and when the appointed day arrived the Field of Mars lived up to its name with so great a throng of Pompey's old troops that the Clodians had no choice but acquiescence or broken heads. The preparations were so thorough that a supremely confident Cicero was sailing back to Italy while the vote was taking place on 4 August, and this time his confidence was not misplaced. On 8 August, three days after his arrival at Brundisium, he received his brother's letter confirming the expected result, and started on what became almost a triumphal journey to the capital from which he had been away for some seventeen months.

Cicero was prompt to give credit where it was due, and among the extravaganzas of gratitude which he gushed at Pompey in the Senate and Forum on the two days following his hero's welcome to Rome on 4 September, he proclaimed his debt to be 'such as it is scarcely lawful for one mortal man to owe another': Pompey 'never has had, has not now,

nor ever will have a rival in courage, wisdom and renown', and he had
given to Cicero 'what he has always given to the whole state – safety,
security, and dignity'. But if Pompey had demonstrated the overwhelming
superiority of his power-base in Italy and particularly in Campania, it
was not a power-base which could be used every day. To be able to summon Italy to Rome was effective but cumbersome compared with Clodius' manipulation of the ever-present urban poor, and Pompey himself
was well aware that he could not keep his veterans from their farms forever. Before the countrymen dispersed, he determined to use them and
the widespread euphoria generated by Cicero's recall to secure for himself
a commission which would combine new authority with the opportunity
to serve the lowest orders of society where Clodius found his support.

It was a stroke of luck that circumstances had played so neatly into
Pompey's hands. The 'incredible influx of countrymen' whom he had
summoned to vote for Cicero's recall and to demonstrate his own power
had exacerbated an already serious shortage of corn in the city. Indeed
the irrepressible Clodius did not miss the opportunity to blame the whole
crisis on Cicero's return, and he soon had hungry mobs demonstrating
against his old enemy outside the Senate and in the theatres. But if it
was Clodius who could claim to have instituted a completely free distribution of corn to any Roman citizen who claimed it, that was little comfort
if there was no corn to distribute, and as the granaries emptied the people
began to recall the similar shortages which had occurred some ten years
before when Mediterranean commerce had been virtually paralysed by
piracy. They also remembered the man to whom they had given command against the pirates, and the magical effect of his appointment
'which had caused the price of provisions to fall so quickly that the very
name Pompey had been enough to end the war'. And now history
repeated itself as the Senate debated, the people demanded, and an oblig-
ing Pompey graciously allowed Cicero to begin repaying his superhuman
debt by proposing that his restorer should take the matter in hand.

Cicero described what happened in a letter to Atticus, who was away
on a business trip:

Pompey was called upon both by the poor and by the better sort to take
the matter in hand, and as he was more than willing and the people asked
me by name to propose it, I delivered my opinion most elaborately. As all of
the ex-consuls except Afranius and Messalla were absent on the pretext that
it was not safe for them to speak, the Senate passed a decree in accordance
with my motion that Pompey should be asked to undertake the matter and
that appropriate legislation should be introduced. When the decree was read
out to the people they applauded the mention of my name, and I addressed
them at the invitation of all the magistrates present except for one praetor and

two tribunes. The next day there was a packed meeting of the Senate including the ex-consuls, and they denied Pompey nothing that he asked for. In requesting fifteen legates he named me first among them and said that I should be his *alter ego* in everything. The consuls drew up a law giving Pompey control over the grain supply throughout the world for five years. But the tribune Messius proposed an alternative bill giving him control over the treasury too and adding a fleet, an army and authority in the provinces superior to that of the several governors. Our consular law is now regarded as moderate, that of Messius perfectly intolerable, and while Pompey himself says that he prefers the former, his friends say that he really favours the latter.

What Pompey really wanted we can never know. His expressed preference for the consuls' Bill could merely have been false moderation on the part of a man 'whose way it always was to pretend as far as possible not to desire the things he wanted most'. It is hard to believe that he would have refused all that Messius proposed if it came his way, and it is possible that he was behind Messius all the time. On the other hand, whether Messius was acting under orders or not, Pompey could have regarded the alternative proposal mainly as a means of demonstrating the moderation of the consuls' Bill. At any rate it appears that Messius withdrew, the consular Bill was passed by the people before the end of September, and Cicero accepted the appointment as one of the proconsul's fifteen assistants.

For Cicero to become an official subordinate of Pompey was of course of symbolic rather than administrative importance to his restorer, who was quite happy to leave him free to stay in Rome and even stand for the censorship if he so wished. It acknowledged a political commitment which Cicero had refused to make when Pompey had invited him to join his land commission in 59, and it was a further instalment in Cicero's repayment of his debt. Another was his proposal of a public thanksgiving of fifteen days' duration for Caesar's victories in Gaul. Because this was half as long again as the public thanksgiving which had been held for Pompey's victory in the East it has usually been seen as a source of antipathy between Caesar and a jealous son-in-law, but there is no reason to doubt Cicero's own claim that 'Pompey, who had himself been preferred to all distinctions beyond other men, was in favour of granting to another a greater distinction than he himself had obtained'. For it is surely incredible that the newly restored Cicero would have proposed superior honours for a distant general who had been less than lukewarm about his restoration if it had not been the wish of his present champion that he should do so. In 57 Pompey still regarded the successes of his protégé as extensions of his own. He regarded Caesar as his creation, and to the extent that the glorification of a creation reflects glory on the creator, he regarded Cicero's public performance as chief acolyte as a further commitment to his own interest, which he himself was now strengthening where it seemed most endangered – not in Gaul or in Italy but in the Forum.

It was not then in competition with Caesar but as a complement to his successes in Gaul that Pompey now set about feeding the urban poor with all the energy of a man who saw advantage to himself as well as to the hungry recipients of the corn which he was about to provide. Nor was that personal interest limited to the prospect of sapping the foundations of the urban power-base which Clodius had created initially in his interest but used against him. He had his eye on the wealth of Egypt which Crassus had so desperately tried to secure while Pompey had been away in the East. Just as the command against the pirates at the time of the corn crisis ten years ago had been Pompey's stepping-stone to the command against Mithridates, so now he hoped that success in feeding the city a second time might well see him sailing into Alexandria with a lucrative commission to restore the King of Egypt.

Ptolemy Auletes, who had secured Rome's recognition by the payment of six thousand talents to Caesar and Pompey in 59, had done nothing to endear himself to his subjects by his exactions to recoup this huge sum, and his unpopularity had been further compounded by his refusal to assist his brother Ptolemy of Cyprus against Roman annexation in 58. Whether he was expelled from his kingdom or left it voluntarily is disputed by our sources, but in the earlier part of 57 he had come to Rome where, from the luxury of Pompey's villa in the Alban Hills, he had immediately set about bribing the Senate to support his restoration. A counter-deputation of a hundred eminent Alexandrians followed him to Italy, but when they landed at Puteoli Ptolemy saw to it that the majority were murdered, and the survivors who reached Rome were silenced by intimidation, bribery or further murders. 'When this became generally known,' says Dio, 'even the Senate was greatly displeased'; but if all the senators agreed to summon the leading envoy who was miraculously still alive, there must have been many sighs of relief and knowing winks when he failed to turn up.

Eventually it appears that the Senate sanctioned the king's restoration on a motion of the consul Spinther, probably in the autumn of 57 at about the time that Pompey was receiving his corn commission. It also seems that Spinther's motion made the governor of Cilicia responsible for the restoration, and since Cilicia was to be Spinther's own province in 56 there were rumours, according to Plutarch, that Spinther had proposed the corn commission for Pompey solely in order to secure the Alexandrian commission for himself. But there is no need to suppose that Pompey had abandoned the possibility of taking Ptolemy back to Alexandria. It had been essential to persuade the Senate to sanction the restoration in principle, and if Pompey temporarily supported Spinther as the man to carry it out because he knew that there would have been much fiercer opposition to his own appointment, it does not mean that he would have refused a popular demand that he should take over the command himself in the new year.

In the meantime this possibility provided an additional incentive to make a success of his corn commission. The population of Rome was now probably approaching a million, of whom perhaps between a quarter and a third were taking advantage of the monthly corn-dole which Clodius had made completely free in 58, and the rest were demanding a regular supply to the market at stable prices. To satisfy these requirements involved a vast expenditure of public revenue and a vast importation of grain, part of which came as tribute from the great corn-growing provinces of Sicily, Africa and Sardinia, and part as purchases either by independent merchants or by contractors appointed by the provincial governors to make special requisitions in times of need. Italy had long since ceased to provide sufficient corn for the imperial city, and while the amounts which came in from good harvests in Etruria to the north and Campania to the south were not inconsiderable, Rome's real lifelines were the shipping-lanes converging on her sea-port of Ostia from where an endless procession of ox-drawn barges carried the imported grain up the Tiber to the wharves and warehouses of the hungry city. And yet the regular supervision of this complex mercantile and distributive network was left to a quaestor at Ostia and to the aediles in Rome, the former on the very lowest rung of the senatorial ladder, the latter too often preoccupied with the provision of circuses to care about the provision of bread. Their task would have been exacting enough if the annual elections had always produced a succession of quaestors and aediles of the highest ability, but as they were not all paragons of administrative efficiency any more than harvests were always successful or contractors always honest, it is not surprising that the Senate had often found it necessary to detail a more senior magistrate to take action in emergencies. But the corn-supply had never known anything like the world-wide, quinquennial, proconsular *imperium* which Pompey now held, and the scale and duration of this extraordinary commission not only reflected the gravity of the present situation but foreshadowed the establishment of the permanent bureaucracy which administered the corn-supply under the Empire.

Whether a bad harvest contributed to the shortages and high prices of 57 is not known. If the Clodian law of the previous year really did absorb a fifth of the annual revenue as Cicero maintains, the free dole must have been enormously more attractive than its subsidized predecessor, and it may be that an increase in the number of takers was itself sufficient to overstrain a loosely controlled system of supply. By 57 whatever reserves had been kept in the granaries of Ostia and Rome were probably exhausted, and while Pompey made it his first task to collect corn from the provinces to meet the immediate crisis, the whole organizational problem was not solved without great expenditure of time, effort and money. Moreover Pompey's very appointment had aggravated the problem, for Dio tells us that large numbers of slaves were freed in anticipation of his success. No doubt many a rich Roman found it convenient to combine charity with economy by letting the state feed elderly and less efficient slaves who were costing more to keep than they were worth, and all these new freedmen 'caused Pompey some delay, because he wished to take a census in order that the grain might be supplied to them with some order and system'. But eventually they were all fed 'thanks to Pompey's wisdom and the large supplies of grain which he collected', and if it took longer to bring down the prices on the open market, those who complained of the high price of food in the spring of 56 at least had some food to buy, and before the end of the year it was so plentiful and cheap that Pompey could accuse a political enemy of ingratitude 'for opposing the man who had made him full to vomiting instead of famished'.

It is frustrating that our sources give us so little detailed information about the organization and negotiation involved in supervising the transmission of corn from the threshing-floors of distant provinces to the markets of Rome and the hungry slum-dwellers of the Subura who subsisted on their monthly dole. All the same, the degree of detail in which Pompey was personally involved, at least at first, is indicated by odd snippets of information like the letter which Cicero wrote to one of Pompey's corn-supply legates in 53. Writing on behalf of a corn-factor named Avianius, Cicero begged the legate to 'accommodate Avianius as to the place and time at which he is to discharge his corn', and he explains that this would be a renewal of a privilege which he had helped Avianius to secure for a three-year period 'when Pompey was personally in control of that business'. But on the whole our sources were interested in only the more sensational of Pompey's achievements, and Plutarch makes the most of his braving the wintry seas to feed the people of Rome in the autumn of 57:

Having been set over the administration and management of the corn-supply, Pompey sent his legates and friends in various directions and sailed himself to Sicily, Sardinia and Africa to collect grain. When he was about to sail home with it and a violent storm blew up at sea, his ship-captains shrank from putting out, but Pompey led the way on board and ordered them to weigh anchor with the cry 'To sail is necessary, to live is not!' And by this exercise of courage and energy combined with good fortune he filled the sea with ships and the markets so full with grain that the surplus of what he had provided for home consumption sufficed also for foreign peoples, and there was an abundant overflow, as from a spring, for all men.

No one would suppose from this brief account that prices were sky-high again the next April, but although the narrative is telescoped there need be no doubt that Pompey did bring back corn in person, that his administration eventually became the cornucopia which Plutarch describes, or even that he uttered the famous words of defiance to the storm which became enshrined in seafaring lore. But when he returned about December from this first round of visits to the three main corn-producing provinces in the hope that he might sail on to Alexandria on the crest of a wave of popularity, he found instead that he was buffeted by political storms at home that were not so easily weathered.

# 2

# THE MONSTER REVIVES

The strife of wits, the rivalry of birth,
Through nights and days to toil beyond their peers
To scale the heights of wealth and master power ...
Lucretius, *On the Nature of Things*, 2.11–13

Late in December 57 or early in January 56 the statue of Jupiter on the Alban Hill was struck by lightning. At once it was decided to consult the Sibylline Books about so alarming a portent, and when these ancient oracles were opened and their Greek hexameters construed, a verse was found to command that 'if the King of Egypt comes requesting aid, refuse him not friendship nor yet succour him with a multitude, else you shall have both toils and dangers'. According to Dio this showed 'an amazing coincidence between the verses and the events of the time', but for Cicero at least the coincidence was too amazing to be either fortuitous or divinely inspired. When he referred to it in a letter to Spinther in Cilicia on 13 January, he did not hesitate to call it 'a religious sham, which the Senate accepts not for reasons of religion but out of dislike and disgust of Ptolemy's regal largess', and when he wrote again a few days later he maintained 'that the introduction of this trumped-up religious scruple is now generally recognized as the work of your jealous enemies, though not so much to hamper you in particular as to prevent anyone wishing to go to Alexandria from a selfish desire for military command'. But the tribune who manipulated the godsend to political use was a protégé of Crassus, and it was to keep military command from Pompey in particular that Gaius Cato frustrated the plans of fellow-tribunes who were Pompey's protégés.

The speed with which Gaius Cato seized on the opportunity did justice to the lightning itself, if indeed the striking of the statue was not a human brainwave too. He ignored the prohibition against making the Sibyl's mysteries known to the people without authorization from the Senate, and in order to make as great an impact as possible on the superstitions of the lower classes he brought the priests before a popular assembly and ordered them to declare the oracle. The whole affair was stage-managed with a flair that was worthy of Clodius himself, who may conceivably have had a hand in its organization since Crassus was behind the pair of them (as Pompey complained to Cicero, and Cicero repeated in a letter to his brother of mid-February). The priests feigned reluctance to speak, and the more they resisted, says Dio, the more the multitude insisted on knowing this enhanced mystery, which was duly translated into Latin and publicly proclaimed before the Senate had even discussed the matter. And by then it was too widely believed to be ignored.

In his letters to the anxious Spinther in Cilicia and to his own brother who was organizing the corn-supply in Sardinia as one of Pompey's legates, Cicero gives a careful account of the Senate's meetings on the Egyptian question and of his own delicate position as a friend of Spinther, who had worked so hard for his return from exile in the previous year, and of Pompey, to whom he was certainly no less obliged. Superficially of course there was no conflict of loyalties because 'Pompey has been advocating Spinther's cause both publicly and privately'; but this was partly self-protection against the stigma of failing to get something which he openly sought, partly to mislead his rivals, partly to keep his own options open as long as possible in case a better opportunity occurred, and partly because it always enhanced a man's dignity to have to be invited to accept great commands against a modest show of reluctance. And when Cicero described to Spinther the big drive which Pompey's friends were mounting to put their chief in charge of Ptolemy's restoration, it is hard to believe he was naïve enough to suppose that they were acting entirely spontaneously. 'The hurried meetings of Pompey's agents and the zeal of all his intimates have created the impression that Pompey seems bent on being appointed, and those who would reject him are no friends of yours because you secured the corn commission for him.... Any desire there is to please me is overwhelmed by the greater desire to please Pompey.... The king himself and Pompey's friends and associates have secretly inflamed the sore.'

Cicero wrote these words early in the morning of 13 January 56, when he further explained that five lobbies had emerged in readiness for the debate on the Egyptian question which was to take place that day in the Senate. His own opinion, supported by Hortensius and Marcus Lucullus, yielded to the religious objections against the use of an army ('for in no other way can our object be attained') but favoured the retention of Spinther as Ptolemy's restorer according to the existing decree which had been passed the previous autumn on Spinther's own motion. Bibulus on the other hand, supported by most of the other ex-consuls, was proposing that the restoration should be entrusted to a commission of three 'private citizens', and this excluded not only Spinther and all other provincial governors but also Pompey, who held proconsular *imperium* over the corn-supply. Crassus also supported a commission of three, but being as subtle as Pompey in disguising his real preference he extended the selection to include those who already held *imperium*, and indeed he may have been prepared to share it with Pompey if he could not get it without him. The fourth lobby opposed the restoration of Ptolemy altogether, and the fifth supported his restoration by Pompey, whose most ardent supporters were the tribune Lupus and the ever faithful ex-consuls Afranius and Volcatius.

It is interesting that Lupus should be the tribune leading for Pompey in the Senate. Only a month ago he had celebrated the launching of his tribunate by firing an oratorical salvo at Caesar's Campanian Land Act of 59, blasting away at its proposer, and peppering Pompey with recrimination. It had only been target practice because those great ironclads were both away, Caesar wintering from active service in Cisalpine Gaul, Pompey fetching corn for the hungry city, but Lupus was obviously plotting a political course that would bring him into glorious collision with their interests after calculating that the enemy fleet was potentially more numerous. But Cicero's account of this occasion reveals that he had miscalculated:

Having brought his speech to a late conclusion he said that he would not ask for our opinions for fear of burdening us with a quarrel. He said that he clearly inferred the feelings of the Senate from the loud protests of earlier days and its present silence. But when he immediately proceeded to close the meeting, he was interrupted by the consul-elect Marcellinus who warned him not to judge from their silence what they approved or did not approve at that moment, for as far as he was concerned – and he believed that he was speaking on behalf of all present – his reason for keeping quiet was that he did not consider it proper to discuss the question of the Campanian land in the absence of Pompey.

It was not the encouraging response which Lupus had expected. A rapid reappraisal of political tonnage convinced him of the greater wisdom of piloting what was very much more than a corn-ship towards Alexandria, and though Pompey would find himself in rough water for a while, Lupus would prove right to have changed political tack before another three months were past.

Before dawn on 15 January Cicero again used the quiet of the early morning to write to Spinther and let him know the result of the debates of the previous two days. Nothing had been decided on 13 January because the greater part of the day had been consumed with the disputes between the consul Marcellinus and the Pompeian tribune Caninius, and though Cicero does not elaborate, it seems likely that the bone of contention was the Senate's right to decide this matter of foreign policy without reference to the people. For on the next day the Senate passed a resolution against the holding of a plebiscite on the issue, and the resolution was promptly vetoed not only by Caninius, who turns out to have promulgated a Bill to grant the commission to Pompey and two lictors, but also by his tribunician colleague Gaius Cato, who was Crassus' man. Also on the second day the Senate proceeded to debate three of the five possibilities which had been canvassed according to Cicero's letter of 13 January: first Bibulus' motion 'that three commissioners should restore the king without an army'; then Hortensius', 'that Spinther should restore him without any army'; and third Volcatius', 'that Pompey should restore him' (possibly without reference to an army). But before the debate was opened on Bibulus' motion, a request was made that he should split it into two parts: that the king should be restored without an army, and that three commissioners should be sent to do it. On the first part there turned out to be no disagreement: the religious objection to aiding an Egyptian king 'with a multitude' was too strong. But on the question of the three commissioners 'a large majority would sooner have voted for anything else in the world', and it was voted out. Then Hortensius came forward to support Spinther, but at this point the tribune Lupus jumped to his feet and demanded that a proposal of his own in favour of Pompey should take precedence. There was a general outcry at this, and it was certainly very irregular for a tribune to seek to take the management of a senatorial debate from the presiding consuls, but as a tribune had the ultimate authority to forbid any motion to be debated, he could effectively paralyse the Senate unless his wishes were met. His reason for wanting to force a vote on his own motion before Hortensius' was to avoid the possibility that the Senate might vote in favour of Spinther purely as a means of stopping Pompey without having to run the risk of being counted in opposition to him, for Lupus reckoned that if his own proposal came first there would be few brave enough to be seen crossing the floor against Pompey's interest. But the consuls took a stand on the issue of precedence, not because they themselves wanted Spinther rather than Pompey but because they wanted neither. If Cicero was right, they privately favoured Bibulus' proposal, but they spoke in favour of Pompey in order not to appear to be against him while encouraging large numbers of senators to give their opinions with the sole purpose of wasting the rest of the day, which duly closed without a division.

That evening Cicero went to dine with Pompey, and the next morning he wrote to Spinther that he had availed himself of the most favourable opportunity he had ever had to 'speak to Pompey in a way that drew his mind from any other line of thought to a proper consideration of your claims to restore Ptolemy'. And Pompey had evidently been most charming and agreeable. 'When I hear him speak himself,' writes Cicero, 'I acquit him absolutely of any suspicion of selfish greed in this matter.' But he also had to admit that Pompey's apparent disinterestedness had abated none of his friends' ardour for gaining him the commission. 'When I look round at Pompey's associates of whatever rank I clearly perceive what must now be obvious to all, that the whole business has long since been corrupted by certain men – and not without the good will of the king and his counsellors.' But if Spinther's prospects were less bright than they had been, Cicero still concluded on a note of optimism. He was ready to do what he could in that day's debate, and he was confident at least that Spinther's opponents would not succeed in giving the command to anyone else by introducing a plebiscite. For though the tribunes Cato and Caninius had vetoed the resolution which the Senate had passed the previous day against the holding of a plebiscite on the issue, the fact that this vote was on record might be expected to act as a deterrent; and even if it failed, Cicero maintained that he had friends ready to prevent any attempt to put a motion before the people either by tribunician veto or by declaring unfavourable omens.

The third consecutive day's debate turned out to be as ineffectual as the second, and because it was the last day available for a meeting of the Senate until 1 February and the whole of February was devoted to receiving and discussing deputations from provinces and foreign powers, it looked as though the Egyptian question would be shelved for at least a month and a half. Cicero's consolation to Spinther was that the proposal to give the commission to Pompey had been talked out again, and he took a typically immodest credit for 'maintaining our position brilliantly among the great variety of arguments and the great jealousy of those who were for taking the king's affair out of your hands and putting it elsewhere'. But in the more realistic appraisal which he wrote to his brother Quintus in Sardinia he was less confident that Pompey would not get the commission, and if he was no more modest about his own 'brilliance' in debate, he admitted that he had been 'as successful in satisfying the wishes of Pompey as of fulfilling his obligations to Spinther'. What he meant by this was presumably that he supported Spinther without opposing Pompey, and whereas he told Spinther that a tribunician plebiscite was unlikely to succeed, he told Quintus that he was very much afraid that Caninius would get his Bill in favour of Pompey passed by violence if there was any opposition more serious than certain senators' hypocritical bleatings that Pompey could not be spared from the superintendence of the corn-supply, or that they feared for his safety. If Cicero still claimed, even to Quintus, that he was not sure what Pompey himself really wanted, 'there is no mistaking what his friends desire'; and in the expectation that Spinther's cause was as good as lost he ended his letter to Quintus with the conscience-salving observation that while he was of course terribly sorry about it all he could not help remembering that Spinther had not been very helpful over the matter of fixing the indemnity which the state had paid him in recompense for the destruction of his house after his exile.

When the Senate met again on 1 February the whole day was consumed by a long and inconclusive debate about the desirability of postponing the foreign deputations in order to concentrate on more immediate problems, but as soon as this had been agreed on the next day, Gaius Cato proposed Spinther's recall from the governorship of Cilicia. And that, Cicero wrote to the unhappy governor, made Pompey's appointment as the restorer of Ptolemy a virtual certainty, though he still promised to make his best efforts not only to oppose Cato's 'execrable proposal' but to salvage what he could of the apparent wreck of Spinther's Egyptian ambitions, 'if that matter is not abandoned or put into the hands of the man to whom it is thought to have been practically assigned'. But Cicero was mistaken in thinking that Pompey's passage to Alexandria was as good as booked. Cato's proposal to recall Spinther had not been in Pompey's interest, and only four days later the colours of Pompey's oldest rival were publicly hoisted at the trial of one of the tribunes of the previous year whom Pompey now helped to defend against a charge of violence.

The defendant was Milo, the tribune who had laid both Pompey and Cicero under an obligation by organizing mobs of his own to counter Clodius' violence. The prosecutor was Clodius himself, now taking a cynical revenge by accusing another of the crime of which he was himself the guiltiest man in Rome. For Clodius had not reformed since Cicero's return from exile. In November 57, for example, when Pompey had been braving the paths of the sea to fetch corn to a hungry city, there was greater danger in navigating the streets of Rome to judge from Cicero's correspondence, which treats a permanent escort of thugs as a routine precaution of everyday life. Justice in Rome was what you could get away with, and in the absence of an independent judiciary and police-force Clodius knew that he was taking only a calculated political risk when he wrecked the site of Cicero's half-reconstructed house, burnt down his brother's next door, attempted to do the same to one of Milo's, and led his gangs in repeated attacks on Cicero and Milo in the streets in daylight. Milo in the meantime tried to bring him to trial, but though Marcellinus, then consul-elect, had tried to bring a resolution for the trial before the Senate, it was talked out by Clodius' brother, the praetor Appius

Claudius, and his cousin, the outgoing consul Nepos. Nor was Clodius'
violence purely a matter of vendetta. His campaign of urban terror was
designed to intimidate the city into electing him to an aedileship, which
would not only immunize him against prosecution during the coming
year but provide him with a magisterial seat from which to launch
counter-prosecutions against Milo and the other tribunes of 57 who
would then be out of office and therefore vulnerable. And time was on
his side. His friends in the Senate argued with his enemies about the precedence of the trial over the elections. Milo was prepared to stop all elections by announcing unfavourable omens on all election days, and though
Nepos played hide-and-seek with him in an attempt to avoid having the
tribune's formal notice served on him until after daybreak, when it would
have been too late, Milo was always there to stop the elections until his
tribunate expired on 10 December. But when the elections were finally
held on 20 January, he was out of office and could do nothing. Clodius
was elected aedile, and having assumed the ludicrously inappropriate
duties of an office which was responsible for keeping the peace as well
as keeping the streets clean, the sewers operational and the people fed
and entertained, he set about prosecuting Milo, who came up for trial
on 2 February 56.

'It was not with the expectation of obtaining a conviction that Clodius
did this,' says Dio, 'for Milo had many strong champions, among them
Cicero and Pompey; but it was a good pretext under which to carry on
his vendetta against Milo and also to insult Milo's backers.' And Dio
goes on to describe how Clodius had trained a claque to shout a one-
word response to a series of versicles of which Plutarch gives a few
examples that were hardly designed to dignify the conduct of a trial.
'Who's the insatiable *Imperator*?'; 'Who's the man who's after a man?';
'Who scratches his head with one finger?' To all these questions and others
like them the answer was always the same, and when Clodius screamed
one out and shook his toga to give the cue, his gang of 'lewd and arrogant
ruffians' yelled 'Pompey!' at the tops of their voices. 'Not surprisingly,'
says Plutarch, 'this was extremely annoying to Pompey who was not
accustomed to vilification and was inexperienced in this sort of warfare',
but according to Cicero he stood his ground against it when he appeared
for Milo's defence on 6 February. 'Against constant heckling and abuse
from Clodius' gangs,' wrote Cicero to his brother, 'Pompey showed great
fortitude, and sometimes even commanded silence by the weight of his
authority.' At any rate he finished his speech, and when Clodius stood
up to speak after him, the defence was ready to return the compliments
with interest, and did so to such effect that Clodius, 'white with rage
at all the filthy doggerel that was hurled at him and his sister', retaliated

with another series of questions that revealed his own political backer. 'Who's the man who starved the people?' he cried. 'Pompey!' yelled his men. 'Who's after a trip to Alexandria?' 'Pompey!' thundered the reply. But then, 'Who do *we* want to go?' And this time the answer was 'Crassus!'

After this first and possibly premature publication of Crassus' now open rivalry with Pompey for the Egyptian commission the proceedings degenerated from verbal to physical abuse.

At three o'clock [continues Cicero], as though at a given signal, Clodius' men began to spit on ours. We flared up in anger. They tried to hustle us out. Our men charged them, and the roughs took to their heels. Clodius was flung off the rostra, and we also made ourselves scarce at that point for fear of getting hurt in the crush. The Senate was summoned to the Curia. Pompey went home. And I gave the Senate a miss too, because I could not go and say nothing, and I did not want to offend the sensibilities of the good sort by defending Pompey, who is constantly criticized by Bibulus and the rest.

Bibulus and his friends were no more in favour of Crassus than of Pompey, but as it was in their joint interest that Pompey should not have the Egyptian commission, Pompey found himself under increasing fire from both sides while Cicero kept his head down and began to assume a more independent role than what he had described as a 'superhuman debt' to Pompey could possibly allow.

In the Senate the next day Cicero admits that Pompey spoke about the violence of 6 February in an impressive manner, and on the following day a decree was passed condemning it as 'contrary to the interests of the Republic', but none of this discouraged Gaius Cato from making a violent verbal attack on Pompey and 'accusing him as though he were in the dock'. Cato also tried to widen the crack which he had discovered between Pompey and Cicero. He knew that flattery would get him everywhere with Cicero, and he laid it on with the metaphorical trowel. But Pompey knew well enough who was behind all this, and he no longer hesitated to refer to his rival in unmistakable terms. 'In an obvious allusion to Crassus,' says Cicero, 'he declared that he would be better prepared to safeguard his own life than Africanus, whom Gaius Carbo had assassinated.' The remark was well chosen. Cicero himself had often called Pompey the Africanus to whom he wished to act the part of Laelius, and Pompey now put Crassus on notice that he would take more care of himself than that earlier conqueror and would-be pillar of the establishment who had collapsed in 129, murdered, as was generally believed, by his political enemy Carbo. And a letter from Cicero to his brother shows that Pompey was more explicit in private about his fear of assassination and the direction from which an attempt could be expected:

> For it seems to me that issues of great moment are developing, and Pompey clearly understands it and talks to me about it – how plots are being hatched against his life, how Gaius Cato is being supported by Crassus, how Clodius is being supplied with money, how the pair of them are being backed not only by Crassus but by Bibulus and the rest of his enemies, and how he is having to take strenuous measures to prevent his being utterly crushed, with a speech-swallowing populace practically estranged from him, the nobility hostile, the Senate unequally divided against him, and the youth of the country totally depraved.

If Pompey exaggerated somewhat in the hope of winning Cicero's sympathy, he was evidently sufficiently rattled by the vehemence of the opposition to prepare for massive retaliation by the method of last resort. If the urban mob was ready to bite the hand that fed it and if too many jealous senators resented his having the Egyptian commission 'for fear that he might become greater still', he saw no alterative but to call up supporters from Italy in sufficient strength to overwhelm any urban violence which Crassus' agents might bring against him. And so we find Cicero writing to his brother on 12 February that 'while Clodius is strengthening his hired gangs, Pompey is calling up men from the country'. Milo's trial was due to continue on 17 February, and since the case had assumed the wider significance of a trial of strength between Pompey and Crassus, Pompey was evidently determined to use superior violence to ensure an acquittal. Cicero wrote that in addition to the veterans from Campania 'a large reinforcement is daily expected from Picenum and Gaul', the former Pompey's own paternal territory where he had raised his private army to aid Sulla in the Civil War, the latter Cisalpine Gaul where Caesar was in winter-quarters at Ravenna south of the Po. With all these forces available to Pompey even the timorous Cicero looked forward with confidence not only to a successful defence of Milo in court but also to the collapse of Gaius Cato's attempts to have Spinther recalled from Cilicia and to do some further mischief to Milo by unspecified legislative as well as judicial means. But curiously enough Cicero's imagination does not seem to have ventured beyond these immediate preoccupations, and when he wrote to Spinther at about this time, he expressed his belief that Pompey had 'dropped the Egyptian business' and that Spinther might get the commission after all.

After Pompey had secured Milo's acquittal Cicero began to let a series of successful court-cases go to his head, and in the middle of February he was already boasting to his brother of having attained 'a position of dignity and popularity' which he 'would hardly have believed possible'.

Forgetting how recently he had 'tasted the bitter fruits of unrestrained free speech' he inclined towards the increasing number of senators opposing both Pompey and his father-in-law, whose victories in Gaul not only aroused the same jealousy as Pompey's in the East but were doubly distrusted as being dangerous extensions of Pompey's power. (For there is nothing in the contemporary evidence to support the anachronistic assumption of the later sources that Pompey was jealous of Caesar's successes.) Cicero admitted two years later that he had 'disregarded Pompey's wishes by remaining faithful to his old political tenets' at this time. He made no direct attacks on Pompey himself, and in a letter to his brother in the second half of March he even complained that the consul Marcellinus was being 'rather too hard on Pompey', whose position was embarrassing to Cicero because 'no other senator stood up for him' and Cicero himself did not want to do so. But he was nevertheless delighted with Marcellinus' success in juggling the calendar of religious holidays to prevent 'Gaius Cato and others who have promulgated outrageous proposals about Caesar from carrying them into law'. He was also pleased that Caninius' proposal to assign the restoration of Ptolemy to Pompey had 'sunk without trace', and when he added that Pompey was to prevent 'Gaius Cato and others who have promulgated outrageous But Cicero would have been less complacently independent if he had suspected the less superficial reasons for the dropping of Caninius' Bill, for the silence of Pompey's friends against constant attacks on him in the Senate, for Gaius Cato's attempted legislation in favour of Caesar, and for Marcellinus' inability to find a single one of the ten tribunes to veto it – a far simpler procedure than going to the trouble of stringing together a whole series of movable feasts in order to paralyse all public business. He had forgotten how he had cheered too soon almost exactly four years ago when Flavius' Land Bill to provide farms for Pompey's veterans had been allowed to sink as completely as Caninius' present Bill to give Pompey the Egyptian commission. He had forgotten that Pompey was never more dangerous than when he appeared to have been beaten, and in the daily excitement of the political battles in the Senate and Forum it never crossed his mind that the Monster of 59 was about to rise like a phoenix from the ashes of a rivalry between Pompey and Crassus which had already been privately immolated on the altar of mutual self-interest.

Early in March Pompey attended the trial of the tribune Sestius to give a character reference, and in his presence Cicero turned his cross-examination of the prosecution witness Vatinius into a political tirade against the legislation of 59, which Vatinius, then a tribune, had helped Caesar to carry in the interest of the three partners. An expurgated version of Cicero's speech still exists, and it contains passages that must have made Pompey seethe at hearing the ratification of his own Eastern settlement, the greatest of his achievements, made a charge against Vatinius. 'Did you not make treaties with states, kings and tetrarchs?' sneered Cicero, and to judge from what he wrote about the occasion two years later the speech as we have it is probably mild compared with the original. 'The whole of my cross-examination was nothing but a condemnation of Vatinius' tribunate, and I spoke perfectly frankly about the rioting, the disregarding of the auspices and the bestowing of royal titles.' And if this verbal bombardment was sweet music in the ears of Bibulus and the other arch-enemies of the coalition of 59 – especially when Cicero added that he 'preferred the glory of Bibulus to the triumphs and victories of all the rest of them' -- it was not an isolated encounter:

For it was not only in that trial that I took this line but constantly and repeatedly in the Senate. On 5 April I personally proposed, and the Senate accepted, a motion to raise the question of the Campanian land before a full House on 15 May. Nothing could have been a more uncompromising invasion of the citadel of their cause. Nothing could have been a clearer indication how completely I had forgotten the days of my trouble and recalled the days of my power. But the result of this expression of my opinion was greatly to excite the minds not only of those who ought to have been disturbed by it but of those whom I should never have thought to be so.

It was easy to be wise with hindsight. At the time Cicero had taken Pompey's apparent submissiveness as genuine, and when he saw none of the tribunes willing to veto Cato's 'outrageous' proposals, it did not occur to him that there was something ominous in the solidarity of those who were agents of Pompey and those who were backed by Crassus. In proposing to bring the Campanian law before the Senate he may have hoped that Pompey would acquiesce in the suspension of the allotments since most of Pompey's own veterans had probably been settled there by now. He could argue that the state of the exchequer could not afford to lose any more rental income from that part of the public land which was still in the hands of tenant-farmers, but everyone knew that his real purpose was to prevent the establishment of another para-military power-base in Campania when Caesar returned from his Gallic campaigns and wanted to provide his demobilized army with farms. He was in fact preparing against Pompey's protégé the same kind of opposition which had soured Pompey's return from the East, but if he expected Pompey to acquiesce, he was very much mistaken.

While Crassus' immediate reaction was to go and see Caesar in his winter-quarters at Ravenna and 'rouse his indignation' against Cicero, Pompey remained apparently unperturbed at Rome; but the letter which

Cicero wrote to his brother in Sardinia on 11 April shows how completely Pompey had thrown him and all his enemies off guard. Cicero told Quintus about the Senate's resolution of 5 April to review the Campanian Land Act on 15 May (though without admitting that he had personally proposed it), and he mentioned that the debate had been heated on account of the high price of provisions and a shortage of money exacerbated by the vote of forty million sesterces to Pompey for the corn-supply. He then described how he had paid a call on Pompey at his gardens after dinner two days later, because he was about to leave Rome himself and wanted to catch Pompey before the latter went off to Sardinia in connection with his corn commission. He had asked Pompey to send Quintus back to Rome as soon as possible, and as Pompey might have been expected to feel that the claims of the corn-supply took precedence over brotherly affection, Cicero was delighted by his affably monosyllabic reply: 'Immediately!' And when Pompey explained that he intended taking ship for Sardinia from Labro or Pisa, Cicero clearly did not have the slightest suspicion of what Pompey intended to do *en route*.

Pompey's actions and their results are described by Cicero in a letter which he wrote to Spinther two years later to justify his rapid abandonment of an independent political line when Quintus returned, as promised, immediately. 'Though Pompey had shown no sign that he was offended,' wrote Cicero, demonstrating his own political naïvety, 'he set off for Sardinia and Africa, and on the way visited Caesar at Luca.' Now Luca was very near the ports of Pisa and Labro from which Pompey had told Cicero that he intended to set sail, and Cicero has been criticized for not wondering why Pompey should go all the way up to north-eastern Italy in order to sail all the way back down again to Sardinia. But Etruria was also an important source of Rome's corn, and there was nothing illogical in a visit to corn-producing areas that began with a northward journey through Tuscany and then proceeded southward by sea to Sardinia, Campania, Sicily and Africa. Cicero had no reason to suspect that Pompey had arranged to meet Caesar and Crassus at Luca, and Pompey must have had difficulty in keeping a straight face at the thought of the message which he was going to give Quintus to take back with him. For 'when Pompey met Quintus in Sardinia a few days after he had left Luca', continues Cicero's retrospective account, 'he exclaimed, "Just the man I wanted to see! Nothing could have been more opportune! Unless you remonstrate seriously with your brother, you will have to pay up what you guaranteed me for his good conduct."' It was a reminder of all the assurances of devoted support which Quintus had made on his brother's behalf before Pompey had finally exerted himself to bring about Cicero's recall in the previous year, and there is no doubt that when Quintus came back from Sardinia, he had in his ear a flea which he intended to transmit to his brother 'immediately'. Not surprisingly Cicero did not care to dilate on what must have been quite a mouthful:

To cut it short, Pompey had complained bitterly about me to Quintus, recounted his own services to me, recalled the repeated discussions we had had with my brother about the acts of Caesar and the promises which my brother had given him in regard to my own support, and called my brother to witness that whatever he had done in the matter of my restoration, he had done with the full consent of Caesar. *In fine*, I was told that if I would or could not support Caesar's interest, I should at least refrain from attacking it. And as if that was not enough, Pompey sent an instruction by another friend of his that I should do nothing about the matter of the Campanian land until his own return.

News of the meeting between Pompey, Caesar and Crassus at Luca, reinforced by the messages received from his brother and Pompey's other agent, left Cicero in no doubt that Pompey had revived the Monster of 59. He did not know how the coalition would operate this time, but to judge from the large numbers of senators who are reported to have gone to Luca when they knew that Pompey and Crassus had met Caesar there, he was not the only one to have decided that fear is the beginning of wisdom. And though he found it embarrassing at the time to have to absent himself from the debate on the Campanian land which he himself had proposed – 'I have run dry on that business', as he wrote to Atticus in the middle of May – he found no difficulty in justifying his total adherence to Pompey, and therefore to Pompey's protégé, in his letter to Spinther two years later:

For my own part, if I saw the Republic in the hands of unscrupulous and worthless citizens, as we know it to have been in the time of Cinna for example, not only should I resist the temptation of material advantages, which carry but little weight with me, but I should refuse to be compelled by any considerations of danger to espouse their cause. But when the state had Pompey for its leading citizen, a man who had gained all his power and glory by the highest public service and the most brilliant military achievements, a man moreover whose dignity I have conspicuously supported from my youth upwards and as conspicuously promoted both in my praetorship and consulship ... I did not think that I had any reason to dread the imputation of inconsistency if in the expression of some of my opinions I made a slight change in my political attitude and contributed my good will to the advancement of a most illustrious man who has laid me under the deepest obligations. In coming to this opinion I was obliged to include Caesar, since the policy and position of the two men were so intimately connected ... And what compelled me most strongly in this respect was Pompey's having pledged his word for me to Caesar and my brother's having done the same to Pompey.

So much for the reasoned justification of retrospect. What compelled Cicero most strongly at the time was a fear so great that he not only renounced his independence but was forced to confess to Atticus, who evidently heard about it from other sources, that he had 'sent a written recantation to a man who was very insistent to have it', and who can only have been Pompey. For Cicero wanted to leave himself 'no loophole for backsliding again', and with a rare admission of fallibility he told Atticus in late April or early May that he had been a 'perfect ass' not to take his advice long ago and 'befriend himself by befriending those who have the real power'. But not all Pompey's opponents were as quick as Cicero to recognize their utter helplessness against 'those who have superiority in resources, arms and power' and now proceeded to show that they had 'superior authority' too by 'gaining through the Senate, with few dissentients, all they thought they were likely to achieve without revolution'. First came requests from Caesar for money to pay his troops and for an increase in the number of his legates, and though Cicero later admitted his private belief that Caesar was 'well able to pay for his own campaigns out of his booty,' he nevertheless 'thought more of the man than the money' and 'not only argued against the opposition but helped to draft the favourable resolution', which was duly passed. But the opposition did not give up. The consular elections for 55 would be coming up in July, and as the law prescribed that the provinces which consuls were to govern after their year of office should be selected by the Senate before the elections, it was now proposed that Caesar's Gallic provinces should be allotted to the two new heads of state.

At first glance this does not appear to be an aggressively anti-Caesarian proposal. It would be over a year and a half before the consuls elected in July 56 would be ready to take up their provincial governorships on 1 January 54, and Caesar's campaigns might not unreasonably have been expected to be finished by then. Moreover the plebiscite of 59 under which Caesar was governing Cisalpine Gaul and Illyricum was due to expire on 1 March 54, and the principal province, Transalpine Gaul, could be reassigned by the Senate at any time without reference to the people since it had not been included in the plebiscite but granted voluntarily by a Senate which had then temporarily despaired of further futile opposition to Caesar's desire for provincial command. But there was more to the present proposal than met the eye. The consul Marcellinus and his friends were now afraid that Caesar would try to secure an extension of his command in Gaul, an ambition which may already have shown itself in what Cicero had termed 'outrageous proposals' made by Gaius Cato and others on Caesar's behalf in March. At any rate the reallotment of one or both of Caesar's Gallic provinces was the latest stick with which the opposition hoped to beat the Monster. To allot both provinces would be more effective of course, but if there were to be objections to the legal difficulty of having two proconsuls in command of one province between 1 January and 1 March 54 because Cisalpine Gaul was subject to the Vatinian plebiscite of 59, it was of course Gaul beyond the Alps that was the seat of Caesar's wars, and if he could only be knocked off it, his whole command would collapse. Although a plebiscite could overrule a senatorial resolution to allot proconsular provinces, the resolution itself was not subject to tribunician veto, and if a majority in the Senate would support it, it might encourage some of the tribunes to join the opposition in thwarting a plebiscite. But when the proposal was made in June, the sight of the obedient Cicero dancing to his new tune helped to deprive Marcellinus of his hoped-for majority. For Cicero gave a long speech against the proposal to allot either both or only one of Caesar's Gallic provinces, and he left no doubt who was calling his tune when he described Caesar's conquests in Gaul as extensions of Pompey's own and urged with schizophrenic conviction that the Senate should rather refuse to allow Caesar to leave Gaul until his work was completed, 'however much he might want to return to his hard-earned triumph, to his delightful daughter and to his illustrious son-in-law'.

It must have been highly gratifying to Pompey to find Cicero so faithful to his new resolution, though he would doubtless have preferred Cicero to oppose the attempt to allocate Caesar's provinces without using the argument that it was more important to get Piso and Gabinius out of theirs. But if it was too much to expect the orator to drop his vendetta against the consuls of 58 whom he blamed for not preventing his exile, the alacrity with which he sprang to the defence of another of the Monster's protégés left nothing to be desired. This was Cornelius Balbus, one of Caesar's officers, whom his accusers sought to deprive of the Roman citizenship that Pompey himself had granted him in recognition of services in the war against Sertorius. The charges against the defendant were irrelevant to his case: Balbus' real crime was that he was Caesar's agent and his principal go-between with Pompey.

Cicero began by pointing out that Balbus had been defended 'by gentlemen of the very greatest distinction' – Pompey and Crassus – and went on to praise Pompey's contribution with a fulsomeness which he normally reserved for his own oratorical efforts:

The impressive gravity with which Pompey spoke yesterday, the eloquence, the fluency, were clearly recognized not only by your tacit approval but by your evident admiration. Indeed I have never heard anything that seemed to me more acute in its exposition of the law, anything more impressive in its recollection of precedents, anything more learned in regard to the law of treaties, anything more brilliant or authoritative concerning war, anything more weighty concerning the affairs of state, anything more modest concerning the speaker himself!

But Pompey could afford to be modest when he had Cicero to praise him, for this was nothing compared with what followed.

Cicero claimed that he had nothing to add to the legal arguments which others had set out so brilliantly. The most important fact was that it was Pompey who had given Balbus his citizenship:

And what does Pompey lack to make anyone believe that any privilege which he has conferred has not been rightly given? Is it experience of affairs, when the end of his boyhood marked the beginning of his wars and his mighty commands, when most of his equals in age have seen fewer camps than he has gained triumphs, when he can count as many triumphs as there are shores and parts of the earth, when he has won as many victories in war as there are kinds of war in the world? Is it ability, when the history of our generation has not been the guide to his policy but the result of it, when he is the object of the highest rivalry between Fortune and his own valour, and when the unanimous judgement of men assigns more credit to the man than to the goddess? Has honour, integrity, duty or industry ever been found wanting in him? Has any man more upright, more moderate, more righteous ever been seen or even dreamed of by our provinces, by free peoples, by kings or by the most distant of lands? What need I say of his prestige, for it is as great as it ought to be in a man of such great virtues and renown? He is a man to whom the Senate and people of Rome have bestowed unasked the rewards of the highest distinction for commands which he tried to refuse, and therefore even to discuss the legality of an act of such a man is not only insulting to him but also to you, gentlemen of the jury, and to the whole Roman people!

And after a great deal more of the same, as well as a great mass of legal arguments which he included despite his earlier claim that the brilliant expositions of Pompey and Crassus made them superfluous, Cicero's last sentence put the legal case firmly in its political nutshell. 'And finally, gentlemen of the jury, keep one thing fixed firmly in your minds: that in this case you are about to judge not an offence of Balbus but a benefaction of Pompey.'

The acquittal of Balbus following on the failure of the attempt to allot Caesar's provinces to the consuls of 55 is eloquent testimony to Pompey's restored authority after his resurrection of the Monster of 59. Indeed, Pompey had openly accused his political enemies of cowardice for attacking a lightweight like Balbus 'in an unequal and unjust contest' because they were afraid to attack Balbus' powerful friends directly in what, by implication, would also have been an 'unequal and unjust contest' but with the advantage on the other side. And when Spinther now wrote from Cilicia to ask about the political situation, Cicero had no hesitation in acknowledging the supremacy of the Pompeian interest:

There is the greatest dissension in the state, but the contest is unequal. For those who have the superiority in resources, arms and power seem to me, through the stupidity and inconsistency of their opponents, to have made such progress that they now also have the superiority in prestige. And so, with very few dissentients, they have gained through the Senate all they thought they were unlikely to obtain even through the people without insurrection, for Caesar has not only been given money for his troops and ten legates by senatorial decree but they easily managed to prevent his being superseded under the Sempronian law.

And the irony is that if Marcellinus and the opposition had only known who the consuls of 55 were going to be, they would hardly have taken the trouble to try to allot them Caesar's Gallic provinces in the first place.

When the consuls prepared to hold the elections of their successors, Pompey and Crassus surprised them with a last-minute decision to stand. Exactly when this was is not certain. The paucity of dated political correspondence from Cicero for the latter part of 56 makes it impossible to reconstruct a reliable absolute chronology for the garbled narrative of Dio and the references in the other non-contemporary sources, but there is no reason to suppose that the elections were not fixed within the usual period, the second half of July. What is certain is that Pompey and Crassus came forward as candidates less than twenty-four days before polling-day, for Dio is explicit that Marcellinus and his colleague refused to accept their candidature on the grounds that 'they had started to seek office outside the period specified by law', and he is not likely to have invented such a detail. The presiding consuls then went ahead with the elections without admitting the late entries to the ballot, but when polling-day came, they received a formal notice of unfavourable omens from the tribune Gaius Cato.

This was exactly how the tribune Milo had stopped the aedilician elections in order to prevent Clodius from standing in the previous year, but it was a serious extension of its application to stop the consular elections and therefore the elections of the other magistrates which followed them in order of seniority. Of course Cato did not say that he was stopping the elections because Pompey and Crassus were not being allowed to stand. A letter from Cicero reveals that Cato had publicly threatened to do as much in March in retaliation for the manipulation of the religious calendar by which Marcellinus had prevented him from bringing Bills before the people, and in so far as the tribune felt constrained to give a secular reason for a religious objection, it was probably electoral revenge for that legislative delay. Pompey and Crassus affected to

acquiesce in the rejection of their candidature to judge from Dio's statement that the postponement of the elections 'was being achieved by other
men on other pretexts', and if most people realized that 'it was really
the work of the candidates themselves', there was advantage to both sides
in maintaining a pretence which might make it easier for the other to
give in without too embarrassing a loss of face.

According to Dio's narrative Cato's action provoked stormy debates
in the Senate and more than one walk-out by indignant members, but
'the strife then subsided for a while', presumably until the consuls again
tried to hold the elections and Cato again announced unfavourable
omens. In an attempt to overawe him they proposed that the Senate
should put on mourning as for a public calamity, and when Cato saw
that the majority were likely to be in favour of it, he rushed out of the
House and tried to bring in some non-senators whose presence would
have prevented the taking of a vote. But other tribunes refused to let them
in, the vote was passed, and on the strength of this success it was further
proposed that the Senate should boycott the public games in protest
against Cato's intransigence. Cato vetoed the proposal. Angry senators
then went home and returned dressed in deepest mourning, but still he
refused to be cowed even when the Senate went down into the Forum
and Marcellinus harangued the people. All the same, Cato was under
heavy pressure, and he welcomed the timely reinforcement of the greatest
rabble-master of them all, the flexible Clodius 'who now leapt across to
Pompey's side in the hope that if he helped him in securing his present
ambitions, he would make him thoroughly his friend'. In the spring Clodius had been leading his mobs in mocking Pompey. Now he became
another of Pompey's agents, and appearing before the people in ordinary
dress he began a verbal counter-offensive that was evidently highly effective in sending the furious senators back to the House. Clodius rushed
back after them, but tempers were running so high that he found himself
surrounded by a threatening crowd of senators and knights and only
managed to save his life by 'summoning the people, who came with fire
and threatened to burn down the Senate House and all the senators inside
it if Clodius should be harmed'.

'It was a close shave for Clodius,' says Dio, 'but Pompey, not at all
alarmed by these happenings, also rushed to the Senate on one occasion
to oppose a vote that was about to be taken, and he succeeded in thwarting it.' What the measure was is not clear from the text. It might have
been an attempt to invalidate Gaius Cato's obstruction of the elections
or perhaps the proposal for a senatorial boycott of the games, but whatever it was, Pompey evidently made such a personal issue of it that Marcellinus could no longer suppose or pretend that the electoral paralysis

was of the tribune's independent making. He determined to attack its roots in the hope that they would wither before the glare of exposed hypocrisy, but when he formally asked Pompey and Crassus in public if they really intended to become candidates themselves, they admitted it. According to Plutarch Pompey 'shuffled' at first with a rather feeble 'perhaps so, perhaps not', but when Marcellinus repeated the question, Pompey confessed, 'though he said he would solicit only the votes of the just citizens and not the unjust'. Crassus more subtly said that he would do whatever was for the good of the Republic, but though Plutarch maintains that this was thought 'less arrogant' than Pompey's reply, its meaning was no less clear. At any rate it was Pompey who bore the brunt of the attack on his ambitions, and when Marcellinus persisted in insulting him and 'was reckoned to be making a strong speech', the offended provider of corn retorted with his famous taunt of ingratitude – that Marcellinus 'was of all men the most unjust because he was ungrateful to one who had made him eloquent instead of speechless, and full to vomiting instead of famished'. And now that Pompey had openly staked his dignity on the issue, he would clearly stop at nothing to succeed.

'Marcellinus and many others were terrified as they observed the preparations and opposing array of Pompey and Crassus', says Dio; and as 'too few went to the Senate to form a quorum for passing any vote about the elections, it was impossible to have any business about them brought forward, and thus the year passed away. The senators did not go back to their usual dress, or attend the games, or celebrate the feast of Jupiter on the Capitol, or go out to the Alban Hill for the Latin festival, but instead they passed the rest of the year as though in bondage and without authority either to have elections or carry on any public business.' A letter from Cicero suggests that he at least was keeping out of harm's way in the country, and he was probably not the only one. 'Since the games are going on for an extra day,' he wrote to Atticus in Rome, 'I shall be all the better for spending that day here', and he proceeds to express sympathy for Domitius, the consular candidate who had been leading the field until the two dark horses entered the race. 'What could be more lamentable,' he exclaims, 'than for a man who had been designated consul from the day of his birth to be unable to become consul, especially as he had only one serious rival at the most?' He even ventured to compare Domitius' fate with his own exile, 'except that Domitius deserved it' – presumably by opposing the Monster so vigorously when he was praetor in 58 and in the Senate in the current year. Nor did Cicero rate his chance of ever becoming consul very high, 'for if it is true, as I suspect it is, that our friend Pompey has in his little notebooks as many pages of future consuls as of consuls past, then Domitius has only one rival in wretchedness – the Republic itself, in whose condition there is not even a hope of improvement'.

So much for Cicero's confessions of his true feelings to his closest and most trusted friend towards the end of 56. When he wrote to Spinther in Cilicia early in 55 he confirmed that 'affairs are so securely in the hands of our friends that it seems unlikely that there will be any change in our generation', and while he still admitted that it had been painful for him to cast off his old political ideal 'especially when it was well and truly founded', he made a virtue of his support for the now invincible Pompey:

I adapt myself to his will because I cannot honourably dissent from him, and in doing this I am no hypocrite as some perhaps think I am. For I am so heavily influenced by the promptings of reason and, Heaven knows, by my affection towards Pompey that whatever is expedient for him and whatever he desires now appear to me in every case right and proper, and in my opinion even his enemies would not go far wrong if they were to make a truce with him since they cannot possibly be a match for him.

But unfortunately Cicero does not tell us how Pompey came to be in that position of unrivalled supremacy, and for that we must rely on the non-contemporary sources.

When the new year opened without consuls the constitution provided for a revival of a vestige of the ancient monarchy in the form of an *inter-regnum*. The patrician members of the Senate appointed one of their number to become sole head of state for a period of five days with the title of *interrex*, and when his five days were up they made further appointments of this 'temporary kingship' until the consular elections could be held. Now that the presidency of the elections had passed from the obstructive consuls of 56 to an *interrex*, there was no longer anything to prevent Pompey and Crassus from competing, if indeed there can be said to have been an element of competition in what was now a foregone conclusion. For all other candidates had withdrawn either in discretion or despair except only Domitius, and even Domitius would have weakened without the exhortations of his irrepressible brother-in-law Marcus Cato, now back from his mission to annex Cyprus with enor- mous sums of money. He was the same old Cato, uncompromising as ever in his opposition to Pompey and still parading his ancestral hatred of pomp with priggish insensitivity. When the consuls had led the Senate down to the river to welcome him home, he had rowed straight past them and brought his six-banked treasure-ship to the official dockyard where the money was to be deposited. And now he urged Domitius not to give in, ' "for the struggle with the tyrants is not for office but for the liberty of the Romans!" ' With these stirring words, reinforced by the more practical observation that ' "those who are keeping quiet now through fear will help us when it comes to the voting" ', Plutarch tells us that Cato 'all but forced Domitius to go down to the Forum' and continue the canvass. But on the day appointed by the *interrex* for the elections, 'Pompey and his partisans, observing Cato's firmness and fearing lest he, having the Senate with him, might alter the good will of the favourable element of the electorate, would not allow Domitius to go down to the Campus Martius, but sent armed men who slew the torch-bearer leading the company and put the rest to flight'. Then it was all over bar the voting, and 'since no one at all opposed them', says Dio, 'and since Crassus' son who was then serving under Caesar's command brought troops to Rome for this very purpose, the remaining two candidates were easily elected'.

Thus Pompey assumed his second consulship and again with Crassus, but this time they displayed greater unanimity of purpose than in 70. For 'having secured the highest offices for themselves', they set about 'making sure that the other magistracies were given to such as were well disposed to them', and since Marcus Cato was not in this category and was standing for the praetorship, they took particular care that he should not succeed to become even more of a thorn in their flesh than the praetors Domitius and Memmius had been in 58. On 11 February, according to a letter which Cicero wrote to his brother later that month, the Senate met and passed a resolution 'concerning electoral corruption'. Tantalizingly we read that Cicero had explained its details to Quintus when they had last met, but since it can hardly have been a decree condoning electoral corruption, it seems a curious means to the consuls' end. And yet it must have been, because its proposer was the ex-consul Afranius, Pompey's protégé from the Eastern campaigns and his faithful mouthpiece in the Senate ever since. Most probably it was what Afranius' proposal omitted which was to the consuls' advantage, for some of the senators tried to add a rider requiring a sixty-day interval between the election of the praetors and their assumption of office, and when the consuls refused to accept this, the Senate reacted 'with a great groan', suggesting that there was more to this refusal than a desire not to deprive the city of the services of its second most senior magistrates for yet another two months. The supporters of the amendment had probably been trying to achieve a chance to prosecute praetors who used bribery in the elections before the guilty parties could gain the immunity from prosecution conferred by their office. In normal circumstances there would have been several months for such prosecutions as praetors were usually elected in the summer before their year of office began, but in this extraordinary situation where the year had opened without magistrates, Afranius had evidently proposed that the praetors should be elected at once, and tried to pre-empt the criticism which underlay the attempted amendment by setting it in the context of a decree against bribery. But for the Senate to pass decrees about bribery was of course useless without the legal means of punishing it, and Plutarch is clearly right in interpreting the resolution as having been aimed particularly against Marcus Cato. For 'on that day', wrote Cicero, 'the consuls' repudiation of Cato was plain. But why should I say more? They have everything in their power, and they want everyone to know it.'

The resolution proposed by Afranius was therefore the very opposite of what it seemed, giving the consuls a charter for bribery without the fear that Cato would challenge the candidates whom they now proceeded to bring forward to the elections 'while they themselves not only offered money for votes, but stood by while the votes were cast'. Even so the first votes to be announced were for Cato, whereupon Pompey declared that he had heard thunder at that moment, and promptly dissolved the assembly to be on the safe side of Providence. He then resorted to more extensive bribery, and when he and Crassus reconvened the electoral assembly in the Field of Mars, his men made doubly sure that all known opponents were removed before the voting began. And this time the gods remained silent as Cato was beaten by Vatinius, the former tribune who had served the coalition's legislative requirements so faithfully in 59 and now earned his reward and a magisterial compensation for the verbal battering which he had received from Cicero's cross-examination at the trial of Sestius the previous March. For Cato there was consolation in being escorted home from the scene of his electoral defeat 'by a greater throng of admirers than accompanied all the successful candidates put together', but it was no compensation for having lost 'a magisterial vantage-point for his struggle against his opponents', which it was truly 'not easy for a private citizen to carry on'.

Once the elections had been held Dio tells us that Pompey and Crassus 'gravely pretended that they wanted nothing more', but while their opponents breathed a sigh of relief, a tribune named Gaius Trebonius was preparing to take their breath away completely by promulgating a Bill to give five-year proconsular commands to both heads of state. Pompey was to have the two Spains, Crassus Syria. They were to be free to make peace and war as they wished, and they might raise as many troops as they required. Needless to say the opposition was immediately up in arms, but as its arms were purely metaphorical they were even less effective now than in 59 when there had at least been a consul to oppose the Monster's will. All the same Marcus Cato found two tribunes who were prepared to make a stand against their colleague Trebonius, and the legislative farce of 59 was re-enacted in 55 with few variations to its inevitable conclusion, probably in May. Trebonius held his popular assemblies at which he invited private individuals to speak before officials, just as Caesar had done in 59. The opposition's tribunes were kept out of the Forum by force, and when one of them spent the night in the Senate House in order to be on the spot in the morning, Trebonius locked him in and kept him imprisoned there while the assembly met on the following day. Cato renewed his experience of being hauled off the speakers' platform, and when it came to taking the vote, desperate cries of thunder and ill-omen were silenced by a hail of blows, and the Bill was passed.

While Trebonius acted as the master of these revels, Pompey and Crassus were not far away, 'keeping an eye on things'; and when one of the opposition tribunes tried to create a stir among the departing crowds by exhibiting his bloodstained colleague and making inflammatory speeches about the sacrosanctity of the people's elect, the consuls moved in and 'intimidated the men with their large bodyguards'. They then summoned another assembly which passed 'the additional measures relating to Caesar', which were principally the extension of his Gallic command for a similar five-year period. Thus each of the Monster's three heads had its slice of the imperial cake to keep the wolves from their political door for the next five years – Caesar continuing in Gaul, Crassus gaining Syria, and Pompey the two Spains, which in his superior way he still pretended to consider rather a bore to a now doubtful Cicero. As for Egypt, which had been the original bone of contention between Pompey and Crassus, King Ptolemy was restored to Alexandria by May 55 after a lightning campaign by the governor of Syria, Pompey's old protégé Gabinius, who relied on his patron to protect him against any political repercussions that might result from his sacrilegious use of 'a multitude'.

The narrative of Pompey's resurrection of the Monster in 56, compiled as far as possible from Cicero's letters and stripped of the interpretations of non-contemporary sources, proves incorrect the motive assigned to him by almost all these later sources and followed blindly by most modern historians. The writers of the Empire are constantly anticipating the estrangement between Pompey and Caesar which led to the Civil War, and they must also have been influenced by living under an autocracy whose ruler bore the name of the victor. Dio is typical when he makes Pompey and Crassus seek the consulship and proconsular commands in self-defence against Caesar, who in Plutarch's *Life of Pompey* even appears to regard his Gallic Wars as little more than a training session for the Civil War. And Suetonius has Caesar 'compelling' Pompey and Crassus to stand for the consulship in defence of his interests. But there is nothing of this from a contemporary like Cicero. To Cicero the so-called triumvirate of Pompey, Caesar and Crassus nearly always presents itself in the dominant personality of Pompey, and when Pompey and Caesar are coupled together, it is as patron and protégé, allied by interest and marriage, the son-in-law seeing the achievements of his wife's father as extensions of his own. If Pompey had been afraid or even jealous of Caesar, he would hardly have intervened so vigorously to protect his command against attempts to reallot it in 56, have introduced and forced through a plebiscite to extend it for another five years in 55, and then have lent Caesar one of his own legions at the end of the following year 'in recognition of the public good and of private friendship' in Caesar's own words. In taking a similar five-year proconsular command in Spain for himself he was not rivalling but complementing Caesar's command in Gaul. Indeed Pompey might not have bothered to take a five-year pro-consulship at all but for Crassus' desire to mount an invasion of Parthia that might give him the belated satisfaction of a military triumph. If Crassus was to have a five-year command in Syria, his fellow-consul must have at least the same elsewhere, not out of fear and still less from any desire to win more laurels but because his dignity demanded it. It was far preferable to Pompey that Crassus should expend his energies in the distant military arena of the securely Pompeian East than in political rivalry at Rome, which was where Pompey himself intended to stay.

The Roman Alexander who had 'gained more triumphs than most men of his age had seen camps' had no desire to undertake another series of lengthy campaigns far from home. His ambition had graduated from the acquisition of greatness on the periphery of the Empire to its enjoyment at the centre, where he had an adoring wife, great wealth, and the envy that properly belonged to the 'prince of citizens'. But one question remains. Despite the evident strength of his political interest in the summer of 56 Pompey had suddenly decided, less than twenty-four days before the elections, that it was imperative for him and Crassus to stand for consulships themselves. Why?

The answer in one word is almost certainly Domitius. Suetonius puts his finger on the reason when he writes that 'when the candidate Domitius openly threatened to effect as consul what he had been unable to do as praetor and take Caesar's armies away from him, Caesar compelled Pompey and Crassus to come to Luca, when he prevailed upon them to stand for a second consulship in order to defeat Domitius, and through their influence he succeeded in having his term extended for a further five years'. That Caesar 'compelled' Pompey and Crassus is as glaring a naïvety on the part of Caesar's biographer as the assumption (followed by almost all the non-contemporary sources and modern historians) that a decision taken at Luca in April was not implemented until after the date for the registration of candidatures, which was at least two months later. All the same Cicero writes later in the year that Domitius 'deserved' his fate when Pompey and Crassus stood against him, and if in the three weeks of frantic canvassing that preceded the elections the leading candidate had openly declared his intention to bring about Caesar's recall and 'do as consul in 55 what he had failed to do as praetor in 58', this could well have been what prompted Pompey and Crassus into their own belated candidature as the only certain way of stopping him.

But had Pompey and Crassus not even thought of standing before? Almost certainly it had been suggested to them, Crassus may well have been in favour of it, and Domitius may even have kept his manifesto muted until after the date for registration had passed because he feared this very danger. But Pompey was probably as reluctant to stand for the consulship now as he had been in 60, largely because he did not want the trouble of being consul and because there was no one whom he wished to dignify with a formal equality of status even if he could trust his loyalty and ability. He would have preferred to counter Domitius in 55 as he had countered Bibulus in 59, but unfortunately there was no Caesar among the existing candidates. Indeed Cicero tells us that Domitius had only one serious rival, presumably supported by Pompey and Crassus, but this anonymous character was evidently not regarded as a sufficient counterweight. And there were compensations to Pompey in making the best of a lesser evil. He was fifty in September 56, and his Theatre was nearly completed. It would perhaps be no bad thing to mark his half-century with formal headship of state, and if he had to share that distinction with Crassus, he could eclipse his colleague not only in technical precedence by polling the higher number of votes but also by the dedication of Rome's first permanent theatre, which would provide him with the opportunity to entertain the people of Rome on a scale which would recall the glory of his Eastern triumph of 62.

But Pompey's public success was marred by a personal grief which portended a greater tragedy in the following year. The election of the praetors had been relatively peaceful, but at the elections of the aediles there was a fight in which Pompey's clothes were spattered with blood, and though he was unhurt himself, his wife fainted when she saw his servant returning home with the bloodstained garments which he had changed on the spot. Julia was pregnant at the time, and the shock was so great that she miscarried. She recovered, but the loss of her child was a great sorrow to her husband and to her father, both of whom were utterly devoted to her and whose political alliance would have been sealed even more securely by a child of this arranged marriage which had turned out to be one of the most successful love-matches of the century. For Plutarch is emphatic that 'even those who found most fault with Pompey's friendship with Caesar could find nothing to blame in the love he bore his wife', and as long as Julia remained alive it is hard to imagine that her husband and father could ever have been irreversibly estranged.

# 3
# PRINCE OF CITIZENS

Come quick and gaze at the empty husks of our dear old
Republic! See cash distributed openly before the elections,
tribe by tribe, all in one place! See the acquitted Gabinius,
smell the whiff of dictatorship, enjoy the holiday
and free-for-all ...
Cicero, *Letters to Atticus*, 4.19

By the late summer of 55 the idea which had prompted Pompey to
commission detailed plans of the open-air theatre at Mytilene on his way
home from the East in 62 had been translated into monumental reality
on the Campus Martius at Rome. Sadly, unlike the Colosseum which
was completed 135 years later, it has few remains today, but though it
was Rome's first example of this genre of architectural glorification of
self and city, it was of such magnificence that even after another two and
a half centuries of imperial megalomania Dio could write of Pompey's
Theatre as 'one in which we still take pride even now'.

Approaching it from the north-west would have brought you to the
middle of the convex exterior of the semicircular auditorium, which most
probably had three storeys of arcades adorned with columns, the lowest
of which has left some traces. The arches themselves were of volcanic
peperino quarried from the Monte Albano. The columns were of red
granite, and possibly, if the Augustan theatre of Marcellus copied Pompey's in this respect as in others, they were of different styles on the three
storeys – Doric on the ground level, Ionic on the second, and Corinthian
at the top. And if Pompey did not actually gild the façade as Nero was
to do 121 years later when the King of Armenia came to receive his
diadem from the imperial hand, there was nothing plain about the stone
arcades, which were embellished not only with ornate columns but
with every possible elaboration in stone and stucco and innumerable
statues in terracotta, marble and bronze.

According to Pliny the open-air auditorium which lay behind that
façade could seat as many as forty thousand spectators on the tiers of
stone seats which radiated upwards from the semicircular *orchestra* in
front of the rectangular stage, which was itself enormous. The diameter

of the auditorium, whose curve is still followed by the tenements of the Via di Grotta Pinta, was some 170 yards, which is not very different from the diameter of the Colosseum (though the latter was a completely oval amphitheatre). The stage, raised a few feet above the level of the *orchestra*, was a hundred yards wide and perhaps twenty deep, and if a playing area of some two thousand square yards seems somewhat daunting by modern standards, it is an indication of what could be done when money and taste were no object. Behind the stage and forming a permanent background to the extravaganzas for which it had been designed was a vast stage-building, rising probably to the full height of the auditorium and giving access to the stage through a huge, arched entrance in the centre and lesser entrances to either side. And this whole monumental background was embellished with every conceivable sculptured and painted refinement – statues in niches, landscapes, Bacchanalian revels, representations of monstrous births and other marvels, and all manner of distractions which would be the despair of a modern producer.

But magnificent as it was, the Theatre itself formed only part of the vast leisure-complex which was Pompey's gift to the Roman people and to his own memory. Beyond the great arch of the stage-building was a delightful park, beautifully laid out and surrounded by a covered colonnade with four parallel rows of pillars. This was Pompey's Portico, some 200 yards long by 150 wide, which became the most celebrated place of amorous dalliance for the polite society of Rome. It was not the sort of place where a lady would remain alone for long, and they were not all refugees from the heat of summer who drifted elegantly among 'the shady columns bright-hung with gold-embroidered curtains, the avenues of thick-planted planes rising in trim rows, and the tinkling streams which sprang from countless fountains' – thus demonstrating to the less romantically disposed that there was at least one department of material culture in which the Romans could improve on the Greeks from whom the idea of Portico as well as Theatre had derived. Nor indeed was the Greekness of Pompey's Portico purely conceptual. It was packed with the finest works of art that wealth and power could acquire from that attractive nation, and for those who had eyes for anything but their companions there was a cultural feast of classical masterpieces which would forever associate the name of Pompey with the sort of refinement over which Pliny was to enthuse more than a century later. Pompey may not have been much of a connoisseur himself, but he wisely sought the expert advice of men like Cicero's friend, Atticus, whom he asked to arrange his statues. And there were of course the cultivated Greeks of his own entourage, notably the historian Theophanes and his secretary Demetrius, the latter so closely responsible for the whole enterprise that he was nastily rumoured to have paid for it all himself from ill-gotten gains in the East and only to have called it after Pompey in order to avoid the odium that would attach itself to the rich freedmen of the Empire. But if Pompey was probably ill at ease discussing the finer points of his art-collection, there were one or two pieces which he would have taken particular pleasure in displaying to a visitor. He might forget the name of Pausias who had painted the sacrifice of oxen with a technique over which Pliny was to wax eloquent, and even the creator of *Cadmus and Europa* might slip his mind. But he would have kept you well informed about the merits of Nicias' portrait of Alexander, and he is unlikely to have been vague about a masterpiece by Polygnotus, the fifth-century painter of Delphi and of the Painted Portico at Athens who was renowned for the expressive features of his females and the delicacy of the diaphanous draperies with which he contrived to clothe them more erotically than if he had left them nude. Artistically and financially the Polygnotus was one of Pompey's best pieces, and it was given an appropriately prominent position gracing the most important part of his Portico – the entrance to the *Curia Pompeii*, the new Senate House which Pompey had built adjoining it.

At first sight it appears very public-spirited of Pompey to have provided his peers with a new meeting-place out of his Oriental spoils, and it was undeniably convenient for meetings which required the attendance of proconsuls and others who could not enter the city-walls without losing their *imperium*. But it was most convenient for one particular proconsul who, pleased to have the command of armies but disinclined to proceed to distant and uncomfortable provinces when his consulship expired, was already setting the pattern of imperial administration to be followed by Augustus. For Pompey had no intention of burying himself in Spain for five years. When he ceased to be consul, he would continue to govern his provinces through the legates whom he had sent out immediately on his appointment, while he himself commuted pleasantly between his villas in the country and the new town-house which he had had the happy thought of incorporating in the plan of the permanent exhibition of his own greatness. For Pompey's new mansion, looking to Plutarch 'like a boat being towed behind a great ship', was set in beautiful gardens adjoining Pompey's Theatre. Pompey's Theatre would entertain the people fed by Pompey's corn. Pompey's Portico would present an artistic reminder of Pompey's benefactions at every turn. Pompey's Senate House would accommodate the Fathers of Rome within strolling distance of Pompey's residence, and in case he happened to be away when they were meeting there, he had thoughtfully installed a large statue of himself to remind his peers that some political animals were in fact more equal than others. It was all a most skilful exercise in imperial public relations which not only gave a new dimension to the glorification of Empire but marked a long stride towards the glorification of Emperor. And though Caesar would pay the price of autocracy at the foot of Pompey's statue, it was appropriate that the new position which Augustus found for it was at the Theatre's great entrance which bore the name of the 'Regal Gate'.

Pompey was clearly aware of the envy which all this self-glorification would generate. Although the giving of costly and elaborate enter-tainments in the most comfortable of settings had long been the *sine qua non* of political advancement and there was no shortage of permanent theatres elsewhere in Italy, in Rome only temporary structures were allowed. A theatre was built by one man for the length of his shows and then dismantled. Personal glory was permissible as long as it was transi-tory, but Pompey's Theatre would be a permanent reminder of his triumph. And because Pompey feared that the Senate might one day – after his death if not during his lifetime – vote to destroy this glorious monument to his greatness on the pretext of a crusade for moral rearma-ment, he decided to sanctify his Theatre by a clever device explained by Tertullian.

'When Pompey summoned the people by edict to the dedication of his citadel of all uncleanness,' wrote that stern Christian some two and a half centuries later, 'he called it not a theatre but a temple to Venus "under which", he said, "we have set seats for gladiatorial shows"!' And that indeed is exactly how it looked from the stage. The central wedge of seats rising from the *orchestra* made a monumental staircase at the top of which, dominating both the inside and the outside of the auditorium, was perched a chapel to a goddess who, far from detracting from the glory that belonged to Pompey, was its presiding and preserving deity. For this was no ordinary Venus stimulating the tender passions in the Portico. This was Venus the Victorious, the divinity under whose guid-ance Pompey had triumphed over the three parts of the inhabited world and under whose protection the monument which he had created from their spoils would be safe from desecration. To modern archaeologists her temple has seemed an architectural eyesore, but she was placed up in the gods for more than the view, and if the structure appeared some-what top-heavy, it was necessary to her protective role. If the temple had been placed at ground-level, the theatre might have been demolished around it, but since the auditorium formed the temple-steps, it was safe. And so, says Tertullian, 'Pompey the Great humbugged morality with superstition' – without adding that any 'morality' which destroyed this 'citadel of all uncleanness' would itself have been humbug from the improbable puritans of Rome's jealous aristocracy.

It was probably September 55 by the time everything was ready for the dedication, and Pompey had spared no expense to obliterate the memory of all spectacles since his own triumphal procession almost exactly six years earlier. In 58 the unprecedentedly extravagant Scaurus had exhibited 150 female leopards for the first time at Rome. Pompey ordered 410. In 93 Sulla had created a sensation with a hundred lions. Pompey had six hundred, of which 315 were maned. And so it went on, with every attraction multiplied and enlarged to produce what Cicero publicly heralded as 'the most sumptuous and magnificent games beyond human memory' and privately described to his refined friend Marcus Marius as tasteless and vulgar. According to Cicero, poor Marius, 'somewhat weak in health as in character', had been far better off where he was, enjoying the beautiful scenery of the Bay of Naples while his Greek slave read him improving literature. It had been too terrible to have to sit through so many farces. One had scarcely been able to keep awake, and one had had to endure simply any old rubbish that Pompey's Lord Chamberlain had sanctioned. It had all been very sumptuous of course, but unlikely to have appealed to Marius' refined taste if Cicero's own reactions were anything to judge by. The actors who had returned to the stage out of respect for Pompey were those who had left it out of respect for themselves. And as for the great Aesop, Marius' favourite tragic actor, his voice had cracked at the height of the drama, and he had been such a flop that no one would have regretted a premature exit. As for the rest of the shows, they had lacked the charm even of more modest productions. The sheer spectacle of such magnificence had taken all the fun out of the thing. For what possible pleasure could one derive from the sight of six hundred mules on stage in the *Clytaemnestra*, or three thousand bowls in the *Trojan Horse*, or all the varieties of arms and armour of the veritable regiments of foot and horse who appeared in casts of thousands whenever a battle-scene was portrayed. It had excited the admiration of the common people, it was true, but ... need one say more?

It must have been as annoying to Cicero's correspondent as it is to us that he did not give a fuller and less affectedly highbrow account of 'the most sumptuous and magnificent games beyond human memory', but he says enough to indicate the scale of the theatrical performances. Great actors were brought out of retirement for the command performances. Supernumeraries and properties were on a scale more appropriate to Hollywood than to Stratford, and if the play required a battle, the glorious array of cavalry and infantry left nothing to the imagination except perhaps the words of the actors struggling to compete with six hundred mules or a squadron of cavalry horses. And drama was only one of the attractions which were spread over many days. Dio lists music, athletics and horse-racing as well as the inevitable gladiatorial contests and beast-hunts, but Cicero's jaundiced eye regarded all with the same studied disdain:

As to the athletics, why should I suppose that you are sorry to have missed them – you who scorned the gladiators. Even Pompey admits that he wasted toil and oil on them. And that really is all there was to it, except of course the beast-hunts, two a day for five days. Magnificent, yes: there is no denying it. But what pleasure can it possibly be to a man of culture when a frail specimen of mankind is torn to pieces by a mighty brute, or when a splendid beast is transfixed by a javelin? And even if this were something worth seeing, you have seen it all before, and I, who was there, saw nothing new in it. The last day was elephant-day, but though the mob was mightily impressed, even they showed no pleasure. Indeed the reaction was a certain compassion and a sort of feeling that those huge animals have a kinship with the human race.

Sadly that is all our irritating eye-witness has to tell us about the greatest show on earth, but for the day of the elephants at least there were obviously other contemporary accounts on which later writers could draw, and from Pliny's careful description it does appear that Cicero was not being merely feline in indicating that Pompey's grand finale had not been an unqualified success. Indeed Pompey always seems to have been rather unlucky with elephants at Rome. When he had returned from defeating Sulla's enemies in Africa and tried to enter the city in a triumphal chariot drawn by elephants in 79, the wretched pachyderms had proved too wide. And now that he wanted to use them in a beast-hunt, they proved too human. At first they provided marvellous entertainment as they defended themselves against their human opponents, who were Gaetulians armed with javelins. 'One animal in particular,' says Pliny, 'disabled by a forest of javelins aimed at its tender feet, had dropped to its knees, but still it advanced against its persecutors, snatched their shields with its trunk, and hurled them in the air in such graceful curves that they appeared to have been thrown by a skilful juggler rather than an infuriated wild animal.' This was a great delight to the enthusiastic spectators, and there was still greater applause for the skilful throw of one of the Gaetulians who killed an elephant with a single javelin that 'pierced the animal just below the eye and penetrated to the vital parts of the head'. But after a while things began to go wrong. The elephants first tried to break out of the iron palisade which confined them, and that caused something of a panic among the close-packed audience (and particularly the quality in the better seats near the front). Then 'having given up all hope of escape, they tried instead to gain the sympathy of the crowd by making indescribable gestures of entreaty and by lamenting their fate with a sort of wailing which caused the people so much distress that they forgot the *Imperator* and the munificence which he had carefully devised for their honour, rose to their feet with tears in their eyes, and invoked curses on the head of Pompey, for which he soon afterwards was to pay the penalty'.

Although this supposed cursing of Pompey is of course as retrospective a flourish as most of history's omens and presages of disaster, there is no reason to doubt Pliny's description of the battle or the 'displeasure' of the spectators to which Cicero refers, and it may well be that they begged Pompey to spare the elephants as recorded in Dio's version of this obviously exceptional example of tender feelings on the part of Rome's bloodthirsty mob. On the other hand there is no reason to suppose that this unfortunate finale soured the memory of the feast of bestial delights which had gone before, not to mention the extravaganzas over which the gentler Muses had presided. For days the people of Rome had been treated to plays, musicals, athletics, races, gladiatorial shows and the excitement of seeing men fighting all manner of less sympathetic wild beasts than the unfortunate elephants. The consumption of lions alone had run at a rate of over a hundred a day for five days, and all the 410 leopards had been put in the arena at once. Moreover Pompey had taken pains to refresh jaded appetites with some animal novelties. He brought baboons and the lynx to the arena for the first time, and he created a sensation with the first rhinoceros, which afterwards became such a firm favourite at Rome that Pliny describes carefully how they were bred to fight elephants and how they prepared for battle by sharpening their horns against a rock. And when it was all over there is no doubt that Pompey had never enjoyed greater popularity and prestige, or Crassus less.

According to Dio both consuls had incurred some unpopularity in raising the levies voted them for their proconsular commands, but Plutarch's account of Pompey's role in escorting Crassus from Rome suggests that by November at least it was Crassus who bore the full force of this particular storm. For the opposition to Crassus' projected campaign against Parthia was intense. There had been no specific authorization of a Parthian war in the plebiscite which had given Crassus the governorship of Syria for five years, but everyone knew that this was what he intended. 'Though extremely upright and no slave to passions in his general behaviour,' says Velleius, 'he knew no bounds in his lust for money and his ambition for glory.' According to Appian he looked upon a war with a supposedly weakened Parthia as 'easy and profitable', and in his desire to emulate Pompey and Caesar in military glory at the age of sixty Plutarch suggests that he was in his second childhood, 'for he made youthful boasts, and flew on the wings of hope as far as Bactria and India and the Outer Ocean'. As he sat through the glittering spectacles in Pompey's Theatre with its fourteen statues representing the fourteen nations over which Pompey had triumphed, his mind had doubtless wandered to the day when he would return covered with glory and loaded with the spoils to celebrate a Parthian triumph 'which would make the successes of Pompey look like child's play in comparison'. But Pompey was less concerned about Crassus the general than Crassus the politician. He was only too pleased to encourage a formidable political manipulator to direct his energies into distant wars, and he felt he had nothing to fear either in reputation or security from Crassus' success (though possibly something to gain from his failure).

But that element in the Senate which opposed all great commands on principle was even more than usually opposed to Crassus' intention 'to wage war against a friendly power'. Leading the opposition was a tribune named Ateius, and to judge from Dio's account he had enjoyed the support of all his tribunician colleagues until they realized that 'their boldness unsupported by arms was too weak to hinder any of Crassus' undertakings'. But Ateius himself could not be cowed. When Crassus offered the customary sacrifices before leaving the city, the opposition spread rumours of unfavourable omens, and on the day of his departure to take command of his army there was such a large and hostile crowd barring his way that he 'begged Pompey to come to his aid and join in escorting him from the city, for great was Pompey's reputation with the people'. Although Crassus could probably have forced his way out of Rome, it would scarcely have been an auspicious start to his expedition to be hissed and abused by an angry crowd, and still less if it had involved the spilling of citizen blood. He therefore swallowed his pride and appealed to Pompey, whose confident appearance caused all hostility to subside like a pricked bubble. 'For when the crowd saw Pompey's beaming face in front of Crassus,' says Plutarch, 'they gave way in silence', and the tribune Ateius was thwarted. But still Ateius did not give up. He ordered Crassus to be arrested, and when other tribunes prevented this, he 'rushed ahead to the city-gate, placed there a brazier, and cursed him with ancient curses', which would no doubt have been forgotten if they had not been fulfilled in one of the most shattering defeats in the history of Roman imperialism.

As Pompey's second consulship drew to a close, he must have felt supremely confident in his position as prince of citizens. He had so far eclipsed the consulship of his colleague that the duality of the office had been no more than a formality in terms of status, and it had marked a gratifying acceptance of his supremacy to have been begged to escort

Crassus from Rome. And Crassus' military ambition had compelled him to dance to Pompey's political tune more than once that year. When, for example, the tax-farmers of Syria had complained to the Senate in the autumn that Gabinius' expedition to Alexandria to restore King Ptolemy had left the province open to pirates, Crassus had initially spoken against Pompey's protégé, possibly because he had money tied up in the tax-farming companies, and more especially to discredit the governor whom he was replacing. But only a few days later Crassus was speaking even more earnestly in Gabinius' defence, and it would be strange if this remarkable change of heart were unconnected with a reminder of his dependence on Pompey's support against the mounting opposition to his military ambitions. As for Caesar's exploits, Pompey still regarded them as familial, and when the news arrived that his father-in-law had conducted an expedition against the mysterious island of Britain ('from which', says Dio, 'he gained nothing for himself or the Republic except glory'), it is hardly likely that the president of the Senate and controller of its agenda was unfavourable to the vote of a public thanksgiving of twenty days.

Looking ahead to the next year, Pompey could be confident of maintaining his interests at Rome because he was going to stay in Italy. While Plutarch maintains in his *Life of Pompey* that this refusal to leave Italy had caused him some unpopularity, in the *Life of Crassus* he says the very opposite, that 'most people wanted Pompey to stay close to the city and were therefore pleased that he, being passionately fond of his wife, intended to spend most of his time there'. If there had been any general unpopularity from an admittedly exceptional arrangement which suggests that Pompey considered himself the guardian of a constitution whose rules applied to others more than himself – and Dio mentions an apparently abortive attempt by political opponents to prosecute the proconsuls' legates – it probably belonged to the earlier part of the year, when Pompey had been riding roughshod over the opposition. Perhaps if he had not been staying in Italy he would have been more concerned about the elections of the consuls for the following year, but as it was, though the elections were not held until the very end of 55, there is no suggestion that he was personally responsible for their postponement or that he interfered in the voting beyond supporting his own candidates in the accepted way. He evidently took no steps to prevent Domitius from standing for the consulship again, and though he was hardly overjoyed at the latter's election, he was unconcerned, not least because the other consul-elect was his son's father-in-law. This was Appius Claudius, whose daughter had become the wife of Pompey's elder son Gnaeus, probably during the course of 55. And since Appius Claudius was the brother of the infamous Clodius, young Gnaeus Pompeius had usefully acquired for an uncle the greatest rabble-rouser and mob-manipulator of them all who had 'leapt over to Pompey's side' with a timely regard for self-interest in the latter part of 56.

Cicero naturally felt less than comfortable about this marriage connection between his arch-enemy and Pompey, whose interest he now considered it essential to support. In the late autumn of 55 the very letter in which Cicero had disparaged Pompey's extravaganzas reveals that the orator had thought it wise to undertake the trial of Caninius, the tribune of 56 who had pushed a Bill to transfer the restoration of King Ptolemy from Spinther to Pompey. And when Crassus had vented his frustration at having to defend Gabinius against the tax-farmers' complaints in a scathing attack on Cicero, Pompey had compelled a public reconciliation. This took the form of a dinner-party which Cicero threw for Crassus just before he left Rome; and though Cicero privately rejoiced at Crassus' inauspicious departure in a letter to Atticus – 'What a worthless rogue he is!' – the new year finds him writing to the East-bound proconsul the sort of 'recantation' which he had made to Pompey in 56. In January 54 we learn that he had been defending Crassus' expedition in the Senate 'in a way that showed everyone', so he wrote, 'that I am your dearest friend', and he begged Crassus to regard this humbug 'not merely as a letter, but as a firm treaty of alliance and friendship between us'. In short, Crassus' absence from Rome had suited Pompey, and Cicero had had to oblige them both by supporting the expedition. Admittedly his letter to Crassus was also something of an insurance policy against an uncertain future – what if Pompey were to die and Crassus return a conquering hero? – but the hard fact remains that Pompey was the proconsul who was staying at home, and it was upon Pompey's favour that Cicero's own security most clearly depended.

For similar reasons Cicero began cultivating the closest possible relationship with Caesar, on whose staff his brother Quintus was serving miserably in outlandish parts of Gaul which the urban Cicero neither knew nor cared to know about provided that fraternal self-sacrifice continued to serve their joint political purpose of keeping close to Pompey's principal protégé. A letter of February 54 contains an enigmatic reference to Pompey which seems to suggest that Africanus was paying uncomfortably little attention to the would-be Laelius, and Cicero is constantly emphasizing the necessity of making himself as useful as possible to Caesar. But by July Cicero was feeling more confident about the following year. 'I am conscious of my resources,' he wrote, 'seeing that I retain the favour of Caesar and Pompey'. And if there is any significance in the order in which the two names appear, it is not that Cicero was putting a higher value on the good will of the absent Caesar. He knew that one way to the good will of Pompey was through his protégé, and he was afraid of 'an outburst of frenzy by our demented friend', namely Clodius. Similarly at the end of July we find Cicero preparing to defend Scaurus, and his acceptance of this brief was hardly unconnected with Pompey's favour since the client had been one of Pompey's officers in the Eastern campaigns, enjoyed a familial connection with Pompey through having married his former wife Mucia and fathered a step-brother to his children, and was now standing for the consulship of 53 with Pompey's support in the most bizarre circumstances. 'There is a vague hope of elections,' Cicero had written only a month ago. 'The Forum is profoundly tranquil, but that is more a symptom of senility in the body politic than of acquiescence, and the opinions which I express in the Senate are such that others agree with them more than I do myself'. But it had been the lull before a storm; and when the storm broke in July over an electoral scandal, the Forum rapidly became the scene of corruption and violence on such a scale that the translation of Pompey's latent, unofficial supremacy into a legalized dictatorship seemed to many a preferable alternative to total paralysis of the constitution and urban anarchy.

The other contenders for the consulships of 53 were Calvinus, Memmius and Messalla, and Cicero commented that he had never seen four candidates more evenly matched. Memmius, like Scaurus, was supported by the Pompeian interest, for though he was the same Memmius who as praetor of 58 had joined his colleague Domitius, now consul, in opposing the Monster's legislation of 59, he had since followed Cicero's example in 'running before the gale'. But with Pompey more interested in Scaurus, and with competitive bribery causing interest rates to double from four to eight per cent overnight, Memmius allowed himself to be paired with Calvinus in a secret agreement with the existing consuls Domitius and Appius Claudius, who pledged their support for these two candidates in return for guarantees of receiving from them the proconsular provinces of their choice. The whole sordid compact was solemnly drawn up in legal form including the names of the priests and others who were to be their accomplices. But so fantastic an agreement could not remain secret for long, and by 27 July Cicero was already telling Atticus that he had 'got wind of a secret arrangement which I dare not commit to writing'. And Pompey was not amused. 'He growls and complains,' wrote Cicero, though whether his concern for the detrimental effect on Scaurus' chances was genuine or not seemed doubtful. 'Ostensibly Scaurus is his man,' continued Cicero, 'but does he mean it?' On the other hand, Pompey made a point of giving a character-reference for Scaurus at the celebrated trial at which Cicero led for the defence, and he was clearly keen to keep him in the running if only to stimulate the competition in bribery and brute force which would eventually require authorized intervention by the one man capable of suppressing it.

With August came a further postponement of the elections to September, but Pompey was now more preoccupied with domestic than public affairs as Julia prepared for her confinement. For after the tragedy of her miscarriage in the previous year she had conceived again, and her husband looked forward to the birth of their child with a mixture of excitement and anxiety that he shared with her father. But the bond between them was not to be reinforced. A child was born alive, but the mother died, and her baby daughter survived for only a few days. Pompey was desolated. His love for Julia had become almost proverbial as an exception to the rule of marital infidelity in that society of arranged marriages, and the aura of domestic romance had sweetened his greatness with an attractive humanity not often found alongside ruthless ambition. As he received the messages of condolence and made the automatic acknowledgements of a mind numbed by grief, his one thought was to lay Julia to rest at their villa in the Alban Hills where they had passed their happiest times. But when the eulogies had been spoken in the Forum and the funeral cortège re-formed to take the body out of Rome, the crowds began to cry out against taking her anywhere but to the hallowed ground of the Campus Martius. And they did more than cry out. They seized the bier and carried it down to that Roman equivalent of Westminster Abbey, and there, at the insistence of the Roman people, the wife of Pompey the Great was laid to rest among some of the greatest names of Roman history.

According to Plutarch's account this took Pompey completely by surprise, and though the hard-headed Dio has doubts that the call for Julia to be buried in the Campus Martius was quite as spontaneous as it appeared, and suggests an element of stage-management by friends of Pompey and Caesar, there is no reason to question the sincerity of the people's enthusiasm to grant this honour to their prince of citizens. When Plutarch maintains that they were motivated more by their pity for the young woman than by any desire to gratify Pompey or Caesar, he is making an artificial conflict of loyalties from an indivisible and unrationalized emotion, and when he adds that 'of the two it was thought that the people gave a greater share of honour to Caesar, who was absent, than to Pompey, who was present', his further subdivision is not only artificial but typically anachronistic. The wave of rejoicing that swept through the whole of Italy four years later on the news of Pompey's recovery from a serious illness shows that even then he still came second to no one in public esteem. Caesar naturally shared in the honour shown at his daughter's funeral in 54, but it was not at Pompey's expense. It was Pompey who had triumphed over the three parts of the inhabited world, and if Caesar was now thrilling the city with news of his second expedition to mysterious Britain, it was no sort of challenge to the glory of a patron who, resting on his own many laurels, was now feeding, entertaining and beautifying the city whose greatness he promoted, protected and personified. And if Pompey was heroic in his achievements, he was also human in his love for his wife, and to suppose that the people suddenly pitied Julia more than the grieving widower is absurd.

But there was one voice raised in opposition to the popular will. According to Dio the consul Domitius objected that it was sacrilegious for Julia to be buried in hallowed ground without a special decree of the Senate, but his pretext was as transparent as his opposition was rash. Incensed at this insult to Julia's memory and his own honour Pompey sought distraction from his grief in political revenge, and a letter from Cicero to Atticus dated 1 October reveals how he achieved it. Ever since June there had been rumours of the scandalous agreement between the consuls Domitius and Appius Claudius and the candidates Calvinus and Memmius, but there had been no proof until now, when Memmius caused a sensation in the Senate by revealing the whole affair 'at the instigation of Pompey'. Why Memmius should have agreed to implicate himself in this way is not clear, except perhaps in the hope of escaping conviction for a crime that was bound to come to light sooner or later, but Pompey was evidently able to put sufficient pressure on him to bring the desired disgrace on that sanctimonious humbug of a consul who had dared to insult his wife's burial with the name of sacrilege. 'To Appius Claudius it makes no difference,' wrote Cicero scathingly, 'for a rogue like that had no reputation to lose. But Domitius is utterly discredited.'

The result was a further postponement of elections and a lawyers' paradise in which all four candidates were indicted for bribery and corruption. But Pompey's concern was more with the trial of Gabinius, on whose behalf Cicero was now called upon to prostitute his forensic skill before the altar of political expediency. Cicero had already undertaken the distasteful task of defending another of Pompey's protégés, Vatinius – the tribune of 59 who had helped Caesar to carry through his legislation and on whom Cicero had heaped abuse at Sestius' trial in 56. In 55 Cicero had vigorously opposed Vatinius' candidature for the praetorship which would have gone to Marcus Cato but for the physical and financial intervention of Pompey and Crassus; but in September 54 Cicero obligingly defended him against the charge of having gained his praetorship by corruption, and when Spinther took him to task for lack of principle at the end of the year he explained blandly that Pompey 'insisted' on a reconciliation and that Caesar had added an urgent request that he undertake the case. 'But why did I eulogize him? You know the political game as well as I do....'

But if it had been distasteful enough for Cicero to defend Vatinius, a reconciliation with this older Pompeian protégé whom he held scarcely less responsible than Clodius for his exile was such a bitter pill that he could bring himself to swallow it only after a long struggle to accept that his political health could be secured in no other way. When Gabinius returned to Rome in the autumn of 54 and appeared before the Senate on 7 October to make his formal report on his governorship of Syria, Cicero helped to 'give him a hot time of it'. And when Gabinius retorted by flinging the hated word 'Exile!' in his face, any prospect of a reconciliation seemed so remote that everyone expected Cicero to lead for the prosecution when Gabinius was put on trial for lèse-majesté – for having offended against the sovereignty of the Roman People by leaving his province and making his unauthorized campaign to restore Ptolemy to the throne of Egypt. But the one-word retort of Gabinius had been enough to remind Cicero of the bitter fruits of political independence, and however nauseating it was to swallow Gabinius' insult, it was less harmful than opposing Pompey, who was determined to secure his protégé's acquittal not only by wholesale corruption of the jury but by making the trial as personal an issue as that of Balbus had been two years earlier. The most Cicero did therefore was to give evidence for the prosecution in a mild form which represented his attempt to save face without offending Pompey or jeopardizing the result. 'I neither trampled Gabinius nor picked him up', explained Cicero to the apprehensive Quintus, 'and after that I kept quiet' – which had been his brother's fervent advice all the time. But while his evidence was clearly mild enough for Gabinius to make no cross-examination, Cicero was still nervous about Pompey's reaction, and when Atticus wrote to ask how Pompey had taken it, he replied with more hope than certainty that Pompey had been 'kind enough to consider my dignity until Gabinius should have made amends' for the public insult in the Senate.

Gabinius was acquitted, and on 24 October Cicero relieved his feelings with the following epistolary explosions to Quintus and Atticus over the result and its political implications:

Gabinius is acquitted! The prosecutor was puerile, the jurors corrupt, but even so it was only the strenuous efforts of Pompey and an alarming rumour of a dictatorship that carried the day. You can see there is really no Republic left, no Senate, no lawcourts, no position of authority for any of us.... Some say I should have undertaken the prosecution.... It would have been political suicide.... Pompey would have regarded it as a struggle not for Gabinius but for his own position.... He would have entered the city, and I should have been like some nimble little flyweight squaring up against the heavyweight champion of the world. He would probably have bitten my ear off, and he would certainly have unleashed Clodius.... And who am I to join battle with the man who stands alone in his omnipotence in an impotent Republic? ... There is no freedom now either in reality or even superficially, but I am not bothered that one man is all-powerful. In fact it is almost a pleasure to see that those who were upset that I should have any power at all are equally choked by his. And there is no doubt that the whiff of dictatorship in the air had a profound effect on the more timid members of the jury.

This is not the first mention in 54 of the prospect that Pompey might become dictator. As early as June Cicero had written to Quintus that 'there is some suspicion of a dictatorship but nothing concrete', and though his comment on the state of affairs at Rome had been excessively, perhaps deliberately, vague, it had conveyed the image of a city over-shadowed by the formidable presence which resided in the monument to its own greatness outside the city-walls.

There followed a flood of the River Tiber which Cicero called a judge-ment of heaven against Gabinius' acquittal, but to Pompey it was a god-send, providing him with work which was not only an antidote to grief but a source of still greater popularity. Torrential rains had brought down such a volume of water that all the lower levels of the city were in-undated, and though Cicero made the stoic resolution not to let it 'trouble' him in the comfortable security of his Tusculan villa, it was not so easily ignored by those inhabitants of the disaster-area who were lucky enough to have escaped with their lives. For Dio tells us that the loss of life and property had been enormous. Many houses and tenements had been swept away together with their occupants, and of those that were still standing there were few not dangerously weakened. But even more critical than the loss of shelter was the loss of food, not only live-stock and the contents of private homes and businesses but the city's corn-supply which had been stored in the granaries down by the docks, and this of course was Pompey's official concern. And while the consular candidates and their cliques continued bribing and battering each other into political paralysis, the prince of citizens devoted his energies to the more useful work of his corn commission, and for much of the remainder of the year Pompey was away ensuring that the city would not starve.

By the end of November Cicero was writing to Atticus in the most lurid colours. 'Come quick and gaze at the empty husks of our dear old Republic! See cash distributed openly before the elections, tribe by tribe, all in one place! See the acquitted Gabinius, smell the whiff of dictator-ship, enjoy the holiday and free-for-all, and observe my equanimity at the rise of interest-rates to ten per cent.' And to Quintus he was even more explicit. Pompey and Caesar had thrown over their former candidates Scaurus and Memmius, and though Calvinus had been involved in the consuls' election-rigging, he had since displayed the right political colours by voting ostentatiously for Gabinius' acquittal, and now he and Messalla were leading the field. But it was no longer the consulship which was monopolizing political conversation. The word on everyone's lips was 'dictator', and though Pompey was openly denying that he wanted a dictatorship, Cicero was not convinced, especially since Lucilius Hirrus, one of the tribunes about to take office for 53, was already rumoured to be framing the necessary plebiscite. 'Ye gods, what a fool he is!' exclaimed Cicero. 'What a lover of himself without a rival!' Yet Cicero had to admit that Pompey had asked him to intercede with another of the tribunes-elect to dissuade him from taking the same line. 'Does he want it, or doesn't he? It is hard to know. But if Hirrus starts agitating for it, he will have a job convincing anyone that he doesn't.'

In early December Cicero was still uncertain of Pompey's real wishes. Pompey's denials had evidently done nothing to kill the proposal, and when Cicero speaks of his certainty that Messalla will become consul in the new year, he treats it as an open question whether the elections will be held by an *interrex*, who will immediately leave office, or a *dictator*, who will not. But 'nothing has actually been done about a dictator yet. Pompey is away. Appius Claudius is mixed up in it. Hirrus is getting ready, though other tribunes are said to be just as ready to veto it. The people are apathetic. The better sort are against it. And I keep quiet.'

But there was one issue on which Cicero was unable to preserve his diplomatic silence, for when Gabinius was again put on trial, this time for provincial extortion in December, Pompey approached him to accept the brief for the defence. In September Cicero had maintained to Quintus that Pompey would never succeed in reconciling him to Gabinius as long as he had 'a particle of independence left'. In October he had said that it would have brought him 'eternal infamy' to have defended Gabinius at the first trial (though he acknowledged that his 'middle course' was an attempt to steer clear of 'eternal infamy' without running on to the rocks of 'dangerous enmities'). And even in early December he was still quoting a Homeric outburst to Quintus against the suggestion that he should have spoken for Gabinius: 'Rather let the earth gape and swallow me!' But all that was now swallowed was his pride. Not surprisingly he did not publish his speech on this occasion, but a fragment of his notes for it suggests that he tried to present his reconciliation with his enemy as an act of humanity, which of course fooled no one and earned him the epithet 'turncoat' which, Dio says, 'was applied to him now more than ever'.

In his letter to Quintus in September Cicero had expressed dismay at his brother's news that Caesar was talking of his joining Pompey's proconsular staff. It would hardly have meant going to Spain and it may not even have involved much work, but it was more than the nuisance which Cicero sought to avoid. It would have lost him that very semblance of independence to which his pride still clung, and in his anxiety to get out of it gracefully he had written to Caesar to ask him to intercede with Pompey on his behalf. At first Caesar had appeared sympathetic, but the agents in Rome whom he had asked to approach Pompey significantly either failed to do so or pretended not to have done so. Caesar was not going to jeopardize his own relationship with Pompey for Cicero's sake, and as soon as he realized that Pompey wished to bring Cicero to heel, he let Cicero's brother convey his congratulations at the news of the appointment. If Cicero wanted to be excused the honour, he could publicly commit himself to the Pompeian interest in Gabinius' trials. In October Cicero had refused, but when the same choice was presented in December he chose 'eternal infamy', and we hear no more of his joining Pompey's staff. 'You know the political game as well as I do....'

Although Gabinius was convicted at the trial – despite Cicero's eloquence, his own bribery, and an address by Pompey who also read out a letter of support from Caesar – the result reflects a diminution of effort on Pompey's part rather than an erosion of the political supremacy which Cicero despairingly calls 'omnipotence'. Pompey was clearly less personally concerned in this trial than in the former, which had been as much a trial of himself as of his protégé, for whereas he was in no way responsible for Gabinius' governorship within his province, he had been directly responsible for the invasion of Egypt.

A lack of relevant political correspondence from Cicero for the next year and a half leaves us depressingly over-dependent on Dio, Plutarch, Appian and other non-contemporary and often garbled accounts. Pompey's sincerity in not wanting the dictatorship seems as probable as his pleasure at the airing of a possibility which it could only increase his prestige to reject. Ever since his return from the East in 62 he had sought to live down the name of Sulla's pupil, and now that his political preeminence was not only recognized but reinforced by a five-year proconsular command exercised uniquely by remote control, he was not likely to want that irregular office whose name was almost as hateful as that of monarchy itself. On the other hand he was quite willing to be called upon to restore law and order in a city paralysed by political strife, and would gracefully oblige as soon as the anarchy had reached the point where his intervention would not be the subject of a plebiscite, which was sure to be opposed, but the object of the pleas of a united Senate and People of Rome. For there was no advantage in being the master of a state when it was possible to be universally accepted as its first servant – and not only as one pillar of the establishment but as an Atlas supporting the whole structure on his shoulders. To have let Hirrus proceed with a Bill to make him dictator at the beginning of 53 would clearly have been premature and counter-productive. Things would get worse before they were better, and if, as seems likely, Pompey himself silenced Hirrus in the new year just as he had silenced one of his colleagues with the same idea in November, it was a sound policy that would slowly but surely bring its rewards.

It is frustrating not to have the guidance of Cicero for 53, a year in which Rome must have been Bedlam. *Interrex* succeeded *interrex* at five-day intervals for seven months before the consular elections were held exactly a year after the usual time. So fierce was the struggle for office, so vast the sums expended to buy it, and so disastrous the result of losing the chance of a proconsular province from which to recoup the expense, that each candidate was determined to use every means at his disposal to postpone the elections until he believed that he could outbribe or out-fight his opponents. It was politics rather than piety which kept the imaginations of tribunes and augurs alert for signs of heavenly displeasure on election-days, and it was jobbery rather than justice that swept the candidates in and out of the courts on charges of which the accusers were as guilty as their defendants. Gang-warfare was now endemic, and the disease was demoralizing. A constitution so perfectly adapted for paralysis could function only as long as its politicians observed an un-written code of conduct, and once the whole religious and legal apparatus had been abused to the limit of what was constitutionally possible, the constitution itself began to be questioned with calls for the revival of anti-quarian curiosities. One, of course, was the dictatorship itself, an office which had been obsolete since the third century until Sulla had revived it in a scarcely recognizable form in 82. Another, if we can believe Dio, was the so-called 'consular tribunate' as an alternative to the consulship. It had fallen in disuse over three centuries ago and its relevance to the present situation is obscure, but since there had been up to six consular tribunes at a time, it might have been argued that more room at the top allowed more ambitions to be satisfied. But multiplying the problem was scarcely the best way of solving it, and 'when no one would heed them', says Dio, 'the tribunes declared that Pompey must be chosen dictator'. And 'by this pretext', he continues, 'they secured a very long delay, for Pompey was away from Rome, and of those who were on the spot there was no one who would venture to vote on this demand, since they all hated that institution because of Sulla's cruelties yet dared not refuse to choose Pompey on account of their fear of him'.

But it is as far from certain that all hated the prospect of Pompey's dictatorship as that all ten tribunes favoured it. Appian may well be representing an increasing body of popular opinion when he suggests that 'many began to talk about the possibility because they believed that the only remedy for the existing evils was the authority of a single ruler', provided of course that they could have the right man. 'There was need of someone both powerful and moderate, they said, thus indicating Pompey, who had a sufficient army under his command and appeared to be both a friend of the people and a leader of the Senate on account of his rank, a man of moderation and self-control, and easily approachable.' And to judge from the rough order of events suggested by Plutarch and Dio it appears that a Bill to bring this about was eventually promulgated by the tribunes Hirrus and Vinicianus, confident presumably that it would command popular support even if they were unsure of Pompey's own wishes in the matter, unless, indeed, Pompey had deliberately put them up to it in order that he could again refuse. Pompey was away at the time of the public announcement, and when Marcus Cato led a strong senatorial lobby in opposing it, Plutarch insists that 'many of Pompey's friends came forward and declared publicly that he neither asked for nor desired that office'. And when Pompey himself returned to Rome, he reiterated the denial and enjoyed the satisfaction of being publicly commended by Cato and urged 'to devote himself to the cause of law and order'.

It was exactly the invitation that he had been waiting for, and though Dio does not elaborate on his statement that Pompey now 'took measures' to bring about the election, it goes without saying that Cato's invitation must have been translated into a formal authorization by the Senate before Pompey employed the same necessarily forceful methods by which he had secured the vote for Cicero's recall in 57 and his own election with Crassus in 55. Nor was such authorization likely to have been delayed, for Rome was still reeling from the news of a catastrophe so great that even the most ardent partisans were temporarily jolted out of their preoccupation with internal politics. On 9 June the expedition of Crassus had met total disaster at Carrhae in upper Mesopotamia. Crassus himself was dead, some 25,000 Roman troops were either killed or captive, and the province of Syria was defended by only a few scattered remnants under the command of his quaestor Gaius Cassius. As the scale of this disaster began to sink into the Roman consciousness, it naturally enhanced the prestige and authority of Pompey, whose invariable success not only invited comparison from the past but gave reassurance for the future. For if the King of Parthia should now turn out to be another Mithridates and invade the Roman provinces of the East, there was only one man who could be safely entrusted with the war – the greatest soldier of the age, whose spoils filled the Theatre and Portico that dominated the Field of Mars where the elections at last took place under his aegis in July 53.

But if Carrhae had been a military disaster on the scale of Cannae, the battlefield was comfortably further away than the site of Hannibal's comparable victory in the heart of Italy, and when the Parthian menace to Syria failed to materialize, the imperial city reverted to its former pre-occupation with the power-struggles at home. For no sooner had Calvinus and Messalla been elected consuls for what remained of 53 than it was time to elect their successors, and the rival candidates for 52 made the struggles of the earlier part of the year seem like drawing-room dis-agreements in comparison. In vain the consuls proposed a senatorial de-cree imposing a five-year period between holding a consulship or praetor-ship and going out to govern a proconsular or propraetorian province. The rationale, explains Dio, was that candidates might 'cease their craze for office' if they lost the prospect of a continuity of command and the means for immediate recovery of their election expenses by extortion. But even if it had been adopted, it was too late to have any effect on the competition for 52. The candidates were already too deeply com-mitted, 'supporting their canvass not only with lavish and unrestrained bribery and popularity-seeking shows but with gangs of armed retainers'. Calvinus himself was wounded in one of the battles, and though both consuls made a public demonstration of their helplessness by 'laying aside their senatorial attire and appearing in the dress of knights as on the occasion of a great calamity', it did no good. Elections were impossible, and another year expired without successors to replace the outgoing magistrates.

Plutarch and Appian maintain that Pompey 'allowed' or 'connived at' this state of anarchy in order that he might become dictator, and Plutarch argues that he wanted to become dictator through fear of Caesar's grow-ing power in Gaul. But they are not convincing. That Pompey 'allowed' the anarchy is clearly true, but it was hardly a sinful omission when he had no constitutional authorization for continuing intervention after the emergency of the July elections. As proconsular governor of Spain he could not even enter the city-walls without special permission; and while he favoured two of the three consular candidates, it was their own ambi-tion which had created the situation. Plautius Hypsaeus was one more in the long list of candidates who had served under Pompey in the East, and Metellus Scipio had an even stronger claim on Pompey's loyalty because Pompey was about to marry his daughter Cornelia, the widow of young Publius Crassus who had perished leading his father's cavalry at Carrhae. But if Pompey preferred Hypsaeus and Scipio to Milo, it was not Pompey's preference but their greed for office which made postponement of the elections so attractive to these two candidates who seemed unable to outbribe or outfight the third. Moreover it was not only the rivalry of candidates for the same office which was creating the deadlock. Milo's candidature for the consulship was even more violently opposed by a candidate for the praetorship, namely his arch-enemy Clodius who was determined not to have his praetorship stifled by a consul who reciprocated his hatred. And with these two specialists in gang-warfare at each other's political throats more violently now than in 57, when their struggle over Cicero's recall had compelled Pompey's first authorized suppression of urban terrorism, Pompey had no need to connive at electoral postponement even if that was what he wanted. As to his desire for dictatorship, it still seems likely that he valued the suggestion more for the distinction of rejecting it than because he really coveted a dangerously monarchical office which he regarded rather with Solonian wariness as 'a fine position but one from which there was no way down'. And the argument that he wanted to become dictator through fear of Caesar is the usual Plutarchian anachronism.

It was Caesar who was afraid for his own position and desperate to keep the favour of Pompey, who could have broken him like a reed at this stage if he had so desired. For Caesar was scarcely shorter of enemies in Rome than in Gaul, and if Pompey had wanted to see him recalled, it might not have been difficult to arrange. And Caesar was fully aware of his dependence. It was no threatening Caesar who sought to restore his marriage-alliance with Pompey after Julia's death by offering him Octavia, his sister's grand-daughter (already married to Gaius Marcellus) and asking for the hand of Pompey's daughter (already betrothed to Faustus Sulla). And it was no frightened Pompey who refused, and married instead the pretty and accomplished young widow of Publius Crassus. Moreover the year 53 had not been easy for Caesar, who had certainly needed the legion which Pompey had readily lent him at the end of 54; and though it had ended in relative tranquillity, it was only the lull before the storm of Gallic nationalism that was about to centre round Vercingetorix in 52 and seemed likely to shatter the vast but fragile structure of Caesar's conquests. It is only with hindsight that Caesar's ultimate victory gains the sanction of destiny, and his clash with Pompey becomes preordained. In 53, and even more in 52, it seemed equally possible that he would share the fate of Crassus. He had more than enough on his hands in Gaul, and it was hardly a self-confident politician who let the severance of his marriage-connection go by without changing the will which he had made in his consulship and under which Pompey was his heir.

For the extraordinary events of January 52 which resulted in Pompey's intervention we are fortunate to have the detailed commentary which Asconius wrote a century later as a guide to Cicero's speech in defence of Milo, and it contains the following sentence: 'Pompeius, the son-in-law of Scipio, and T. Munatius, tribune of the plebs, had not permitted a motion to be brought before the Senate for the convocation of the patricians to nominate the customary *interrex*.' Now this, if correct, throws a different light on Pompey's responsibility for the prevailing anarchy, but the identification of this 'Pompeius' with the son-in-law of Scipio, i.e. Pompey, is open to question. For Pompey had no authority parallel to that of the tribune Munatius Plancus for preventing a meeting of the Senate, and while the sentence is sometimes taken as meaning that Pompey was behind the tribune's veto, that is not its natural interpretation. The text clearly suggests that Pompeius and Plancus jointly prevented the meeting in the same way, and since the tribune Plancus had a colleague Pompeius Rufus who is constantly coupled with him in joint actions during the coming weeks, it seems almost certain that the insertion of 'son-in-law of Scipio' after the name of 'Pompeius' here is either the result of Asconius' misunderstanding of his own sources or, much more probably, a marginal note by a later scholar which a copyist subsequently incorporated into the text which has come down to us. The purpose of the two tribunes' action in preventing the appointment of an *interrex* was simply to postpone still further the elections which Milo seemed likely to win, and while this further step to total anarchy brought the intervention of Pompey much nearer, it was not Pompey who was responsible for it. Milo's rivals and enemies needed no encouragement, and the very last thing that Pompey wanted at this juncture was to stain his public image of constitutional rectitude.

On 18 January the crisis was precipitated by a fatal encounter between Clodius and Milo on the Appian Way, the former riding back to Rome from a visit to Aricia, the latter driving out to Lanuvium. As they passed each other, one of the gladiators in Milo's armed entourage picked a quarrel with one of Clodius' slaves, and when Clodius looked round to see what was happening, he was spitted by a javelin. The Clodians carried their wounded leader into a wayside inn, but Milo had him hauled out and finished off in the middle of the road. Milo probably calculated, as Dio suggests, that he would be more easily acquitted on a charge of murder with Clodius dead than for assault with Clodius alive. Or perhaps the hatred of his old enemy simply carried him away. At any rate he took care to kill or scatter all the Clodian eye-witnesses, and he freed all his own slaves in order that they might not only keep a grateful silence but be secure from having the truth forced out of them by the examination under torture to which a defendant's slaves were usually subjected. As for the body, it was left where it was in the middle of the Appian Way, to be found and recognized later by a passing senator who carried it on to Rome. But having taken the corpse to Clodius' sumptuous mansion on the Palatine, that prudent traveller could not get out of Rome fast enough, and 'returned at once from whence he came'.

As the news of the murder spread through the tenements and taverns of the Subura the crowds began to gather at Clodius' house, where his frenzied widow displayed his naked body and screamed for vengeance. Overnight the whole apparatus of the guilds and clubs had been mobilized, and by the morning the crowds had multiplied into a surging, chanting, many-fisted Fury wanting only official direction for its destructive energy. And that was soon provided by the tribunes Pompeius Rufus and Plancus, eager not only for revenge but for the chance to assume the leadership of the organization through which Clodius had moulded the urban poor into a political instrument which only Pompey's soldiers could control. Taking Clodius with them they led the way to the Forum, where they displayed his dead body for all to see, naked except for the red leather shoes which signified his senatorial rank. They exhibited the wounds, and spoke what Dio calls 'appropriate words', which are not hard to imagine. But the mob scarcely needed reminding of the heady days of 58 when Clodius had begun his tribunate with the institution of a free corn-dole and the legalization of the underground clubs and guilds. As the personification of proletarian power Clodius was the victim not only of Milo but of the establishment, and when the mob now surged into the Senate House and began piling up benches and books in the middle of the floor, they were making the symbol of aristocratic self-interest into their champion's pyre. The body was perched on the top, the pile was lit, and the whole Senate House was burnt to the ground with Clodius inside it.

It was not, Dio observes, a mob impulse but a carefully contrived gesture, and while the Senate House still smouldered and the mob filled the Forum with a funeral feast for Clodius, the Senate met anxiously on the Palatine Hill and authorized its patrician members to appoint an *interrex*. And this time there was no veto from Pompeius Rufus and Plancus. On the contrary, these partisans of Milo's rivals were all eagerness for the elections now that their enemy's candidature seemed as dead as his victim, and Aemilius Lepidus had no sooner been installed as *interrex* than crowds began besieging his house with the demand that they should be held immediately. But it was unconstitutional for the first *interrex* of the year to hold elections, and when the besiegers found Lepidus intransigent, they seized the consular *fasces* from their sacred depository and carried them first to the homes of Scipio and Hypsaeus and then to Pompey's house outside the city-walls. For Pompey was also the people's friend. If it was Clodius who had made the corn-dole free, it was Pompey who had provided it. If it was Clodius who had raised the lowest of the people above the highest of the Senate in his tribunate, it had been Pompey who had restored the tribunate to full potency after its emasculation by Sulla; and it was Pompey who had conquered as the people's general, whose spoils had been devoted to their entertainment, whose towering greatness had its foundations in the popular will. It was forgotten how relatively recently Clodius had been the bane of Pompey's existence. All that mattered now was that Clodius had leapt over to Pompey's side in 56, and that he had since become the uncle of Pompey's elder son. Pompey would surely see to it that justice was done on the murderer, and as the crowds outside his house hailed him alternately as 'Dictator' and 'Consul', he must have imagined the agonizing among his peers with pleasurable anticipation.

The *interrex* Lepidus, in the meantime, remained in a state of siege which continued with increasing exasperation for all five days of his *interregnum* and nearly cost him his life. At one stage the mob actually smashed down his outer door, and having enjoyed themselves overturning the statues of his ancestors which stood in the hall, they armed themselves with the weapons which decorated the walls and smashed their way into the bedroom of his wife, 'a lady of exemplary chastity' who would have lost more than her reputation but for the timely arrival of one of Milo's gangs. At once Milo's men joined battle with the Clodians and the partisans of Scipio and Hypsaeus who had been demanding the elections, but if their distraction had rescued Lepidus, that was not why they had come. Incredible as it may seem they too were now demanding elections, for contrary to the expectation not only of Scipio and Hypsaeus but of a great many moderate senators who hoped that Milo had gone into exile and thus rid the city of not one but both of its most violent politicians, Milo was back in town and showering largess from both hands – bribes from one and hush-money from the other.

In the hope that the burning of the Senate House would swing the indignation of the propertied classes away from the mere murder of one electoral candidate by another, Milo had stolen back into Rome on the night after the conflagration. Moreover he had nothing to lose and everything to gain by continuing his canvass for an office which would not only render him immune from trial but restore the fortune which he had squandered in bribes and the expenditure of 'three inheritances' on public shows, the last of which had cost a million alone. His town-house had not escaped attack, but its garrison of gladiators and slaves had saved it from destruction, and the fact that his own residence proved more secure than that of the temporary head of state was reassuringly symbolic. And he was not without powerful friends. He had earned the devotion of Cicero ever since he had fought Clodius in support of Cicero's restoration from exile, and after the events of 18 January Cicero regarded himself as being under a double obligation to the avenger of his disgrace. Marcus Cato's faction was also backing him against the Pompeian candidates, and one of the tribunes named Caelius, perhaps not without financial inducement, was as devoted to him as Rufus and Plancus were to his rivals. On the other hand his personal feud with Clodius had now become a blood-feud with one of the greatest families in Rome, to which Pompey was now related through his elder son.

Milo tried to see Pompey, but Pompey refused to be compromised. When Milo sent him a message offering to resign his candidature if Pompey so wished, Pompey replied with cold propriety that he 'urged no one to stand or to abstain from standing, nor would he interfere with the power, design or will of the Roman people'. And his refusal to see Milo was given a sinister significance by the tribune Rufus before a mass-meeting the next day. ' "Milo has given you someone to cremate in the Senate," ' he thundered. ' "He will next give you someone to bury on the Capitol" '; and this suggestion that Pompey's life was being threatened by a political enemy was a clever stratagem in the war of words between the rival factions. It discredited Milo now as effectively as it had discredited Clodius in their very different political alignments of 58, and when Pompey subsequently divulged the evidence for this accusation (whether he believed it or not) at another public meeting summoned by Rufus and Plancus, he knew that it would accelerate the authorization for him to defend himself and the state in 52 as surely as in 57.

When a massive distribution of largess had emboldened Milo to appear in person at a public meeting of his own, the tribune Caelius obligingly summoned one for him. Both Caelius and Cicero devoted their eloquence to arguing that Clodius had been killed in self-defence, and Milo said the same while openly maintaining that the state was better off without 'that desperado and friend of the desperadoes who had set fire to the Senate House and burnt it to the ground over his dead body'. But these words were scarcely out of his mouth before those same desperadoes stormed into the Forum under the leadership of Rufus and Plancus, and in the battle which ensued Caelius and Milo managed to escape with their lives only by disguising themselves as slaves. And it was more than a political faction-fight. The urban poor on whose frustrations Clodius had capitalized did not pause to inquire into the political sympathies of a well-dressed man with a gold ring. When gangs of hooligans burst into private houses on the pretext of looking for Milo's adherents, they had a sharper eye for portable property than political persuasion, and 'for many days', says Appian, 'they made Milo the excuse for an orgy of burning, stoning, looting and every sort of crime'. In vain successive *interreges* tried to hold the elections that would give the state two consuls who could then be authorized 'to see to it that the Republic shall suffer no harm'. There was only one man with the power to do that, and as the city spun faster and faster into total chaos, the Senate finally authorized Pompey to act.

The actual form of the Ultimate Decree authorized the *interrex* and the tribunes as well as Pompey 'to see to it that the Republic shall suffer no harm', but of course the *interrex* and the tribunes either could or would do nothing. The five-day *interrex* was only a stop-gap, and the divided tribunes were the instigators rather than suppressors of anarchy. It was to Pompey, alone in all but name, that the Senate had committed the restoration of order, and the seriousness of the situation is reflected in its additional decree that he should 'levy troops throughout Italy' and that 'all young men of military age should be conscripted'. At once Pompey's recruiting officers fanned out over the peninsula, and to the worried Caesar wintering in the Po valley the opportunity to recruit more troops was a god-send: for as he admitted in his memoirs, 'when the situation in Rome was brought under control by the excellence of Pompey', he promptly took them with him over the Alps where he needed every man he could lay his hands on to deal with the rising of Vercingetorix, whose cause now gained additional strength from the news that anarchy reigned in the imperial capital.

But Pompey did not wait for others to do his recruiting for him. He went out himself, and as he was not away long, he no doubt went direct to Campania where his veterans of the Eastern campaigns had their farms. With a large and devoted force he swiftly returned to Rome, turned his gardens outside the city-walls into an armed camp, and waited for the Senate to respond to the increasingly insistent demands that he should be made dictator. For it was no longer simply a question of sending in troops to quell a riot, or even holding elections under armed supervision. To have held elections from the existing candidates whose rivalry had been largely responsible for the crisis would have been to perpetuate disunity. If Milo and one of his enemies were to be elected joint heads of state, the result would be political schizophrenia, and in any case Pompey was not prepared to see Milo win. The Claudii Pulchri wanted justice done on their dead kinsman, and Pompey was determined to see that they would get it. But the situation would be little better if Milo were defeated. The election of the two candidates whose supporters had joined forces against his would neither unify the loyalties of a divided city nor secure it against any act of desperation on the part of Milo. For Milo was dangerous, and if he were to be faced with the wreck of his fortune and the certainty of condemnation there were many who saw him as another Catiline, however much Cicero might play down the danger of an attempted *coup* which would of course require the assassination of Pompey if it were to have a chance of success. What Rome needed was a strong head of state with the prestige to command a peaceful return to the rule of law and with the power to enforce it. But Pompey was as reluctant to revive the image of Sulla's pupil as to share the first place with a colleague. He preferred the singularity of the dictatorship but the constitutionality of the consulship, and since many of his peers were equally anxious not to have a dictator but painfully aware that his troops would not share their scruples, they agreed to the sort of compromise which is the essence of statesmanship. Pompey was to become sole consul.

According to Plutarch this constitutional innovation was a last-minute attempt by Cato's faction to deprive Pompey of the dictatorship, but the fact that the proposal was made by Bibulus and seconded by Cato does not mean that Pompey was either surprised or disappointed at being offered a unique office which Appian calls 'a combination of the power of a dictator with the responsibility of a consul'. It was another 'first' in a long career of political one-upmanship. At twenty-six, when still too young for even the lowest senatorial office, he had become the first Roman knight ever to celebrate a triumph. At thirty-five, with an army at the gate, he had jumped direct from equestrian rank to his first consulship with Crassus. And now at fifty-three, already the first proconsular governor to govern his provinces by remote control – once again with a large force at the gates but no Crassus – he reached the zenith of his authority as the first sole consul to be appointed in the history of Rome. In his own Senate House, guarded by his own veterans, his peers universally acknowledged him as their prince of citizens on the proposal of those very diehards of the senatorial establishment who had opposed him tooth and nail ever since his return from the East in 62. And Pompey must have found it hard to keep a straight face when he heard Cato – the same Cato who had scorned a marriage-alliance ten years ago – now acknowledging to the whole House that 'in this state of disorder there is no one who would govern better than Pompey the Great'.

# 4

# STATE PHYSICIAN

For just as the aim of the helmsman is a successful voyage, of
the physician, health, and of the general, victory, so too the
guardian of the Republic has as his goal for his fellow-citizens
a happy life, fortified by wealth, rich in resources, great in
glory and honourable in virtue. I want him to bring to
perfection this achievement, which is the greatest and best
possible among men ...

Cicero, *Republic*, 5.8

Pompey entered his third consulship with the energy of a great specialist
entrusted at last with the sole management of a chronically sick patient
who had not wanted to come to him until the disease had become insup-
portable. Within three days he published his diagnosis and his first pre-
scription in the form of two laws, *On Violence* and *On Corruption*. His
diagnosis was that the Roman body politic was corrupted by bribery and
convulsed by the violence of unrestrained appetites for wealth and power.
His remedy would be the physic of law backed by the threat of the knife
if the patient failed to respond to the immediate treatment of the latest
and most acute symptoms, among which he specified the murder of Clodius, the burning of the Senate House, and the attack on the house of
the *interrex* Lepidus. But if these were the running sores that required
immediate medication, they were only the latest eruptions from a deep-
seated cancer which had been poisoning the system for decades. Old
lesions must also be investigated, malignant cells attacked, and the patient
subjected to a regimen which, if it could not extirpate a disease whose
roots were deep in human nature, might at least keep it under control
by a combination of remedial and preventive measures that should avoid
the need for a further course of such intensive care.

To judge from the accounts of Asconius and Dio his laws *On Violence*
and *On Corruption* were drafted to ensure not only that justice was done
but that it was both done and seen to be done quickly and efficiently.
He not only increased penalties and specified certain crimes that were
to be investigated but designed a streamlined court-procedure that would

bring law and justice into a closer relationship than they had enjoyed for a long time. Under the new regulations the duration of a trial, which would be heard under the presidency of a judge or examiner to be elected by popular vote, was to be precisely four days. The first three were to be spent on the examination of witnesses, the fourth devoted to the speeches for the prosecution and the defence. The prosecution was to have two hours, the defence, which spoke last, three. Then the jury would vote. And there were to be no more character-witnesses. 'All too often,' says Dio, 'guilty men had been snatched from justice by the eulogies of prominent personages', and Pompey's new courts were not to be deflected from the evidence by a string of glowing panegyrics that bore no relation to the specific charge. But there were of course other pressures which could be brought to bear on a jury, and since court-procedure had been subject to the same pernicious influences of bribery and violence as the electoral struggles which had provoked the most urgent cases that were now to be tried, Pompey endeavoured to curtail both physical intimidation and financial inducement. The intimidation he could stop by policing the courts with his troops, but as bribery in its less overt forms was less easy to prove, he designed intricate procedures to make it as difficult as possible.

First he drew up a new panel of 360 jurers with a relatively irreproachable impartiality that compelled the admiration of Asconius, 'for it was generally agreed that more famous or more upright men had never been proposed'. That at least avoided the obviously unprincipled and debt-ridden who were most susceptible to corruption, and in accordance with the Aurelian law, which had been passed in his first consulship eighteen years ago to minimize the dangers of class interest, he made up his 360 by selecting 120 from each of the three propertied orders, the senators, knights and so-called *tribuni aerarii*. All the same it was impossible to guarantee that a jury appointed from even the least obviously corruptible 360 Romans would be proof against bribery in all cases. In messy and politically sensitive cases it needed only a few to succumb for the result to be prejudiced, and as jurors were certain to be approached as soon as they were named, Pompey determined that the names would not be known until it was too late to bribe them. He therefore required the whole panel of 360 potential jurors to sit through the first three days and hear the presentation and examination of the evidence, even though only eighty-one would sit on the fourth day after a selection by lot of twenty-seven from each of the three classes at the opening of the final session. But still there was a danger that the drawing of lots would not exclude personal or political enemies, and Pompey took account of this by incorporating into his system the standard procedure of the challenging of individual jurors by both plaintiff and defendant, though not *ad in-finitum*. Like all good principles the right to challenge jurors had been abused, and in order to avoid its degeneration into a delaying mechanism he instituted a simple, compulsory rejection by both sides of fifteen jurors each, five from each of the three classes, so that the eighty-one which had been chosen by lot from the original 360 were further reduced to fifty-one just before the vote.

These regulations were to apply to all cases of corruption and violence according to Dio, but the *cause célèbre* for which everyone was waiting was the trial of Milo, overlaid as it was with blood-feud, political rivalry and even class antagonism. The prosecution was launched by the two young Appii Claudii, nephews of the dead Clodius and of the very much alive Appius Claudius. They charged their uncle's murderer with violence, corruption and illegal association, and their efforts were backed by the Clodian tribunes Plancus and Rufus, who not only kept the proletariat seething with outrage at the murderer of its champion but reinforced and broadened their appeal by bringing to the rostra more and more witnesses to Milo's supposed conspiracy against Pompey himself. And all this (including the apparently superfluous addition of 'illegal association' to the list of charges) is a clear indication that conviction on the principal charges was not to be taken for granted, for Milo could still count on such powerful supporters as Marcus Marcellus, Cicero and the tribune Caelius. Marcus Marcellus was a rising star in the political firmament, solid rather than scintillating perhaps, but a formidable orator who had defended Milo against a similar charge of violence brought by Clodius himself in 56 in the classic case of the pot calling the kettle black. Cicero remained determined to defend the friend who had fought and killed the enemy who had exiled him, and while Marcellus prepared to cross-examine the witnesses for the prosecution and Cicero worked busily at the final speech for the defence, the tribune Caelius continued to oppose his Clodian colleagues in the Forum for reasons that owed more to passion than to politics.

There had been no love between Caelius and the Clodian family ever since he had tired of the favours of Clodius' insatiably debauched sister. This was the 'incomparable Lesbia' of Catullus who had expressed his infatuation in poetic agonies over the death of her sparrow, but to the irreverent Caelius who replaced the spurned poet in her bed 'the lustrous goddess of the delicate step' was only a 'Threepenny Clytaemnestra', who soon became a bore. But Clodia had been more used to jilting than to being jilted, and when Caelius treated her to the experience which she had so often inflicted on others, the woman scorned vented her fury in organizing his prosecution on a great list of charges including complicity in the murder of the Alexandrian envoys who had come to Rome in 57 to protest against the proposed reinstatement of King Ptolemy. With Cicero's help Caelius had been acquitted, but the vendetta had continued, and he had become a natural adherent of Milo, on whose behalf he now tried to use his tribunician veto against the enactment of Pompey's legislation which would make the trial more difficult to rig. He argued that the law *On Violence* was unconstitutional because it had been drafted *ad hominem*, and that the trials were being unreasonably accelerated. But Pompey would not stand for such trifling. If the physic was not acceptable, he would resort to the knife, and when Caelius persisted in his attack, Asconius tells us that 'Pompey went so far in anger as to say that if he were forced to it, he would not hesitate to defend the state in arms'.

Pompey was determined not only to bring Milo to justice but to see him convicted and exiled as soon as possible. Although his marriage-connection involved his personal and familial dignity, his overriding concern was the rapid restoration of law and order in the city, and he rightly regarded Milo's continuing presence as incompatible with that aim. In retrospect he could not help regarding the murder of Clodius as one of the best things that could have happened both for himself and for Rome. It had not only produced the crescendo of violence which had made his intervention possible but had made his task incomparably easier by removing one of the chief troublemakers and providing the perfect excuse for getting rid of the other. With Milo gone his para-military force of gladiators and armed slaves would disintegrate, the Clodian mobs could be warned that they had no more excuse for agitation, and Pompey would all the sooner be able to abandon the threat of superior force. For Pompey did not want to appear a military dictator. He knew that the longer he policed the city with his troops, the greater was his risk of being stigmatized as Sulla's pupil, and having been recognized as a Pericles he had no wish to use the methods of Pisistratus for longer than was absolutely necessary.

How seriously Pompey regarded the testimonies of Milo's conspiracy against him is hard to judge, but it was to his advantage to encourage them as a means of discrediting Milo and of justifying still further his own large military establishment as being necessary not only for the restoration of order generally but to deter Milo from revolution and to deal with him if he did break out.

By the end of March Pompey's laws had been passed and the judges elected for the separate trials for violence and for corruption. On 4 April Milo was summoned before both of them simultaneously, and as he could not be in two places at once, Marcus Marcellus appeared for him before the corruption tribunal to beg an adjournment while Milo presented himself before Domitius, the ex-consul of 54 who had been elected to preside over the more serious charge of violence. On 5 April Milo faced the first day of his first four-day trial under Pompey's new regulations while their author stationed himself in the Treasury with a large body of troops in case of trouble. Pompey was as determined to keep the appearance of impartiality as the reality of peace, and since the Treasury was in the Temple of Saturn just outside the Forum beneath the Capitol, the court was not inhibited by his formidable presence and yet he was near enough to intervene rapidly to restore order if called upon to do so by the presiding judge. And he could probably guess what was going on even without his regular reports. The attempt of Marcus Marcellus to cross-examine the first witness for the prosecution was greeted with so threatening a roar from the Clodians that both Marcellus and Milo begged the judge's protection, and though the trial managed to continue after they had been given sanctuary on the tribunal itself, Domitius could not face another day like that. He 'begged Pompey to come to the court in person', and on the next day Pompey did so, flooding the Forum with his troops and ordering troublemakers to be dispersed with flat swords. Even so the Clodian hooligans jeered at the troops, but the jeering soon changed to screams of terror when a flick of the wrist brought the blade into play, and after a short session of blood-letting Pompey's message had permeated even the thickest skull: the trial was to proceed without further interruption.

The evidence that was presented on that day and the next ranged from the lucid to the lachrymose. Accomplished men of the world, gliding smoothly through eloquent expositions, knew how to negotiate tricky questions with a nimble irrelevance if lost for a more carefully meditated impromptu. Red-faced rustics stammered through testimonies about the murder of the landlord of the roadside inn, and Clodius' widow and daughter-in-law gave suitably emotional expression to their bereavement. But far more remarkable than what was said, which was more or less expected, was that it was said and listened to at all. It was the sort of trial which Rome had forgotten. There were none of the interminable delays, the gang violence or the overt bribery which had made a mockery of justice for so long. Once the two sides had realized that a law which specified three days for the examination of evidence meant exactly what it said when it was Pompey's law, they had concentrated on the case with an energy that recognized any attempt to delay or disrupt as a virtual admission of guilt. And on the evening on 7 April the whole city was tense with expectation and suppressed violence as it waited for the fourth and final day on which Milo's fate would be decided.

As soon as the court had been dismissed, the tribune Plancus had held a public meeting at which he had incited the people to demonstrate against Milo and 'let their indignation be seen by all the jury' on the following day, and while Pompey was probably not averse to a peaceful demonstration for that purpose, he was determined to prevent violence from either side. Overnight he planned his dispositions, and strong detachments of troops were patrolling the Forum and all its approaches long before dawn. All shops and taverns in the city were shut and barred. The Forum filled like a reservoir after a storm, but when the lots were drawn to select the eighty-one jurors from the whole panel of 360 who had sat through the proceedings of the previous three days, the Forum was 'as silent as a forum can ever be'. As the sun rose, the court gleamed with the helmets of picked troops watching for signs of suspicious groupings among the crowds; the patrols guarding all the approaches stood ready for any last-minute attempts by Milo's private army, and Pompey resumed his neutral position in the Treasury. The prosecutors divided their two hours between them, but the defence rested all its hopes on Cicero alone, who had prepared a long and cunning speech arguing not only that Milo had acted in self-defence but that Pompey's insistence on a fair trial revealed the sole consul's concern to see the acquittal of an innocent man. But Cicero was already trembling like a leaf at the sight of so many troops, and when he rose shakily to his feet, a terrific howl of indignation from the Clodians completely shattered his nerve. According to the charitable Asconius he 'failed to speak with his customary resolution', but Dio is probably nearer the mark when he says that Cicero 'merely garbled a few words which all but died on his lips, and was only too glad to retire'. And that was the end of Milo. In the old days his armed gangs would have broken up the court long before this, but now he had no choice but to sit still and wait impatiently for his fate to be sealed. The compulsory rejection of fifteen jurors before the final vote was of no use to him. The remaining fifty-one condemned him by a large majority in each class, and he went into exile in the south of France, where he derived little consolation from reading the speech which Cicero had intended to give. For Cicero salved his conscience by sending a copy on to him, and so earned himself a sarcastic reply. 'I am relieved you did not give this after all,' returned Milo, 'otherwise I should never have known the excellent red mullet of Marseilles.'

If Cicero had been prepared to analyse his real feelings at the moment of his nervous collapse, he would have had to admit that it was not just the sight of so many troops and the anger of the Clodians which had unmanned him but the knowledge that the stubborn defence of a lost cause would have been tempting too far the providence of a man 'whose character and fortune are such that he has been able to achieve what none other could achieve'. This tactful remark in his speech for Milo was a tribute to Pompey's Herculean achievements in empire-building, but it was equally applicable to Pompey's emulation of that hero in swilling away the Augean accumulations of unpunished corruption and violence in the imperial capital. For Pompey now opened every legal sluice-gate to swell the torrent of litigation that might scour not only the recent offal but the long-dried encrustations of the last eighteen years. If Appian may be believed, he 'brought forward a law that any citizen who chose might call to account anyone who had held office from the time of his own first consulship', and when taken to task for 'raking up old troubles that were best forgotten', he replied with the medical metaphor that he had 'gone back so far in order to effect a complete cure for the ills from which the Republic had been wasting away for so long'. According to Dio he further encouraged the purge 'by rousing against all who practised bribery those who had been convicted of a similar offence, for if anyone secured the conviction of two men on charges similar to the one against himself, he gained pardon for himself'. These were powerful stimulants to the action of the remedial measures already prescribed, and with their aid Appian tells us that Pompey 'rapidly restored the sick commonwealth'. Plutarch adds that he set a personal example by 'acting himself with dignity and impartiality in most cases', though it would be wrong to see Pompey as a paragon of impartiality: the qualification 'in most cases' refers to an instance of favouritism which may not have created much of a stir at the time but provides another example of the attitude which earned him Tacitus' condemnation as 'the maker and breaker of his own laws'.

The contrast was pointed by Pompey's treatment of Milo's rival candidates for the consulships of 52, Metellus Scipio and Plautius Hypsaeus. Both were arraigned on charges of corruption of which they were both manifestly guilty, and when Hypsaeus begged Pompey for help on the score of friendship and loyal service on his staff in the East, Pompey refused to interfere in the workings of justice with a decisiveness which was more praiseworthy than polite. According to Plutarch a desperate Hypsaeus waylaid him one evening as he was returning home from the baths and clasped his knees in supplication, but Pompey simply shook himself free, 'telling Hypsaeus contemptuously that apart from spoiling his supper he was accomplishing nothing'. With Metellus Scipio, on the contrary, Pompey was anything but unhelpful. Scipio's prosecutor was Gaius Memmius, himself convicted for electoral corruption as a result of his scandalous agreement with the consuls of 54 to rig the elections for 53. He was eager to take advantage of Pompey's law offering pardon to those who secured the conviction of two others on a similar charge,

and in attacking Scipio in particular he may have had the additional
motive of paying Pompey back for deserting him after persuading him
to reveal the secret compact to the Senate. But if Memmius thought that
Pompey would let him harm Scipio, he was mistaken. Where Pompey
had sacrificed Hypsaeus to a hot supper, he not only put on mourning
in protest at the indictment of Scipio but invited all 360 potential jurors
to dine with him. And when as a result 'the prosecutor saw the whole
lot escorting Scipio from the Forum', says Plutarch, 'he simply abandoned
the case'.

Pompey's marriage to Scipio's daughter had almost certainly taken
place after his entry to Rome as sole consul, probably just after the condemnation and exile of Milo had allowed him to relax the military precautions which he had taken to protect his own life. His bride was 'well
versed in literature,' says Plutarch, 'in playing the lyre and in geom-
etry, and she had been accustomed to listen to philosophical disputa-
tions with profit; but she was nevertheless free from that officiousness
which such accomplishments are apt to impart to young ladies, and her
father's birth and reputation were beyond reproach'. All the same it is
hard to believe that this combination of blue-blooded and blue-stock-
inged virtues would have won her the position of Rome's first lady if
she had not also enjoyed youth and beauty, for if her new husband was
twice the age of Crassus' dashing son who had left her a widow in the
previous year, there were more than faded laurels to commend Pompey
as a lover even at the age of fifty-three to judge from the mutual devotion
which made this fifth marriage almost as famous a love-match as his
fourth. Of course there were critics who said that Cornelia's youth made
her a more fitting bride for one of Pompey's sons, and that he had no
business 'decking himself with garlands and celebrating nuptials in
neglect of the unhappy condition of the city which had chosen him as
its physician and put itself under his sole charge: he ought instead to
be in mourning for the calamity of a consulship which would never have
been given to him if the Republic had been prosperous'. But Pompey
proved anything but neglectful of the city's ills, and having spared no
efforts to effect a cure in the shortest possible time, he restored the duality
of the consulship in July by taking a colleague and then holding elections
of successors for the following year. 'He had won the glory which lay
in the passing of the vote which made him sole consul,' observes Dio,
'and he wished to avoid the envy attaching to it.' And if it was hardly
impartial to secure the election of his own father-in-law as his colleague
for the last five months of 52, even the most pessimistic constitutionalist
was forced to admit that he had feared far worse from Sulla's pupil.

But if Pompey now had a new father-in-law to promote politically, he did not neglect his old one, and it was a disappointment to Caesar's many enemies that Pompey resisted their campaign to prepare for the conqueror of Gaul an even more frigid political welcome than had greeted the conqueror of the East ten years ago. Pompey was too big a man to feel anything but admiration for the conquests of his protégé, and he entertained a soldier's contempt for the unmilitary Catos and Bibuluses who spent their time campaigning at home against men who sought glory for themselves and their country in war. If Caesar had made fools of them in his consulship of 59, they had only themselves to blame, for if they had not opposed Pompey's own legitimate demands on his return from the East, Pompey might never have promoted Caesar as his political agent. Let Cato and Bibulus seethe with jealousy at achievements beyond their reach. No man knew better than Pompey what it meant to carry the sole responsibility for great campaigns, and when in the spring of 52 Caesar had set out to face the rising of Vercingetorix which threatened to bring the whole structure of his conquests crashing about his ears, there had never been a time when he could be more certain of Pompey's support, as Cicero reveals: 'Pompey, who had prolonged Caesar's tenure of his provinces in 55 and championed his cause in his absence, now again in his third consulship, when he began to be the defender of the constitution, fought to get all ten tribunes to propose a bill admitting Caesar's candidature [for another consulship] in absentia.'

What Caesar wanted when he came home was not only a triumph but a guarantee of political security, and this combination was what Pompey now sought to secure for him. The triumph itself would be no difficulty. On the contrary, Caesar's enemies in the Senate would be only too pleased to get him into the city as soon as possible, for once the excitement of his triumph had died down they intended to prosecute him for the illegalities of his consulship in 59 and any number of other charges which their fertile imaginations could find as excuses to cripple his political career. And it goes without saying that his attempts to secure a ratification of Gallic settlements and to provide farms and pensions for his veterans would be fought tooth and nail. Since the only immunity against prosecution was that conferred by public office, Caesar needed to pass directly to a second consulship after losing the immunity of his proconsular imperium which would end the moment he passed through the city-walls. And as consul he would be as well placed to provide for his own troops and provincial settlement as he had been to provide for Pompey's in 59. But the special dispensation which would allow him to stand for the consulship in absentia could certainly not be relied upon with so many enemies in the Senate.

It was a refinement of the dilemma which had confronted Caesar in 60 when he had returned from Spain. The Senate had refused him permission to stand *in absentia* for the consulship of 59, and he had had to choose between entering the city to stand in person or staying outside and waiting to be granted a triumph. Then, of course, he had chosen the consulship, but now there was nothing that would make him forgo the triumphal procession at which he would display the accumulated captives and spoils of so many years of war, and unless he could gain permission to stand *in absentia*, he would have to forgo the consulship or lay himself open to prosecution – and not only for the prescribed three weeks before the election, for while that would be the most dangerous time because he could then be prosecuted on any charge, even a consul-elect could be prosecuted for the electoral corruption which was the prerequisite of success.

Pompey sympathized with Caesar's predicament to the extent of securing for his protégé the necessary dispensation in advance by an enactment of the people which would be proof against any senatorial decree or tribunician veto. This was something which Caesar had already urged Cicero to support from his winter-quarters at Ravenna, and though Cicero later claimed that he had urged Pompey against the idea, Pompey had insisted, and used his unique position of supremacy and influence in the chaotic first weeks of his consulship to put pressure on all ten tribunes to propose the necessary measure. Even so it was 'a struggle' to get them all to agree, and when the young Caelius proved particularly stubborn, it was Cicero himself, anxious to mitigate Pompey's dissatisfaction at his support of Milo, who persuaded him to abandon his opposition to Pompey's will.

In pushing through this so-called 'law of the ten tribunes' Pompey could not have been fairer to Caesar, and while there were some people for whom he could never have been too unfair to his protégé and others for whom he could never have been fair enough, there is no sign whatever that Pompey ceased to trust Caesar in 52 despite the usual anachronism of the non-contemporary sources anticipating their estrangement. According to Appian, for example, there were some who regarded the legislation admitting retrospective prosecutions for bribery and violence back to the year 70 as 'an attempt to cast reproach on Caesar' for his consulship of 59, but if so, it is hardly likely that the indignation which Pompey expressed at the insinuation was only 'pretended' when he had just gone to the trouble of immunizing Caesar against prosecution. Similarly we may believe Dio that when a subsequent law was passed on regulations governing the magistracies, the inclusion of a standard clause requiring personal candidature at elections was seized upon by Caesar's enemies as a contradiction of the special dispensation granted by the law of the ten tribunes. But again it was no 'pretended indignation' which caused Pompey not only to declare the validity of Caesar's exemption but to emend the general provision of the second law (which had already been inscribed on bronze before some pettifogging nitpicker had noticed the political possibilities in the apparent contradiction) by adding the obvious exclusion of 'those who had been granted the privilege by name'. And just as Pompey's third consulship had begun with a defence of his protégé's interests at a vulnerable time, so it would end with a twenty-day public thanksgiving for Caesar's victory over Vercingetorix – the longest ever awarded except only for his similar one in 55, when Pompey had also been consul. All the same, if Pompey's third consulship still shows no symptoms of the mistrust of Caesar which our non-contemporary sources have been seeing for years, the very remedies and prophylactics prescribed by Pompey to cure the corrupted Rome in 52 were already producing dangerous side-effects which, though unrecognized at the time, were a sinister indication of a far more serious illness.

While the purgative litigation produced an immediate rash of convictions, the restoration of the censors' powers enacted by Pompey's fellow-consul and father-in-law Scipio proved even more inflammatory when they were applied two years later to expel undesirables from the Senate. The vermin which thrived on corruption and disorder fled from the relative sterility of Pompey's Rome to find a more congenial host in Gaul, and the effect of this accumulation of parasites on Caesar's already hyper-thyroidal condition was a dangerous stimulation of the persecution-complex which he began to indulge as convenient justification of increasingly anti-social behaviour. For in his desire to have everything his own way in Rome as he had had it in Gaul for so many years, Caesar convinced himself that he had never had anything his own way. 'All these measures have long been in the course of preparation against me', he would tell the troops of Pompey's Spanish armies in 49 when about to receive their surrender in the Civil War. 'Against me were commands of a new kind set up so that one and the same person might preside over public affairs outside the gates of Rome while holding in absence two of the most warlike provinces for so many years. Against me the rights of magistrates have been subverted, so that they are not sent into the provinces after holding their praetorships and consulships but as appointed and elected by a small clique ...' But this distortion of cause and effect is one that is more obvious than observed by historians, who are still too easily gulled by the revisionism of Caesar's revolutionary propaganda. It is scarcely more credible that Caesar regarded Pompey's legislation of 52 in this light at the time than that he would have been justified in doing so, and while there was no shortage of disgruntled exiles seeking to poison his mind against the scourge of corruption in Rome, even Appian admits that 'he cheered them up and spoke well of Pompey'.

The law which would carry the burden of Caesar's complaints three years later was Pompey's enactment of the measure proposed by the consuls of 53 to establish a five-year gap between the holding of a consulship or praetorship and the governorship of a proconsular or propraetorian province, but it was no more aimed at Caesar when it was passed in 52 than when it had been proposed in the previous year. It was a genuine constitutional reform designed to break the vicious circle of electoral corruption and 'craze for office' which had spiralled into anarchy. For if the prospect of a provincial governorship immediately after the year of office meant the chance to recover unlimited electoral expenditure, the prospect of electoral defeat was more likely to mean financial ruin, and candidates trailing in the election race had used any means to lengthen it until they might outbribe or outbatter their way into the lead. But with a five-year gap between consulship and proconsulship a candidate might think twice before squandering his own fortune, bankers would certainly think twice before lending him another, and the provinces might even find themselves governed by men with more in their heads than the thought of personal profit. Admittedly Pompey himself was exempted from this as from his other regulations. The Senate extended his proconsular command in Spain for a further five years, that is until he would be eligible for it under his own five-year law, whereas Caesar could no longer expect an automatic provincial governorship after the second consulship for which he was now intending to stand. But why should Caesar want another province so soon? If some grave emergency occurred in the empire he might be interested in resuming the path of glory, and the Roman people could at any time grant him or anyone else a special command by plebiscite, but a routine provincial governorship so soon after Gaul would surely be the last thing to appeal to a man whose 'long and laborious contest against most warlike foes' now left him free to return home 'to his honours, his sacrificial duties and his relaxations'.

Caesar would have been away from Rome for nearly a decade by the time he returned to stand for his second consulship, twice as long as Pompey had been in the East, and Pompey had already granted him far more security than he himself had enjoyed in similar circumstances ten years ago. Thanks to Pompey's efforts Caesar would have the opportunity to go immediately to the headship of state, secure in his political dignity, immune from prosecution, and with a whole year to press from the top for the provision of farms and pensions for his troops and the satisfactory organization of the conquered territories. Pompey would continue as proconsul, it is true, unless he chose to resign his Spanish command, but what had Caesar to fear from the man who had just done so much for him – provided of course that Caesar remained content to do what his chief political agent Balbus still claimed to be his desire three years later: 'to live without fear with Pompey as first citizen'? And in so far as Pompey regarded Caesar as a threat, it was to less powerful men than himself, old political enemies such as Cato and Bibulus who now satisfactorily regarded Pompey as a lesser evil than his protégé. For if Pompey fell short of the ideals of the guardian of Cicero's idealized *Republic*, which was published and acclaimed in the following year, he had nevertheless cleaned up the Sink of Romulus more effectively than any other man could have done.

We have already seen that he did not always practise what he preached. His relentless rooting out of corruption stopped short at his new father-in-law. He had forbidden character-witnesses at trials, but when the tribune Plancus was prosecuted for violence the moment his office expired in December, Pompey sent a written eulogy to be read out in court. The five-year gap between consulship and proconsulship was to apply to others rather than himself, and the presence of election candidates would not be required of his protégé Caesar. But Pompey's laws deserve more praise than his exceptions warrant blame. Gang-warfare and overt electoral and legal corruption were suppressed, their perpetrators purged by each other, and the constitution freed from paralysis. That Pompey took Scipio as his consular colleague was less important than that he restored the duality of the consulship and held elections for the next year. And while the handing over of the headship of state to two new consuls at the end of the year left him 'none the less the supervisor, ruler and all-in-all at Rome', even Appian admits that it was a role in which he had deserved to be confirmed after his outstanding performance as physician of the sick commonwealth, especially since another epidemic of the same ills seemed to be building up in Gaul.

If the supervisor, ruler and all-in-all could afford to remain relaxed about the return of his protégé, there was an increasing number of his lesser peers who dreaded the stifling political influence which the conquering hero would wield. They feared the golden stream of plunder which Caesar was already channelling from Gaul into popularity-seeking shows, prestigious public works, funeral games in honour of Julia and the pockets of promising political allies. They saw the political promotion of their own families and friends swamped by the influx of votes which Caesar would be able to command by wealth or procure by a patronage far wider than their own. They shuddered at the prospect of his demobilized veterans pensioned off on Campanian farms, ever ready to march to Rome to vote by numbers in support of their old general's legislative and electoral interest. And it was not only his patronage over existing citizens that they feared. The Romanization of Gaul would bring new citizens, a trickle at first but an increasing stream all bearing the name of Julius. The already highly Romanized Transpadane Gauls from that part of his Cisalpine province which lay between the Po and the Alps still possessed only the second-rate 'Latin' status, and the full enfranchisement of these communities was a cause which it was as much in Caesar's interest to promote as in the interest of his enemies to prevent. It was also a cause which raised many more Roman hackles than almost any other. It challenged the same mentality that had preferred to fight all Rome's Italian allies nearly forty years earlier than to admit them to citizenship in an empire they had helped to build, and it was a legacy of the resulting wars, which had been fought by a Caesar and a Pompeius and had been won as much by their concessionary legislation as by their efforts in the field. For it had been a law of Lucius Caesar, consul of 90, that had granted full citizenship to all the Latins, and it was the law of Pompey's father, consul in the next year, that had granted Latin rights to the towns beyond the Po, which had remained candidates for full enfranchisement ever since. Their cause had been championed by Crassus who tried to enrol them on the citizen-lists in his censorship of 65, and when this attempt to extend his political power-base against the absent Pompey had been resisted by his colleague, Crassus had tried again in 63 through the agency of the tribune Rullus. But again he had been thwarted, this time by an edict forbidding non-citizens to be present in the city on the day of the vote, and so it was to Caesar that the Transpadane Gauls now looked for the reward which would be to their mutual advantage. And it was this that the senior consul of 51 made it his business to oppose as a flanking attack in his campaign to get Caesar disarmed and away from Gaul.

The consul in question was Marcus Marcellus, the same who had defended Milo the previous April. He had been chosen consul along with Sulpicius Rufus in the elections which Pompey had held as soon as possible after taking Scipio as his colleague in July, and they had beaten Marcus Cato, who had stood undisguised on a violently anti-Caesarian platform. But Cato had ruined his own chances by endeavouring to carry meritocracy into Utopia in what were already the cleanest elections for years. He had not only proposed an extremely unpopular decree forbidding the use of canvassing agents but had then disdained to canvass in person with any of the smooth-talking, hand-shaking, baby-kissing techniques which were the tiresome but mercifully temporary duty of candidates at democratic elections then as now, and when the electorate had responded by leaving such uncompromising virtue to be its own reward, Pompey was no doubt both amused and relieved. But Pompey was less amused when his successors took office in 51 and Marcellus began to attack Caesar's position with a Catonian intensity which challenged him to defend not only the interests of his protégé but the validity of his own legislation.

Marcellus had probably taken his cue from a request by Caesar to the Senate for a prolongation of his provincial commands beyond the expiry date, which is still the subject of perennial controversy among historians but was almost certainly in 50 and most probably 1 March in that year. Caesar's victory over Vercingetorix had not been the end of Gallic resistance, and Caesar's continuing concern is reflected by his wintering in Transalpine Gaul instead of crossing the Alps to hibernate as usual in northern Italy. He had stayed instead at Bibracte in Burgundy, and though his troops were drooping with exhaustion after the hard fighting of 52, a shower of largess had revived them sufficiently to undertake a winter campaign of atrocities designed to crush the guerrilla warfare to which the surviving Gallic leaders had reverted. But the Gauls were tenacious, and though the spring of 51 saw Caesar in firm control over a devastated wasteland in Central Gaul, the Belgic tribes found a guerrilla leader of their own, and it was probably when they rose, perhaps in April, that Caesar sent the request which is recorded by Appian. No doubt he hoped that he would not need an extension of time, but he would feel happier if it were available, and since the Gauls knew as well as he did that his term was expiring, the prolongation might have a demoralizing effect on the enemy that would help to make it unnecessary. But the consul Marcellus was unsympathetic. He not only spoke against an extension but urged that Caesar should be recalled 'even before the end of his term' on the grounds that 'the war was ended, peace established, and the victorious army ought to be disbanded'. Marcellus in turn was opposed by his fellow-consul Sulpicius 'who did not approve of replacing a magistrate before his term had expired', and this was also Pompey's position. According to Appian he told the Senate that it 'should not put an indignity on a distinguished man who had performed such great services for his country on account of a short interval of time', and though Appian adds his usual observation that this was yet another 'pretence of fairness' on Pompey's part, it is hard to see why Pompey should have troubled to pretend a fairness which he did not feel. For even if he 'made it plain that Caesar's command must end immediately on its expiry', he did not maintain this position as the year progressed, and to have appeared too indulgent to Caesar at this juncture might well have been counter-productive. He could not in fact have done fairer than to stand by the law which he and Crassus had jointly proposed in their consulship of 55, and when

Marcellus now forced his motion to the vote recorded by Hirtius, it was no doubt satisfactory to Pompey to see 'the majority of the Senate trooping across to the other side'.

Rebuffed by that vote and Pompey's strong opposition, the hard-liners not only shelved their attempts to truncate Caesar's command but hesitated even to propose the appointment of the successors to take over his provinces when the command expired. In late May the ex-tribune Caelius wrote to Cicero that 'Marcellus has so far brought no motion before the Senate about the succession to the Gallic provinces and has put off doing so, so he told me, until 1 June'. His letter also reminds us how dangerously Rome was prey to rumour in the days before instant communication. There was even a story going the rounds that Cicero had been murdered by his old enemy, the ex-tribune Plancus, but what was both more credible and more cheering to Caesar's enemies was a report of grave difficulties in Gaul. Caelius amused Cicero with his description of 'the little clique whose names you need not guess', gloating over their open secrets while Domitius 'puts his finger to his lips before he speaks'. But if the clique of Cato, Bibulus, Domitius and their ilk was now soft-pedalling the question of appointing successors with the growing hope that Pompey would soon have no protégé to protect, they had nevertheless pressed their attack on the enfranchisement of the Transpadanes, which was an issue that had clearly been red hot before Cicero had left Rome early that month for Brundisium to take ship for his 'colossal bore' of a province, Cilicia. It had united an aristocracy worried about a dilution of its traditional patronage with a chauvinistic populace opposed to sharing its privileges, and though the Senate's desire to publish a decree formally forbidding this enfranchisement had been frustrated by a tribune's veto, the resolution was nevertheless written up as an 'authority' recording the fact that the will of Caesar in this matter was not the will of his assembled peers.

Cicero was full of this when he left Rome in early May, and when he wrote to Atticus from Pompeii on his way south to Brundisium he complained that 'not enough has reached us about Caesar's reaction to the senatorial opinion, and there is a rumour that the Transpadanes have been instructed to elect boards of four', which were the magistrates appropriate to a Roman colony. 'If that is true,' continued Cicero, 'I fear great ructions. But I shall learn something from Pompey.' For Pompey turns out to be at Tarentum at this time, and Cicero is looking forward to a long talk with the great man who in the heel of Italy is evidently more closely in touch with what is happening in Gaul and in political affairs generally than any of Cicero's correspondents in Rome itself. And when Pompey invited him to spend three days with him, Cicero was delighted at the prospect of 'hearing much fine discourse on public affairs and getting some useful advice about this wretched business of my own', by which he meant his unwelcome governorship of Cilicia. He also promised Atticus a full account of his discussions with Pompey, and Caelius wrote eagerly for the same: 'If you find Pompey disengaged as you hope, please write a full account of your impressions of him, what he has to say, his pretended wishes ... he says one thing and means another, but he is not really clever enough to hide his real desires.' But Cicero disappointed Caelius. 'I spent three days with Pompey talking nothing but politics,' he replied tantalizingly, 'but our conversation could not and should not be repeated in writing. Let this suffice: Pompey is an excellent citizen and ready both in heart and mind to take all precautions in the interest of the state. Give yourself to him heart and soul....'

What Pompey had said to impress Cicero so is not recorded, for if Cicero ever wrote his promised account to Atticus, it has not survived: there is only a brief note telling his friend that he was leaving in Tarentum 'an excellent citizen perfectly prepared to ward off the dangers that are feared'. But it is not hard to imagine the wide-ranging discussions covering the whole political spectrum from the candidates in the forthcoming elections, the likelihood of renewed corruption and violence and the current trials to the issues connected with Caesar's position, the dangers inherent in the Transpadane question and the determination of the anti-Caesarian lobby to precipitate the appointment of new governors for the Gallic provinces. Nor is it hard to imagine Pompey's replies in the spirit of firm moderation appropriate to the elder statesman or *rector* of Cicero's *Republic*. He would impress upon Caesar the need to be less provocative over the enfranchisement of Gauls. He would counter the extremism of Marcellus and support the moderation of Sulpicius, who had already discoursed on the horrors of civil war. And he might well go to Spain.

The efficacy of Pompey's threat to leave Italy is repeatedly and unwittingly proved by Cicero's correspondence. By the beginning of July Cicero had heard from Atticus that 'Pompey is determined to go to Spain', and his reaction was unequivocal. 'I am emphatically not in favour of his doing so,' he replied, 'and in fact I easily persuaded Theophanes that nothing is better than that Pompey should go nowhere.' But it is hard to believe that Pompey needed the encouragement of his Greek historian not to leave the luxury of his Italian villas, his delightful Cornelia and his role of elder statesman in order to subject himself to the rigours of a campaign in that remote land which had provided him with a triumph in his youth. To govern Spain by legates and fight its wars by remote control added greatly to his dignity, provided a military power-base to support his authority at Rome, and gave him a useful source of patronage which was not restricted to furthering the careers of young men of senatorial rank seeking appointments on his military staff. In all the talk of high politics at Tarentum Cicero had remembered to find out that Pompey proposed to make five prefectorial appointments to each of his Spanish provinces as sinecures designed merely to exempt equestrian businessmen from jury-service, and this was obviously something in which Atticus had a close interest to judge from the references to it in the letters. But for Pompey to have gone himself to Spain and started campaigning in person on the scene of youthful victories would be a step backwards. Any setback there would be too damaging to his prestige, and no second Spanish triumph could be other than second-rate compared with his own Oriental spectacular of 61 or what Caesar was planning by way of celebration of his conquest of Gaul. What Pompey wanted by declaring his intention to go to Spain was to hear exactly what he had heard from Cicero, that Rome could simply not manage without him. It was a threat which he was to make more than once in the next year and a half, and each time it evoked the satisfactory response until Caesar's agents began to demand that he should carry it out and were met with the unequivocal refusal that preferred civil war.

But in the June of 51 Pompey still maintained an attitude of protective paternalism towards his protégé and recoiled with disgust at Marcellus' public flogging of a distinguished Transpadane Gaul from Novum Comum, a town which Caesar had founded with Latin status at the foot of the Alps. 'It was an ugly gesture,' wrote Cicero from Athens on 6 July in reply to Atticus' news of the incident. 'Even if the man turns out not to have been an ex-magistrate he was still a Transpadane Gaul, and I imagine Marcellus has angered our friend as much as Caesar.' Pompey was indeed offended, not only by the slight to Caesar but by the insult to his own semi-patronal status which he had inherited from his father's grant of Latin rights to the Transpadanes. The purpose of the consul's brutal action had been to emphasize that the Transpadanes were not Roman citizens, who alone enjoyed exemption from corporal punishment; but in practice if not in law the Latin allies had long been accorded a similar immunity, and what made this case even more shocking was the possibility that the victim was in fact an ex-magistrate of the Latin community and therefore entitled to Roman citizenship *ex officio*. But Marcellus' concern was to press home the Senate's resolution against the mass-enfranchisement of the Transpadanes, and when the flogging was over, he had told the bleeding victim 'to go and show his scars to Caesar'.

This outburst in June may well have been a frustrated reaction to Marcellus' failure to make any progress over the question of appointing successors to Caesar. We know from Caelius that he had planned to bring it before the House on the first of the month, and it seems likely that he had to postpone it because Pompey was away, for if Pompey was still at Tarentum on 22 May it is unlikely that he was back at Rome for June. But he did return for a meeting on 22 July at which the payment of his own troops was to be dealt with, and his presence provided the occasion for the 'political development' which Caelius had 'long ceased to expect'. The anti-Caesarian lobby began to quibble about the legion which Pompey had lent to Caesar at the end of 54. They wanted to know whose legion they were supposed to be voting money for. To what contingent did it belong? How long did Pompey intend to leave it in Gaul? And an angry Pompey 'was eventually compelled to say – not immediately but only after many insinuations and outcries from his detractors – that he would withdraw it'. Even so he avoided giving a date for the withdrawal and in fact did nothing about it until the next year, but his special relationship with Caesar was coming under increasingly heavy pressure, and the hard-liners gave him no respite. For he was next 'interrogated about the appointment of successors to Caesar', and since Caelius quotes him as 'coming out with the statement that it is the duty of all men to obey the Senate', he had evidently been asked to comment on the hypothesis that Caesar would resist being replaced. As far as Pompey was concerned this statement was probably no more than a politician's platitude designed to play out time in an embarrassing debate, and he was clearly successful since the session ended with a resolution 'that Pompey should return to the city as soon as possible in order that the succession to the provinces might be dealt with in his presence'. But it was seized upon by Caelius and the other anti-Caesarians as a remark of far greater significance: that Pompey would see to it that the Senate's decision was implemented.

Caelius explains that Pompey 'was just about to go to his army at Ariminum and promptly did so', but we are left to speculate why. It is unlikely that this journey is the one referred to by Dio as 'setting out as though to campaign in Spain', for no one would go to Spain from the Adriatic port of Rimini. The troops assembled there may well have been preparing to march to one of the western ports for embarkation, and Pompey's concern with them may have been a useful reinforcement to his expressed intention to go there himself eventually; but this visit was probably connected with Ariminum's geographical location just south of the border of Caesar's Cisalpine province and at the terminus of the Aemilian Way, the great trunk-road running north-west across the Po Basin and providing the most rapid line of communication with Caesar beyond the Alps. From there Pompey would not only be able to investigate the Transpadane question at close quarters but obtain much clearer information about Caesar's progress in Transalpine Gaul. He would have ascertained that the Gallic resistance had now centred on the siege of Uxellodunum, where Caesar was making a massive effort commensurate with the stubbornness of the defenders, who knew that it was his last summer in Gaul. What communications thundered up and down the Aemilian Way between Pompey and Caesar we cannot know, but from what follows it appears that Pompey concluded that once Uxellodunum had fallen there would be no military justification for extending Caesar's command beyond 1 March 50, which already left him over six months to make his final arrangements to hand over a thoroughly conquered province.

Another reason for Pompey's leaving Rome at this juncture could well have been the imminence of the consular elections, which took place at the end of July. The fact that he was inspecting 'an army' might usefully give pause to any who contemplated violence in his absence, and his absence itself would reinforce his image of the impartial elder statesman, ostensibly superior to party-struggles but guaranteeing the freedom of others to pursue their political ambitions within the constraints of the law. And when he heard the results, he was not displeased. For 50 as in 51 a hard-liner was paired with a moderate, and the moderate again came top of the poll. The counterpart to the Sulpicius who had countered his colleague's anti-Caesarian campaign in the current year was to be Lucius Aemilius Paullus, who was clearly not 'the bitter enemy of Caesar' described by Appian. On the contrary, Paullus was one of the many Romans financially indebted to Caesar (as indeed was Cicero), and when Caelius wrote to tell Cicero of the election results on 1 August, he was 'dying to hear what Paullus would have to say' when the question of Caesar's provinces came up. But there was no doubting what his colleague would say. The successor to Marcus Marcellus was to be his cousin Gaius, and Gaius Marcellus really was a bitter enemy to Caesar 'even though he was related to him by marriage', as the unnecessarily puzzled Dio remarks, failing to observe that this was the very reason for the vendetta. For it was this Marcellus whose pretty young wife Octavia, Caesar's great-niece, had been regarded by Caesar as the ideal replacement for Julia in the marriage-alliance with Pompey. Pompey of course had rejected the suggestion, but the proud Marcelli had neither forgiven nor forgotten Caesar's insult to their house, and they were bent on revenge. Thus Pompey could wait to learn how effective Caesar had been in stamping out the embers of Gallic resistance in full confidence that there would be one of the heads of state ready to support whatever line he then decided to take.

During September Pompey will have heard that Caesar had succeeded in the way described by his officer and historian Hirtius. Uxellodunum had fallen, and 'relying on the fact that his natural clemency was so well known that he need not fear the reputation of cruelty from a severe action', the paragon of humanity had graciously allowed the wretched defenders to keep their lives but not their hands. It was an 'exemplary punishment intended to deter any further rebellious designs', and it worked. Sporadic pockets of resistance were soon crushed by Caesar's legates, and Caesar himself, 'seeing that matters were going well in every region and judging that in the campaigns of previous summers the whole of Gaul had now been conquered', decided to spend the end of the campaigning season in Aquitania, which he had never visited in person, before going into winter-quarters. And since the Aquitanians promptly gave hostages, there was no reason whatever why Caesar should need an extension of his command, and the crystallization of this opinion into a firm line at Rome is clear from Caelius' letters to Cicero, to whom he describes the Senate's meetings of that month.

On 1 September the Senate debated the question of Caesar's provinces for the first time since Pompey had been embarrassed by his interrogation on the subject on 22 July. Caelius had expected the debate to be resumed on 13 August when Pompey would be back from Ariminum and the elections would be over, but it had been further postponed by the trial of the consul-elect Gaius Marcellus, who became the object of a vindictive prosecution by a failed rival. And even on 1 September Pompey still proved reluctant to take a strong line. The news of the fall of distant Uxellodunum had probably not come through by then, and even if it had, it would be a little time before the repercussions would be known for certain. He therefore declared 'that no decree on the subject of Caesar's provinces should be passed at this time', and though he refused to be more specific himself, he was almost certainly speaking through the mouth of his tame father-in-law who proposed 'an adjournment of the whole question until 1 March'. On the face of it the adjournment of any decision on the appointment of Caesar's successors until the expiry-date of his command was a generous concession, involving as it did an inevitable period of grace after that date. For if successors were appointed beforehand they would be ready to take over immediately his term ended, whereas successors chosen only on or after 1 March 50 would need two or three months to organize themselves to get up to Gaul, and Caesar would of course remain in command until they arrived. But even so 'it made Balbus very unhappy', says Caelius, and when he adds that Caesar's principal agent had 'expostulated with Scipio over it', it is a clear indication that what Caesar now wanted was to remain in formal command of his provinces and armies until the very end of the year in which he was elected consul. And this was something that Pompey was not prepared to countenance, as Caelius shrewdly realized: 'Pompey clearly does not want Caesar to keep his provinces along with his army and to be consul-elect at the same time.

It was not that Pompey was trying to retract the privilege which he had worked so hard to secure for Caesar in the previous year. By the law of the ten tribunes Caesar had been guaranteed the right to stand for the consulship *in absentia*. But the right to stand *in absentia* did not imply, as Caesar later claimed, that he was to be allowed to keep his provinces and armies beyond the legal termination of his governorship. The loss of the provinces and armies over which a proconsul had exercised his *imperium* did not invalidate the *imperium* itself, which he retained until he re-entered the city. If therefore Caesar's successors were appointed on 1 March 50 and arrived, say, in June, he could be back at Rome in time to receive a hero's welcome outside the walls just before the elections in late July, and he would then have five months in which to organize his triumphal entry into the city at the end of December, when he would exchange the *imperium* of proconsul for the *imperium* of consul on 1 January 49. And Pompey was prepared to accept this. But Caesar wanted more. He was no longer happy about handing over control of his armies and keeping only a token force for the purpose of his triumph. *Imperium* stripped of the means to exercise it seemed a chilling prospect to the armour-plated proconsul whose word had been law in Gaul for nine years. It might protect him from prosecution, but would he win the election as easily when the velvet glove no longer contained a mailed fist? With an enemy like Gaius Marcellus presiding over the elections might he not find his candidature rejected on some other excuse, or face constant postponements for which the will of heaven could take the blame? And what if he was allowed to stand, but lost? He would no longer have the ultimate sanction to compel. He could not postpone his triumph for another year and hang about outside Rome in order not to lose his proconsular *imperium* until he could stand again in the following July. He would have to do what Pompey had done in 61, and enter the city in triumph without the security of a consulship to step into. Caesar was not prepared to risk it. He did not want to be a Pompey of 61 but a Pompey of 52, when the anarchy in Rome had made a consul out of a proconsul who was still in command of his provinces and armies. And while he was not of course seeking a sole consulship or, for the present at least, the uniquely simultaneous consulship and provincial governorship which Pompey had then held, his reluctance to hand over his provinces and armies until he actually became consul was not only a vote of no confidence from protégé to patron but the beginning of a campaign to rival the prince of citizens.

Caelius already foresaw the resulting deadlock in his letter to Cicero about the Senate's debates on 1 and 2 September 51, which in fact proved inconclusive because there was no quorum for a vote. 'The Gallic provinces,' he wrote, 'which have a vetoer in readiness, are being brought into the same category as all the other provinces.' What this meant was that Caesar had a tribune ready to veto any attempt to decide the succession to his own provinces, and that the Senate would respond by making the allotment of all the other provinces dependent on it, as Caelius explained more fully in a letter later that month. 'You know the usual scenario,' he wrote. 'There will be a decision about the Gallic provinces. There will be someone to veto it. Then someone else will get up to obstruct a decision on the other provinces "unless the Senate be allowed a free hand to decide on *all* the provinces". And so there will be a huge and lengthy farce, so lengthy indeeed that it could drag on for more than a couple of years in these entanglements.' But by the end of the month Caelius was more hopeful of an end to the deadlock because Pompey had taken a firm line, and he could not believe that Caesar would not back down.

By then Pompey will definitely have heard that there was no military justification for granting Caesar an extension of his command over a Gaul so thoroughly subdued, and he no longer hesitated to align himself openly with the suggestion mooted by Scipio at the beginning of the month. And it was only now, 'when it had been clearly ascertained that the inclination of Pompey was to the side of a resolution that Caesar should leave his province after 1 March', that the Senate felt confident enough to confront the issue squarely and to pass such a resolution. On 29 September the Senate met in the Temple of Apollo outside the city-walls in order that Pompey might attend, and after a lengthy debate in which Pompey made his views known the following decree was passed and carefully recorded by Caelius for Cicero's benefit:

Whereas the consul Marcus Marcellus has opened the question of the consular provinces the Senate gave the following opinion on the matter:

That Lucius Paullus and Gaius Marcellus [the consuls-elect for 50], when they shall have entered their term of office, after the nineteenth day of the month of February which shall fall in their year of office shall bring the matter of the consular provinces before the Senate and shall not after the first day of March in the said year give precedence to any other motion nor shall any other motion be brought before the Senate in combination with that motion;

That they shall hold a meeting of the Senate for that purpose on comitial days as on any other and shall make a decree of the Senate, and when this matter is brought before the Senate by the consuls it shall be lawful to summon such of the senators who are on the panel of jurors without their incurring a penalty....

In other words Caesar was being warned that he must not expect an extension of his command after 1 March 50 when it expired. The Senate was making it clear that on and after that date it would not allow any other business of whatever urgency either to postpone or be combined with the allocation of consular provinces, and since his own provinces were of course consular and would then be free for reallocation, he should not expect to keep them. In order that the debate begun on 1 March might continue uninterrupted by adjournments until the decision was reached the Senate exempted itself from the usual regulation prohibiting sittings on days available for electoral and legislative assemblies of the people. And in order that there might be no danger of losing a quorum or suffering from rival attractions the senators on the jury-panel were to be exempted from the penalties normally incurred for a failure to appear at court. But if this was a warning to Caesar that he must prepare to leave his provinces once his existing term had expired, it was also a guarantee and a concession. The guarantee was that the Senate would make no attempt to curtail his command before its expiration. The concession was that the appointment of his successors would not be made sufficiently far in advance for them to be in a position to take over in Gaul immediately on 1 March, and he could therefore count on a period of grace before he would actually have to leave his provinces, even though he would only be caretaker governor until they or their representatives arrived. And the fairness of this decree based on Pompey's opinion is reflected by the fact that not even the most ardent of Caesar's supporters among the tribunes attempted to veto it, unlike the further resolutions which the Senate wished to make on the following day.

On 30 September the Senate endeavoured to provide against a tribunician veto of whatever would be decided when the debate was actually held in five months' time, or indeed of the debate itself when the consuls of 50 would try to act in accordance with the first decree. The House supported a motion that 'anyone who shall have obstructed or prevented the holding of a debate or the making of a decree shall be considered to have acted against the interests of the Republic', but four tribunes immediately vetoed this resolution. And even the authors of the motion can hardly have been surprised. It would have been as unreasonable for the tribunes of 51 to agree to neutralize the vetoes of their successors on an unknown resolution to be taken in the future as it would have been for them to have vetoed the last resolution to hold the future debate, or indeed for the Senate to have resolved in advance what was to be resolved at that debate in five months' time. But it was a further warning to Caesar that the Senate did not mean to be trifled with once his command had expired, and it was reinforced by two further resolutions. The one sought to authorize any of Caesar's troops who had served their full time to apply to the Senate for discharge; the other to degrade Cilicia from a consular to a praetorian province, and to provide for the appointment of praetorian governors to that province and to the eight existing praetorian provinces by a casting of lots among ex-praetors who had not yet taken governorships. These were both anti-Caesarian measures. The former would have begun the gradual demobilization of Caesar's armies at once and made the Senate and not the general the benefactor of the discharged veterans. The latter would not only have removed Cilicia from the number of provinces available as alternatives to Gaul in the allotment of proconsular provinces but would have indicated that the number of proconsular provinces to be allotted need not be limited to the usual two as under the old system before the enactment of Pompey's law of 52 requiring a five-year period to elapse between the holding of a magistracy and the promagisterial governorship of a province.

Under the old system it had been necessary each year to provide only two proconsular provinces for the two consuls to be elected for the following year. And presumably it was envisaged that only two proconsular provinces would again be allotted annually once five years had elapsed and the consuls of 52 would be eligible for governorships, if they wanted them. But the interim arrangements whereby provinces were to be allocated to ex-consuls who had failed for whatever reason to take up provincial governorships after their term of office made it possible to appoint new governors to more than two proconsular provinces at a time, and while only two had been appointed in 52 (Cicero for Cilicia and Bibulus for Syria), the resolution which now proposed the simultaneous allotment of nine praetorian provinces required the appointment of more praetorian governors than the annual number of eight praetors. It was in fact a proposal for a clean sweep of all praetorian provinces, and since its implementation would set the precedent for extending the annual allocations of proconsular governorships beyond the number of annual consuls, it would become even less likely that Caesar's Gallic provinces would escape allocation. Of course this does not mean that the Caesarian tribunes who opposed this resolution believed that its failure would make the Senate any more inclined to leave Caesar in the governorship of Gaul. Nevertheless five months was a long time, and if in the meantime two other proconsular governorships became vacant by death or illness or Ciceronian agitation to return or even some emergency requiring Pompey's redeployment from his governorship of Spain, it might be useful to have prevented the establishment of a precedent invalidating the argument that only the traditional number of provinces should be allocated and therefore Caesar should remain where he was. All the same the veto of the Senate's resolutions of 29 and 30 September 51, except for the first one postponing the debate on the consular provinces until a fortnight before the expiry of Caesar's command on 1 March 50, did not prevent their being formally recorded as 'opinions' rather than 'decrees'; and this left Caesar in no doubt that the majority of the Senate was determined to have his provinces and armies under new governors before the elections of July 50 at which Caesar was expected to stand for consulship of 49, and that any attempt to hold on to them until the very end of 50, when he might enter the city as consul if he stood successfully, was likely to be regarded as 'acting against the interests of the Republic'.

The attitude of Pompey towards Caesar in all this, though less friendly, was anything but hostile. He had consistently resisted the attempts of Caesar's enemies to curtail his command. In July he had gone to Ariminum to make his own evaluation of the likelihood that Caesar would require an extension of his command in order to complete the pacification of Gaul, and in August he had been keeping the hard-liners quiet by talking again of going to Spain, as Cicero reveals in his reply to a letter from Appius Claudius that month. 'Please write more about the political situation,' he pleaded; 'I am very anxious when you tell me that Pompey is going to Spain.' And it was only in September, when Pompey learnt of Caesar's success in beating out the last flames of Gallic resistance and realized the unlikelihood of further outbreaks, that he formally committed himself to supporting the appointment of successors to take over from Caesar after the expiry of his command. By then he had also realized that Caesar wanted to keep his provinces and armies as well as his residual *imperium* beyond 1 March 50, not for the purpose of completing an unfinished conquest but in order to rest his candidature on legions rather than laurels, force rather than friendship, and the security of continuing to govern Gaul if he were prevented from governing Rome.

But if Pompey was determined to concede nothing to Caesar the rival, he was still prepared to protect the interest of Caesar the protégé, and he remained adamant against even allowing Caesar's successors to be appointed before his legal term expired. ' "I cannot," ' he declared in the Senate on 29 September, ' "without offence decide about Caesar's provinces before 1 March, but after that date I shall not hesitate." ' ' "But what if vetoes are interposed on that day?" ' someone asked. ' "It makes no difference whether Caesar is going to refuse to obey the Senate openly or puts someone up to obstruct its decrees," ' replied Pompey. And Pom-

pey clearly believed that Caesar would climb down. ' "What if he
wants," ' asked another, ' "to be consul-elect and to keep his army at
the same time?" ' ' "What if my own son raises a stick to me?" ' replied
Pompey with what Caelius describes as the utmost mildness. It was inconceivable, but if the inconceivable happened, there would be only one
remedy. But Caelius did not believe that it would come to that any more
than Pompey did, although he was aware that their relations were not
as cordial as they had been. 'All this makes people think that there has
been a bit of trouble between Pompey and Caesar,' he wrote to Cicero.
'What Caesar wants is to reduce the whole matter to a simple alternative:
either to remain in his province and not have his candidature considered
in this [electoral] year, or, if he will be able to become consul-elect, to
give up his province.' In other words, if the Senate wanted him to leave
his provinces, it had to allow him to stand while still in command of
them on the assurance that he would hand them over after his election
to successors whose appointment could then proceed without obstruction
by tribunes loyal to his interest. Otherwise he would not stand at all for
the elections of 50, and would continue to use tribunes to obstruct the
reallocation of his provinces. He hoped that the Senate would concede
the former as a lesser of two evils, but it was a piece of blackmail which
Pompey was not prepared to connive at.

But soon there was something else to worry about besides Gaul. Ever
since Cicero had taken over his unwanted province of Cilicia in August
he had been flapping about the Parthian peril, and the worthy Bibulus
was showing anything but enthusiasm to reach his own province of Syria
which had been without a proconsular governor since the defeat and
death of Crassus in 53. But that was just as well. The delay of Bibulus left
Crassus'old quaestor Cassius in command, and when King Orodes' son
Pacorus led a Parthian army into Syria in September 51, that able officer
not only defended Antioch but counter-attacked so effectively early in
October that the prince withdrew to Cyrrhestice for the winter and left
a temporarily tranquil province for Bibulus to take over in December.
Cicero in the meantime had advanced to defend his own eastern border
with his two skeletal legions, and when he reached the Amanus mountains
his relief at learning of Cassius' success (for which he later took outrageous credit as having terrified the Parthians by his mere approach!)
emboldened him to exercise his troops against the mountain tribes who
lived by plundering all but the most heavily armed caravans. But even
as he was writing an account of this to Caelius in mid-November and
urging his assistance in lobbying to gain the distinction of a triumph from
the really rather trivial victory which he had just gained over the hereditary
robbers of Amanus, this improbable *Imperator* was under no illusion

that the Parthian withdrawal from Syria was anything but a temporary lull, and he was desperate to be out of his province before the storm broke again in the following spring.

In the same week in which Cicero wrote to Caelius, Caelius wrote to tell Cicero how Rome was reacting to the recently arrived reports of the Parthian invasion of September. 'One man would send Pompey; another would not have Pompey withdrawn from the city; another would send Caesar in command of his army; another the consuls. . . .' And while it was no doubt gratifying to Pompey to hear men saying that the conqueror of Mithridates was the obvious choice to defend the East from Orodes if only he was not so indispensable at Rome, this was one overseas assignment which he may genuinely have wanted to take. To have gone campaigning in Spain would have been a step backwards to the scene of youthful victories, but to take on a new enemy in the East and win the glory of avenging Crassus' disgrace was a different thing altogether, and there is no reason to doubt that, when he wrote to Cicero in December and told him not to worry about the next year because 'this will be my affair', he meant exactly what he said. And the implications of this decision went far beyond Cicero's immense relief that he would not be facing the spring offensive which Pompey's old protégé King Deiotarus of Galatia assured him was bound to come. For if the danger had materialized and Pompey had gone to wage war in the East, it might have postponed if not avoided the self-destructive madness condemned by Lucan –

> When Rome abandoned Crassus' ghost
> Still unavenged in Babylon
> To haunt the heaps of Roman spoils,
> And chose to feast barbarian eyes
> With Roman blood from civil wars
> That could no triumphs win.

# 'ARES ALIKE TO ALL'

All this has made Caesar so strong that all hope of resistance
now depends on one man. I should rather that that citizen
had not given him such great power in the first place than
that he should be resisting him now at the height
of his strength.
Cicero, *Letters to Atticus*, 7.3

On 1 January 50 the consul Gaius Marcellus assumed leadership of the
hard-liners from his cousin Marcus, 'but if there was one man who more
than anyone else applied the flaming torch which kindled the Civil War',
says Velleius, 'it was the tribune Gaius Curio'. We last heard of him in
59, the year of Caesar's consulship, when he was one of the young hotheads
accused of complicity in a plot to assassinate Pompey. Like Caelius he
was a young friend of Cicero, and when Curio had been elected to the
tribunate for 50, Caelius had written to Cicero that he would be likely
to support the Senate and 'the good', by whom he meant the anti-Caesarian
lobby. 'Certainly he is bubbling over in that direction,' observed Caelius,
'largely because Caesar, whose habit is always to enlist at whatever cost
the friendship of all the most worthless men, has gravely insulted him.'
And in September 51 Caelius reported that Curio was preparing 'total
opposition to Caesar' if Caesar failed to yield over the appointment of
his successors.

But Curio was not a natural supporter of the Senate's authority. He
saw himself as a great popular legislator in the Gracchan tradition, and
he began drafting a whole series of Bills which he proposed to introduce
as the tribunician successor to Clodius, in whose widow he found a wife
more than ready to encourage a demagogic career. There was a massive
programme of building roads, a rather more useful equivalent of famine
walls, over whose construction he was to be superintendent for five years.
There were to be more farms for the urban poor, to whom more of the
Campanian land would be parcelled out as freeholds. And the whole
kingdom of Numidia was to be annexed by the Roman People. It was
a programme as little likely to appeal to the majority of the Senate now
as Crassus' attempt to secure an overseas power-base by the annexation

of Eygpt in 65 or the similar schemes of his tribune Rullus which Cicero had squashed in 63. And it certainly had no appeal for Pompey, who was not only hereditary patron of the African monarch but bristled at the prospect of a further eviction of Campanian tenants that would leave Caesar a free hand with farms for his veterans so near to Rome. But Pompey needed to do nothing to oppose Curio personally. There was such over-whelming opposition to his schemes from the rest of the Senate that the tribune made no progress at all in the first two months of 50, and as 1 March drew nearer, and with it the prohibition against discussing any other business but the appointment of Caesar's successors, he retaliated through the pontificate by trying to browbeat his fellow-priests into insert-ing an intercalary month into the calendar in the latter part of February. But if the trailing sun smiled on Curio's efforts to help him catch up with the Roman calendar, the Senate saw only a political challenge which threatened to postpone the debate on Caesar's provinces for a month, and when Curio was violently attacked over this in February, Caelius tells us that he 'crossed to the democratic side and started speaking for Caesar'.

According to Dio and Appian Curio had been bought by Caesar long since, and his only motive in producing obviously unacceptable measures was to gain an excuse for changing sides. But while Cicero claimed 'not to be surprised' by Curio's volte-face when he received Caelius' letter, the proposed legislation need not have been uninspired by a genuine reformer's zeal even if the intercalary month was deliberately provoca-tive. And perhaps the Pompeian poet Lucan was right to give Curio the benefit of the doubt when he looked back to the origins of the Civil War from the reign of Nero over a century later:

> No son of Rome had such promise displayed,
> To no one the state had such debts to be paid
> As to him for the time that he trod the right road.

But there is no doubt that Caesar saw a most effective tool in this frus-trated reformer, for whom he no longer felt contempt. Here was his new Clodius, married to Clodius' widow, and financially embarrassed after constructing the amazing contraption described by Pliny – a pair of revolv-ing wooden theatres in which he had been able to treat the electorate to two plays simultaneously in the morning before swinging the two halves round to produce an amphitheatre for gladiatorial and bestial extrava-ganzas after lunch. And once Curio had washed away his independence in the 'golden stream' from Gaul, 'it was not just the gladiators', says Pliny, 'but the whole Roman people that fought for its life in the funeral games which he gave at his father's tomb', as Lucan goes on to explain:

> For as years of corruption our state did corrode
> So his wavering spirit was borne on the stream
> Of largess and luxury, wealth beyond dream;
> But the power of such riches is most to be feared,
> And by Curio's course revolution was steered,
> For Curio's favour proved easy to hold
> With plunder from Gaul and Caesarian gold.
> For the sword in the past had made laws of its own
> With its point at our throats – and not Sulla alone,
> But Cinna and Marius and all Caesar's line,
> Ferocity, cruelty, time after time –
> But to whom before now had such power been doled,
> For they bought the country which Curio sold?

How Curio staged his début in this new role over the question of Caesar's provinces is revealed by Appian. The consul Gaius Marcellus opened a debate on the subject in accordance with the Senate's decree of the previous September, presumably on 19 February, and 'proposed sending successors to Caesar, for his term was expiring'. But Marcellus was not supported by his fellow-consul Paullus, whose silence was eloquent testimony that Caesar had reached the price which this extravagant builder of self-glorifying public works had placed on his political integrity. Curio on the other hand was anything but taciturn, and having first gratified Marcellus by agreeing with his proposal as though maintaining his former anti-Caesarian stance, he proceeded to wipe the smile from the consul's face by adding 'that Pompey should also resign his provinces and army exactly like Caesar, for in this way the Republic would be made free of fear all round'. At once there was uproar in the House. Speaker after speaker condemned this suggestion as outrageous because Pompey's command had not expired, and the two cases were not comparable. But Curio maintained that Pompey and Caesar were now 'suspicious of each other', that 'lasting peace could be secured only by the ending of all extraordinary commands', and that 'he would personally oppose the sending of successors to Caesar unless Pompey should also lay down his command'. And he said this, says Appian, 'because he knew that Pompey would not give up his command and because he saw that the people were incensed against Pompey on account of the prosecutions for bribery'. The Sink of Romulus had been too well scoured by Pompey's caretaker consulship of 52. If there was still no shortage of corruption at the highest levels of society, the urban mob was missing the rich pickings to which it had grown accustomed from the frenzied electoral bribery of the last few years, and there was not even the fun of running amuck in the name of democracy or the satisfaction of thumbing noses at the establishment. Pompey, once the popular champion, was now the personification of senatorial establishment, and when Curio coupled his Clodian programme of popular legislation with a personal attack on Pompey's command, the people admired their tribune's pluck, 'for nothing was considered more perilous than to get on the wrong side of Pompey the Great'.

Thanks to the Senate's opposition to Curio's schemes and Curio's retaliation with a paralysis of senatorial business, 1 March came and went without any decision on the succession to Caesar's now expired provincial command. The greater part of March seems to have been taken up with stormy public meetings convened by Curio and with blocking tactics by the consul Paullus, who, though similarly suborned to Caesar's cause – 'a nasty business about Paullus and Curio', wrote Cicero when he heard – was otherwise totally opposed to all Curio's own legislative schemes, and employed every constitutional device to deprive him of comitial days on which he could present them to the people. But in April the debate on the provinces was at length resumed, and a letter from Caelius of the latter part of that month reveals an attempt by Pompey to break the deadlock by offering Caesar exactly what he wanted: 'Pompey seems to have thrown his weight behind a proposal that Caesar should relinquish his provinces on 13 November.' Nothing could have been fairer or more statesmanlike, for it removed the final plank on which Caesar might have based a justification for blocking the appointment of his successors after 1 March. It recognized the fact that the new rules for the allotment of provinces enacted into law by Pompey in 52 had removed an assumption on which Caesar might previously have relied. Under the old system, whereby consuls went out to provincial governorships immediately after their year of office in Rome, the obvious successors to provinces held under an extraordinary command expiring on 1 March 50 would have been the consuls of 50, who would not have been ready to take command of them until the end of that year. But since the introduction of the new system in 52 Caesar had no longer been able to count on nine months' grace, and Pompey was prepared to support a further concession granting to Caesar all that he could have expected under the old system. For the Senate to decree that Caesar should relinquish his command on the Ides of November would have the effect of granting a formal extension of his command in order that he might stand for the consular elections in late July 50 not only *in absentia* but still in command of his provinces and armies, which he would have to leave only at the last practical date to allow time to come down to Rome and put the final touches to the organization of the triumph in which he might enter the city and a new consulship on 1 January 49. It seems to be exactly what Caesar had been trying to achieve the previous autumn, and what Pompey had been determined not to concede. But now that Pompey was prepared to concede it, unenthusiastically perhaps but unequivocally, Caelius tells us that 'Curio is determined to submit to anything rather than this'.

The reason for Curio's opposition was that Caesar was now against the fixing of any specific date on which he must relinquish his command even if he would be able to stand for the consulship before then. Once successors had been appointed to take over on a fixed date, Caesar would lose the last shred of legality for holding on to his command when that date came. For while it was undoubtedly an abuse of the constitution for tribunes to veto the appointment of successors to Caesar, it was not unlawful, and as long as no successors had been appointed, Caesar might remain in command on the simple principle that provinces and armies could not be left ungoverned. As for the consulship, Caesar was no longer sufficiently confident that he could win the elections of 50 even if he retained his governorship and armies over the summer. He may even have doubted that his candidature would be accepted when the time came, for while he could discount the danger of a successful repeal of the law of the ten tribunes guaranteeing his right to stand *in absentia*, his enemies might find other objections. Or they might contrive to postpone the elections to the end of the year or into the next, when other proconsuls would have taken over his provinces and legions. It was a risk which Caesar was simply not prepared to take.

Perhaps Pompey urged his latest concession with a shrewd idea that it would prove as unacceptable to Curio as to the hard-liners in the Senate, but he had at least formally and publicly committed himself to a concession which he was reluctant to make if we may rely on Caelius, who described this development to Cicero. 'This is the new scenario,' he wrote in April. 'Pompey, as if he were not attacking Caesar but making an arrangement which he considers fair to him, says that Curio is seeking excuses for discord [in not accepting it]. But the fact is that Pompey does not really want Caesar to be designated consul before he has handed over his army and his provinces, and clearly fears that prospect.' It may even be true that Pompey offered this concession with an eye to blocking the elections until after 13 November, and this suspicion may have reinforced Caesar's inclination to distrust the proposal. But equally it could have been made in good faith to break the deadlock. To have accepted it would have meant that Caesar trusted Pompey to continue to play fair by him. That he rejected it was an acknowledgement that he did not trust him, and after this the old bonds of friendship between the two men began looking very dangerously frayed.

Not satisfied with rejecting Pompey's concession, Curio launched all-out verbal warfare on Pompey himself. 'Pompey is taking a lot of flak from Curio,' observed Caelius, 'and the whole of his third consulship is under violent attack.' Pompey retaliated by sharpening his own oratorical rapiers which had become somewhat blunted in long years of unchallenged supremacy. But he was not able to battle for long before he succumbed to a recurrent illness, possibly malarial, which was nearly fatal. To judge from Cicero's note to Atticus in early June Pompey was evidently unwell in April, and when Cicero referred to the 'hateful things' which he had heard about Curio and Paullus he added, with typical confidence in the Republic's guardian, 'not that there is anything to fear whether Pompey stands up or sits down as long as he keeps his health'. But Pompey's health did not hold, and when he took a break at Naples, he experienced so severe a relapse that 'all Italy prayed for the safety of her leading citizen'.

When he eventually recovered, the ripple of rejoicing that radiated from Naples throughout the length and breadth of Italy recalled the welcome which had greeted his return from the East nearly twelve years before. 'It began when the Neapolitans offered sacrifices of thanksgiving for his preservation,' explains Plutarch.

Their example was taken up by the neighbouring communities, and thus it spread throughout all Italy so that every city, small and great, held festival for many days. No place could contain all those who came from all quarters to greet him, but roads and villages and ports were all filled with sacrificing and feasting throngs. Many more, with garlands on their heads and lighted torches in their hands, escorted him on his way and pelted him with flowers so that his progress and return to Rome made a most brilliant and splendid spectacle.

But it was a dangerous tonic to his morale, if Plutarch's judgement is sound:

For this is said to have done more than everything else to bring about the Civil War. Such universal rejoicing made Pompey so over-confident that he disregarded calculations based on hard facts. Throwing to the winds the caution which had so far always given security to his career of success and achievement, he was indulged in unlimited self-confidence and contempt for Caesar's power, and he convinced himself that he would need neither armed force to oppose Caesar nor any irksome labour of preparation but that he would pull him down much more easily than he had raised him up.

But while it was undoubtedly heartening to Pompey to be carried back to Rome on the crest of a wave of universal affection, he nevertheless repeated in person before the Senate a statement which he had sent it in writing from his sick-bed, and which appears to have been another genuine attempt to defuse the potentially explosive situation. According to Appian, what he had written from Naples was a long letter

praising Caesar's exploits, recounting his own from the beginning, and saying that while he had been invested with a third consulship and with provinces and armies, these had not been solicited by him: he had received them only on being called upon to serve the state, and since his provinces had been accepted unwillingly, he would gladly yield them to those who wished to take them back, and would not wait for his command to expire.... And when Pompey returned to Rome, he spoke to the Senate in the same way, and repeated his promise to lay down his command. As a friend and kinsman by marriage of Caesar he declared that Caesar would cheerfully do the same, for his had been a long and arduous contest against warlike peoples, and having added greatly to the Republic he would now come back to enjoy his honours, his sacrificial duties and his well deserved relaxations.

Appian calls this letter 'an artifice by which to demonstrate his own fairness and excite prejudice against Caesar', but it is doubtful that this was its only purpose.

It was of course humbug for Pompey to maintain that he had accepted his third consulship and an extension of his command as burdens to be shouldered by a devoted servant of the state, but it does not follow that his offer to resign his command if Caesar would do the same was not fair or genuine. It was in fact exactly what Curio had suggested in February, and while Pompey might now have offered this further concession in the expectation that the majority of his peers would reject it, he could not have been certain. Moreover the offer was made not only in a letter which he wrote from Naples when he may have feared that he would become a permanent invalid but when he had recovered and returned to Rome in a blaze of glory. Let the Senate appoint successors to his own provinces as well as to Caesar's. Let them both return to private life. It was too late for Caesar to stand at the elections of the current year which were coming up in late July, but the ten tribunes' law of 52 was still in force to grant him candidature *in absentia* in the next year if he was so afraid of prosecution that he preferred to remain outside the city-boundaries and postpone his triumph until he could become consul. On the other hand he could do what Pompey himself had done, and enter the city in triumph as soon as he returned. Even if he risked prosecution when he entered the city, he would not necessarily be convicted. A glorious triumphal procession into a city sighing with relief at a crisis averted would hardly be conducive to the successful prosecution of the *triumphator* immediately afterwards, and with Pompey's support he would have every expectation of enjoying 'his honours, his sacrificial duties and his well-deserved relaxations', if that indeed is what he wanted. Pompey may well have envisaged going out in great state to greet the returning Caesar just as Sulla had gone out to greet a loyal young general returning from defeating the Marians in Africa nearly thirty years ago. He may have seen himself proposing in person the senatorial resolution to authorize Caesar's triumph with the same good-natured patronage with which Sulla had smiled at the rising sun and bent his own rules to indulge a deserving protégé. And he may still have regarded the danger that Caesar would march on Rome as no more likely than his own supposed intentions in which Sulla had been foolish enough to believe, if confident enough not to fear. At any rate Pompey was prepared to give Caesar the benefit of the doubt, and when he publicized his willingness to agree to a joint handing-over of armies and provinces in the early summer of 50, he was offering Caesar a last chance to justify his confidence in him and reciprocate his trust.

But Caesar did not trust Pompey. After nine years of supreme authority in Gaul he trusted nothing but his army, and he was no longer prepared to hazard his position on Pompey's favour, which meant acknowledging Pompey as first citizen. The conqueror of Gaul was no longer the protégé of the conqueror of the East. A letter from Balbus to Cicero in the following year claiming that 'Caesar wanted nothing more than to live without fear with Pompey as first citizen' was greeted with the derision which it deserved. Caesar had remarked more than once that 'as he was now the first citizen, it was harder for his enemies to push him down from first to second place than from second to bottom', and Curio's response to Pompey's agreement to the demand which he had made in February finally snapped the last frayed threads of the old relationship between Pompey and his protégé. Simultaneous disarmament by Pompey and Caesar was apparently not enough: Pompey must disarm first.

Pompey was furious. Who did this arrogant young tribune think he was to stand up in front of the Senate and say that he, Pompey the Great, proconsul of the Spains with a legal commission that still had three years to run, should give up his armies before the proconsul of Gaul, his own protégé, a man whose command had already expired? How dare he say that Pompey 'was aiming at tyranny', and that 'unless Pompey laid down his command now, while he had the fear of Caesar before his eyes, he would never lay it down at all'. If this was the way his concessions were to be flung in his teeth, Pompey would make no more. Nor would he stay to be insulted. Apoplectic with anger he leapt to his feet, 'threatened Curio, and swept out of the house to his palace', where he waited to hear how the Senate reacted. And the vast majority reacted satisfactorily. Even those who regarded Pompey only as the lesser of two evils thought that he was 'the better republican', and that 'it would not be safe to deprive Pompey of his power until after Caesar had laid down his'. For Curio to insist that they 'needed Caesar against the power of Pompey' proved counter-productive, and when he eventually returned to his former demand for simultaneous disarmament, it was too late. 'The Senate would not agree with him,' says Appian, and having been left in no doubt that he would lose if he put a proposal to the vote, 'Curio dismissed the House and left the whole matter in the air'.

Encouraged by the Senate's hostility, the anti-Caesarian lobby now sought to browbeat Curio into withdrawing his veto on the appointment of successors to the Gallic provinces. In a letter of June 50 Caelius told Cicero how this was formally proposed by Marcus Marcellus, the ex-consul of 51 and cousin of the present consul Gaius, who is unlikely to have been unaware of what Marcus would suggest when called upon to give the first opinion. '"The Senate,"' he declared, '"should treat with the tribunes"', which presumably meant warning them that their action was 'against the interests of the Republic'. When the Senate had voted in the previous September to postpone debating the appointment of Caesar's successors until 1 March, it had also recorded the opinion that any obstruction or prohibition of the matter after that date should be regarded in those terms, and to that extent Marcellus was now proposing no more than the reactivation of a decision taken nine months ago but vetoed, and now more than three months overdue. But while the majority of senators were against any suggestion that Pompey should lay down his command, which they regarded as a bulwark against a Caesarian autocracy, they were not for trying to prise Caesar away from Gaul and his army there without granting him the right to stand for the consulship first. 'The view they had come round to,' wrote Caelius scathingly, 'was that the candidature of a man who was inclined to surrender neither his provinces nor his army should be admitted.' They shrank from the hard line of Marcellus as being unnecessarily provocative at this delicate stage. They feared giving Caesar the battle-cry that the rights of the people's tribunes were being overborne, and when the proposal 'to treat with the tribunes' was put to a division, a large majority voted against it. It was exactly what Caelius had foreseen in April: 'if they try to crush Curio in everything, Caesar will be defended, and if they shy away from the vetoer, as they look like doing, Caesar will stay on as long as he wishes'. And unless he was being even more than usually sarcastic, Caelius expected Cicero to be pleased at this result. But if Cicero held the same opinion at the time as he did with hindsight in the following December, he thought this appeasement a grave mistake: 'Curio would have collapsed if they had once started treating with him, but the Senate would not support the proposal, and no successors to Caesar were appointed.' But what Cicero thought in distant Cilicia was less important than what the first citizen thought at Rome, and Caelius promised to report Pompey's reaction as soon as it was known. 'The fact is,' he sniggered, 'that Pompey's appetite is so jaded at present that he cannot find anything palatable ... how he will take this I shall let you know when I find out ... and what the Republic's future will be after that, you rich old men will have seen for yourselves.'

Unfortunately the letter in which Caelius reported Pompey's reaction has not survived, but there is no doubt what line he took. When we next hear from Caelius in August he reiterates what he has already 'repeatedly' told Cicero in what must have been a spate of correspondence. 'I cannot see peace lasting out the year,' he writes. 'The issue on which those who control power are going to fight is this. Pompey is determined not to let Caesar be elected consul unless he has handed over his provinces and army. Caesar is convinced that he has no hope of safety if once he quits his army. He therefore proposes this compromise: that both should give up their armies.' But this was something that Pompey would no longer contemplate. It was now a matter of 'face', that almost untranslatable commodity expressed by the Latin *dignitas* which these proud and powerful men valued more highly than life itself. It was one thing for Pompey to offer to bestow favours on a forgivably prodigal son. It was quite another for those favours to be demanded under the threat of unrepentant force, and with Caesar now sitting in Cisalpine Gaul and demanding to remain another whole year in an expired command unless his former patron disbanded his own legal one, Pompey's rhetorical question of the previous year was no longer hypothetical. 'What shall I do if my son raises his stick to me?' now required an answer.

What messages passed between Rome and Ravenna during the summer of 50 we do not know, but the result is clear enough. 'So much for their famous affection, their detestable alliance,' crowed Caelius. 'It is not merely receding into a private quarrel behind the scenes, but erupting into open war.' And that was a prospect which called for a serious political reassessment from a shrewd opportunist like Cicero's spendthrift young correspondent:

As long as a struggle is carried on constitutionally and without recourse to arms one is bound to follow the more honourable course; but when it comes to war and taking the field, then one judges that cause to be better which is also the safer. Amid all this discord I see that while Pompey will have on his side the Senate and all those who settle disputes at law, all who live a life of fear or have but little hope will join Caesar, for his army is altogether beyond compare. I only hope we have time to consider the resources of each and choose the right side. After all, each of the two is well prepared in resolution and resources, and if it could only be managed without personal risk to yourself, a spectacular and entertaining drama is being staged by Fortune for your benefit.

The only chance which Caelius could see of avoiding civil war was the continuation of the foreign war which might require one of Rome's two best generals to go to the East; but even as he was writing this opinion in August, the possibility was already dead. In the early summer the Parthian army had again invaded Syria as Cicero had feared. Cicero had once again led his two legions to defend the eastern frontier of his own province, but Bibulus in Syria had had little of the vigour of Cassius whose energy had repelled the invasion of the previous year. Indeed, Cicero maintains that the former consular colleague of Caesar was no more willing to emerge from Government House in Antioch while the Parthians were outside the walls in 50 than he had been to put his nose out of doors in Rome while Caesar had been on the political rampage in 59, and it was small thanks to this star-gazing specialist that the Parthian armies rolled back across the Euphrates – unless it really was a diplomatic initiative by Bibulus that created the diversion, as Dio maintains. At any rate, whether it was due to Bibulus' good management or Cicero's 'incredible good fortune' the Parthians retired of their own accord to fight a civil war of their own at home. But if it seems ironic that a Parthian civil war should have removed the main hope of avoiding civil war at Rome, it is doubly so in providing the occasion for a transfer of one of Caesar's legions to Pompey. For when the Senate had responded to Bibulus' bombardment of requests for reinforcements in the early summer by decreeing that he should be sent two legions, one from Pompey's army and one from Caesar's, Pompey had chosen to send the legion which he had lent to Caesar in 54.

At the time of course this was not necessarily the unfriendly act which the non-contemporary sources claim, still less the calculated purpose of the Senate's decree in the first place as it was misrepresented by Caesar's subsequent propaganda. The situation in Syria had been very serious. Reinforcements were needed urgently, and though it is true that Pompey had command of several cohorts raised in Italy in the emergency of 52, these were not formed into legions. Pompey's only battle-ready legions were in Spain, and since it was a great deal quicker to recall a legion which he had sent to Gaul there could be no objection to his decision, especially since the legion was no longer needed in Gaul. What is significant is not that Pompey now withdrew this legion but that he had not done so before, despite the pressure which had been put on him in the Senate in the previous year. Moreover there had been no attempt to veto the decree, and when Caesar received Pompey's request to return the legion, he did not demur. He rewarded the troops handsomely and sent them back to Pompey along with a legion of his own. But by the time the legions arrived the danger for which they had been summoned had long receded, and instead of being embarked for Syria they were sent into winter-quarters at Capua among the veterans of Pompey's Eastern campaigns. And in view of the degeneration of the relations between Pompey and Caesar by the autumn, it was clear that Caesar's own legion was now to be listed along with the one which he had borrowed from Pompey as major contributions to the forces immediately available for the defence of Rome.

But Pompey still believed that Caesar would back down if treated with sufficient firmness, and he was less worried about Caesar the general than Caesar the politician. For once it had become clear that Caesar would return not as his ally but as his rival, Pompey had determined not only to stop him becoming consul without first handing over his provinces and armies but to stop him becoming consul at all. The consulship of 59 had demonstrated Caesar's unscrupulous effectiveness as a political manipulator, but then it had been serving Pompey's purpose. To allow a repeat performance directed against Pompey's interest by a Caesar of independent means was unimaginable. If Caesar came back in peace, he must come as a private citizen. If he would not do that, it was better that he should return in a war which Pompey was entirely confident of being able to win.

'When some said that if Caesar should march on Rome they did not see any forces to defend it,' records Plutarch, 'Pompey replied as follows: "In whatever part of Italy I stamp on the ground there will spring up armies of foot and horse."' When the young Appius Claudius (the censor's nephew) arrived back with the Pompeian legion which he had gone to bring from Gaul, he told Pompey that 'he could put down Caesar with Caesar's own troops the moment he appeared before them, so great was their hatred of Caesar and their affection for Pompey'. And no doubt much more of the same was said by Pompey and his friends without necessarily implying the rash over-confidence which Plutarch deduces from his anecdotes. It was exactly what was needed to stiffen the spines of the senatorial moderates who were prepared to accept Caesar the consul only because they feared Caesar the rebel even more. If Pompey was to scuttle the concession which he had now rejected, that Caesar should be allowed to stand for the consulship before he had given up his armies, he must convince the timid majority that war was preferable to a false peace, that confrontation was really safer than appeasement, that instead of yielding to Caesar's 'impudent demands' they would do better to authorize Pompey to stamp on the ground. Those who criticize Pompey for not levying troops earlier seem to forget that as the constitutionalist he had no authority to do so. He had first to embolden the Senate to defy Caesar and overbear the tribune opposing the appointment of successors to his provinces. Once that had been done, the authorization to stamp on the ground would follow automatically, and then it would be up to Caesar to decide on war or peace on Pompey's terms.

This was all part of the cold war which intensified throughout the second part of 50 after the summer elections, at which Pompey's determination to humble Caesar either politically or militarily was reflected in the capture by hard-liners of both the consulships for 49. At the top of the poll came another Gaius Marcellus, the third Marcellus to reach the headship of state in three successive years and no less ardently an anti-Caesarian than his cousin Gaius of 50 and his brother Marcus of 51. About his colleague Lucius Lentulus there may initially have been less conviction, and there were rumours over the ensuing months that his massive debts were tempting him to join the increasing number of spendthrift heretics queuing up for baptism in Caesar's golden stream, but if he was tempted, he did not succumb. And certainly Caesar had not supported Lentulus in the elections. Caesar's candidate was Servius Galba, one of his former legates in the Gallic campaigns of 57, and it was highly gratifying to Pompey to see Galba trounced by Marcellus and Lentulus. But if it was a blow to Caesar to have both heads of state against him in the year to which he had now postponed his own candidature, the important thing was to have a stalwart tribune to succeed Curio and maintain the veto against the appointment of his successors, and this he achieved though the election of a vigorous young officer named Marcus Antonius, better known to history as Mark Antony. With the backing of Caesar's gold and the voters of the Cisalpine province whom Caesar paid to go to Rome and support him, Antony not only became tribune-elect for 49 but beat the anti-Caesarian Domitius for a vacancy in the college of augurs. Admittedly the augurate carried more prestige than direct political power, but the contest was nevertheless 'fought on party-lines', and Antony's success in both these elections reveals once again the underlying elements of class-conflict and political ideology. For while the anti-Caesarians could get both their candidates elected consuls by the assembly of centuries in which the voting system was biased in favour of the wealthier classes, they were less successful in the more egalitarian assembly of the plebs, which elected the ten tribunes, or the tribal assembly which elected augurs. The Caesarian interest was projected as

the democratic opposition to senatorial government. For the urban poor
it offered a revival of their Clodian aspirations, and it was the obvious
recourse of men of gentle birth who looked to revolution for an escape
from the pecuniary and political frustrations to which mischance or their
own imprudence had brought them in Pompey's too sterile Rome. 'All
persons under legal sentence or censorial stigma are on Caesar's side,'
observed Cicero in December, 'as are all who deserve one or the other,
nearly all the youth, all the desperate city-rabble, some tribunes, all the
debt-ridden. In fact Caesar's side lacks nothing but a cause: all else they
have in abundance.'

Cicero's mention of 'censorial stigma' refers to the multiplication of
malcontents by the improbable agency of Clodius' own brother, the irrepressible Appius Claudius, father-in-law of Pompey's elder son and a
close personal and political friend. For Appius had been elected censor
in 50, and though he had as his colleague the father-in-law of Caesar,
his greater energy and determination were usually more than a match
for the mild protestations of Piso. He purged the senatorial roll with a
partisan vigour which Caelius likened to 'treating his office as a sort of
soap that would cleanse the stains on his own record'. Dio tells us that
he was all for striking off Curio's name, tribune or no tribune, if he had
not been prevented for once by Piso, who was himself supported by the
consul Paullus. Even so he told the Senate exactly what he thought of
Curio in terms so insulting that Curio attacked him and tore his clothes,
whereupon the consul Marcellus saw another chance to get rid of Curio
and his veto simultaneously. He ordered the unruly tribune to be arrested,
and though it was of doubtful legality for a consul to order the arrest
of a sacrosanct tribune, there was the precedent of the Pompeian tribune
Metellus Nepos in 62. At any rate Marcellus apparently proposed that
Curio should be suspended from office with high hope of success, but
Curio knew better, and instead of trying to veto the debate he boldly
defied Marcellus to do his worst. Curio judged that the majority of the
Senate was so afraid of provoking Caesar into war and giving him the
battle-cry that the rights of the people's tribunes were being overborne
that they would do nothing against him. And he was right: he remained
tribune, and his veto remained in force.

This was the last straw for Pompey. It was now nearly December,
Caesar was back in his Cisalpine province after attending a great series
of military reviews beyond the Alps during the autumn, and the Senate
was still too flaccid to stand up to him. Pompey was tired of trying to
talk guts into cowards at home and competing with Caesar in outflatter-
ing provincial governors like Cicero, who had told Atticus in October
that he had received letters from both of them on the same day, 'each

saying that there was no one in the world whom he valued more'. If only the Senate could be coaxed or driven to the point of authorizing mobilization, Pompey knew that their determination to oppose Caesar would stiffen with the momentum of his military preparations, and it was to try to carry the Senate across this psychological watershed that the consul Marcellus reopened the debate on the appointment of successors to Caesar on or about 1 December. After all, it was now nine months since Caesar's command had expired, and even under the old system of allocating proconsular provinces he would have been preparing to hand over to the consuls of the current year, who would have succeeded him on 1 January.

For obvious reasons Marcellus framed two separate questions to put before the House, and in order to pinpoint Caesarian sympathizers and cowards he asked each member in turn to state his answers openly. He first asked, ' "Shall successors be sent to Caesar?" ' and then, ' "Shall Pompey be deprived of his command?" ' And when the majority answered 'Yes' to the first and a resounding 'No' to the second, the consul believed that he was home and dry. But once again Curio had the better of him. Curio proposed that both Pompey and Caesar should lay down their commands simultaneously, and when he put this question to a division, only twenty-two voted against and 370 in favour 'in order to avoid civil war'. But it was a vote for peace at a political price that Pompey and twenty-two others were not prepared to pay, and Marcellus promptly dismissed the House with an explosion of disgust at their cowardice: ' "Enjoy your victory," ' he exclaimed; ' "you have won Caesar for your master." '

The frustration felt by Pompey and the hard-liners at this overwhelming vote for peace at Caesar's price is not hard to imagine. The prospect of obtaining the Senate's authority for the urgently needed raising of troops seemed remoter than ever, and unless some sudden shock jolted the timid peers into a revulsion of feeling against Caesar, some other method would have to be found even at the risk of giving Caesar the 'cause' which Cicero claimed to be the only thing that he lacked. 'Then suddenly,' says Appian, 'false rumours swept the city that Caesar was marching on Rome.' There had been similar scares before. On 15 October Cicero had written Atticus a letter 'on the day you say that Caesar is moving four legions into Placentia', which turned out to be a misunderstanding of an order which he had given for a military review at the similar-sounding Nemetocenna. The Belgic town of Nemetocenna, the present-day Arras, was several hundred miles north of Placentia in the Po valley, and if so stable and well-informed a Roman as the banker Atticus had been prepared to believe that Caesar, then known to be beyond the Alps, was already making what would have been an extremely provocative move by sending four legions into northern Italy, it is hardly surprising that Rome was ready to believe a rumour of his imminent attack now that he was back in his Cisalpine province. It was exactly the shock that the Pompeians had wanted, and though they may not have been responsible for starting the rumour, they lost no time in making use of it. Marcellus convened the Senate for an emergency session and proposed 'that Caesar be declared a public enemy, and the army at Capua be sent against him'. Curio was on his feet at once, declaring the rumour untrue and promising to veto any such resolution. But this time Marcellus was not waiting for a discussion which would almost certainly give Caesar the benefit of the doubt when it came to a vote. ' "If I am prevented by a general vote from taking steps for the public safety," ' he thundered, ' "I shall take steps on my own responsibility as consul" ', and with that he swept out of the House to the amazement of the crowds waiting outside for news and to the perplexity of most of his peers. Preceded by his lictors, followed by a large number of senators, and attracting an increasingly large crowd of lesser folk as word of his outburst spread through the tense city, he must have had half Rome with him by the time he reached his destination, which was Pompey's palatial residence outside the city-walls. And this was no spontaneous decision. Even if the rumour of Caesar's imminent attack had not been manufactured for the purpose, its exploitation had been carefully concerted, for Marcellus would not have risked leading a procession to Pompey's house only to find the great man not at home. Pompey was neither out nor surprised at a visit by the head of state, and when he emerged to receive Marcellus, the excited crowds fell silent in order to hear what he would say. And there, against the backcloth of Pompey's palace, portico, parks, playhouse and all the other monuments to his greatness, the consul handed him a sword and declared in a loud voice, ' "I hereby command you to march against Caesar on behalf of the Republic. I give you for this purpose the army which is now at Capua and in any other part of Italy, together with any other forces which you may care to levy." '

It was a breach of constitutional practice if not of theory for a consul to authorize the raising of troops for the defence of Italy without the support of a senatorial decree, but while Pompey accepted the consul's order to march against Caesar with the proviso 'unless there is some better solution', he lost no time in taking over command of the two legions at Capua and starting to recruit fresh forces from among his veterans in Campania. And on 10 December he met Cicero, who was making his way up to Rome from Brundisium where he had landed in late November after leaving his quaestor to look after Cilicia until a successor could be appointed. In the letters which he had written to Atticus on the long journey from the East he had agonized about the political situation like a character in a Russian novel, and though he was terrified at the prospect of civil war ('I shudder at the news from Rome ... I see the greatest struggle there has ever been'), he had at last convinced himself that the only honourable course was to support Pompey in the Senate, even though he 'would vote in his heart for peace at any price', and would do his best to dissuade Pompey from war. But when Cicero actually met Pompey on 10 December for the first time in over a year and a half, he found him in no mood for such dissuasion. 'On the political issue,' Cicero reported to Atticus, 'Pompey talked as though war were a certainty, and there was nothing to suggest any hope of agreement.' And as proof of Caesar's total estrangement from him Pompey told Cicero how he had been snubbed by one of Caesar's agents just before he had left the city. 'Hirtius, a very close friend of Caesar, had come from Caesar to Rome but had not gone near Pompey. He had arrived on the evening of 6 December, and Caesar's agent Balbus had arranged a meeting with Pompey's father-in-law Scipio to discuss the whole situation, but Hirtius had disappeared again in the middle of the night.' Admittedly Hirtius may have felt that there was nothing left to discuss after hearing what Marcellus had done, or that the situation was now so changed that he needed to inform Caesar at once and obtain fresh instructions, but 'to Pompey it seemed a further proof of Caesar's estrangement'. But even now Cicero could still not bring himself to believe that Caesar 'would be mad enough to risk everything when even his enemies have granted him a second consulship and Fortune has given him the greatest power'. He had evidently not yet appreciated that Pompey was no longer prepared to see Caesar consul whether he gave up his army or not.

For the next fortnight or more Cicero stayed on his estates at Formiae, a pleasant seaside resort on the Gulf of Gaeta some eighty miles southeast of Rome down the Appian Way. From there he directed a stream of letters to Atticus in Rome, and though he is tiresomely repetitive in cataloguing all the past follies (other people's, naturally) which had been responsible for this lamentable crisis, he not only provides a glimpse of Pompey's active preparations but an unconscious acknowledgement of their success in promoting confidence and even belligerence among men who had previously been for peace at any price. 'Roman senators and knights are using the bitterest language about the conduct of affairs in general and about this trip of Pompey's in particular,' wrote Cicero on 16 December, presumably in reference to Pompey's journey to Capua to take over command of the two legions there. 'Peace is what is wanted. Victory will bring with it many ills, including the certainty of a despot.'

And Cicero now doubted Pompey's ability to resist Caesar. 'It is more expedient to concede Caesar's demands than to fight, for it is too late in the day for us to resist a force which we have been building up against ourselves for ten years.'

'Pompey and his council' – of which the Cilician *Imperator* was significantly not a member – 'have decided to send me to Sicily,' exploded Cicero on 19 December after observing with high satisfaction that the vote for his triumph seemed to be in the bag. 'The reason they give is that I have *imperium*. It is crazy. I have no mandate from the Senate or assembly to command in Sicily. Or if the state leaves all this sort of thing to Pompey, why send me rather than a private individual? If this *imperium* of mine is going to prove a nuisance, I shall walk into Rome by the first gate!' It was evidently part of Pompey's strategy to secure the corn-growing province of Sicily which could feed or starve the city of Rome, and as the name of Cicero had been revered there ever since his successful prosecution of the notoriously oppressive governor Verres in 70, his appointment was an obvious one. Nor was his having *imperium* as irrelevant as he tried to make out. It is true that he lacked a formal mandate to exercise it in Sicily, but as long as the appointment of provincial governors remained blocked by tribunician veto there was no possibility of his getting one, and if Sicily lacked a governor, it was infinitely more justifiable for Pompey to propose a man who already held the authority to govern a province than someone who did not. But Cicero did not want to be anywhere but at Rome or to do anything that might involve more than a verbal commitment to Pompey, and since Pompey had no authority to compel him, a sensible proposal was killed. It was an example of what the champion of the Republic would have to suffer from his independent-minded peers in organizing resistance to a rebel general whose word was law to his own followers.

'If only we had stood up to Caesar while he was weak,' lamented Cicero, criticizing Pompey's constant support of his old protégé over the last ten years while conveniently forgetting his own toadyings. 'Now we have to deal with eleven legions, all the cavalry he wants, the Transpadane Gauls, the city populace, so many tribunes, our demoralized youth, and a leader so strong in prestige and daring.' Admittedly Cicero goes on to reiterate his intention of supporting Pompey in the Senate, but it seems less from confidence of defeating Caesar than from fear of what Caesar would do if he won, for while Cicero still talks of 'slavery' whoever wins, the domination of Pompey is evidently a less frightening prospect than the mastery of Caesar, 'who will be no more merciful than Cinna in his slaughter of leading citizens and no more temperate than Sulla in plundering the rich'. But a week is a long time in a crisis, and after Cicero had met Pompey again near Formiae on 25 December, his report to Atticus was in a very different vein:

> On 25 December Pompey overtook me at Lavernium and we went on together to Formiae, where we talked privately from 2 o'clock until evening. You asked if there is any hope of peace. The answer so far as I could see from Pompey's conversation, which lacked neither detail nor length, is that there is not even the desire for it. Pompey's view is that if Caesar is made consul even after giving up his army, it will mean the subversion of the constitution.

A week ago this declaration from Pompey that he had no desire for peace would have reduced Cicero to a nervous wreck, but what follows suggests that Pompey's own confidence was now as infectious as his preparations were reassuring:

> Pompey further thinks that when Caesar hears that preparations are proceeding energetically he will give up trying for the consulship in this [electoral] year and just try to hang on to his army and province. But if Caesar should take leave of his senses, Pompey was quite contemptuous of the man and confident in his own and the Republic's forces. And all in all, 'though I often thought of Homer's phrase 'Ares is alike to all' [a quotation from the *Iliad* which the philhellenic Atticus would have no difficulty in capping 'And the slayer of him who slays'], I nevertheless felt relieved as I heard such a man, courageous, experienced and supreme in prestige, discoursing in such a statesmanlike fashion on the dangers of a false peace.

'The dangers of a false peace' is a far cry from Cicero's 'peace at any price' only a week ago, and he proceeds to reveal another reason for the sudden revulsion of feeling against Caesar when he refers to the draft of a speech which the new tribune Antony had given on 21 December. Pompey had it with him when he saw Cicero on 25 December, and Cicero was suitably horrified by its sheer offensiveness. 'It contained a denunciation of Pompey from the day he came of age, a protest on behalf of persons condemned in the courts, and threats of armed force. "How do you expect Caesar to behave if he gets control of the state when his feckless nobody of a quaestor dares to say such things?" Pompey asked. In short, so far from seeking a peaceful settlement, Pompey seemed to dread it.' In a more reflective mood on the next day Cicero sent Atticus a decision-tree covering what seemed to be all the eventualities of peace or war, but while he still argued that Caesar should be allowed to stand for the consulship if he gave up his army first – and still hoped that this was what Caesar would do – he now maintained that war was preferable to letting him stand at the elections without giving up his army. But the hard-line Pompeian view was adamant against letting Caesar stand under any circumstances. 'Certain persons think that we have nothing to fear more than Caesar as consul,' Cicero wrote to Atticus. ' "Better that, " you will say "than for him to come with an army." Surely, but your "that" is exactly what someone considers a great evil, and there is no help for it. "You must allow it if Caesar wants it," you argue; "you put up with him once, put up with him again." "But he was young then," comes the reply, "yet more than a match for the whole Republic." What do you think he will be like now? And if Caesar becomes consul, Pompey is resolved to stay in Spain.' Significantly there is not even a mention of the suggestion that Pompey should give up his command. On the con-trary, Cicero's fear is of losing the counterweight of Pompey's presence, and that counterweight would hardly hold down Caesar's consular *imperium* without the gravity of proconsular *imperium* backed by the army in Spain. Moreover the possibility of Caesar's giving up his com-mand seemed remote. 'It we eliminate this possibility which they say Caesar cannot be brought to accept, what is the worst of those that remain? Surely to concede what Pompey calls his most impudent demands. For could impudence go further? You, Caesar, have kept for ten years provinces not given to you by the Senate but by yourself through factious violence' – a barbed reference to the forcing through of the Vatinian plebiscite in 59 against the sky-watching objections of Bibulus, which were still argued to have invalidated the legislation that had given Caesar his command.

The time has expired – time not set by law but by your own pleasure, but let us say it was by law for the sake of argument. It is resolved that you should be succeeded in command. You obstruct and say, 'Admit my right to stand.' What about our rights? Who are you to keep an army any longer than the people ordained and against the will of the Senate? 'I shall have to fight if you refuse to give me what I want.' Very well, we shall fight too, and in good hope, as Pompey affirms, of victory or death as free men.

This apostrophizing epistle sent by Cicero to Atticus on 26 or 27 December may provide a fairly accurate encapsulation of the rival argu-ments and the prevailing view among the Senate. Pompey had been right to believe that the momentum of his military preparations would generate increasing resistance to Caesar among the moderates; and even the most timid were increasingly outraged by the unsubtle threats of Antony, who lacked the relative finesse with which Curio had directed his attack on Pompey and tried to present Pompey as the greater danger to the Re-public. To judge from the speech which Cicero had seen, Antony had not only been attacking Pompey with insults but browbeating the Senate with 'threats of armed force' ever since the tribunician year had begun on 10 December, and when the new consuls Lentulus and the other Gaius

Marcellus entered office on 1 January 49, the Senate which they summoned to the traditional opening debate on the state of the Republic was
a very much more robust body than that which had voted so nervously
for simultaneous disarmament by Pompey and Caesar only a month ago.
The consuls were rightly confident of carrying a motion appointing successors to Caesar and of dealing with the tribunes who would inevitably
veto it, and though Pompey's *imperium* as proconsul of Spain prevented
his attending this meeting on the Capitol, his father-in-law Scipio was
ready to act as his understudy in a debate for which the protagonists had
almost certainly rehearsed their parts in Pompey's palace. But as the consuls entered the chamber on 1 January, they were disconcerted by the
appearance of Curio who publicly presented them with a letter from
Caesar to be read out to the assembled peers.

According to non-contemporary sources Curio had gone to Caesar immediately on the expiry of his tribunate on 10 December and urged him
'to summon his whole army at once and lead it to Rome' before Pompey
had time to prepare adequate resistance, but Caesar 'still thought it best
to try to seek terms', and offered a compromise under which he would
yield Transalpine Gaul and the greater part of his army on condition
of being allowed to retain Cisalpine Gaul and Illyricum with two legions.
And Appian further maintains that a compromise on these lines was acceptable to Pompey, who was prevented from accepting it only by the
consuls. But if such proposals really were made – and as they were
apparently not made officially to the Senate there is room for doubt –
it is scarcely credible that Pompey was prepared to entertain them when
Cicero maintains that he considered Caesar's consulship 'the worst of
all evils' whether Caesar laid down his armies or not. At any rate these
were not the proposals contained in the letter which Curio was now sent
back to Rome to deliver to the consuls. Wisely he waited until they were
in the House before handing it to them for fear that it would otherwise
have been suppressed, but even so the consuls refused to have it read
out, for they were adamant against any form of compromise. But the tribunes Antony and Cassius demanded that it should be read, and when
they finally had their way after a long argument, the Senate was treated
to another lengthy recital of Caesar's services to the state and a repetition
of the proposal which had been so well received when Curio had first
presented it a month earlier, that Caesar and Pompey should disarm
simultaneously. But this time the proposal was presented less as a request
than as an ultimatum with the sting in the tail: 'but if Pompey should
retain his command, I shall not lay down mine but come quickly and
avenge my own and my country's wrongs'. That, at any rate, is Appian's
account, and while such an ultimatum is hardly in line with 'the most

moderate requests' to which Caesar refers in his own history of the Civil War, it may be vindicated by the fact that the letter became a public document, by Caesar's obvious interest in historical self-justification, and by Cicero's description of it as 'threatening and disagreeable'. And nothing could persuade the consuls to present this proposal again. They had their plan and they were determined to keep to it in the confidence that Antony could not stop them. For while he might propose the motion himself, there were other tribunes ready to veto it, and if he tried to veto the whole debate on the Republic, the outrage would simply play into their hands.

According to Caesar's subsequent account of the debate of 1 January the consul Lentulus 'promised that he would not fail the Republic provided that the senators were willing to express bold and resolute opinions, but if they paid regard to Caesar and tried to curry favour with him as they had done so often before, he would decide what was best for himself and ignore the authority of the Senate: he too, he said, had been a recipient of Caesar's friendship and fortune'. And when he called upon Pompey's father-in-law to express his opinion, Scipio 'took the same line: Pompey, he said, was not minded to desert the Republic if the Senate backed him up, but if there was any more shilly-shallying or soft-pedalling, they would ask his help in vain if they needed it again in the future'. These were vague threats as they appear in Caesar's account and perhaps they were intended to be, but it is doubtful whether Lentulus and Scipio would have made political principle so obviously subordinate to self-interest. What need not be doubted is that Scipio was 'speaking straight out of the mouth of Pompey' when he proposed 'that Caesar should be ordered to demobilize his army before a fixed date, and if he failed to comply, he should be regarded as an enemy of the Republic'. Marcus Marcellus proposed the postponement of the whole provincial question, but if Caesar was reduced to citing him as one of the two examples which he gives of senators 'who expressed milder opinions', the majority view must now have been very belligerent indeed. Even Caesar indicates that Marcellus was not opposed to the ultimatum but only to its timing because he wanted the military conscription to be completed first, and he may well have urged the Senate to satisfy itself for the time being with confirming the legality of the recruitment which had been authorized by the consuls a month ago, for though the then consuls-elect had joined in that authorization, it would not only be more constitutional but more effective if backed by a senatorial resolution. At any event Caesar names only one senator who actually spoke up for him, and this was Calidius, an unsuccessful rival of the Marcelli for the consulships of 50 and 49. Calidius proposed 'that Pompey should go to Spain and remove the cause of the dissension', but the consul Lentulus refused to put this motion before the House, and Marcellus also withdrew. The only motion which Lentulus would propose was that of Scipio, and having ordered a division to be taken so that senators would have to stand up and be counted, he watched with satisfaction as all except two voted in favour. Only Caelius and Curio stood alone in the opposition lobby, and a triumphant Lentulus now looked inquiringly to the bench of tribunes to see if Antony and Cassius would still dare to oppose the will of the whole Senate save two of its junior members.

When Antony and Cassius pronounced the veto, there was uproar. There was no longer any hesitation about 'treating with the tribunes', and if Marcus Marcellus had any second thoughts about it, they were only regrets that the Senate had not taken his advice seven months ago and treated with Curio before the tribunician opposition had become so deeply entrenched. While even the mildest of former doves indulged in threat-displays, the leading hawks swooped ever more menacingly on the recalcitrant tribunes with speeches of increasing viciousness, but Antony and Cassius remained as immovable as a pair of exceptionally thick-shelled armadillos until the House rose at sunset. But their respite was a short one. That night Pompey summoned all the senators to his home just as he had invited all 360 jurors to dinner before Milo's trial in 52. He praised the enthusiasts and encouraged them for the future. He castigated the more reluctant and spurred them on. He was preparing for the break-through that would turn the political battle into a military one which he might lead from the front, and though he did not attend the Senate himself, his formidable presence surrounded by troops outside the city-walls was enough to hearten Caesar's frightened enemies, out-frighten those who feared both, and cause a recalculation of the odds by those who thought no further than their own security. He heard with amusement how the Senate had voted to put on mourning as a public demonstration against the tribunician veto, how Antony had vetoed even that, and how the senators had defied him as an earnest of what they were ready to do to his more serious veto unless he relented. He listened with satisfaction to reports of the increasingly anti-Caesarian speeches, and he made his own through Scipio. But it was Antony himself who became Pompey's most effective advocate, especially on 3 and 4 January when the political battle moved to the Forum because these were comitial days on which the Senate did not sit. Antony's demagogy became so violent that even the most timid of appeasers now recoiled in horror at the prospect of Caesar's consulship, and if they turned to the gods as men usually do in a crisis, there was reassurance from Venus the Victorious for the success of a cause in which patriotism, privilege and property were now inextricably blended with the preservation of Pompey's greatness over which she presided.

When Cicero finally appeared outside the city to claim his ridiculous triumph and play the peacemaker, he found 'a very conflagration of civil discord, or rather civil war'. If he tried to arrange compromises, as Plutarch maintains, on the basis of allowing Caesar to keep one or two of his provinces and two or one of his legions until he was chosen consul, his attempts were swept aside 'by the passions of certain men on both sides who wanted war', as were the requests of Caesar's father-in-law Piso to be allowed six days to inform Caesar of the Senate's opinion and report back. On 7 January Pompey finally achieved the ultimatum that he desired. Two years ago the Senate had used its Ultimate Decree to authorize his intervention against internal chaos, and he had soon afterwards become sole consul. Now the Senate was convinced that it needed him against an external threat which he was ready to counter with the vindictiveness that only the shattering of an old friendship can generate, and when on 7 January, in a city bristling with his troops, the Senate again authorized 'the consuls, praetors, tribunes and proconsuls to see to it that the Republic shall suffer no harm', Pompey the Great could now lawfully see to it that a former protégé who 'could no longer endure a superior' would never be his equal.

# 6

# GOVERNMENT IN EXILE

Demented fool! It is not you whom all things flee
But I whom all things follow.
                    Lucan, *Pharsalia*, 2.575

For Pompey's generalship in the first phase of the struggle which now ensued 'for personal domination at the risk and peril of the state' we are heavily dependent on our two contemporary sources, the memoirs of his military enemy and the letters of an exceptionally unmilitary friend. Caesar's memoirs are detailed and thorough, but inevitably biased in his own favour. Cicero's letters are legion, but he had no grasp of strategy, his horizon was bounded by the walls of Rome, and his military usefulness and reliability were correctly assessed by his exclusion from Pompey's confidence. If the pen really had been mightier than the sword, Cicero could have taken on Caesar's legions single-handed. As it is, we have to beware of valuing his judgements according to the weight of his words or the excellence of his epistolary style, for while he eventually glimpsed the wood rather than the trees (and pretended to have seen it all along), the judgements which he made at the time were often invalidated by the very facts on which he based them. If his information is stripped of the comment it reveals a very different picture of 'a man whom I knew to be a failure as a statesman and now find to be an equally bad general', and Cicero's very failure to understand Pompey's strategy as it unfolded is a tribute to the skill with which it was implemented, for its success depended on its being disguised as long as possible.

Pompey feared nothing more than peace at Caesar's price, and having exuded sufficient confidence to carry the Senate across its psychological watershed on 7 January 49, he proceeded to sweep it down into the valley of war with a momentum that would be difficult to stop. According to Caesar their meetings were now held 'outside the city', clearly in order that Pompey might attend and very probably in Pompey's own Senate House adjoining his Portico and Theatre. 'Pompey commended the courage and constancy of the Senate. He set forth the strength of his forces. He declared that he had ten legions ready for action and that he had discovered Caesar's troops to be so ill-disposed to their general that

they could not be persuaded to defend or follow him.' If this is really
what Pompey said, and it is likely enough, it was more than wishful thinking. It was a continuation of the same confident line which had carried
the senators to the point of passing their Ultimate Decree, and it now
emboldened them to proceed to the appointment of Caesar's successors
before their courage failed. With the tribunes Antony and Cassius on
their way to join Caesar, there was no longer anything to prevent this
appointment, which was now made together with the overdue appointment of the new governors to all provinces. Transalpine Gaul and
Syria were declared proconsular and lots were drawn for them, though
Caesar says that not all the names of eligible ex-consuls were included, and judging from the result it is hard to believe that the divine
will was left to operate unaided even among those names that were in
the urn.

   Transalpine Gaul went to Marcus Cato's brother-in-law Lucius Domitius, who had once been as hostile to Pompey as to Caesar. Pompey had
defeated and destroyed Domitius' brother in Africa in the last Civil War
between Sulla and the Marian government, and Domitius himself had been
squeezed on to the rails in the consulship stakes for 55 by Pompey and
Crassus after declaring that he would devote all his efforts to securing
the recall of Pompey's protégé from Gaul. But Domitius had become consul in 54, and now it was with Pompey's blessing that he became Caesar's
successor to the proconsular governorship which he had always regarded
as a family inheritance from his grandfather, the consul of 122 whose
victories in the Rhône valley had laid the foundations of the province.
The name of Domitius was borne not only by the Domitian Way but
by many citizens of the colony of Narbo founded by his father in 118,
and if there was any hope of raising against Caesar that part of Gaul which
carried the highway from Pompey's legions in Spain, Domitius was the
obvious choice. And if Domitius was the obvious choice for Gaul, it was
more than luck which allotted Syria to Pompey's own father-in-law Scipio,
whose name should not have been in the urn in the first place because
he was strictly ineligible for a governorship for another three years under
Pompey's own law of 52. But Pompey was anxious to secure familial control over an Eastern province which he had won for Rome, and which
would be critical if it became necessary to implement his grand strategy
of world war.

   The praetorian provinces were allotted next. Caesar's Cisalpine
province, now downgraded to praetorian status, went to Considius
Nonianus. More significantly Sicily went to Cato, and the security of the
other main corn-producing provinces was entrusted to Tubero and Cotta,
the former receiving Africa, the latter Sardinia. There were also proposals

designed to secure the support of the North African kingdoms. Faustus
Sulla was suggested as an emissary to Mauretania where he had inherited
a special relationship with the royal house from his father, who had
brought the Numidian Wars to an end by persuading King Bocchus to
surrender Rome's enemy King Jugurtha. Faustus could count on being
well received by Bocchus' sons, Kings Bocchus II and Bogud who had
divided their vast inheritance, and it would have been useful to secure this
line of communication between Roman Africa and Pompey's legions in
Spain. Similarly we can see Pompey's influence behind a parallel proposal
to declare his personal friend King Juba of Numidia a Friend and Ally,
but both the motions were opposed, the former by the consul Marcellus,
the latter by a tribune. Perhaps they considered it a confession of weakness
to be panicked into courting African kings by a rebel general in Gaul. Sicily,
Africa and Spain had been the graveyards of the government forces in
the last Civil War when Sulla had driven the Marians out of Italy and
Pompey had pursued them to win his early greatness by destroying Carbo
in Sicily, Domitius' brother in Africa and Sertorius in Spain. Was this
government preparing for flight too ? Pompey did not press the proposals.
No one knew better than the corn commissioner how effective the weapon
of starvation could be if it became necessary to evacuate Italy, but it was
obviously not a prospect which he was anxious to advertise until he knew
for certain if he would have time to recruit the troops necessary for a
defence of Italy.

If Pompey declared that he had ten legions ready for action, he did
not of course say that they were ready for action in Italy, or that those
which were available in Italy were a match for Caesar's battle-hardened
veterans. Neither he nor his more intelligent hearers took too seriously the confident assurances that Caesar's troops would not be led
into rebellion, and if the Senate was reluctant to court the Kings of
Numidia and Mauretania, it did not hesitate to authorize the levying
of troops in Italy to the number of 130,000 if Appian's apparently precise
figure is reliable. Numerically the legionary strengths of Pompey and
Caesar were about the same, but Caesar's ten or eleven veteran legions
were more easily brought from Gaul than Pompey's seven from Spain,
and of the three legions which Pompey had under his command in Italy
two were of doubtful loyalty and one had not seen action. The two of
doubtful loyalty were those which had been brought from Gaul for the
Parthian emergency the year before, and while one was Pompey's own
legion which he had lent to Caesar in 54, it had fought for Caesar for
three years, and was scarcely more certain to fight against him than its
companion legion which had been Caesar's all along. The third was made
up of cohorts levied in 52 and more recently, which had never fought

together as a tactical unit in battle. Admittedly Caesar himself had only one legion on this side of the Alps, but the fact that two more had arrived from Burgundy, some six hundred miles away, by February indicates that they had been summoned in early December. Even if Pompey did not know that they were on their way he must have realized that they soon would be, and he lost no time in organizing an intensive recruiting effort throughout the peninsula as soon as the Senate had voted the levy and 'all the money in the treasury and their private money too if it was needed for the payment of troops'.

Even Cicero was emboldened by Pompey's preparations. 'The state has never been in greater danger,' he wrote to his friend Tiro on 12 January, 'and disloyal citizens have never had a leader who was better prepared. But very thorough preparations are being made on our side too thanks to the authority and energy of our Gnaeus, who rather late in the day is beginning to be afraid of Caesar.' He then reveals a glimpse of Pompey's organization: 'Italy has been divided up into regions showing who is in charge of each, and I have taken Capua.' Magistrates, promagistrates and legates were fanning out to their stations to raise the 130,000 men, and with the equivalent of some twenty-five legions of normal strength it should not be impossible to cow or coerce the recalcitrant Caesar into submission. But when Cicero wrote again on 18 January, his confidence had evaporated. He was leaving Rome 'before daybreak, in order to avoid being laughed at with my laurelled lictors'. The government had been ordered to abandon the city, Pompey had already left, and 'unless I am out of my mind there has been nothing but folly and recklessness.'

It was probably on 15 or 16 January that news reached Rome of Caesar's advance across the little River Rubicon which divided his province of Cisalpine Gaul from Italy. By 10 or 11 January at the latest Caesar will have heard of the Senate's Ultimate Decree passed on 7 January, the flight of the two tribunes who had protected his interests, and the measures that had followed it. His bluff had been called, and he was left to select the least of a series of evils. He could submit and hand over his provinces and armies. That was unthinkable. He could continue to try to negotiate a political settlement without taking offensive action, but that would be regarded as weakness, and with every day that passed his bargaining position would be weaker. He had only one legion, the 13th, and some five hundred cavalry with him at Ravenna. He had sent for two more legions, the 8th and the 12th from his Transalpine province, but they would not be with him for at least another three weeks, and by the time he had three legions, Pompey might have raised a dozen. Admittedly Sulla had proved that a few veteran legions ably led were more than a match for many times their number of new recruits, but Sulla had not been fighting Pompey.

Caesar had his own recruiting ground in his Gallic provinces, but Pompey had the whole of Italy, and the recruitment of Gauls might only stiffen the resistance of the Italian towns to 'the fury of Gaul pouring over the wintry Alps' and turning civil into foreign war. And if Caesar could count on the loyalty of his old legions now, would that loyalty last as the legions arrayed against them multiplied, as Pompey's army began to advance from Spain, and as the reality of rebellion began to sink into the minds of his own men? The only alternative to submission in a situation of diminishing returns was to risk an invasion before the government forces could be raised. And so it came about, says Appian, that Caesar, 'accustomed to rely on the terror caused by the speed and audacity of his movements rather than the scale of his preparations, decided to take the offensive in the great war with his five thousand men, and to anticipate the enemy by seizing advantageous positions in northern Italy'.

On 13 January Caesar was in Ariminum, which he had cleverly infiltrated with reliable centurions in mufti before advancing on the town himself after taking elaborate precautions to disguise his intentions. Not surprisingly Caesar does not admit to such subterfuges in his memoirs. He wished to present a picture of an open crusade joyfully welcomed by the first Italian municipality to which he came, but Appian's account is more credible, not least because it explains how Caesar was able to take bloodless control of Ariminum. Pompeian troops had been stationed there at least as recently as the summer of 51 when Pompey had gone to inspect them and evaluate for himself Caesar's situation in Gaul, and an Ariminum forewarned might well have shut its gates, though it does not seem to have been forearmed. We hear of no Pompeian cohorts in the town or warships or troop-transports in the harbour, and it appears that Pompey had withdrawn his troops long since, possibly in order not to seem provocative but mainly because so northerly a town could not be defended against a veteran legion without the commitment of about half his immediately available forces, which might then be cut off from Rome. If Caesar waited in Cisalpine Gaul to collect his legions, Pompey would be able to protect even the most northerly towns. If Caesar invaded immediately, Ariminum must take its chances. And when its citizens were taken by surprise, they chose to keep their lives by opening their gates. Thus Caesar took possession of a most important maritime town at the junction of the Via Flaminia, which ran due south to Rome, and the Via Aemilia, which carried his line of communication and reinforcement north-westwards through the Cisalpine province to his legions beyond the Alps. He had set the example of acquiescence to the cities of Picenum further down the coast where the government's recruiting effort was being concentrated, and when the tribunes Antony and Cassius met him at Ariminum, he made the most of the opportunity to generate some useful propaganda. He presented these supposedly sacrosanct officials dishevelled to the troops and townspeople 'as having been disgracefully driven out', though we learn from Cicero that they had in fact 'left of their own accord' and that 'no violence had been offered to them'.

According to Plutarch and Appian the news of Caesar's advance fell like a bombshell on Rome, and to judge by Cicero's frantic reaction we need not doubt them. Pompey became the object of bitter recrimination. 'The Senate went to him *en masse*,' says Plutarch. 'Where were the forces for the defence of Rome? Why had he deceived them about his preparedness or the loyalty of Caesar's troops?' The answer was that Pompey had wanted them to push Caesar into submission or war, though of course he did not say so. He had hoped that Caesar would have waited to concentrate his legions from beyond the Alps, but he was hardly surprised that Caesar was invading at once. And though Plutarch says that the praetor Favonius' sneer at Pompey's previous remark that he had only to stamp his foot for armies to spring up was 'borne with meekness by its victim', Appian gives a different account. ' "You will have them", retorted Pompey, "if you will follow me and not be horrified at the thought of leaving Rome, and Italy too if need be." ' And on 17 January Pompey and the consuls left Rome, while nearly the whole Senate prepared to do the same.

Although Appian's account of the exchange between Favonius and Pompey may be more apocryphal than accurate, an airing of the possibility of an evacuation of Italy is indicated by Cicero's panicky letter of the following day, the first of an almost daily correspondence to Atticus which was Cicero's sole contribution to the war-effort. 'I swear I don't know what I am doing or am going to do. I am so confounded by our crazy decision. What Pompey has decided or is deciding, cooped up in a daze in those country towns, I don't yet know. We shall all be with him if he makes a stand in Italy but if he gives it up, that is another matter....' But the fact that a dazed Cicero did not know what Pompey was doing does not mean that Pompey was in the same condition. It was exactly because Cicero was not the only senator reluctant to leave Rome, let alone Italy, and because the prospect of abandoning the land they were supposed to be defending was not likely to assist the recruitment of troops, that Pompey and his intimates concealed their evacuation strategy. Cicero rarely mentions the possibility of Pompey's leaving Italy in the following three weeks, and when he does so it is on the assumption that Pompey would go to his army in Spain. But Pompey was not going to take himself to that graveyard of lost causes. The conqueror of three parts of the inhabited world would secure all three, but he would go himself to Greece, to the bridge that would connect him with the scene of his greatest feat of empire-building from where the wealth and power of the Oriental provinces, kings and nations could be summoned to his service. He would isolate Italy between Spain, Africa and the East, control the seas as he had done in the war against the pirates, and starve the capital into submissiveness before returning like Sulla from Greece to deliver the final blow: ' "Sulla could do it; shall I not do the same?" '

One of the immediate reactions to the news of Caesar's invasion of northern Italy was inevitably a demand for peace-negotiations, not least it appears from Volcatius who had been one of Pompey's staunchest adherents among the ex-consuls in past years, but Appian is emphatic that 'the consuls resisted all accommodation'. Pompey himself on the other hand seems to have sent two of Caesar's friends as unofficial envoys to his old protégé. One was Lucius Caesar, Caesar's second cousin twice removed and the son of one of Caesar's legates. The other was the praetor Roscius, who with Caesar's father-in-law, the ex-consul Piso, had begged in vain for six days in which to visit Caesar and report back before the Senate proceeded to its Ultimate Decree of 7 January. Such relatively junior members of the Senate were clearly not an official embassy, and when Caesar maintains that they came to him at Ariminum to 'make excuses for Pompey' and transmit some stern paternal advice, there is no reason to doubt that Pompey sent them even if Caesar's version of their message is open to question. They may not have come together, but Caesar indicates that they delivered similar messages from Pompey, and he was clearly unimpressed. 'Pompey wished to be cleared of reproach in the eyes of Caesar. Caesar should not construe as an affront to himself what Pompey was doing for the state. Pompey, who had always put the advantages of the state before personal claims, urged Caesar to do the same, and begged that Caesar would not be so grievously angry with his enemies that he injured the state in the hope of injuring them.' But according to Dio that was not all they said, and since Caesar fails to elaborate on 'the rest of the speech which was Lucius' reason for coming', it is hard to believe that he did not gloss over a more constructive peace-initiative from Pompey than the part of the message which he chose to quote. Caesar wanted posterity to believe that all serious efforts to achieve a negotiated settlement came from him, and he makes much of the contrast between Pompey's unhelpful humbug and the self-sacrificing proposals which he himself sent back to Pompey and the consuls by these two men, who 'by taking a little trouble to perform this service for him might put an end to serious disputes and free all Italy from fear'. But this was humbug too, for neither Pompey nor Caesar wanted peace. Pompey was trying to retard Caesar's advance in order to secure the maximum time for the recruitment of legions to take to the East. Caesar was trying to retard Pompey's recruitment in order that Pompey might be as weak as possible for a battle in Italy, which he still hoped to force on him, or for evacuation to the East, which was Caesar's main fear once he knew that Pompey had left Rome.

To Cicero the abandoning of Rome was as incomprehensible as it seemed reprehensible, but once he had reached the peace of his villa at Formiae he had to admit that it had two salutary effects. 'What do you think of Pompey's line?' he wrote to Atticus on 21 January with affected sprinklings of Greek. 'Why has he abandoned Rome? I am completely *dans l'embarras*. At the time nothing seemed stupider. And yet, to judge from the indignation in the country-towns and the talk of people who come my way, it looks as though it may achieve something after all. The public outcry is amazing at the thought of Rome without magistrates, without Senate. And Pompey taking to flight affects men marvellously. In short, the case is altered. People are now dead set against any concessions to Caesar.' And three days later Cicero admitted the other advantage, emotional rather than practical, of having handed over the capital undefended. 'For what will Caesar do, or how, without Senate or magistrates? He will not even be able to pretend to do anything *constitution-nellement*.' But if these were both useful results of abandoning Rome, they were not the only reasons for Pompey's insistence on it. Pompey was not going to raise many troops by stamping his foot in the Forum, and he was simply not prepared to go stamping in Italy while the majority of the senators stayed at Rome. The best chance of raising troops rapidly was to spread the authority of the state through the peninsula in the persons of magistrates and senators, who could exert the maximum amount of influence in the vicinities of ancestral estates. He also wanted to seal their commitment to the war-effort by getting them away from the capital and involved in recruiting before the threat to their property came too close. 'House walls do not make a Republic,' agreed Cicero, echoing Themistocles' famous exhortation to the Athenians not to defend their city against the Persians but take to the wooden walls of their fleet. 'But altars and hearthstones do,' he added sourly, and there were presumably others who were reluctant to leave their property and might not have done so if they had not hoped that they might be back in time to defend the city before Caesar arrived. Pompey may also have argued that Rome was safer if they left it undefended, for if the government stayed, it would have acted like a magnet to Caesar and proved disastrous to Pompey's plans whether it had been defended or not. Pompey could not be sure how his peers would react to a rapid advance on the city by Caesar. If ardour cooled and a sufficient number decided that they would prefer to keep their property with Caesar than lose it with Pompey, Pompey might find himself the champion of a lonely cause, or even outlawed in his turn. If ardour intensified into a determination to defend Rome at any cost against this Roman Hannibal, it would be equally fatal. For if Caesar marched straight on Rome, Pompey could not defend it, and Rome was on the wrong side of Italy for the evacuation to the East – a plan obviously unpublishable but already made, as the distribution of his existing forces will soon reveal.

Having reinforced persuasion with the threat that he would 'treat as partisans of Caesar any senators who remained behind' Pompey had been glad to ride out of Rome on 17 January and leave the chaos which his orders had created. He passed country-folk streaming in to the false security of the capital only to meet the city-folk streaming out, roads jammed with every sort of conveyance, tearful partings between men and their families who were to remain or follow them later. But not all who left were as reluctant as Cicero, nor did they all leave their families behind. A few days later even Cicero had to confess himself 'impressed by the evidence that all the good men have left Rome, and have their ladies with them. And Plutarch explains why. 'Even amid the terrors of that hour Pompey was still a man to be envied for the good will felt towards him, for while there were many who blamed his generalship, there was no one who hated the general: indeed you would have found that those who fled the city for the sake of freedom were not so numerous as those who followed because they could not forsake Pompey.' Plutarch also finds excuses for Pompey's 'bad generalship': 'No one had been willing to let Pompey follow his own judgement. Whatever emotion anyone had felt, whether fear or distress or perplexity, he had infected Pompey's mind with it. Opposite counsels had prevailed in the same day, and it had been impossible for Pompey to obtain any reliable information about the enemy, since many reported whatever they happened to hear and were vexed if he failed to believe them.' But Pompey had not wavered in strategy from the moment he had heard that Caesar had crossed the Rubicon. He had known exactly what he wanted, and he had got it all except one thing, the lack of which would lose him an army – the supreme command.

According to Plutarch it was the arch-republican Marcus Cato who had proposed this for Pompey before his peers. Forgetting, if indeed he had ever been aware, how his own and his friends' small-minded opposition to Pompey on his return from the East in 62 had been responsible for Pompey's promotion of Caesar as his political pugilist two years later, he gloated over the fulfilment of his self-fulfilling prophecies. ' "If any of you had listened to me when I was forever forecasting and warning you against the dangers of Caesar's growing power, you would not now be fearing one individual or pinning your hopes on another." ' But since the worst had happened, Cato at least had the sense to propose that Pompey should be appointed commander-in-chief, if only because 'the men who cause trouble should also finish it'. But his peers would not agree. The ghost of Sulla's pupil had been raised again, and while they wanted victory over Caesar, they wanted it without 'the certainty of despotism' which Cicero's letters of December 50 had been predicting as the outcome of a war whichever side won. Even among the hard-liners there were few who were anxious to see Pompey formally in supreme command, and it was not something on which Pompey himself could insist without losing credibility as the champion of freedom, guardian of the state, and moderator of the aristocratic republic in which equals took turns in ruling and being ruled, embodying their corporate supremacy in what a Hellenistic monarch's ambassador had once termed an 'assembly of many kings'. Although Pompey had succeeded in bringing the Senate to declare war against Caesar and had persuaded the majority of the legal government to abandon Rome, he nevertheless remained only one of several proconsuls whose activities he could direct only by recommendation, not command.

While the other magistrates and commanders spread out to their various recruiting stations Pompey and the consuls had ridden straight down the Appian Way to the nearest and most fertile stamping-ground, where they made Capua 'the seat of war'. Ironically that is exactly what Cicero had declared it would become if the tribune Rullus, backed by Crassus, had been allowed to carry his Bill to settle colonists there in 63. And though Cicero had written to Tiro on 12 January that he had assumed responsibility for Capua, four days later when he knew that Caesar had crossed the Rubicon he promptly exchanged it for a seat on the fence. 'I declined Capua,' he wrote later, 'not because I shirked the post but because I did not wish to be a leader without an army. I told Pompey to his face that I would do nothing without men and money.' The whole purpose of the exercise was to raise men and money, but Pompey seems to have restrained his desire to tell Cicero exactly what he thought of him. Militarily he could do without Cicero, but politically Cicero still had great prestige, and Pompey now offered him a general supervision of the coastal area of Campania – evidently enough of a sinecure to enable the *Imperator* to spend his days bombarding his friends with agonized letters from the comfort of his villa at Formiae. But this was the second time that Cicero had funked a responsibility. He had refused to go to Sicily in December, and he now resisted becoming actively involved in the war-effort in Campania. And in the frustration of trying to run a war without the supreme authority to compel a cowardly proconsul to accept his recommendations Pompey's only consolation was that the negative attitude of a man like Cicero was at least less dangerous to the success of his strategy than the non-co-operation of more aggressive co-equals whose independent energy might raise a large number of troops but could also lose a great many more.

The news that followed Pompey and the consuls down to Capua was mixed. The bad but hardly surprising news was of Caesar's continuing offensive. Having secured Ariminum he had divided his legions's ten cohorts. He remained where he was with two of them and organized a levy of new troops, but he sent five under Antony south-west to take Arretium while the other three were sent further down the coast to Umbria to occupy Pisaurum, Fanum and Ancona. In his memoirs Caesar pretends to have made these further moves only after the government had left Rome and he had received impossible replies to the peace-proposals which had had sent to Capua by Lucius and Roscius, but thanks to Cicero we know better, and a glance at the map of Italy reveals his frustrated strategy. He had almost certainly been planning a swift march on Rome by the Via Flaminia, which was the shortest and most obvious route, running more or less due south to the capital from where it left the Adriatic coast at Fanum Fortunae. But Caesar could not strike inland down the Flaminian Way without securing his line of communication and reinforcement from Gaul. It would be fatal to march south through Umbria only to find a government force speeding northwards through Etruria, along the Via Cassia. The Cassian Way entered Cisalpine Gaul to intersect the Aemilian Way at Faventia some forty-five miles before it reached the Adriatic at Ariminum, and if Faventia were taken by forces raised in Etruria, Caesar would be cut off from the legions marching to join him across the Alps and might find himself surrounded. Similarly he had to guard his rear from the possibility of a northward advance by the government armies being raised in Picenum, and that was why he seized Ancona. Arretium and Ancona would form the edges of the protective umbrella under which he might safely hurl the 8th and 12th legions against Rome as soon as they arrived, whereupon Antony would have been instructed to advance his half of the 13th legion from Arretium. The strategy was a good one. The obvious way to win the war quickly was to capture the centre of government before the government was strong enough to defend itself, and if the government had stayed in the centre Caesar would have succeeded. But even while Caesar was implementing this plan, Pompey was frustrating it by removing the government which could have legalized Caesar's successful *coup de main*. All the

same, the news of Caesar's offensive was still bad. It would be deflected
but not discontinued, and with Caesar obviously out for a quick kill Pompey's own strategy would be a race against time.

The good news was that Caesar had been deserted by Titus Labienus,
his most able and trusted legate, who had served in Gaul as long as
Caesar himself. According to Dio his motives for abandoning Caesar
were scarcely uplifting. 'One might feel surprised that after having always
been so highly honoured by Caesar he should have done this.... The
reason was that when he had acquired wealth and fame he began to conduct himself more haughtily than became his rank, and Caesar, seeing
that he sought to put himself on the same level with a superior, became
less fond of him. Labienus therefore changed sides, for he was not happy
at Caesar's changed attitude towards him and feared lest he should suffer
something untoward.' Some modern historians have swallowed all this
unquestioningly, and looked to Napoleon's marshals for parallels of such
unmerited arrogance by inferiors. Others have made Labienus virtually
a secret agent for Pompey for the last ten years simply because he seems
to have been born in Picenum where Pompey had ancestral estates. But
while human motivation is seldom simple and there may be something
in Dio's cynicism, it is surely not incredible that one of Caesar's generals
simply refused to be a rebel. As long as Caesar fought Gauls and Britons
and other barbarians, he had no lieutenant more loyal. But when he
ordered Roman to fight Roman in civil war against the legal government,
he forfeited the loyalty of at least one man who did, as Cicero says, 'the
better thing', exactly as Caesar's own father-in-law Piso had done by joining the government at Capua and publicly condemning his daughter's
husband 'as a criminal'.

'I expect Labienus is regretting his action,' wrote the feline Cicero in
a letter of 22 January informing Atticus that Labienus' rumoured defection was now official. 'It is less useful and impressive than it might have
been because there is no one in Rome.' But by the next day he had changed
his mind. 'Labienus I call a hero. The finest political action we have seen
for a long time! If he achieved nothing else, he made Caesar smart.' But
Labienus did achieve other things. If he did not bring more than a handful
of horsemen with him – another fact which may suggest that his decision
was made at the last minute when Caesar had taken the offensive – his
arrival was more than a moral reinforcement for the government, important though this was. For he provided Pompey with a helper whose con-
vert loyalty was matched by his ability, and while we may doubt that
Dio's dramatic 'revelation of all Caesar's secrets' amounted to much
more than confirmation of Caesar's having summoned more forces
from Transalpine Gaul, there was no one better qualified to confirm the

loyalty of the government's two legions which had served so long in Gaul.

We learn from Cicero that when Labienus met Pompey and the consuls on 22 January they were not at Capua, as he had no doubt expected, but at Teanum Sidicinum, a town some twenty miles nearer Rome on the Latin Way. We also learn that Pompey had arrived there the previous day, and the evidence which Cicero provides for Pompey's movements is critical to our understanding of his strategy. Cicero had met the consul Lentulus and Pompey's legate Libo at Formiae that day, clearly on their way to Teanum Sidicinum, and they had told him that 'Pompey is making for Larinum, where there are some cohorts, as also at Luceria and Teanum Apulum and in the rest of Apulia'. That Pompey had visited Capua before returning to Teanum Sidicinum where he met Labienus is not certain, though it would be strange if he had left for Apulia without having put in a personal appearance at the town which was to be the temporary centre of government and the focus of the recruiting effort among his own veterans. What is absolutely clear is that only four days after leaving Rome he was already on a journey that would take him eastwards across the Apennines to join cohorts in Apulia, and since these cohorts turn out to be the two legions which had served under Caesar in Gaul, we can begin to appreciate for how long Pompey had been preparing his strategy of evacuation to Greece. These legions had been sent to Capua when they had arrived in Italy in the previous year, but they were now split up in winter-quarters in Apulia, and they had obviously not been sent there after Caesar had crossed the Rubicon. The most likely time for their transfer was when Pompey had been given command of them by the consul Marcellus at the beginning of December 50 in exasperation at the Senate's continued reluctance to authorize a full-scale mobilization. If Pompey had been intending to defend Rome at any cost, he would have left them in Capua. As it was, he had evidently decided at least two months ago to put them in 'the most sparsely populated area in Italy, the most remote from the onset of the war, and the coastal region most convenient for flight.' If it came to war, Caesar would either invade immediately or wait to amass more forces from across the Alps, and in either event these two government legions were better placed in Apulia than in Campania. If Caesar waited to gather more legions of his own, Pompey would have ample time to redeploy them after mingling them with newly recruited legions of more reliable loyalties. If Caesar invaded at once, as he did, these legions could not be trusted to fight so soon against their former commander and comrades-in-arms, and they were therefore best placed there for the rapid evacuation which was clearly no panic decision by Pompey. It was carefully planned as part of a Mediterranean strategy which would isolate Italy and soften it up by starvation in readiness for a reinvasion from East and West. It was another part of the same strategy that had sought to send Cicero to Sicily in December, to control one of the main sources of the grain that kept Rome alive. And it was a strategy which even Cicero would eventually understand, but without realizing how long it had been in preparation.

Pompey's sole concern now was to accumulate the largest possible number of men to take or send overseas, Caesar's to stop his recruiting and bring him to battle in Italy before he could leave. To accumulate troops Pompey could not advertise the fact that he was deserting Italy, and to concentrate them for the evacuation he had to rely on recommendation as well as instruction. But he had able officers whom he could trust besides Labienus, and he used them not only to recruit directly for his own army but to keep an eye on the magistrates and try to stimulate and co-ordinate their efforts. One was Scribonius Libo, the father-in-law of his younger son Sextus. We know from Lucan that Pompey had sent him into Etruria, possibly with the serious intention of raising troops with which to try to cut Caesar's line of communication with his Transalpine province but more likely as a decoy to divert the enemy from the main recruiting effort in Picenum, from where the new levies could be more easily channelled down to Brundisium for embarkation to the East. It could have been Libo's activities that encouraged Caesar to send Antony with half his legion to Arretium, and when Antony arrived, Libo evidently returned at once to where he could be more useful. Cicero saw him passing through Formiae on 21 January on his way to Pompey at Teanum Sidicinum, and when Pompey set out for Apulia with Labienus two days later, he left Libo in Campania along with Titus Ampius, another loyal and energetic legate whom Cicero calls 'the clarion of civil war'. Their job was to maintain the momentum of the consuls' recruiting effort round Capua, and they clearly worked hard at it, for Cicero was relieved to find them 'busily recruiting' and therefore not in need of his reluctant involvement when he visited Capua about 25 January in response to Pompey's expressed wish that he 'should go there and help with the levy in which the response from the Campanian settlers had been far from enthusiastic'.

At least two more of Pompey's most reliable adherents deserve special mention. One was Faustus Sulla, Pompey's son-in-law: he held an independent commission *pro praetore* rather than a legateship under Pompey, but he could be counted on to accept Pompey's recommendations as commands and he raised a legion for his father-in-law. The other was Vibullius Rufus, a prefect under Pompey's direct command who was now entrusted with one of his general's most delicate and critical missions.

Pompey's orders to Vibullius were to go to Picenum and make sure that the cohorts being raised there were safely brought to him in Apulia before they could be overrun by Caesar's redirected offensive. For Pompey knew that Caesar would have guessed what he was planning the moment he heard of the government's withdrawal from Rome. And indeed Caesar had recalled Antony from Arretium and was concentrating all available forces in Ancona for a thrust into Picenum and down the eastern side of Italy.

In the meantime there had been further action on the diplomatic front. Caesar had sent Lucius and Roscius back to Pompey and the consuls with detailed proposals for peace. Pompey not only encouraged the Senate to agree to Caesar's terms but published a personal reply which fooled at least Cicero. 'Lucius brought Caesar's message to Pompey on 23 January, when he was with the consuls at Teanum Sidicinum,' Cicero wrote. 'The terms were approved, but with the proviso that Caesar withdraws his troops from the towns he has occupied outside his province. If he does that, he was told that we shall return to Rome and settle matters through the Senate. I hope there is a chance of peace in the present circumstances, for Caesar is regretting his madness and Pompey the weakness of our forces.' What the terms actually were is almost irrelevant because they were neither offered by Caesar nor accepted by Pompey with any sincerity, but basically they involved a commitment by Pompey to go to his province in Spain, the disarmament of all recently levied troops and garrisons in Italy, Caesar's surrender of his Gallic provinces to his successors, and his standing for the consulship in person rather than *in absentia*. With a purpose other than brevity Caesar's memoirs fail to mention his own commitment to hand over his provinces or the promise to stand for the consulship in person. He wanted posterity to believe that these were demands made in reply by Pompey and the Senate, and that he was being asked to sign a blank cheque. But posterity has the letters of Cicero, and we need not doubt him where he has no reason to falsify his account, for he clearly believed that the diplomacy was genuine, and was ardently hoping that Caesar would ratify terms 'which were after all his own'. He observed at the time that 'many people are saying that Caesar will not keep to his terms and has only put forward these demands in order to stop us making preparations for war', but his own opinion remained what he wanted to believe – that Caesar was sincere and would withdraw – until disillusionment struck in the form of a letter which he saw from Curio. Curio ridiculed Lucius' embassy for what it really was, just another gambit in the war-game, and Pompey had felt safe in calling Caesar's bluff. It should have been clear even to Cicero that Pompey had not the slightest intention of going

to Spain; but Pompey evidently gained some propaganda value by pretending agreement, for Cicero was pleased by the public's enthusiastic
reception of his formal reply even though he complained that it had not
been drafted by Pompey himself, 'who is a good writer', but by an author
whose style was frigid enough to give his readers a chill. Otherwise it
changed nothing. Caesar continued recruiting, the government continued recruiting, and Cicero took the precaution of writing to assure one
of Caesar's friends that he was not recruiting. And it was perhaps as
well for Cicero that Pompey did not intercept the *Imperator's* correspondence, though he would also have found amusing evidence of his success
in disguising his evacuation strategy, for even after he had left for Apulia
Cicero was still writing to Atticus that 'in the event of war' he would
send his boys to safety 'in Greece'.

Pompey's prefect Vibullius arrived in Picenum in time to transform a
virtual rout into an orderly withdrawal. The praetor responsible for recruitment round the Umbrian town of Iguvium had fled before the advance of Curio whom Caesar had sent ahead with the three cohorts from
Ariminum and Pisaurum. Caesar himself in the meantime had moved down
the coast-road to Ancona, and having been rejoined by the jubilant Curio
he advanced on Auximum, 'which was being held by Attius Varus
who was sending round senators and organizing the levy in Picenum'.
Ironically it was at Auximum thirty-four years ago that Pompey had
begun recruiting his private army to support Sulla's invasion from Greece
against the forces of the Marian government in the Civil War of his youth.
He had been only twenty-two then, not even a senator and with no
present or previous authority to levy troops, but the Picentines had
flocked to his revolutionary colours, and they had set him on the path
to early greatness. Now he was fifty-six, long acknowledged as the prince
of citizens, champion of the lawful government against a rebel general
from Gaul, but though Lucan was probably right that 'Italy favoured
Magnus more and loyalty strove with the menace of danger', the actual
appearance of danger in the shape of Caesar's battle-hardened veterans
was 'quick to change men's minds, and the turn of events swept away
their wavering allegiance'. The decurions of Auximum warned the praetor
that he could not expect them to risk the sack of their town by trying
to hold out against the legions which had conquered Gaul, and Varus
withdrew his new recruits. But he was too slow. Caesar's flying column
caught up with him, forced him to an engagement, and won without a
fight because his men deserted. And soon the government forces were
in retreat everywhere as Caesar rushed through the whole of Picenum.
Cingulum threw open its gates despite its obligations to Labienus, its most
famous son who had 'built up and beautified his home-town at his own

expense', as Caesar gloatingly observes. 'Caesar requisitioned troops,' he continues in his laconic style; 'they sent them'. Then the 12th legion arrived from Gaul to join the 13th, and when Caesar led both of them against Lentulus Spinther in Asculum, Spinther beat a hasty retreat with his ten cohorts. Ten newly levied cohorts were no match for twice the number of veterans, and though Caesar seems to be exaggerating even on his own figures when he maintains that most of Spinther's troops proceeded to desert to their homes, it was as well that Vibullius arrived in time to stop the rot. Pompey's able prefect took immediate command, withdrew the cohorts in good order, and conveyed them safely to Corfinium after increasing their number to fourteen on the way. There he found twelve more under the command of Caesar's would-be successor in Transalpine Gaul, the proconsul Domitius who had raised them from the tough Marsi and Paeligni around Alba Fucens. To these came another five from Camerinum under Pompey's legate Lucilius Hirrus either with or without Vibullius' help, and when Pompey received word on 10 February that thirty-one cohorts were setting out to join him from Corfinium, he reckoned on having the raw material for over three new legions in addition to the two veteran legions from Gaul and the numerous cohorts being raised in Campania.

Ever since Pompey had left Campania for Apulia on 23 January to make his headquarters at Luceria, from where he might most conveniently liaise with the recruiting-effort in Picenum while securing the route of evacuation to Brundisium and organizing the formidable logistics of provisioning and transhipment, he had endeavoured to conceal his strategy in order to maintain the momentum of recruiting as long as possible. Cicero had found the recruiting effort in full swing at Capua when he went there to pretend to help at Pompey's request about 25 January, and Pompey sent him a morale-boosting dispatch which he received three days later. Pompey may not have expected to get much active participation from Cicero, but he knew how effectively that epistolary gossip would disseminate any information which he received, and he was happy to use him in the capacity of a Roman Reuters. And sure enough Cicero had wasted no time in spreading the news. 'Pompey has written that within a few days he will have a strong army, and holds out the hope that if he once gets to Picenum, we shall get back to Rome. Labienus is confident of the weakness of Caesar's forces.' But the real plan could not be disguised forever. The consuls had already convened a meeting at Capua for 5 February, and by then even Cicero was beginning to suspect the truth. On 7 February a message arrived asking the consuls to return to Rome and fetch all the money from the Treasury which they had closed but not emptied when they had left. And on the next day

Cicero wrote that 'Picenum has fallen, Caesar will be in Apulia any minute, and Pompey will be sailing away'. But the Pompeian propaganda maintained the old line. On 9 February Cicero received a letter from his wife's freedman Philotimus in Capua with the news that 'Domitius has a strong army, the cohorts from Picenum have joined him, and Caesar can be, and is afraid of being, cut off.' But Cicero feared it was all fancy. 'I believe the other tale is true,' he told Atticus. 'We are all prisoners, Pompey is leaving Italy, and Caesar – the bitter end! – is said to be pursuing Pompey. Caesar pursuing Pompey, do I say? For what purpose? In order to kill him? I find it shattering. Why aren't we all throwing our bodies in front of him?' Clearly there was now enough uncertainty to stifle the recruiting-effort even at Capua, and Cicero, far from throwing himself in front of Pompey, made ready to drop off his fence at Caesar's feet. 'Many people say that Caesar is well satisfied with me,' he concluded.

On 10 February Pompey wrote personally to Cicero with the news of the large forces that were on their way to join him from Corfinium:

GNAEUS MAGNUS PROCONSUL TO MARCUS CICERO IMPERATOR

Greetings. Quintus Fadius came to see me on 10 February. He reports that Domitius is marching to join me with twelve cohorts of his own and fourteen brought by Vibullius, that he intended leaving Corfinium on 9 February, and that Hirrus is following with five cohorts. I advise you to join us at Luceria, as you will be safest there.

This is only one of hundreds of letters and orders that must have streamed out of Pompey's headquarters as he tried to concentrate everyone for the evacuation, and Cicero was hardly at the top of his list of priorities. But if Cicero was worse than useless militarily, Pompey did not want him being cajoled or coerced into lending his legitimizing political influence to the government which Caesar would try to re-establish when he had gone. He therefore tried to entice him to Luceria by appealing to what he knew to be Cicero's overriding concern, his personal safety. But the implication caused offence to the timid *Imperator* whose protesting over-reaction was more damning than any open confession of Pompey's perceptiveness. 'I am writing at once to tell Pompey that I am not just looking for the safest place I can find,' he snapped to Atticus, to whom he also complained of the brusqueness of Pompey's letter as though Pompey had the leisure to labour over lengthy epistles to anyone in the middle of a war, let alone a broken reed whose own letters admit that he was now widely criticized, unjustly of course, for appearing 'less punctilious than I might have been'. And needless to say he wrote nothing of the sort in his reply to Pompey. Instead he favoured him with military advice about the desirability of holding the Campanian coast. It was the very last thing that Pompey needed from Cicero, but it was only an excuse to stay on the fence and avoid the commitment to leaving Italy which his joining Pompey at Luceria would involve, as Atticus could see from Cicero's offended letter. The excuse: 'Pompey should not lose the coastal areas if he wants to be supplied with grain.' The truth: 'Clearly the plan is to concentrate at Luceria and not even make a stronghold there but prepare for flight.'

It was not the end of the world for Pompey that Cicero refused to accept his recommendations, but Cicero was not the only one, and as the situation grew daily more critical Pompey became increasingly frustrated by his lack of supreme command. Even Cato, the very man who had urged the Senate to make him generalissimo, proved unco-operative. When Pompey had left for Apulia he had wanted Cato to go at once to Sicily just as he had wanted Cicero to go there in December, but Cato had refused. If the peace-negotiations with Caesar came to anything, Cato did not want to miss the Senate's debate. Someone else could go to Sicily instead, but the first someone else refused to go without Cato, and so it fell to a third person to take belated command in that island-granary. This was no way to run a war, and it must have driven Pompey to distraction. He could rely on the consuls to do what they were told as long as it meant marching away from danger, but when he sent them the message to return to Rome and empty the Treasury on 7 February, they refused. Cicero sympathized with them of course. 'Having abandoned the capital they are now supposed to go back without a military garrison. They replied that they would go to Rome when Pompey went to Picenum.' In fact they could have gone to Rome perfectly safely at this point exactly because Caesar was so preoccupied in Picenum, and if we may believe Caesar's memoirs they would not have needed to go to Rome at all if they had not been needlessly panicked into leaving the money in the first place. On the other hand it is hard to believe that Cicero would have refrained from snide comments about it if they really had decamped without the ingots after hearing a false report of Caesar's arrival. As it is, he says only that the Treasury had been closed, and the desire to treat the evacuation of Rome as a temporary measure and to disguise the ultimate strategy of evacuation to the East is sufficient reason for the Treasury to have been left shut but not emptied until later. But if sins of omission were bad enough when motivated by timidity, they were worse when backed by bravado, and Pompey was now horrified to hear that the proconsul Domitius, supposedly marching to join him with thirty-one cohorts, had decided to make a stand against Caesar at Corfinium.

The news of this proud folly reached Pompey on 11 February. The outburst with which it was greeted would no doubt have been unprintable if it had been recorded, but Pompey mastered his fury for long enough to send off an immediate message appropriate to a fellow proconsul whom he could coax but not command, though he could not disguise his astonishment that Domitius had not even informed him of his decision but let him hear of it indirectly. He knew the pride of 'pugnacious Domitius' who wanted the glory of defeating Caesar with Pompey's help rather than by helping Pompey. Vibullius had been too successful. With only his own twelve cohorts Domitius would not have risked it, but with thirty-one he regarded himself as too strong to be expendable and believed that he could blackmail Pompey into bringing his two legions to assist him. But Pompey knew better the art of the possible, and tried desperately to inculcate some sense into his colleague.

Luceria, 11 February 49

GNAEUS MAGNUS PROCONSUL TO LUCIUS DOMITIUS PROCONSUL

Greetings. I am greatly astonished that you write me nothing and that I am informed on these public concerns by others rather than yourself. With our force split we cannot be a match for the enemy. By concentrating our forces I hope that we may be able to serve the Republic and the common good. Therefore I am completely at a loss to understand what the reason can have been for your change of mind when you had already decided, as Vibullius had written, to set out from Corfinium on 9 February and come to join me. The reason which Vibullius conveys to me, that you delayed because you heard that Caesar had advanced from Firmum and reached Castrum Truentinum, is valueless, for the more the enemy starts to draw near, the faster you should have acted in order to join me before Caesar was in a position either to interfere with your march or cut me off from you. Accordingly I once again beg and beseech you, as I have continually asked you in earlier letters, to come to me at Luceria on the earliest possible day before those forces which Caesar has mustered have been concentrated in one place so as to cut you off from us. But if there are men who are holding you back in order to save their properties, it is only fair that I should request you to see that I am sent those cohorts which have come from Picenum and Camerinum and have already abandoned their possessions.

Pompey was on tenterhooks waiting for the reply, and on 16 February he knew the worst. He wrote again, desperately trying to ease some tactical sense into Domitius' head while privately wishing that he could wring his neck.

Luceria, 16 February 49

GNAEUS MAGNUS PROCONSUL TO LUCIUS DOMITIUS PROCONSUL

A letter from you arrived by the hand of M. Calenius on 16 February. In it you write that you intend to observe Caesar's movements, and if he begins to advance in my direction along the coast you will immediately march into Samnium to join me, whereas if he remains in your vicinity you wish to resist him if he approaches near.

I think that you are acting with great courage and high-mindedness in this matter, but we must be all the more careful to avoid a situation in which we are divided and therefore no match for the enemy, since he has large forces and will soon have larger. It would ill befit your foresight to consider only how many cohorts Caesar has against you at present without regard to the size of the forces, both of horse and foot, which he will soon draw together. The evidence for this is a letter which Bussenius has sent me. He writes, as do other correspondents, that Curio is mustering the garrisons which were in Umbria and Etruria and is marching to join Caesar. If these forces shall once become concentrated in one place, with part of his army being sent to Alba and part advancing against you, and Caesar not offering battle but repelling attacks from positions of his own choosing, you will be stuck, unable alone with your present force to stand against such numbers in order to go foraging.

Accordingly I earnestly exhort you to come here as soon as possible with all your forces. The consuls have decided to do the same. I sent you word by M. Tuscilius that I must guard against letting the two legions into Caesar's sight without the cohorts from Picenum. Do not therefore be distressed if you hear that I am retiring if Caesar happens to march against me. I feel I must beware of being caught in a trap. I cannot take the field because of the time of year and the disposition of my troops, nor is it expedient to collect the garrisons out of all the towns in case I lose my line of retreat. And for that reason I have gathered no more than fourteen cohorts at Luceria. The consuls will bring down all the garrisons or go to Sicily, for we must either have an army strong enough to allow us to feel confident of breaking through or we must hold areas from which to fight back. At the moment we happen to have neither of these things, because on the one hand Caesar has occupied a large part of Italy and on the other we do not have an army as ample and as great as he does. We must therefore be careful to take account of the greatest advantage to the Republic. Again and again I urge you to come to me as soon as possible with your whole force. Even now we can put the Republic on its feet again if we only organize our affairs with a concerted plan of campaign. If we are divided, we shall be weak. That is my fixed opinion.

But it was too late. Before this letter had gone off the next morning, a second dispatch arrived from Domitius with word that Caesar had reached Corfinium and pitched camp before the walls. Domitius begged Pompey to come to his assistance, and Pompey sent his reply in a post-script to the letter he had already dictated: 'After I had written this letter

I received your letter and message. As to your request that I should come there, I do not think I can do it because I have no great confidence in these legions.' It was as much as Pompey could bring himself to write until he had calmed down, but later that day he wrote a formal reply with a final exhortation to Domitius to extricate his army and bring it down towards Brundisium if he possibly could:

Luceria, 17 February 49

GNAEUS MAGNUS PROCONSUL TO LUCIUS DOMITIUS PROCONSUL

Greetings. I refer to your letter which arrived on 17 February in which you write that Caesar has pitched camp before Corfinium. What I thought and predicted is happening, with the result that he does not want to join battle with you at present, and having concentrated all his forces he is hemming you in with them in order that you might not be able to march to join me and thus combine your own regiments of the very best citizens with the legions here of whose loyalty we are doubtful. I am therefore all the more disturbed by your letter. For I simply do not have sufficient confidence in the enthusiasm of the troops which I have with me to stake all the Republic's fortunes on one pitched battle, and the troops which have been conscripted for the consuls have not yet come together. Therefore do your best, if even now you can find some way of managing it, to extricate yourself and to come here as soon as possible before all the enemy forces come together. For the men from our levies cannot be concentrated here rapidly, and even if they could, it will not escape you how little confidence we can place on new recruits, who do not even know each other, against veteran legions.

The coaxing and flattery have stopped. Domitius is revealed as a stubborn fool. He has got himself into the mess by ignoring Pompey's advice, he must get himself out of it without Pompey's help and must not expect the government's whole cause to be sacrificed on the altar of his pride. But Pompey did not really expect Domitius to be able to extricate his troops now. Caesar was too good a general to let Domitius get away now that he had bottled him up in Corfinium, and Pompey had already signalled a change of plan to the consuls. The plan to reinforce Sicily must be given up. In the expectation of having more troops than he could conveniently tranship to Dyrrachium the consuls had been going to take the cohorts levied in Campania to Sicily together with Domitius and the twelve which he had raised around Alba, but now that Pompey was to lose the nineteen cohorts which Vibullius and Hirrus had been bringing him from Picenum and Camerinum, all available forces must be concentrated at Brundisium, and Pompey informed the consuls accordingly. As soon as Domitius' unhappy dispatch had arrived on 17 February, Pompey sent them a copy with a covering letter preserved by Cicero, who himself saw a copy of it at Formiae on 20 February and promptly communicated its contents to Atticus in Rome:

I refer to a letter which I received from Lucius Domitius on 17 February, a copy of which I append. In the present circumstances I shall not tell you because you will realize of your own accord how vital it is to the public interest that all forces be concentrated into one place and at the earliest possible moment. You will take steps, if you see fit, to join us as soon as possible and leave at Capua as large a garrison as you judge sufficient.

To Cicero it appeared that the unspecified 'one place' on which Pompey wanted all available forces concentrated was Luceria in order that they might go to rescue Domitius, but after a night's reflection he wrote again to Atticus to say that he believed that Pompey was 'going to leave Domitius in the lurch', although he later pretended to have continued to misunderstand Pompey's letter to the consuls as an excuse for failing to join Pompey himself despite the specific 'recommendation' which he had received on 10 February. But to the consuls of course there was no ambiguity. Even if Pompey's written note had not been made more explicit by a verbal message – and it would have been strange if Pompey had not sent one of his most trusted officers to co-ordinate strategy with the consuls – the message which he had sent by Laelius a few days earlier had made it clear that the one place to which all forces must now be concentrated was Brundisium. If Pompey had not been prepared to stand against Caesar in Italy with the forces at his disposal before Domitius had allowed himself to be ensnared, he was not going to do so now on ground of Caesar's choosing even if there was time to get to Corfinium before it collapsed. But Pompey neither needed nor desired to make his plans explicit to anyone who was not already privy to them. If the dispatch had been intercepted, it might have proved as misleading to the enemy as it was initially to Cicero and many others on the government side who might have been less likely to obey the consuls' order to follow if they had known that they were being taken from Italy. 'He left us without a word,' lamented Cicero later, 'without any part in so momentous a plan.' The consuls could reveal as much or as little as they saw fit, just as they could leave as strong a garrison at Capua as they judged 'sufficient'. They would in fact leave little or no garrison at all, and Pompey had not intended that they should. But only he and they and their trusted associates knew that. They responded accordingly and so rapidly that on 20 February, only three days after he had sent the message, Pompey was writing to Cicero that 'the consuls have joined the army under my command in Apulia', and 'advised' him to come quickly to join them at Brundisium.

Once the consuls were on their way Pompey had written them a longer and more careful letter which they could circulate among senators and officers to explain the true plan and his justification for not going to the rescue of Domitius:

Luceria, 19[?] February 49

GNAEUS MAGNUS PROCONSUL TO GAIUS MARCELLUS AND LUCIUS
LENTULUS CONSULS

Being of the opinion that while we are scattered we can neither be of use to the Republic nor any protection to one another I wrote to L. Domitius, first that he should come to me with his whole force, but that if he should feel any hesitation on his own account he should send me the nineteen cohorts which were on their way to me from Picenum. What I feared has happened: Domitius is ensnared, and he has neither the strength to take the field himself, since he has distributed my nineteen and his own twelve cohorts between three towns (for he stationed some at Alba and some at Sulmo too), nor is he able to extricate himself if he so wishes. Now you must know that I am in the greatest anxiety. For while I desire to rescue so many excellent men from the danger of a siege, I cannot go to their assistance because I do not think that these two legions of mine can be sufficiently trusted to be taken there; and anyway I have been able to muster no more than fourteen of their cohorts because I have sent a garrison to Brundisium and I did not think that Canusium should be left without garrison while I am absent. In the hope that we were going to have larger forces I sent D. Laelius with the message that, if you saw fit, one or other of you should join me, that his colleague should set out for Sicily with the force which you have raised in Capua and its environs and with the troops which Faustus has enrolled, that Domitius should be attached to this force together with his own twelve cohorts, and that all remaining forces should be concentrated at Brundisium and transported from there to Dyrrachium by sea. But now, as I am no more able to go to help Domitius than you yourselves at this time ... we must not allow the enemy to meet my fourteen doubtful cohorts or overtake me on the march. I have therefore decided (and I see that I have the approval of M. Marcellus and the other members of the senatorial order who are here) to take this force which I have with me to Brundisium. I urge you to gather together all the forces you can and to come to Brundisium as soon as possible. I consider that you should equip the troops which you have with you with the arms which you had been going to send me; and if you will have all remaining arms carted to Brundisium, you will have been of great service to the Republic.

I should be grateful if you would inform all our people of all this. I have myself sent word to the praetors P. Lupus and C. Coponius to join you and bring you all the troops they have.

Pompey wrote this just before leaving Luceria for Brundisium, probably early on 19 February. We know that he reached Canusium the next day because he dated his letter from there to Cicero with the formal 'recommendation' to join him at Brundisium, and the day after that he was on the road again himself. And he was wise to get away when he did, for Domitius surrendered Corfinium that very day, and Caesar lost no time in pursuing Pompey in a desperate attempt to prevent him leaving Italy.

Domitius' débâcle as described in Caesar's memoirs is exactly as Pompey had feared. Domitius was evidently taken by surprise by the speed of Caesar's advance. He had sent five cohorts to demolish the bridge over the river which formed a natural barrier some three miles from the town, but they were overrun before they could complete the task, and after a brief skirmish they were in headlong flight from Caesar who chased them back to Corfinium and immediately started fortifying a camp outside the walls. Domitius tried to put heart into his men by promising them four acres apiece from his own vast domains. He sent Pompey the plea for assistance which reached him on 17 February, and he prepared to withstand the siege which Caesar was already preparing to lay. Domitius placed artillery on the walls, and carefully assigned each man a specific task in the defence. Caesar strengthened his camp and sent Antony with five cohorts of the 13th legion to Sulmo, for Domitius had not even concentrated his forces in Corfinium, and Sulmo contained seven of his cohorts. But seven cohorts of new recruits were no more eager to take on half a veteran legion than the town's inhabitants wanted to suffer a siege, and while they surrendered, their two generals jumped from the walls in despair. Antony was back with Caesar the same day, and found him organizing the construction of siege-works to prevent Domitius' escape and sheds and mantelets under which his troops could storm the walls as soon as reinforcements arrived. In the meantime Domitius was prevented from foraging, exactly as Pompey had predicted. After three days Caesar's 8th legion arrived with twenty-two cohorts newly levied in Gaul and three hundred cavalry. Caesar now had fifty-two cohorts, the equivalent of over five legions, of which three were veteran. Domitius had less than half that number, and all were new recruits.

Even if Pompey had arrived with his fourteen cohorts, it would have been too little and too late. Caesar constructed a second camp on the far side of Corfinium, put Curio in command of it, and surrounded the town with a line of earthworks and redoubts which was already finished by the time Domitius received Pompey's reply. Domitius concealed the truth and told the troops and townspeople that Pompey was on his way to help them, but 'his looks belied his words, his actions were marked by more haste and timidity than he had displayed on previous days, and he began much secret conversation with his friends'. Suspicion spread through the town like an enervating gas. The troops and their officers decided that Domitius had betrayed them, and they sought to save themselves by surrender. Only the Marsi disagreed, men of that tough Italian tribe who had proved such formidable opponents to Pompey's father in the Italian War of Pompey's youth. They were just as reluctant to desert a cause for which they had taken up arms now as then, especially since they were fighting on their own territory – unlike the recruits from Picenum whose land had already been overrun, as Pompey had pointed out to Domitius in his dispatch of 11 February: 'if there are men who are holding you back in order to save their properties, it is only fair that I should request you to see that I am sent those cohorts which have come from Picenum and Camerinum and have already abandoned their possessions'. But even the Marsi finally agreed to surrender once they were convinced of Domitius' decision to escape. Domitius was arrested by his own officers, and envoys were sent to treat with Caesar under a flag of truce.

Caesar's response was undoubtedly astute. Anxious as he was to take advantage of this opportunity to win a swift and bloodless victory before largess or false news caused any change of heart – 'for he reflected that in war the most enormous changes can so often result from trivial causes' – he was even more afraid to let his troops enter the town at night and risk an uncontrollable orgy of looting and destruction that would stiffen the resistance of other Italian towns. He therefore threw so tight a cordon around Corfinium that it was impossible for individuals, let alone cohorts, to get away, and about the first watch he was approached by Spinther, the former governor of Cilicia who had been Pompey's frustrated rival for the task of restoring King Ptolemy to the throne of Egypt seven years ago. Spinther grovelled, if Caesar may be believed, and Caesar reassured him about his own safety and the safety of all the troops and senators in the town. After all, Caesar wanted those troops for his own army and he was not going to jeopardize the political side of his war-effort by murdering senators. And at dawn he received the formal surrender. Domitius begged for death, but Caesar not only refused him the satisfaction of martyrdom but restored to him the six million sesterces of public money which he had brought to the town, and sent him away both unharmed and in funds as an example of Caesar's clemency. He wanted to persuade as many of the fence-sitting senators as possible that there was a soft landing on his side, as Lucan observes in his version of Caesar's response to Domitius' demand for death:

> 'Then live against your will, and see the rising sun
> By Caesar's grace. In you your friends will find a cause
> For hope when they are conquered too.'

But Pompey's propagandists projected what Caesar called his 'new style of conquest with the weapons of mercy and generosity' as an old sham, and they reminded men how Sulla 'down to the moment of his victory had shown himself more moderate than could have been expected, but when once he had conquered, his cruelty had been unprecedented'.

Domitius' proud folly had not only lost Pompey thirty-one cohorts but Sicily as well. Cato eventually went to take command in the island, but he had to start recruiting troops there and in the toe of Italy, while Domitius' twelve cohorts, which should have gone there as government troops, now went as Caesar's men under Curio. Caesar himself raced on to Brundisium in pursuit of Pompey with six legions, three veteran and three newly raised. But he was too late to prevent the first transhipment of troops to Greece: 'He found that the consuls had already gone to Dyrrachium with a large part of the army, and that Pompey was remaining at Brundisium with twenty cohorts.' In his memoirs he pretends that he was unaware of Pompey's intentions. 'It could not be discovered for certain whether he had remained there for the sake of holding on to Brundisium in order that he might more easily control the whole Adriatic from the extremities of Italy and the shores of Greece and so carry on the war simultaneously from both sides, or whether he had stayed behind for lack of ships; but fearing lest Pompey should think that he need not abandon Italy, Caesar determined to block the exits and stop the working of the harbour.' But Caesar is hardly convincing, for all that he writes in the third person to give a pretence of objectivity while ensuring that the reader reads his name as often as possible. If he wanted posterity to believe that he drove a reluctant Pompey into the sea, there was nothing that he feared more at the time, and he did all he could to prevent Pompey's evacuation to the East. For there was more than wishful thinking in the words which Lucan gives to Pompey:

> 'Demented fool! It is not you whom all things flee
> But I whom all things follow.'

Even Cicero now had to revise his opinion of Pompey's 'lack of wisdom, organization and power'. The logistics involved in concentrating some 27,000 men and transporting over half of them across the Adriatic at one sailing were formidable, and Pompey had not been wasting his time 'cooped up in country towns' in Apulia. He had collected so many ships that Caesar admits that there was hardly a vessel to be found between the Po valley and Sicily with which to follow him. The two legions which had served under Caesar in Gaul had no doubt been part of the forces with which the consuls had crossed on 4 March, and the twenty cohorts with which Pompey was holding Brundisium until the

fleet's return will have been loyal troops recruited from the families of
his old veterans in Campania and conveyed to Brundisium by the consuls
in response to Pompey's recommendations of 17 and 19 February. But
for Domitius he would have had even more troops to take to Greece,
though he had probably not intended to take more than another ten
cohorts because he had planned to send Domitius' twelve and a large
part of the Campanian levy to Sicily. He would have taken the nineteen
cohorts which Vibullius and Hirrus had been bringing from Picenum and
Camerinum, but as it was he took Campanian troops instead, and Cato
would have to fend for himself in Sicily. What Pompey would have done
if Domitius had managed to break out of Corfinium after Caesar's arrival
and convey his thirty-one cohorts to Brundisium we can only guess. If
Caesar had been so close on their heels that it would have been impossible
to redeploy them by land, Pompey would have needed three sailings to
get them all across the Adriatic, but there is little doubt that he would
have endeavoured to get them all away by sea either to Dyrrachium or
to Sicily and would have resisted any demands by Domitius for a pitched
battle. Evacuation was and had always been Pompey's strategy ever since
Caesar had crossed the Rubicon, and despite Domitius' ineptitude he had
concentrated no fewer than fifty cohorts of legionaries to form the
nucleus of a powerful army which he could train at leisure in Macedonia
while starving Italy into submission by cutting off the grain-supply
and the provincial revenues. And all this compelled the belated and still
grudging admiration of Cicero, who failed to conceal it even under
the thickest veneer of outrage at Pompey's supposed plans for a Sullan
dictatorship:

> The plan is to strangle Rome and Italy with hunger, then carry fire and sword
> through the countryside and dip into the coffers of the rich.... Pompey is even
> stronger than we thought. If only his health holds, he will not leave one stone
> unturned when he returns to Italy.... I have no doubt of the destruction that
> lies ahead, to be introduced by famine.... All his fleet from Alexandria,
> Colchis, Tyre, Sidon, Aradus, Cyprus, Pamphylia, Lycia, Rhodes, Chios,
> Byzantium, Lesbos, Smyrna, Miletus, Cos, is being collected with the object
> of cutting Italy's lines of supply and occupying the grain-exporting provinces.
> How angry Pompey will be when he returns!... The grain-supply in Italy can-
> not be managed without revenues from the provinces.... What part of Greece
> will not be plundered?

In the East Pompey's name would command unlimited supplies of money,
cavalry and light-armed troops. All he would be short of there were
Roman legionaries, for though there were considerable numbers of
veterans who had chosen to settle in the eastern provinces after their

Pompey's Theatre: an aerial photograph of the modern buildings in the Campus Martius
shows how they still follow the outline of the theatre-complex.

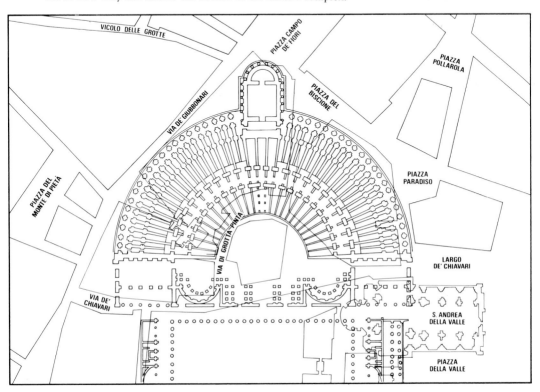

VICOLO DELLE GROTTE

PIAZZA CAMPO
DE' FIORI

PIAZZA
POLLAROLA

VIA DE' GIUBBONARI

PIAZZA DEL
BISCIONE

PIAZZA DEL
MONTE DI PIETÀ

PIAZZA
PARADISO

VIA DI GROTTA PINTA

PIAZZA
DELLA VALLE

LARGO
DE' CHIAVARI

VIA DE'
CHIAVARI

S. ANDREA
DELLA VALLE

This representation of Rome's port at Ostia would have been appropriate to Pompey the corn commissioner: Neptune presides while the captain of a merchant-ship on the left offers sacrifice for a safe voyage, barges are loaded on the right, and the lighthouse blazes behind.

Roman infantry foraging for corn in the fields.

ABOVE Cicero (106–43). ABOVE RIGHT Caesar (100–44). BELOW LEFT Cato (95–46).

BELOW RIGHT King Ptolemy XII 'Auletes' of Egypt (80–58, 55–51), who owed his recognition and restoration to Pompey's patronage. His son ordered Pompey's assassination.

BELOW CENTRE King Juba I of Numidia (60–46), Pompey's hereditary ally, defeated Curio's invasion of Africa in 49 but was himself defeated by Caesar in 46.

Roman cavalry charging barbarians.

A wintry view westwards on the likely site of the Battle of Pharsalus from the position of the advancing Caesarians. Pompey's camp was on the slopes of Mt Dogantzes on the right. The River Enipeus flows north-westwards behind the village of Hyperia which can be seen to the left of the tree.

campaigns, there was not of course the inexhaustible supply of Italy. Not surprisingly therefore Caesar now set out to do everything in his power to stop Pompey and his twenty cohorts from getting away.

According to his memoirs Caesar had already sent one of Pompey's captured officers ahead to Brundisium with proposals for a personal conference. This was Numerius Magius, Pompey's prefect of engineers, who may have been on his way to join Pompey's army in Spain when he was intercepted. The message he took to Pompey was reasonable enough in principle. 'It is in the interest of the state and the common good that Caesar should have a meeting with Pompey. When men are separated by long distances and terms of agreement are conveyed by third parties, the same results are not gained as would be secured if they were to discuss all the conditions face to face.' But when Caesar arrived at Brundisium, his memoirs claim surprise and disappointment that Magius had not been sent back to him. Thanks to Cicero we know better. Cicero quotes a letter which Caesar had written to Balbus, his principal political agent now in Rome, on 9 March, the date he arrived before Brundisium. 'Pompey is in Brundisium,' Caesar wrote. 'He sent Magius to treat of peace. I replied as I thought fit. As soon as I see any hope of compromise, I shall write.' In fact neither Caesar nor Pompey wanted peace except through victory. Caesar had sent Magius to Brundisium in the hope of undermining Pompey's resistance or enticing him into a trap. Pompey sent Magius back in the hope of slowing down Caesar's siege-works, but Caesar omits Magius' return from his memoirs to make Pompey appear unco-operative. What he does record is that he made a second peace-initiative at a great sacrifice of time, for 'his frequent attempts to reach an understanding were hindering energetic action and military planning'. He sent a personal friend of Scribonius Libo, the father-in-law of Pompey's younger son, to urge him to persuade Pompey to 'come for a personal interview', and Libo duly transmitted the message. But when Pompey replied with diplomatic regret that 'since the consuls were absent it was impossible to enter into negotiations for a settlement, Caesar finally decided that he must abandon an attempt so often made in vain and apply himself to war'. Again Caesar gives the impression of a frustrated seeker after peace, but again the sincerity of his later claim to have let his peace-initiative 'hinder energetic action and military planning' is revealed as humbug by Cicero, who was naïvely horrified to compare two of Caesar's letters. When he saw the letter which Caesar had sent to Balbus for dissemination on 9 March he had thought it bad enough that 'Pompey has sent Magius to sue for peace and is still besieged', for all that Balbus wrote that he was 'on tenterhooks for the success of the negotiations'. But it was the end of illusions when on the same day he received a copy of another letter which Caesar had written to someone in Capua:

> Pompey shuts himself up in the town. We camp at the gates. We are attempting a big job which will take many days on account of the depth of the sea, but there is nothing better to be done. From both wings of the harbour we are sinking moles in order either to force him to tranship the forces which he has at Brundisium as soon as possible or to prevent him from getting out.

'Where is the peace Balbus was on tenterhooks about?' exploded Cicero. 'Could anything be more cold-bloodedly ruthless?' But neither had Pompey slackened his military efforts for a second, and the negotiations were humbug on both sides.

The city of Brundisium was well fortified with walls and towers and had water on three sides, for an arm of the main harbour projected inland on either side of the town. Caesar threw siege-lines round the three landward sides and outside the two inlets in order to prevent Pompey's escape by land, but if Pompey's fleet returned safely and he was able to get himself and his army across to Greece this would be so much wasted effort. Caesar's only way of stopping escape by sea was to block the harbour-mouth, and since the channel to the open sea was fairly narrow, he was able to exploit as a weakness the very feature which gave the port its commercial strength as a safe haven for shipping. Working simultaneously from both sides he threw out piers and a mole from either shore, but as the water deepened he extended them by means of pontoons. He constructed a large number of rafts thirty feet square, and having fixed a pair of them at the end of each breakwater with anchors at each corner he proceeded to add more and more of the same size and to cover them with earth, in order to form a floating causeway which he protected with screens and fascines. On every fourth raft he raised towers two storeys high from which missiles could be hurled down on attacking ships or fire-rafts, and it was not long before they were in action, for Caesar was not fighting a Domitius now. Pompey had been a master of siege-warfare before Caesar had gone to Gaul, and he was not sitting idly by while his former protégé closed his exit to the East. As the moles and their projecting pontoons crept slowly closer from each side of the deep-water channel, Pompey commandeered some merchant ships and built great towers on their decks. With literal one-upmanship Pompey made his towers three storeys high against Caesar's two, and having equipped them with artillery and missile-weapons of every kind he deployed them against Caesar's rafts and moles. Unfortunately Caesar does not elaborate on the 'fighting which took place every day with much discharging of slings, arrows and other missiles', but he rarely elaborates on his own

failures, and the success of Pompey's counter-measures is clear from the
fact that the fleet apparently had no difficulty in sailing back into the
harbour without loss. Caesar now accelerated his efforts to try to block
the channel before Pompey could embark, and it is possible that this was
the time of his last attempt to bring Pompey to a personal conference
through the intercession of Libo. But if so, it was in vain.

Pompey was in his element now. He was no longer dependent on
distant incompetents to whom he could send only recommendations. At
Brundisium he was in sole command, revelling in the excitement of the
action and gratified to find that none of his old skill had deserted him.
The final stages of the evacuation were faultlessly planned and executed.
While his armed merchantmen intensified their attacks on Caesar's pontoons, he took measures to delay an attack by the besieging forces during
the embarkation of his own, and even Caesar was impressed:

> To prevent Caesar's troops from breaking into the town Pompey blocks the
> gates, barricades lanes and streets, digs trenches across the thoroughfares and
> makes them into man-traps by filling them with stakes and sharpened timbers
> before levelling them over with light hurdles covered with earth. He also shuts
> off the approaches and the two routes leading to the harbour outside the walls
> with stockades of huge timbers fixed deep into the ground. Having made these
> preparations he bids his heavy-armed troops to embark in silence, and replaces
> them on the battlements and towers with light-armed men drawn from the
> reserves, archers and slingers. These he arranges to recall at a given signal
> when all the other troops have embarked, and he leaves them some merchant
> vessels ready in a convenient place.

But it was not only Caesar's troops with whom Pompey had to contend.
It was impossible to hide the preparations for evacuation from the citizens
of Brundisium, and they signalled to the besieging forces from the upper
windows of their houses. 'They are embittered by the wrongs inflicted
on them by Pompey's soldiers and by the insults of Pompey himself,'
wrote Caesar pompously, as though the townspeople were not more
afraid of what Caesar's toops would do to them when Pompey had left
unless they ingratiated themselves with the enemy general. But Pompey
was on top of the situation. Caesar prepared scaling-ladders and armed
his men, but he could do nothing until the trumpet blew at midnight,
the ships loaded with legionaries began lurching out of the harbour, and
the light-armed troops left their station on the walls and 'raced down
to the waiting vessels by familiar routes'. The Caesarians hurled their
ladders against unmanned walls, but they were brought up short by the
blind stockades and man-traps. They did not fall into them because they
were warned by the townspeople, but by the time they had been guided
down to the harbour by circuitous routes, the Pompeian armada was

streaming out to sea with a loss of only two ships which had fallen foul of Caesar's pontoons and been overrun. It was 17 March, two days after the Ides – an unlucky day for Caesar in 49 and destined to be a fatal one four years later, though only after Pompey's own famous good fortune, 'wearied by his triumphs, proved untrue'.

# 7

# 'WAR THROUGHOUT THE WORLD'

Thus Fortune made the rival leaders smart in turn,
Mixed failure with success for both, and kept them matched
With equal strength for Macedon.
                            Lucan, *Pharsalia*, 5.1–3

'Other people count Pompey's sailing away among his best stratagems,' observes Plutarch, 'but Caesar was astonished that when he was in a strong city, expected his forces from Spain and controlled the sea, he gave up and abandoned Italy.' But whatever official opinions Caesar might have given to provide the basis for Plutarch's statement, it is not even necessary to read too carefully between the lines of Caesar's memoirs to appreciate the frustration which their author felt at Brundisium on 17 March 49:

Caesar, in the hope of finishing the business, particularly approved the plan of collecting ships and following Pompey across the Adriatic before he could strengthen himself by overseas support, yet feared the delay and length of time involved because Pompey, by collecting all the available ships, had robbed him of any present opportunity of following him. It remained to wait for ships from the most distant parts of Gaul and Picenum, and from the straits. This, owing to the time of year, seemed a protracted and difficult process. In the meantime Caesar was unwilling that in his absence a veteran army and the two Spanish provinces, one of which was closely tied to Pompey by the great benefits received from him, should be confirmed in their allegiance, that auxiliary forces and cavalry should be prepared, or that Gaul and Italy should be tampered with. For the present therefore he gives up his plan of following Pompey and determines to go to Spain.

In short Caesar did the only thing he could, and his analysis of the situation is a muted but clear admission of the success of Pompey's strategy. Pompey had put himself beyond pursuit for long enough to be able to concentrate the military and monetary resources of the vast Eastern empire which it had been his greatest achievement to defend, extend and organize in the sixties. He need not fear that Caesar would pursue him round the Adriatic by land and down through present-day Yugoslavia. It was a long and difficult march through tribes as hostile as their terrain, and it would only invite a counter-invasion of Italy by Pompey's legions in Spain. Nor did he fear that Caesar would stay in Italy. On the contrary, there was nothing that he would have preferred to see than Caesar sitting in a starving capital, struggling to organize an illegitimate government and wondering how to pay an increasingly demoralized army while it waited to be crushed by a simultaneous invasion from East and West. But Pompey was under no illusions that Caesar would give him that satisfaction, and because he knew that Caesar could not afford to lose the momentum to which he had owed his success in overrunning Italy, he had already sent the loyal and able Vibullius Rufus to Spain in order to co-ordinate a vigorous defence by the Pompeian legions there. At best this might destroy Caesar, and at least it would delay him from following to Greece where the mobilization of the East would be Pompey's personal preoccupation while he waited for news of a distant war-game which he could play only by proxy.

The weaknesses in the government's position were less the result of Pompey's strategy than of his lack of supreme control over its implementation, and this was seen most immediately in the vulnerability of Sicily. If only Cicero had taken command there when Pompey had suggested it four months ago, that grain-producing island might have been impregnable by now. If Cato had not delayed after being assigned its governorship in January, he would still have had over two months in which to raise land and naval forces for its defence. If Domitius had not refused Pompey's 'recommendation' to withdraw from Corfinium, his twelve cohorts would now be holding it for the government instead of preparing to capture it for Caesar, and a large contingent of the consuls' Campanian levy would have been with them. As it was, Cato was having to levy troops almost from scratch in a hopeless race against time before Caesar could gather enough ships to send his ready-made army against him.

By Caesar's own account his first orders at Brundisium were for the concentration of ships, partly for his long-term plan of following Pompey across the Adriatic but also for the rapid transhipment of a smaller army across the much shorter distance to Sicily, for while he maintains that ships were available at the Straits of Messina, it is not likely that Cato's recruiting efforts in the toe of Italy would have left them there for long. Caesar also authorized a crash building-programme of warships on both the Adriatic and Tyrrhenian coasts. He appointed admirals at once in order that their land-bound frustration might speed the work that would take their flags to sea, and he appointed Curio to take four of the newly enrolled legions to Sicily and then to Africa. For while Sicily and Sardinia were his priorities in securing the vital supplies of grain, he intended to have Africa too, and Curio's task was exactly that which Sulla had entrusted to the young Pompey in the last Civil War, though Curio was not destined to enjoy the same success.

After he had distributed his forces between the towns of Brundisium, Tarentum and Hydruntum – 'to guard Italy' according to Appian, but also 'to close the ways out by sea' for senators like Cicero who was now beginning to regret that he had not gone with Pompey while the going had been good – Caesar moved up to Rome to try to legitimize his *coup d'état*, only to find that Pompey's evacuation had been as much a moral as a military success. Early in March Cicero had noted 'how the country towns are making a god of Caesar … you can imagine their deputations and official compliments'; and while he admitted that 'they might well be frightened', he had thought they 'would be even more frightened of Pompey'. But if Cicero had been right about Caesar's general popularity before Pompey sailed for Greece, Pompey's absence evidently made men's hearts grow fonder, and when Caesar arrived at Rome at the end of the month

> … no joyful crowds
> Came forth to greet his glorious approach,
> But men looked on with silent fear.

It was the reaction to the realization that the consuls, Pompey, and the greater part of the governing class had been driven from Italy by a rebel general. Men's minds recoiled as the implications sank into them, and even Cicero found his backbone when he was brought face to face with Caesar who passed through Formiae on 27 March.

Even before he had reached Brundisium Caesar had alarmed Cicero with the request that the latter should join him in Rome. 'As I trust that I shall be coming to Rome soon,' he wrote about 5 March, 'I beg you most particularly to let me see you there and allow me to have the use of your advice, influence, standing and help in all matters.' But Cicero had realized that Caesar wanted his sanction for illegal elections in the absence of the consuls, and by the time he actually met Caesar towards the end of the month he had steeled himself not only to reject that role but to recognize even neutrality as a false haven, 'a course of non-action that makes for dishonour without security'. When Caesar now urged him again to come to Rome, Cicero flatly refused. Caesar complained that this 'was tantamount to passing judgement against him', and that 'the rest would be slower in coming if Cicero refused'. He invited Cicero 'to come and work for peace', but even if Cicero had not already returned the philosophical treatise on that subject which he had so fatuously borrowed from Atticus some time ago, he was not stupid enough 'to step into Caesar's trap'. He did not make the obvious retort that if staying away implied condemnation of Caesar, going to Rome would imply approval. He asked instead if his peace-making efforts could be undertaken at his own discretion. ' "Naturally," ' said Caesar. ' "Then I shall take the line that the Senate does not approve of your making an expedition into Spain or of your transporting armies into Greece," ' declared Cicero, adding for good measure that ' "I shall have much to say in sympathy with Pompey." ' Caesar protested that that was 'not quite what he had in mind', and asked Cicero to think it over. But Cicero had already thought, and finally decided: 'I am determined to join Pompey.'

It would be pleasant to think that Cicero had at last shed hypocrisy and taken his decision to do or die with Pompey in a spirit of dedication to principles nobler than self-preservation, but the toothless leopard had not changed his spots. 'Affection comes to the surface,' Cicero had written grandly on 18 March, but elsewhere he cannot decide whether he is more loyal to the man or the cause: 'Unless Pompey wins, the name of the Roman People will inevitably be blotted out.' He presents Pompey as the lesser of two evils. 'The Republic is not at issue: this is a fight for a throne, in which Pompey is the more moderate, upright and clean-handed.' And he may have been right, although Pompey's record scarcely suggests that 'his victory would be after Sulla's example and fashion'. But it was neither affection for Pompey nor selfless devotion to a cause that touched Cicero most closely. 'I must be off,' he confessed to Atticus, 'because I simply could not endure the talk of your friends in Rome. . . . I can't face the Senate.' In other words, Cicero did not mind being a humbug but being called a humbug. For the writer of the *Republic* to have appeared in Caesar's Senate would have made him the laughing-stock of Rome and deserved the contempt of friends and enemies alike. Nor was it only his 'face' that Cicero sought to save. For all his scorn of Pompey's policy of evacuation he was now convinced that Pompey would win. 'He is even stronger than we thought' . . . 'We have it for certain that Pompey is on his way through Illyricum to Gaul' . . . 'Do you really believe that if Spain goes Pompey will lay down his arms? Certainly not. His entire plan is Themistoclean. He calculated that whoever holds the sea is bound to be the master. That was why he was never interested in holding the Spanish provinces for their own sake. His main care was to fit out a navy, and when the time comes he will put to sea with huge fleets and land in Italy.' But to join Pompey was now easier said than done, and Cicero soon found that orders had been given to prevent his or anyone else's leaving Italy for the East, for he was not alone in having decided that too much of Caesar was more than enough.

When Caesar arrived in Rome about the end of March, the tribunes
Antony and Cassius 'convened the Senate from which they had so recently
been expelled', and Caesar gave what Dio enigmatically terms 'a long
and reasonable speech'. But though he had the support of 'every disreputable character in Italy' – the types who had so horrified Cicero when he
had met 'the whole half-human crew of them' at Formiae ('I knew them
all but I had never seen them in one place before') – Caesar was disappointed by his reception. He had reason to hope for something better.
Even while he was still besieging Pompey in Brundisium, there had been
something of a return to normality in government and business, and it
had brought Cicero crashing back to reality from his state of suspended
belief: 'A Roman army besieges Pompey, and Rome still stands, praetors
sit on their bench, aediles prepare their games, supposed loyalists book
their receipts!' And Plutarch adds that Caesar had been pleased 'to find
the city more tranquil than he was expecting, and with many senators
in it'. But it was a sham Senate anyway with the heads of state and some
two hundred of its members away in Greece. Many of the senators still
in Italy followed Cicero's example and refused to attend, and of those
who did attend not all were prepared simply 'to record the utterance of
a private individual': a few turned out to have stayed in Rome precisely
for the purpose of opposing him even at the risk of their lives.

According to Caesar's own memoirs he 'urged the sending of envoys
to Pompey to effect a settlement', but it hardly rings true when he adds
that 'no one could be found willing to go, each refusing the embassy
through fear because Pompey on leaving the city had said that he
would regard those who remained in Rome in the same light as those
who were in Caesar's camp'. It was ridiculous to suggest that Pompey
would not respect ambassadors, and if Caesar had really believed that
Pompey would not receive senators who came better late than never, he
would scarcely have taken so much trouble to guard the ports to prevent
their leaving Italy. Dio is more convincing when he maintains that Caesar
made his proposal only after finding the Senate as a whole unimpressed
by his long-winded attempts at self-justification, 'displeased at what was
happening and suspicious of the multitude of soldiers'. It was merely an
attempt 'to encourage and tame them, in order that he might prevail at
least in their quarter until he could bring the war to an end'. Plutarch
agrees that 'no one would listen to him because they thought that he did
not mean what he said but was talking humbug'. And according to Dio
he soon proved it, 'for though envoys were in fact chosen to effect the
so-called reconciliation, they never set out, and Caesar's father-in-law
Piso was once called to account for so much as referring to them'.

By now the proconsul of Gaul must have felt like the Gauls who had sacked Rome in 390 and found senators sitting so immobile in their seats that they had thought them statues until an experimental tugging of beards had animated them. But if Caesar could beard them, he could not massacre them as the barbarians had done, and he soon realized that he would have to carry out his threat 'to administer the state by himself if they refused to take up the burden of government and administer it with his help'. And he seems to have had little more success with the popular assemblies. Just as he had tried to sweeten the Senate with peace-initiatives, he bribed the people by promising doles of money and grain, but even the feckless democracy of Rome was not entirely slave to its belly. 'Remembering the behaviour of Marius and Sulla,' says Dio, 'the many benevolent phrases addressed to them by those men and the contrast with the treatment they had received in return for services rendered, and perceiving Caesar's present need, the people of Rome were unable to trust his words or be cheered by them.' Nor were they greatly impressed by a promise of largess from a man who at the same time was helping himself to 'the funds and inheritance of the Roman people in order to support his troops', and when he demanded all the money from the inner reserves of the public Treasury which the legitimate government had not removed, he found himself opposed not only by 'three days of discussion and excuses' in the Senate but by a veto of a popular tribune named Lucius Metellus. In his memoirs Caesar does not even mention the financial demands and pretends that Metellus' opposition was directed against his peace-initiative, but our other sources reveal the true story. 'Metellus opposed the proposal about the money,' says Dio, 'and when his efforts were unavailing, he went and stood guard before the doors of the Treasury', to which the absent consuls had the keys. It was a brave action. By interposing his veto Metellus had given Caesar a taste of the nasty medicine with which Caesar's tame tribunes had dosed the government over the last year and a half, and when he placed his sacrosanct person before the Treasury doors, he was defying Caesar to practise what he preached, and respect the rights of the tribunes in whose defence he had supposedly mounted his invasion. Metellus told Caesar that he would have the money only over his dead body. ' "That is easier done than said," ' replied Caesar shortly, and signalled his troops to cast Metellus aside and smash down the doors.

Cicero heard about this from Curio, who visited him about 14 April on his way to take up his command in Sicily. 'It had been touch and go,' Curio reported. 'Caesar had been carried away with anger over Metellus and wanted to have him killed, in which case there would have been a bloodbath. Caesar is not clement by nature.' And while Dio is no doubt right that Caesar succeeded in 'arranging everything in the city and the

rest of Italy to his own advantage', the qualification 'so far as circumstances permitted' suggests that even the veneer of legality was not always
intact. It is far from clear to what extent Caesar had secured senatorial
or popular approval at this stage for recalling all the exiles convicted
by the courts which Pompey had introduced in 52, for allowing the
proscribed to canvass for office, or for appointing men like Curio to provincial commands either as governors or legates. What is clear, though,
is his anger and frustration at Pompey's moral victory *in absentia*. 'Caesar
hates the Senate more than ever,' reported Curio, 'and he had not even
dared to hold a public meeting before he left.' And Caelius told Cicero
the same: 'Caesar left Rome angry with the Senate. He is thoroughly incensed by these vetoes. Believe me, the time for vetoes will soon be past.'
Caelius warned Cicero not to jeopardize his own safety. 'If you suppose
that Caesar will continue his policy of letting opponents go free and offering terms, you are making a big mistake. He thinks and talks nothing
but ruthless severity.' And the words of Curio and Caelius were not lost
on Cicero. He realized at last that those who were not with Caesar were
against him, and that the only refuge for those who were against him
was with Pompey.

By the second week in April Caesar was on his way to Spain and Curio
to Sicily. He had found the praetor Lepidus willing to collaborate by looking after Rome in his absence, he had put his old legate, the tribune
Antony, in command of the forces left in Italy with instructions not to
let anyone in or out. He had also appointed Antony's brother, Gaius
Antonius, to try to establish a bridgehead across the Adriatic and keep
watch on Pompey's movements, but there was nothing significant that he
could do to undermine Pompey's mobilization of the East, and though
he released Aristobulus from house-arrest in Rome and sent him to try
to regain the Jewish throne from which Pompey had expelled him, it was
a vapid hope that soon expired in assassination. But in the West Caesar's
career of conquest seemed unstoppable, for Sardinia succumbed without
a fight, and even Cato evacuated Sicily before Curio arrived. Caesar's
memoirs maintain that Cato gave a public denunciation of Pompey
'for having undertaken unprepared an unnecessary war,' but none of the
other sources says anything of the kind, and it is highly unlikely that Cato
would have publicly insulted the champion of the cause for whom he had
himself proposed supreme command and to whom he was about to sail.
Cicero typically criticized Cato for not resisting. 'Cato could have
defended Sicily without difficulty,' he wrote airily, 'but instead he left
Syracuse on 23 April. Let us hope that Cotta holds Sardinia as they say
he will. Cato will cut a poor figure if he does!' But Cotta followed Cato's
example, though evidently not, as Caesar implies, the moment he heard

that Caesar was sending an army against him. Whether Cotta took many
troops with him on his flight to Africa is not known, but Appian's narrative certainly suggests that when Cato 'sailed off to Corcyra and thence
to Pompey', he took with him the considerable armament which even
Caesar admits that he had managed to raise in a short time; for he had
'repaired old warships, requisitioned new ones, raised levies from the
Lucanians and Bruttians of southern Italy, and exacted infantry and
cavalry from the Sicilian towns'. Cato was wiser than Domitius had been,
and though it was humbug to claim that he had decided 'not to make
resistance in Sicily in order to spare lives,' there was sound military sense
in sailing away in time to swell the forces which Pompey was rapidly
assembling in the East.

Pompey cannot have been surpised at the loss of Sicily and Sardinia
but he was justifiably angry, though more because it could so easily have
been avoided if only his colleagues had co-operated than because it was
either catastrophic or irreparable in terms of his overall strategy. Curio
himself had admitted to Cicero that 'he was afraid of Pompey's fleet,
and if it put to sea, he would leave Sicily'. But Pompey was not yet prepared to divert any of his resources from the massive build-up of power
in Greece. Sicily and Sardinia would be driven back into the fold soon
enough when the time came to loose new dogs of war from the East,
or even earlier if his seven battle-trained legions in Spain succeeded in
winning this war for him entirely in the West despite the superior forces
which Caesar was now concentrating against them. For while Caesar
began marching three newly recruited legions from Italy about the middle
of April, six more were on their way from Gaul, three from Narbonne
and three from Macon. From Narbonne it was only a short march to
the Pyrenees, and Caesar had ordered his legate Fabius to take the three
legions from there and secure the mountain passes in readiness for the
arrival of his own three and the three from the Saône which were accompanied by large forces of cavalry. But Pompey's legates in Spain remained
calmly confident of their own resources and their familiarity with the
terrain which had helped Sertorius to resist Pompey himself for five
years, and they were soon cheered to hear that Caesar had received a
setback *en route* which was not only diverting the three legions which
he was bringing with him from Italy but shattering the myth of his
invincibility.

The rock which stood fast against the flowing tide of Caesar's success
was the city of Marseilles, the ancient Massilia. It was a Greek city of
great antiquity, a colony which had grown rich and powerful on five and
a half centuries of trade throughout the Mediterranean and up the valley
of the Rhône. It had been founded by citizens of Phocaea on the coast

of Asia Minor about 600 when Rome was still a primitive city-state under
Etruscan domination in a largely hostile Italy; and though it had seen
Rome grow to become mistress of the Mediterranean world, it had
retained its liberty, and its commerce had thrived on the Roman peace.
It was indebted to both Pompey and Caesar for grants of land and local
suzerainty during their campaigns in southern Gaul, and when Caesar
now 'pleaded with the Massilians not to let the first outbreak of hostilities
come from them', they gave what Dio rightly terms a 'noteworthy reply'
– 'that as allies of the Roman People they felt friendly to both sides ...
and would therefore receive both in peace but neither in war'. What motivated this response is not certain. Partly, as Cicero believed, it may have
been the conviction that Pompey would win, for as a mercantile people
they were no doubt influenced by their memory of his brilliant success
in sweeping the seas clear of pirates in forty days, and they believed that
the vast naval forces which he was assembling in the East would prove
decisive. Partly, perhaps, they were influenced by Pompey's presence in
Greece, his benefactions to the Greek cities of Asia Minor and his mastery
of the wealth of the East, of which the Massilian merchants were as well
aware as anyone east of the Adriatic. But the sheer tenacity of their resistance suggests a deeper motive, a pride in freedom which made them support the lawful government of the Roman People whose allies they were
glad to be but not the slaves, let alone the slaves of a rebel general. This
was not a sudden decision. Pompey had urged this course of action three
months earlier through the agency of some Massilian envoys, 'young men
of noble birth', who had been in Rome when he had abandoned the
city in mid-January, and by the time Caesar arrived outside Massilia
with his demands and three legions, the Massilians had amassed a huge
store of provisions against the prospect of a siege, established arms-
factories, strengthened their fortifications and summoned their subject-
tribes from the mountains of the hinterland. Even while Caesar was
'trying to talk them back to sanity' as he chose to express it, Domitius
arrived by sea with seven merchant-ships full of his own slaves,
freedmen and tenants, and the Massilians not only let him enter their
harbour but put him in charge of the defence. After all, Domitius was
the legal governor of the province in which they resided, though 'they
alone of all the peoples who inhabited Gaul refused to collaborate with
Caesar'.

  With his typically Assyrian attitude to obstacles in his path Caesar
made preparations to besiege the city by land and blockade it by sea.
According to his own account he did not wait to launch an attack in
person, but Dio says that he actually tried and failed to take the city by
storm, and the omission of this failure from Caesar's memoirs does not

disprove it. But whether it was knowledge or merely right opinion that convinced Caesar of Massilia's impregnability to anything but a long and difficult siege, he left his legions there under the command of legates while he sped on to Spain with his personal bodyguard of nine hundred horsemen. He had already wasted too much time at Massilia. Every day he spent there strengthened Pompey's army in Spain but weakened his own position morally as well as militarily, for the world was waiting to see Caesar falter, and if a single Greek city in the south of France was allowed to halt the momentum of his success, the repercussions throughout Gaul and Italy could be disastrous.

Even without the three legions which he left at Massilia the force with which Caesar was invading Spain was formidable both in size and skill. All six legions were veterans of the Gallic Wars, and they were supported by five thousand auxiliary infantry and six thousand cavalry, half of which had been with Caesar throughout the Gallic Wars and half were native Gauls, 'the most conspicuous in rank and courage'. But they were by no means irresistible by Pompey's army of seven legions under his three legates, Afranius, Petreius, and Terentius Varro. Afranius commanded three legions in Nearer Spain, the province which Pompey had governed in the war against Sertorius and which was particularly closely attached to his name. Petreius and Varro divided Further Spain between them with two legions each, the former in Andalusia, the latter in Lusitania and the Tagus valley. And all three men had proved themselves in high command. In the long war against Mithridates Afranius had been to Pompey what Labienus had been to Caesar in the conquest of Gaul; and though his political acumen had proved inversely proportional to his military ability during his consulship of 60, he was in his element again now, and the last five years had given him experience of Spain's peculiar difficulties which were powerful allies against invasion by conventional armies even when led by versatile generals. About Petreius we know less. He was in the war against Catiline in Italy, but if it is not clear how he had become so closely attached to Pompey to secure the appointment to Spain, the events of the next few weeks will prove that Pompey had known his man. As for Varro, he was one of Pompey's oldest friends and adherents: the same Varro who had composed a brief guide to consular duties for Pompey's benefit when the conqueror of Sertorius had suddenly leapt to the headship of state on his return from Spain in 71. Although Varro is better remembered today as a man of letters than of war, his military record belies the image of the absent-minded academic reflected by his enormous output of learned tomes on almost every subject from farming to philosophy. He had served as one of Pompey's legates in the Pirate War of 67, and he had been highly decorated after holding command of the naval and land forces in the Ionian sea from Delos to Sicily.

It is not recorded what instructions Pompey had sent to his three legates in Spain by Vibullius, but the results of their council of war may well have reflected his general advice, though detailed strategy could clearly be decided only by the commanders on the spot. Varro was to remain in Further Spain with his two legions in order to hold that province and raise fresh forces and supplies. Petreius was to join forces with Afranius in Nearer Spain, and their combined strength of five legions would dig in at some readily defensible position between the Ebro and the Pyrenees. In numbers of legions and cavalry Afranius and Petreius were inferior to Caesar – they had five legions against his six and five thousand horse against his six thousand, which was also of better quality – but they were probably superior in auxiliary infantry, of which they had both light and heavy native units made up of those tough mountain-tribes who had provided Sertorius' guerrillas. But wars on this scale are not won or lost by an extra legion or a thousand cavalry. The Pompeians had the advantages not only of terrain but of time. Knowing that Caesar's interest was to seek and destroy them as soon as possible, they could pick their own ground, fight at their own advantage, and otherwise refuse to fight in the confidence that they were well supplied in a country in which small armies are defeated but large armies starve. They had the moral advantage of defending a country against an invader, their native auxiliaries were fighting on their own ground against Gauls as well as Romans, and the whole province 'was under deep obligations to Pompey for great benefits' which he had conferred on its cities and inhabitants after his governorship in the seventies. And last, but not least, they carried the talisman of Pompey's name, which was legendary throughout the whole peninsula. The only name that living memory held in greater awe than that of Sertorius was that of his conqueror, and when Caesar arrived to find the provinces alive with the rumour that Pompey himself was marching to Spain through North Africa at the head of his legions, it is hard not to suspect Vibullius as the author of this propaganda effort, which also added the promise of future benefactions to the recollection of past obligations and present inducements to continuing allegiance to an absent governor.

When Fabius crossed the Pyrenees with the first three of Caesar's legions he found Pompey's generals encamped outside the city of Ilerda, the present-day Lerida in Catalonia; and if, as seems likely, he found no opposition in the mountain passes, the explanation is almost certainly that 'the natural advantages of their position', which were admired by Caesar himself, made Pompey's generals only too eager to draw the

enemy into their trap. Ilerda was an exceptionally strong and well-forti-
fied city on the west bank of the River Segre as it flows south-westwards
from the Pyrenees to meet the Ebro on its eastward journey to the Mediterranean. To the west of the city stretches a great triangle of land formed
by the Segre and the more westerly Cinca, which are some thirty miles
apart at that point but converge to an apex just before their confluence
with the Ebro some twenty miles to the south. To the east the city was
defended by the unfordable river flowing beneath its walls, although its
own access to the east bank was secured by a stone bridge well fortified
against both natural and human assault, 'fit to withstand the winter
floods and spanning the river with a mighty arch'. The Pompeians' camp
was about three hundred yards to the west of the city. The city itself
was their fortified supply-base, and while a hostile army would find little
left to eat between the Segre and the Cinca, Ilerda's bridge gave its
defenders an all-weather access to fresh supplies from across the Segre
itself. And if this may seem relatively unimportant when Fabius must have
been heading his dispatches with dates in late June by the time he was
approaching Ilerda, his unreformed Roman calendar was running so far
ahead of the seasons that it was still early April by our reckoning, the
corn was not ripe, and the rivers were likely to rise in sudden floods that
would carry away all but the strongest bridges.

With only three legions against the Pompeians' five, Fabius wisely made
no attempt to fight until the other three should arrive. He encamped on
a hill about two miles north of Ilerda and battled instead with the problems of supply, which meant crossing to the eastern bank of the Segre.
His engineers constructed two bridges, one opposite his camp, another
about four miles upstream, and in the days that followed there were
constant skirmishes between the troops protecting the foraging parties
of both armies until the river itself joined forces with the Pompeians by
sweeping away Fabius' lower bridge in a storm and leaving two of his
legions and all his cavalry on the far side. At once Afranius led four of
his five legions across Ilerda's stone bridge and began to engage the
stranded Caesarians, who would have had no chance of survival if Fabius
had been unable to reinforce them. But Fabius now had at least four and
probably all six legions under his command, and as the higher bridge
still stood, he was able to send two more legions to the rescue. It meant
an eight-mile forced march for the relieving forces, but the embattled
troops were able to hold out for that long, and when Afranius saw the
new eagles approaching, he promptly withdrew from what had become
an equal contest which he could not afford to risk.

Two days later Caesar arrived to take personal command of his army.
Realizing that time was his worst enemy he advanced at once towards

Ilerda and offered battle on a piece of level ground below the city and the Pompeian camp. But it was a futile hope that Afranius would be mad enough to accept his challenge. The Pompeians drew their battle-lines on the slopes immediately in front of their camp, and when they offered Caesar an uphill struggle instead, it was Caesar's turn to decline. But he did not withdraw. He started to dig in where he was, and in the course of three difficult days of dividing his army between wielders of spades and wielders of swords against the constant skirmishes of the Pompeians, he succeeded in constructing a new camp with perhaps a thousand yards of fairly level no-man's-land between his own and the Pompeian lines. But there was all the difference in the world between the strengths of the rival positions. The Pompeians were scarcely more than three hundred yards from a city full of food and a stone bridge across the river. Caesar was now further than ever from the sources of supply, and though he had ordered 'huge supplies' to be fetched from Italy and Gaul, it was a long and difficult business to bring wagon-trains across the Pyrenees. What he needed was a rapid success which would encourage the Catalonian towns to defect from Pompey, but as he could neither attack the Pompeian camp with any hope of success nor lay siege to Ilerda with the Pompeian army encamped alongside it, he made a desperate attempt to separate the two by sending a picked detachment to seize a mound that lay between them.

So rash an action was exactly what Afranius had been waiting for, and though it is not the sort of thing that Caesar would acknowledge in his memoirs, it is more than likely that Afranius had deliberately left that hillock unguarded in the hope of enticing Caesar to try to occupy it. Caesar's troops had scarcely begun their charge when a Pompeian detachment was racing to anticipate them, and in the irregular struggle that ensued even Caesar grudgingly admits that his men were 'thrown into confusion' by the 'barbarous kind of fighting' which the Pompeians 'had learnt in their continual wars with the Lusitanians and other barbarous peoples'. In other words it was a triumph for flexibility over regimentation. Caesar confesses that his whole line was panic-stricken, the legion which he had sent up in support of his task-force was in retreat, and it was only by bringing up fresh legions that he could stop the rout. Even so he was outmanoeuvred. The Pompeian cohorts retreated as nimbly as they had advanced, and when Caesar's ninth legion raced in pursuit, they suddenly turned and held it at bay below their fortified town, from which they could receive a continual supply of fresh men and missiles in safety while the Caesarians were cut off from cavalry or infantry support by the nature of the ground. For five hours the Pompeians rained missiles on to the struggling legion, and it was only by an uphill charge of desperate bravery that the survivors managed to cut themselves out of their impossible position and push the Pompeians back into Ilerda for long enough to receive the cavalry support that could cover their withdrawal.

According to Caesar both sides claimed a victory, but the greater justification for the Pompeian claim is apparent when he goes on to say: 'the enemy fortified the hill for which they had fought with great entrenchments, and placed a garrison on it.' And what followed showed the soundness of the Pompeian strategy in general and the choice of Ilerda in particular, for two days later the rivers rose again as torrential rain swelled the meltwater from the Pyrenees and swept away the bridges which Fabius had built over the Segre, as Caesar relates:

This caused serious difficulties to Caesar's army. For since his camp was situated, as has been described above, between the two rivers Segre and Cinca, thirty miles apart, neither could be crossed, and his whole army was necessarily confined in this narrow space. The states which had entered into friendly relations with Caesar could not supply provisions, nor could those foraging parties which had travelled to any distance return, being cut off by the rivers, nor could the huge supplies which were on their way from Italy and Gaul reach the camp. Moreover it was the most difficult season of the year, when there was no corn left in the winter-stores, the crops were far from being ripe, the local communities were exhausted because Afranius had conveyed nearly all the corn to Ilerda before Caesar's arrival, and whatever they had left had been consumed by Caesar during the previous days; also the cattle which could have provided a secondary reserve against want had been removed to a distance by the neighbouring states because of the war. The men who went out to collect fodder or corn were followed by light-armed Lusitanians and skirmishers from Nearer Spain who were acquainted with the district and also had no difficulty in swimming the rivers, for it is their universal custom never to join the army without bladders. But Afranius' army had abundant provisions of every kind. Much corn had been provided and collected previously. More was being fetched from the whole province, and there was a great supply of fodder. The bridge at Ilerda and the untouched districts across the river, which Caesar was now completely unable to reach, gave opportunities for all these things to be done without risk.

Caesar's situation went from bad to worse. His frantic attempts to repair the bridges were frustrated by the river and by the Pompeian patrols on the far bank. He received word that his supply-trains from Gaul and Italy were approaching from the north-east, but they could no more cross the swollen river than his own foragers, and if they had not been accompanied by sufficiently large forces of Gallic cavalry to cover their withdrawal to the hills, they would have fallen prey to the Pompeian legions which Afranius threw across the Segre to destroy them. While the price of corn rose fifty times in Caesar's camp, Afranius and Petreius wrote enthusiastically to their friends in Rome, crowds thronged their houses there, and congratulations were offered for a success that seemed assured. Caesar's popularity had not been great when he had left Rome, and it had been deteriorating ever since. The resistance of Massilia had reinvigorated anti-Caesarian sentiment. On 6 May Cicero had written to Atticus that 'the Massilians know what they are about. . . . Their action is not only intrinsically valuable but proof to me that everything is all right in Spain.' He also mentioned anti-Caesarian demonstrations in the theatres, and widespread disaffection in the legions newly recruited in Italy. On 14 May he was himself approached by the centurions commanding three cohorts at Pompeii. They were ready to hand over the town to him, and if he had not promptly convicted himself of the cowardice with which he had so recently charged Cato by making himself scarce, he might even have raised Italy against Antony. And all that was several weeks ago. By now Cicero had succeeded in getting away to join Pompey, and when the latest news arrived from Spain many more senators followed his example, 'some in order that they might show themselves the first to bring him such news, others that they might appear not to have waited for the issue of war and to have been the last of all to come'. But even as Pompey was receiving congratulations for having ended the war by remote control, the tide of fortune turned again and swept Caesar clear of imminent disaster.

It is perhaps the most admirable characteristic of Pompey's opponent that he was never more determined than when nearest to disaster. As the weather began to improve he made boats of hides stretched over a wooden frame, sent a detachment of troops across the river twenty-two miles upstream, and secured a bridgehead which rapidly became a bridge before the Pompeians discovered it. It was a very long way from his camp, but it enabled him not only to bring in his supply-train but to deploy his now massively superior cavalry against the Pompeian foragers to the east of the Segre. And soon he was able to add a tonic from Massilia to the invigorating effects of sunshine, food and action which were heartening his demoralized army. Domitius had fought a naval battle against Caesar's newly built squadron, and though the Massilian fleet of seventeen warships and numerous other vessels was superior in size and seamanship, the Caesarians contrived to neutralize these advantages by using grappling-irons and fighting a land-battle at sea. Although Massilia itself was not taken, the defeat of its fleet was a timely success for Caesar, and the news influenced a number of towns and tribes of northeast Spain to go over to him. The pretence that Pompey was on his way to Spain through North Africa could no longer be maintained. The enormous power that Pompey was building up at the other end of the world had less reality for the local tribes than Caesar's tangible presence, and when Caesar began fighting the river itself like Achilles in the *Iliad*, Afranius and Petreius decided that the time had come to leave Ilerda and withdraw into the Celtiberian highlands. There the terrain would neutralize Caesar's enormous superiority in cavalry, reinforcements and supplies would be readily available both locally and from Varro, and 'the name of Caesar was still only dimly known' among tribes which Caesar divided into only two categories: 'for those which had been conquered in the Sertorian war feared the name and authority of the absent Pompey, and those which had stayed loyal were devoted to him for his great benefactions'.

Caesar's battle against the river took the form of digging a series of huge channels to divert part of the water and make the main stream fordable at a point only three miles above his camp. As the work could be done from only one side of the river the Pompeians could not prevent it as they might have prevented the building of a bridge, and once Caesar's formidable cavalry could cross the river almost as quickly and easily as the Pompeians instead of facing a twenty-two-mile march to the first bridge, Ilerda would virtually lose its main sources of fresh forage and fodder. But while the Caesarians were digging for victory three miles up the Segre, the citizens of Octogesa some thirty miles to the south were collecting hundreds of boats and fastening them together to make a floating bridge that could carry the whole Pompeian army to the safety of the highlands across the Ebro. The Pompeians began their withdrawal at a time when only Caesar's cavalry had proved able to cross the ford, and that with great difficulty, but they had reckoned without the extraordinary tenacity of Caesar's hardened veterans. The weaker men and one legion were left to guard the camp, and with the help of the cavalry and lines of pack-animals strung out above and below the crossing point the rest of Caesar's army succeeded in crossing to the eastern bank and began the pursuit.

The Pompeians had a good start, but they were slowed down by the need to fight constant rearguard actions against Caesar's cavalry, and the pursuing legions caught them up when they were only five miles from safety. If only they had reached the narrow defiles that would have taken them securely across a mountainous watershed down to the Ebro and their waiting bridge of boats, further pursuit would have been ineffective. As it was, the Pompeians were as exhausted as their pursuers, and both armies pitched camp for the night on nearby hills. According to Caesar it was a fatal mistake for the Pompeians not to have struggled on and reached the passes, but his own narrative reveals that they planned to steal a march on him under cover of darkness, and were prevented from doing so only by his lucky interception of a watering-party which disclosed the plan. By ordering his own trumpeters to sound the order to break camp Caesar signified to the Pompeian generals that their silent departure was no longer secret, and they decided to remain where they were until morning rather than face a night engagement. Moreover they had their baggage-train with them whereas the Caesarians were marching light, and they were confident that the enemy 'could not hold out for long against privation'.

The next day was devoted to reconnaissance by both sides. The Pompeian army was firmly entrenched on the shortest and easiest route between Caesar and the safety of the mountains, and when the following day dawned to reveal the Caesarians breaking camp and then marching off in a different direction, Afranius and Petreius congratulated themselves on the apparent success of their decision to stay where they were. But the enemy was wheeling round to outflank them, and though this involved a much longer march over more difficult terrain, the Pompeians' more level ground made them prey to Caesar's cavalry. The race to the mountains was won by the enemy, whom they found drawn up across their line of march. In an attempt to secure an alternative route to the Ebro across a ridge Afranius sent his light-armed cohorts to seize a commanding height, but Caesar's ubiquitous cavalry was upon them before they could reach the safety of the hills, and they were annihilated piecemeal before the eyes of both armies after a long and desperate resistance.

A single day had reversed the positions. It was impossible for the Pompeians to stay where they were on a waterless hill but to advance would be futile when all the passes through the hills were sealed off by Caesar's army, and they could not even return to their former camp without giving Caesar the chance to bring them to battle with superior forces on superior ground. But despite his own men's demands for a battle, Caesar was still not prepared to risk it with only an equality of legions, and since his great superiority in cavalry had made hunger and demoralization his allies, he let them fight for him instead. The Pompeians were therefore able to return to their camp without a battle, but though their baggage-train was there and they were able to secure access to water by running a line of earthworks from the camp to the source of supply, foraging was hopeless against Caesar's cavalry, and the provisions they had brought with them were running dangerously low. The legionaries still had a few days' supply of corn with them, but the auxiliaries had none, and began defecting in considerable numbers to Caesar who had pitched his camp nearby and received them with his usual cordiality. And soon it seemed that another Pompeian army would capitulate without a fight. While the

two generals were out supervising the earthworks, there was fraterniza-
tion between the hostile camps. Semi-official deputations passed between
them to negotiate terms, and the full horror of civil war was revealed
in the mutual hospitality of friends and even relations in the rival armies.
Afranius himself was inclined to give up an increasingly hopeless struggle
against a guarantee of security for himself and his army and a promise
that they would not be required to fight against Pompey, but he had reckoned without Petreius, whose tenacity in the face of defeat was as fierce
as Caesar's own. For when Petreius returned to find that he had been
fortifying what looked like a holiday-camp, he exploded with fury at the
army's cowardice:

> 'You soldiers who forget your country's claims,
> Unmindful of the name your standards bear,
> If now your arms no longer can uphold
> The Senate's cause and win you lasting fame
> By freeing Rome as Caesar's conquerors,
> You can at least be conquered for her sake.
> While hands hold swords and fate is still obscure,
> While blood remains to flow from many a wound,
> Will you prostrate yourselves before a master's feet,
> Bear standards which you once condemned, beseech
> An equal treatment with his other slaves? ...
> It seems you now regard our oath as cheap
> That binds us to a lawful cause and gives
> You hope of pardon. Alas that honour dies
> So foul a death! Even now great Pompey works
> To raise the world in arms and summons kings
> To serve Rome's cause, unknowing yet
> That we desert him here in Spain, and have
> Perhaps already made his life a clause
> In shameful treaties with Rome's enemy.'

That Lucan's poetic imagination was cramped by authenticity is
decidedly unlikely, but whatever Petreius really said he certainly produced a revolution of sentiment which he drove home by leading his personal bodyguard through the camp and slaughtering every Caesarian
soldier he could lay his hands on. He shamed his colleague back to loyalty
(if indeed the tradition of Afranius' disloyalty is more than vindictiveness
enshrined for the deception of posterity in Caesar's memoirs). He made
every officer and man from Afranius downwards swear a solemn oath
'not to desert the army or take measures for their own safety apart from
the rest'. He ordered all Caesarians who had been hidden by their friends

to be produced at headquarters for public execution, and though some were saved by friends who smuggled them out of the camp at night, enough were put to death to 'remove all prospect of immediate surrender'. But having recovered the will to fight on, the Pompeians still had to find a way to a well-supplied stronghold, and with their passage to the Ebro now blocked the choice seemed to lie between a dash back to Ilerda or the much longer march to Tarraco, the present-day Tarragona on the Mediterranean coast some fifty miles to the south-east. Maritime Tarraco would obviously have been better at this stage than depleted Ilerda, but when any distance was too far, over fifty miles was inconceivable. They therefore settled for Ilerda, broke camp, and set out on a nightmarish march dogged by Caesar's legions and continually harried by his cavalry against which their own was now helpless.

Progress was slow and painful. Going uphill was not too bad because the terrain favoured the retreating army, but descending slopes and crossing valleys required costly rearguard actions to try to disperse the pursuing cavalry for long enough to enable the main body of the army to make a dash for the next defensible position. After four miles of this gruelling process the Pompeian generals attempted to steal a march by stratagem. They pretended to begin fortifying a camp on a suitable hill, watched with satisfaction as Caesar began doing the same, and suddenly marched off again as soon as Caesar's cavalry had disappeared on foraging duties. But Caesar was determined not to lose contact. He recalled his cavalry and foragers but set out with his legions without waiting for them or taking any baggage which would impair his speed. The packs could be brought up later. The important thing was to catch the Pompeians, who soon found themselves so hard pressed from the rear that they were forced to make a stand, and dug in once more. Caesar entrenched a camp close by, and though the Pompeians improved their position by extending their fortifications throughout the night and the next day, they secured a military advantage only at the price of moving further from their water-supply. Caesar in the meantime began to fence them in with siege-works, and when they became dangerously short of water on the following day, nearly the whole army marched to the river to fetch it while a garrison held the camp. But desperate as they were, they no longer talked of surrender while there seemed a chance of a fair fight, and on the third day they drew their battle-lines before the camp. According to Caesar it was merely a sham to halt his siege-works, but his explanation is a transparent excuse for his own failure to accept their soldierly challenge. He drew up his own lines 'in order not to appear to have shunned a battle against the general sentiment of his troops', but he kept them on the hill-side in front of his camp, and the pains which he takes to justify his refusal to meet the Pompeians on the intervening plain reveal a clear embarrassment. Militarily of course he was right not to risk a pitched battle even with superior forces when hunger would do his work for him in another day or two, but he was always sensitive to any suggestion of cowardice, and he was genuinely afraid of losing.

The next day it was all over. Unable to provoke Caesar into giving battle anywhere but on a hopelessly unfavourable position the Pompeians tried to ford the falling river, but Caesar sent his cavalry and light-armed troops across first and gave them no more chance to flee than to fight except on terms of certain annihilation. And since there was now nothing they could do that would be of the slightest advantage to Pompey or the Senate, their generals begged Caesar for a private conference. Caesar granted the conference but not the privacy. If they had anything to say, they must say it openly between the two armies, and that is what they did. Afranius begged for an honourable surrender in words which Caesar gloatingly terms 'humble and submissive'. In return he was treated to a lengthy justification of Caesar's decision to make war, but the result was all he could have hoped for. No Pompeian was to be punished for having done his duty. The generals were to go free, and the whole army was to be demobilized. It was another example of Caesar's famous clemency that was common sense paraded as virtue. These veteran troops of Pompey's Spanish army were not like the government's recruits which had surrendered in Italy only weeks or even days after being enrolled. The *esprit de corps* which they had developed over five years of living and fighting together as Pompey's army in Spain made it dangerous if not impossible to incorporate them in Caesar's army. Any terms of surrender requiring them to turn their arms against their former commander-in-chief might well have provoked them to a final struggle, inevitably suicidal but still damaging to Caesar militarily, morally and quite unnecessarily now that they were prepared to be demobilized.

It was 2 August, and according to Caesar's memoirs only forty days after he had first arrived at Ilerda. His victory was a triumph for bigger forces under a better general, but his opponents were not unworthy of him, and he had come nearer to disaster in this campaign than at any time in his career. For without his timely reinforcement in cavalry and supplies it is doubtful that he would have extricated himself from Ilerda and improbable that he could have prevented the Pompeians from reaching the Ebro if he had done so. But history is not what might have been. The shock-waves from the surrender of five Pompeian legions north of the Ebro shattered old loyalties throughout the peninsula, and though Varro still had two legions and numerous auxiliaries in the further province, the natives refused to continue a hopeless struggle, city-gates closed against him, and he surrendered too. Both provinces had fallen into Caesar's lap like ripe plums in a gale, and after appointing a new governor and holding a few suitably imposing victory-parades in important cities, he was free to return to Italy and carry the war to the East without fear of a counter-invasion from the West.

On his way back through the south of France he also received the surrender of Massilia, which had been the object of one of the most stubbornly contested sieges in Roman military history. For over two months the Massilians had resisted the efforts of three legions to batter, shell, overrun or undermine their walls. But eventually the besiegers constructed a six-storey artillery-tower of brick, and by using its commanding height to cover hundreds of sappers advancing to the base of the walls under a protective wooden tortoise fireproofed with earth, they succeeded in dislodging some of the foundations and bringing down part of the fortifications. The Massilians then asked for an armistice until they might surrender to Caesar himself on his return from Spain, but even this proved to be a case of diplomacy carrying on war, for they observed the truce only for long enough to strengthen their weakened defences and let the besiegers grow careless with inactivity. They then made a sortie and succeeded in destroying the tower and all the siege-works within artillery cover of their own walls. But the struggle was hopeless. The Massilians had gained time in which to pray for the miracle that alone could save them, but nothing more miraculous occurred than the speed with which the besiegers constructed new earthworks of such indestructibility that the defenders finally despaired, Domitius escaped by sea, and the citizens renewed their offer to surrender on the same terms. But this time they were disarmed while waiting for Caesar's clemency, which left them alive and free yet deprived of something more important than the territory and colonies that were taken away from them. For the freedom held on sufferance is not the same as the freedom claimed as a right by a people capable of defending it by force of arms, and even if the Massilians had been able to keep their lands and colonies, they would not have fought for nothing.

How Pompey reacted to the news of the capitulation of his army in Spain and the fall of Massilia we do not know. If his better nature regretted the need to pay a higher price in Roman blood for a victory which he might have won without further effort if Caesar had succumbed to arms, illness, assassination or any other act of man or god in the West, he may nevertheless have felt a certain satisfaction that fate was reserving his rival for destruction at the hands of his creator. And since Caesar's complete sucess in the West was balanced by complete disaster in the Adriatic and in Africa, Pompey's confidence in ultimate victory was in no way diminished by the sum total of the news that reached his headquarters in northern Greece in 49.

The campaign in the Adriatic and on the coast of Illyricum was evidently as much a triumph for Pompey's naval superiority as Caesar's Spanish campaign had been a victory for superior land forces, but there is unfortunately no similarly detailed or even coherent account in our surviving sources from which to recover with certainty much more than the final statistics. Before leaving for Spain Caesar had ordered the construction of two new war-fleets in Italy, one on the Adriatic sea, the other on the Tyrrhenian, and had appointed Dolabella and Hortensius as their admirals. In the meantime it appears that Dolabella had been collecting troop-ships, and as soon as he had a sufficient force he convoyed an army under Antony's brother, Gaius Antonius, across the Adriatic, partly to establish a bridgehead on the Illyrian coast for Caesar's future invasion of Greece and partly to monitor Pompey's movements in case he decided to launch a counter-invasion of Italy in Caesar's absence. Dolabella seems to have established bases on the mainland, Antonius on one of the many offshore islands that pepper the Dalmatian coast, most probably 'Black Corcyra', the modern Korčula, which lies more or less midway between Dubrovnik and Split. But they did not escape the attentions of Pompey's Adriatic fleet for long. We learn from Orosius that Dolabella was the first to encounter Pompey's admirals Octavius and Libo, and though he gives us no details of the battle or the size of the forces involved, the Pompeian victory was unequivocal since Dolabella 'was stripped of all his forces and fled to Antonius'. Antonius in the meantime seems to have been reinforced to the extent of two legions and the co-operation of Hortensius' Tyrrhenian fleet which now sailed round into the Adriatic 'to help in a concerted action', but they only made his disaster all the greater. The Pompeian admirals blockaded him on Korčula, and having shattered the enemy fleet they let starvation and the unfriendly natives reduce his army which now had no hope of relief. In desperation his men constructed rafts in an attempt to reach the mainland, but only a few got away, and Antonius himself finally surrendered with fifteen cohorts, which Libo took to Dyrrachium for incorporation in Pompey's army.

Although we have so little information about these important campaigns, we can at least avoid the historians' usual trap of misunderstanding the one bizarre incident which happens to be recorded in any detail – the fate of one of the rafts intercepted by the Pompeian navy. The Cilician sailors in Pompey's fleet – presumably former pirates who had not lost their old skills during their peaceful resettlement – had snared this wretched craft with underwater cables, but when they closed in to secure it in the morning, they were confronted with a floating heap of several hundred corpses. The story of this mass suicide pact is dramatized most colourfully by a passage of Lucan in which purple predominates, and it concludes with a tribute to their devotion to Caesar and an expression of the world's amazement

That any leader should command such loyalty.

But it is not too cynical to observe that fear of the law is more likely to have been the beginning of this folly. It was not that Pompey's clemency was less great than Caesar's, for Pompey now incorporated the fifteen captured cohorts in his legions as readily as Caesar had enrolled the government's recruits who had surrendered to him in Italy. And it is Lucan himself who unwittingly suggests the most probable explanation of the terror which drove these men to prefer the certainty of a quick death to the uncertainty of surrender. He mentions that they were all Opitergians, and since Opitergium is a town of the Transpadane Gauls, we need only remember the bitter political opposition to their proposed and covert enfranchisement by Caesar to realize what they were afraid of. Almost certainly these men were not Roman citizens (or citizens whose credentials would have been accepted by the government in exile), and though there had been general revulsion in the Senate when the consul Marcus Marcellus had publicly scourged a Transpadane visitor to Rome as part of his anti-Caesarian political campaign in 51, feelings had hardened since the outbreak of war. The unhappy Opitergians may well have feared that a Senate embittered by exile would devise some far worse punishment to make an example of them and demonstrate contempt for Caesar's illegalities, and they preferred the certainty of a quick death at each other's hands 'like the seed which Cadmus sowed'. But if Caesar derived some propaganda benefits from this heroic madness that could be interpreted as extraordinary devotion, it was his only consolation from a disastrous campaign in which he had lost forty ships, a legion and a half captured, and possibly as many men killed.

Such welcome news from Illyricum must have done much to counter the depressing effect of the reports reaching Pompey's camp from Spain and Gaul, and the news from Africa did even more, not least because it recorded a suitably bloody end to the career of Curio whose political defection to Caesar in the tribunate of 50 had never been forgiven. At first it had seemed that Curio could not go wrong. He secured Sicily without out a fight in the wake of Cato's withdrawal, and having organized the island's defence, seen to the security of the corn-supply and collected sufficient ships, he embarked two of his four legions and some five hundred horse for Africa with the intention of wresting the third and greatest of Rome's corn-producing provinces from Attius Varus who was holding it for the government. Varus was a former governor of Africa who had gone to take command of his old province after his recruiting effort in Picenum had been overwhelmed by the speed of Caesar's invasion of Italy earlier in the year. According to Caesar's memoirs he had gone there of his own accord, but while it is true that he was not the Senate's appointment to the governorship of Africa and that he drove the official governor out when that worthy finally arrived, it is more than likely that he acted with the blessing of Pompey.

At any rate it was Varus whom Curio found defiant in the provincial capital of Utica, but despite the strength of Utica itself and the fortified camp which Varus had constructed adjoining the city-walls, Curio seemed destined to do for Caesar what the young Pompey had done for Sulla, and in as short a time. Even on the sea-voyage his escorting warships had dispersed a Pompeian squadron and captured its flagship. When he then marched his army to Utica and sent his cavalry to plunder the terrified civilians struggling to carry their possessions into the safety of the town, he scored an immediate victory against the thousand Numidian horsemen whom Varus sent out to try to protect them. He then ordered the merchant-ships in the harbour to ferry all the cargoes destined for Utica across to his own position, and since the arrival of his own warships ensured compliance with his instructions, he struck a double blow against Varus and seemed to be well on his way towards deserving his troops' premature salutation of 'Imperator'. But the very fact that an army was so premature in its congratulations revealed its potential weakness. Curio's troops were not veterans like the legions which Caesar had taken to Spain, nor were they fighting alongside veteran legions of great loyalty and experience. They had been enrolled only a few months ago in the Senate's name by officers who were now with Varus, and while only a few defected at once, many more began wavering as they weighed the news of Caesar's distant victory in Spain against the immediate threat of King Juba, who was reported to be sending or bringing reinforcements to Varus. But Curio acted quickly to try to defeat Varus before the royal army could arrive. After sending his own cavalry to intercept the advance guard of Juba's horse and foot and challenging Varus to a pitched battle, which the latter accepted in the hope of wholesale defection, he succeeded in defeating Varus in the field and driving his army back into Utica. He then prepared to follow up his victory with a siege, and since the citizens of Utica had none of the Massilians' freedom to defend, they began badgering Varus to surrender until messengers arrived from the king himself to tell them to hold on.

King Juba rejoiced to hear that Varus' failure to defeat Curio 'had left the glory of the campaign for his own arms'. He was not only a hereditary friend of Pompey but a personal enemy of Curio ever since the latter had proposed legislation to annex his kingdom in 50. Indeed his only concern was that Curio might be afraid to meet him and fight the pitched battle which would give him revenge. He therefore sent a detachment of his army ahead under another general and spread the word that he had himself been recalled with his main forces to deal with trouble on his borders. Curio believed what he wanted to believe, and instead of waiting for the other two legions which he had summoned from Sicily, he rushed to meet what now appeared to be a manageable army, and was in the trap before he realized it. The king's superiority in cavalry put Curio's legions in exactly the same predicament as Pompey's in Spain except that Juba, unlike Caesar, had no intention of offering surrender. He surrounded the Roman army, wore them out, and slaughtered them in so tight a square that the corpses are said to have remained standing like stooks of hay. Only a few horsemen escaped to warn the troops which Curio had left guarding his camp. They tried to persuade local merchants and fishermen to carry them off by sea, but the few boats that responded were so overloaded that many of them capsized, and the unscrupulous captains of others discharged their human cargo into the sea after stripping them of their possessions. The majority of Curio's garrison threw themselves on Varus' mercy, but though Varus accepted their surrender, he was himself at the mercy of his royal ally who arrived to 'claim them as his booty'. Juba put nearly all of them to death, wrote a glowing report of his victory to Pompey, and returned to his kingdom in a state of high satisfaction which was shared by Pompey and the Senate when they heard not only that Africa was secured by the annihilation of two enemy legions but that Curio himself was dead. For Curio's tribunate of 50 had made him as hateful to Caesar's political enemies at Rome as to King Juba in his threatened kingdom, and it seemed to both that he had met his just deserts:

> What profit now to Curio for having stirred
> The frenzied forum, stronghold of the tribunes' power,
> In which his banner claimed the people's right
> To arm the nations of the world? What profit now
> To have betrayed the Senate's rights, to have compelled
> A man to meet the father of his wife in arms –
> A battle he would never see?

Pompey himself had not seen any action in 49. While Caesar had been in Spain Pompey had devoted his energies to the mobilization of forces in the East, and Caesar catalogues his opponent's achievements with an admiration which needed no dissembling since it enhanced the glory of his own ultimate victory:

In a year of peace Pompey had gathered a large fleet from Asia and the Cyclades, from Corcyra, Athens, Pontus, Bithynia, Syria, Cilicia, Phoenicia and Egypt. He had put in hand a massive ship-building programme in all places. He had requisitioned a large sum of money from Asia and Syria, from all the kings, potentates and tetrarchs, and from the free peoples of Achaea. He had compelled the tax-farming corporations of all the provinces which were under his control to pay over their revenues to him. He had made up nine legions of Roman citizens, comprising the five which he had transhipped from Italy, one of veterans from Cilicia which he had formed by amalgamating the two legions there and renamed the Twin Legion, one newly enrolled from veterans who had settled in Greece and Macedonia after being demobilized by their former generals, and two from Asia which the consul Lentulus had raised. He had also distributed among these legions by way of supplement a large number of men of Thessaly, Boeotia, Achaea and Epirus, and he had mingled with them the men who had surrendered under Gaius Antonius in Illyricum. He was also expecting two more legions from Syria. He had archers from Crete, Sparta, Pontus, Syria and other states to the number of three thousand. He had two cohorts of slingers, six hundred strong, and his cavalry numbered over seven thousand.

There is no need to doubt the accuracy of these statistics, or even the estimates of five hundred or six hundred ships given by our other sources for Pompey's entire navy as long as we remember that not all these ships were necessarily first-raters; but Caesar must not be allowed to get away with his exaggerated impression of the non-Italian preponderance in Pompey's army. There were certainly large numbers of Greek and Asiatic auxiliaries attached to Pompey's legions, but Appian makes it clear that 'Pompey did not intend to use all these native troops for fighting: some were employed in garrison duties, in building fortifications and in other services for the Italian soldiers in order that none of the latter need be kept away from the battlefield'. Similarly with the seven thousand cavalry Caesar lists the contributions of native kings and dynasts, but when their total comes to 3,600 he dismisses the rest simply as 'men of other nations and states' without mentioning that the single biggest contributor was Rome herself. For Pompey had with him the greater part of Rome's aristocracy – the sons of senators and other Roman knights whom Plutarch calls 'the flower of Rome and Italy, pre-eminent in lineage, wealth and virtue' – and since Caesar sought to present Pompey to posterity as the leader of Oriental nations against Italians, he chose to suppress the fact that in cavalry at least he was himself far more dependent on Gauls and

Germans than Pompey was on Greeks and Asiatics, even if it is true that

> So many kings had never served one man before,
> Nor had so many nations met, so different
> In dress or so diverse in speech.

The list of royal contributors to Pompey's cavalry reads like a roll-call of the kings and rulers who held their thrones by grace of Pompey's great settlement of the East, and some of them not only sent contingents to his army but commanded them in person or sent their sons.

> Deiotarus had brought six hundred Galatians, and Ariobarzanes five hundred from Cappadocia. Cotys had provided the same number from Thrace and sent his son Sadala. From Macedonia there were two hundred under the command of Rhascypolis, a man of excellent courage. Pompey's own son [Gnaeus] had brought with his fleet five hundred more from Egypt, mainly Gauls and Germans whom Gabinius had left as a garrison with King Ptolemy. Pompey himself had collected eight hundred from his own slaves and herdsmen. Tarcondarius Castor and Domnilaus had provided three hundred from Gallograecia, one of them coming in person with his men, the other sending his son. From Syria two hundred had been sent by Antiochus of Commagene, on whom Pompey had bestowed large rewards, and among them were many mounted archers. To these Pompey had added Dardani and Bessi, partly mercenaries, partly secured by his authority or influence, also Macedonians, Thessalians and men of other nations and states to complete the number of seven thousand mentioned above.

To have arranged not only to concentrate such massive and miscellaneous forces in Thessaly but to pay, feed and train them is clear proof that Pompey had lost none of his organizational ability or capacity for staff work, and yet he was no more remote from his men now than thirty-four years ago when he had stood in the market-place of Auximum and enrolled his first recruits for Sulla. If he had to spend enormous amounts of time hearing reports, issuing orders, receiving ambassadors, settling disputes and using all his qualities of leadership to redirect the natural rivalry of proud rulers and Romans into a more productive competition to serve him best, he not only organized the training of his men but trained with them, and Cicero could have had no more worries about Pompey's health when he arrived in Thessaly and saw the supreme commander in action in the great training-camp which he had set up at Beroea, some forty-five miles south-west of Thessalonica. 'People flocked there,' says Appian, 'as keen to see Pompey's military exercises as a theatrical spectacle', and Plutarch explains why:

> When Pompey exercised his army, he did not sit idly by but took part in all their exercises himself, as if he had been in the prime of life. And indeed

it gave a great boost to the men's morale when they saw Pompey the Great, who was now fifty-eight [sic], nevertheless competing in full armour as an infantryman and then riding with the cavalry, drawing his sword without difficulty at full gallop and sheathing it again with practised ease. Likewise in hurling the javelin he not only displayed accuracy but also vigour in the length of his cast, which many of the young men could not surpass.

And this was not time wasted. Pompey had no higher priority than forging his miscellaneous legions into a disciplined army capable of standing up to veteran legions which had served Caesar in so many campaigns over so many years. They needed drill and the confidence inspired by exceptional leadership, and Pompey, who turned fifty-seven in September, provided them with both.

When Caesar returned to Rome at about the beginning of December 49 he took the offensive in a bogus battle of legalities. With the help of the praetor Lepidus, who procured a plebiscite authorizing the appointment, he became dictator, and though he held the office for only eleven days it gave him the authority to hold the elections for the consulships of the following year. He stood in person with Servilius Isauricus as his running-mate, and not surprisingly they won, thus making the most of the constitutional advantages of being in Rome. For while the senators in exile could realistically claim that they were the only true Senate, they could not pretend that the people were anywhere but in Rome, and consequently they could not hold elections. The best they could do was 'to employ the same officials as before but as promagistrates rather than magistrates', reaffirm the invalidity of all political activity in Rome, and maintain the formality and protocol of a meeting held towards the end of the year, when the consul Lentulus gave his retiring speech:

'Brave senators of Rome,
If through your veins still runs the ancient Latian blood,
Consider not the land in which we meet nor all
The miles that stretch between this place and home.
Observe instead the aspect of your glorious throng,
And having power to order what you will, decree
This first of all – a fact already known to kings
And nations numberless – that we the Senate are,
And where we are must State and Empire also be....
In Caesar's Rome the sorrowing buildings stand forlorn,
Her empty mansions grieve, her laws are stilled, her courts
Are closed by our decree of dismal holiday.
The Senate House sees none but those whom we expelled
Before we left, for every member not with us
Is exiled. Today the Senate sits in Thessaly.'

But after a year of civil war the legalities were becoming increasingly blurred, as Dio observes:

> For the following year the Romans had two sets of officials at once. . . . Those in the city had chosen as consuls Caesar and Servilius along with praetors and all the other officers required by law. Those in Thessalonica made no new appointments, although they are reputed to have had two hundred of the Senate and also the consuls with them . . . but employed the same officers as before and merely changed their titles of magistrates to those of promagistrates. . . . Nevertheless the officers were officers of the two parties in name only. In reality Pompey and Caesar were supreme, and though they bore the legal titles of proconsul and consul respectively, their acts were not those which their offices permitted but whatever they themselves pleased.

And Lucan says the same, though less explicitly. For while the introduction to his poetic dramatization of the Senate's meeting in Thessaly stresses how

> That noble body taught the world that Pompey was
> But one of them, not they his partisans . . .

the first thing that Lentulus proposes to his peers after reaffirming their authority seems somewhat incongruous with that avowed aim:

> 'You Senate to whose power no limit can be set,
> Consult the common good, make Pompey now your chief.'
> Then great was their applause for Pompey's name,
> And into Pompey's hands they placed the fate of Rome
> And thus their own with no dissenting voice.

In other words, Pompey at last became commander-in-chief, but if it was sound military sense that the Senate's best general should enter the final trial of strength with the authority to command and not merely recommend other proconsuls to carry out his strategy, the recognition that it would take one autocrat to beat another made the war seem more than ever a simple struggle for power between two men. It seemed less and less a struggle of legitimate government against rebellion or an ideological battle between aristocrats and democrats, establishment and revolutionaries, supporters of the Senate's authority and demagogues, or republicans against a prospective monarch. All these elements were involved, but as the war developed its own dynamic, justification became almost irrelevant: the world was about to witness a duel between the warlords of East and West. And while we cannot be sure what Pompey said in reply to his appointment, he cannot be left to face his supreme

challenge without a speech, and the one which Appian gives him seems
appropriate to the occasion:

'Like us, gentlemen, the Athenians once abandoned Athens for the sake of
freedom when they were fighting against invasion because they believed that
it was not buildings that make a city but men; and after doing this they presently recovered Athens, and made her more renowned than ever. So too our
own ancestors abandoned Rome when the Gauls invaded it, and Camillus
hastened from Ardea and recovered it. All men of good sense know that their
country is wherever they can preserve their liberty. This was what was in our
minds when we sailed here, not as deserters of our native land but in order
to prepare ourselves to defend it gloriously against one who has long conspired
against it and suddenly seized it with the help of bribe-takers. You have decreed
him a public enemy, yet now he sends governors to take charge of your provinces and makes other appointments over the city and throughout Italy – such
is the audacity with which he deprives the Roman people of their own government! And if he does these things while still at war and struggling on in fear
of the punishment which we shall, please God, inflict upon him, what cruelty,
what violence will he be likely to abstain from if he wins? He has accomplices
in committing his crimes against our beloved country, and they are men who
have been bought with the money that he obtained from our province of Gaul
and who prefer to be his slaves than his equals.

'I have not failed, nor will I ever fail, to fight with you and for you. I give
you my services both as soldier and general. If I have any experience in war,
if it has been my good fortune to remain unvanquished to this day, I pray the
gods to continue all these blessings in our present need and to grant that my
destiny may prove as happy for my country now that she is endangered as
when I was extending her empire. We must trust in the gods and in the justification of our war, which has for its noble and just object the defence of the
ancestral constitution. In addition to this we may rely on the greatness of the
forces which we now have both on land and sea: they are increasing all the
time and will increase still more as soon as we come into action. For we may
say that of the nations of the East and around the Black Sea all, both Greek
and barbarian, are with us. And all the kings who are friends of the Romans
or of myself are supplying us with forces, arms, supplies and all the other
necessities of war. Come then to the task that lies ahead with a spirit worthy
of your country, of yourselves and of me – remembering always the arrogant
ambition of Caesar and acting swiftly to carry out my commands.'

Whatever Pompey really said to the Senate and army at the end of
December was no doubt received with Appian's 'vociferous applause and
a clamour to be led to do whatever he wanted done', but for what that
was we must look to Caesar. 'Pompey decided to put his army into winter-
quarters in Dyrrachium, Apollonia and the other towns of the Adriatic
coast', and while he began marching westwards from Thessaly along the
Egnatian Way, his fleet was already deployed throughout the Adriatic

and Ionian seas under the overall command of Bibulus, who stationed himself on Corcyra, the present-day Corfu. Curiously both Appian and Dio maintain that Pompey wintered in Thessaly and neglected to defend the coast against the possibility of an invasion by Caesar which he considered unlikely until the following spring, but their judgements are called into question by their mistake over his movements. It would indeed have been remiss of Pompey if he had stayed where they say for the winter, but the fact that he left his comfortable and well-supplied camp in Thessaly to distribute his army in the coastal towns, which will clearly have been provisioned for the purpose well in advance, proves that he was certainly not discounting the possibility that Caesar would try to cross to Greece before spring and that he had been organizing his precautions for some time. For Pompey knew well enough that an inactive winter in Italy would only increase Caesar's difficulties, not least in terms of supply. Pompey had had a whole summer in which to stockpile corn 'from Thessaly, Asia, Egypt, Crete, Cyrene and other districts', to quote Caesar's own catalogue of Pompey's sources of supply in which he could evidently not bring himself to include Africa which Curio had failed to secure. Caesar in contrast had found it necessary to make an emergency distribution of corn 'to the starving people' the moment he returned to Rome, and if the capital was running short already (and the calendar was two months ahead of the seasons), he cannot have relished the prospect of struggling to feed not only the capital's civilian population but his own vast armies if they were to stay inactive in Italy throughout the long winter that stretched ahead.

Moreover it would be mistaken to suppose that Pompey's dispositions of land and naval forces were entirely defensive. He knew from Cicero and all the other people who had joined him from Italy during the year that discontent was rife among the occupying forces, and even if he had made allowances for the exaggerations of the latecomers anxious to ingratiate themselves by telling him what he most wanted to hear, the news of the mutiny of Caesar's veteran legions at Placentia in November had probably come through by now. Admittedly this mutiny had been suppressed, but if even a veteran legion could contemplate defection, the more recently enrolled ones would be even less reliable, and Pompey wanted to be in a position to capitalize on any general rising against Caesar in Italy now that he had accumulated sufficient forces and the navy that could tranship them. That is not to say that he was definitely planning to invade Italy even in the spring if nothing had happened in the meantime. He would obviously prefer Caesar to face the perils of transporting his army across the sea and either succumb to a superior navy or escape destruction at sea only to find himself cut off from supplies and reinforcements on a coast defended by Pompey himself with nearly all his forces. But Pompey wanted to be prepared for any eventuality, and though Caesar may not have known that Pompey was already marching west to his destined positions on the Adriatic coast at the beginning of January 48, he would probably have guessed that he would soon be doing so. But whether Pompey would have taken the same risks in Caesar's position is less certain, for when he was still about seventy miles east of Dyrrachium he was surprised to hear that Caesar had sailed from Brundisium on 4 January and had landed amazingly intact on a remote part of the coast some eighty miles to the south, from where he was already advancing northwards to threaten Apollonia and Dyrrachium itself. The war in the East had begun.

# 8

# UNLAURELLED IMPERATOR

Today would victory have been with the enemy if they had
had a victor in command.
Plutarch, *Life of Pompey*, 65

A poet can usefully remind a historian that of Vergil's two components
of war, 'the arms and the man', the latter is not without more tender
passions:

> So strong the bond of married love which tightly binds
> Two gentle hearts that even Pompey found himself
> Made anxious and afraid of battle by his love.
> His wife alone he wished to save from that fell stroke
> That overhung the world and destiny of Rome.
> With mind made up he yet could find no words,
> Preferring sweet delays, postponing what must come,
> And stealing brief reprieves from fate. But when the dawn
> Began to banish sleep, and edging closer in their bed
> Cornelia clasped her husband's breast so full of cares
> And sought his lips, he turned from her to try to hide
> The tears that wet his cheeks, and she fell back in fear,
> Amazed to find great Pompey weeping silently.
> He sighed and said, 'Dear wife, more dear to me than life
> When life was sweet and not the drudge I find it now,
> The day has come that I put off too long and yet
> Not long enough – the day that we must part. By me
> The war with Caesar must be fought but not by you,
> For Lesbos knows no war and thither you must go.
> No, not a word entreating me to change my mind!
> I have already spurned my own heart's tender pleas,
> And we shall not be long apart. The crisis comes,
> The mighty crash of falling fortunes will resound
> Throughout the world: for you it must suffice to hear
> Reports of all the dangers Pompey must incur.'

But if it was dramatically satisfactory to Lucan that Pompey should send Cornelia to safety only at the last minute before joining battle with Caesar, it is much more likely to have been at the end of the calendar year, when Pompey was preparing to leave his summer camp in Thessaly and the consuls had called the last great meeting of the exiled Senate before their term expired. As Pompey began marching westwards to winter-quarters on the Adriatic coast, his younger son Sextus was probably escorting Cornelia and other women and children in a naval convoy from Thessalonica to Lesbos, which was an appropriate haven for the wife of Pompey the Great. It was at the city of Mytilene that Pompey had listened to the contest of poets celebrating the greatness of his conquests as he returned from the East in 62. He had declared the city free in honour of Theophanes, his Greek secretary, historian, confidant and now prefect of engineers, who had been born there. And he had taken its theatre as the model for the much grander pleasure-palace which he had constructed in Rome. But according to Lucan the charms of that lovely island in the north-east Aegean where burning Sappho loved and sung were lost on Cornelia, for she too burned, though with a more wholesome passion:

> How often, dulled by sleep, she clasped the empty couch
> With cheated arms, and sought her husband in the dark,
> But though the fires of love consumed her inmost heart
> She would not toss her eager limbs across the bed
> But kept from touching Pompey's side in fear that he
> Was lost to her ...

For Pompey the separation was easier because he had no time to think about it once he heard that Caesar had landed safely with seven legions and six hundred horse at a place called Palaeste on the treacherous coast of north-west Epirus above Corfu. According to Caesar the news was carried to Pompey by none other than Vibullius, who had become Caesar's prisoner-of-war twice in one year after surrendering first at Corfinium and then in Spain. Caesar claims that he sent Vibullius to Pompey with peace-proposals the moment he landed, and since Vibullius was anxious to warn Pompey of Caesar's arrival, Caesar gives the impression that he had been really rather sporting in making Pompey aware of his landing in Epirus – just as if Pompey's own coastguards or the garrison at Oricum to the north would not have sent messengers to the commander-in-chief the moment Caesar's ships had been sighted. Caesar was surely attempting to retard Pompey's counter-offensive, for however remote the possibility that Pompey would take his peace-initiatives at face value, it was worth a try to secure a breathing-space in which the ships which he had immediately sent back to Italy might return with the rest of his army.

As soon as he knew of Caesar's landing, Pompey guessed at once what the enemy would try to do. Caesar could not have brought much with him in the way of provisions, and his only chance of maintaining so large an army on so barren and hostile a coast was to move rapidly northwards and try to seize some of the supplies which Pompey had accumulated in the maritime cities which were to have been his winter-quarters – first Oricum, then Apollonia, and then Dyrrachium itself. It was not long before Pompey heard that he was right. Caesar had set out for Oricum on the very day he had landed, and after a night's march of extreme difficulty and chaos he arrived before its walls the next day to demand its surrender. The officer commanding Pompey's garrison had closed the gates, but Caesar maintains that the Greek inhabitants refused to fight against 'authority conferred by the Roman people' and dutifully admitted the consul, presumably without considering for a moment what seven desperate legions might otherwise have done to them. But while Caesar found valuable supplies at Oricum, he did not have everything his own way, and it is interesting that we learn of his frustration only from Appian. When Caesar mentions that there was a naval squadron of eighteen Pompeian ships in the harbour, it is only to observe their cowardice in failing to put out to sea and fight his own escort of twelve. Appian explains that they were guarding a convoy of Pompey's corn-ships, and when Oricum surrendered, they scuttled all those they could not save before withdrawing in good order to Dyrrachium.

But the loss of Oricum was bad news for Pompey, and the loss of Apollonia was even worse. When Pompey heard that the citizens of that larger city had similarly failed to support his local commander against Caesar's legions – or, as Caesar has it, 'against the decision of the whole of Italy and the Roman people' – he redoubled his efforts to reach Dyrrachium in the knowledge that Caesar would be doing the same thing. 'If only we can get possession of Dyrrachium,' Caesar told his troops, 'we shall have in our hands all the things they have collected by the labour of a whole summer', and Appian describes the race that ensued as Pompey led over thirty-five thousand legionaries, numerous auxiliary troops and several thousand cavalry westwards along the Egnatian Way while Caesar pushed northwards from Apollonia with perhaps fifteen thousand legionaries and six hundred horse:

If either army saw any dust or fire or smoke in the distance, they thought it was caused by the other, and they strove like athletes in a race. They did not allow themselves time for food or sleep. It was all effort and speed, the shouting of guides leading them by torchlight, and the resulting tumult and fear as the hostile armies drew ever closer. Some of the troops threw away their burdens through sheer exhaustion, others hid in ravines and were left behind, exchanging their fear of the enemy for the rest which the moment craved.

The relief which Pompey felt when he came in sight of Dyrrachium and found it safe needs no emphasis, and when Caesar heard that Pompey had won the race, he advanced no further but fortified a camp on the south side of the River Apsus which separates the territory of Apollonia from that of Dyrrachium. According to Caesar the Pompeian troops had been morally and physically shattered by the speed of their advance 'which had been more like a flight', and it may be true that when Pompey finally pitched camp near Dyrrachium his army needed a vigorous declamation from Labienus to restore its confidence. All the same it was not an army that Caesar was prepared to attack, and when Pompey advanced to the Apsus and pitched camp opposite Caesar on the northern bank, he found Caesar disinclined to fight. According to Dio's account Pompey did try to cross the river and withdrew only because the risk proved unacceptable, but Caesar does not mention any such attempt, and Appian speaks of cavalry skirmishes but no general engagement. If Caesar had offered him a pitched battle on level ground Pompey might have accepted it, but otherwise he was happy to stay where he was in the conviction that time was a better ally to him than to the enemy.

Although Caesar maintains with altruistic humbug that he was concerned to give protection to Apollonia, Oricum and the other communities to his rear 'which had deserved well of him', his decision 'to winter there in tents and wait for the rest of the legions to cross from Italy' is a confession of the real weakness of his position which he sought to disguise by bombarding Pompey with bogus peace-initiatives. Dio rightly suspects that they were specious, though they were more than 'attempts to show that he was neither holding back through fear nor making the first move in war'. If it sounds eminently reasonable for Caesar to send Vibullius with the message that 'this was the one time for making peace, when each had confidence in himself and both seemed equally matched', the statement was clearly untrue, and Pompey was right to treat Caesar's approach as 'another snare'. Pompey was much stronger at this stage. He had a larger force of legionaries, admittedly not a veteran army like Caesar's but nevertheless a trained force whose confidence would increase the longer they saw the master of mobility apparently immobilized by fear. He had massive superiority in cavalry. He had a vast arsenal of supplies at Dyrrachium which could be replenished by sea as fast as he depleted it. He could look forward to the arrival of Scipio from Syria with two experienced legions brought up to strength by drafts of his own veterans and with huge supplies of money from Syria and Asia to pay them. Caesar on the other hand had fewer, if tougher, legionaries, very few cavalry and very little food to keep them all going. Although he had captured Oricum and Apollonia and no doubt filled Apollonia's Treasury with money which he had taken from the Treasury in Rome to pay his men, money was no use if there was nothing to eat. Both towns were cut off from supply by sea, their stocks would soon be exhausted, and it would be many months before the next harvest. Caesar's hopes rested entirely on the arrival of Antony with the legions which he had left behind at Brundisium, for while they would be more mouths to feed, they would give him the military superiority to beat Pompey in the field. But Pompey was confident that his fleet could prevent any reinforcements from reaching Caesar by sea, and he was content to sit still and avoid unnecessary risks when he could do what Caesar himself had eventually done to the army in Spain by letting famine do the fighting for him.

If Pompey had been disappointed that his fleet had not intercepted and sunk Caesar and his seven legions before they had reached Epirus, he was not displeased at the result, which was the division of Caesar's forces by about eighty miles of sea which would not easily be crossed a second time. Now that Caesar had landed, Pompey's fleet could concentrate its vigilance on a much narrower stretch of coast than the hundreds of miles which it had patrolled before. Pompey also knew that his admiral Bibulus would stop at nothing to prevent Antony from crossing with reinforcements from Brundisium, and though Caesar accuses Bibulus of 'carelessness' in allowing him to get through in the first place, he knew as well as Dio 'how much more his own voyage had owed to luck than good management', and he would eventually admit it when trying to hearten his defeated troops with confidence in his lucky star.

Bibulus had been at Corcyra with 110 ships when Caesar had crossed, and as soon as he had word from his coastal patrols, he had put to sea in the hope of intercepting some of the loaded troop-ships – 'only to fall in with them empty', as Caesar records with obvious satisfaction. But Caesar found it less amusing at the time, for Bibulus not only destroyed thirty of his returning transports that were so badly needed to bring the reinforcements but proceeded to maintain so close a blockade of the coast from Korčula in the north to Sazanit in the south that Caesar sent a desperate message to Brundisium to tell his reinforcements not to sail, 'for all harbours and shores were occupied by the enemy's fleets'. Bibulus himself remained at sea in all weathers, and it was only an extraordinary mischance that cheated him of the revenge for which he had longed so bitterly ever since Caesar had made a mockery of their joint consulship in 59. Caesar's depleted fleet had taken on board the rest of the cavalry and legions at Brundisium 'as far as the supply of ships allowed' and was already clearing the harbour-mouth when Caesar's messenger sailed up signalling frantically in the nick of time to turn it back, and all obeyed except for one solitary ship which sailed on to meet the fate which Bibulus had prepared for them all. 'On such fine timing,' says Caesar, 'and so great a stroke of luck did the safety of a whole army depend.'

But if Caesar was relieved to hear that the rest of his army had been spared a watery grave, they were still no use to him in Italy, and the prospect of their ever getting across to him must have seemed remote as Bibulus intensified his blockade. It must also have been depressing to reflect that for Pompey's fleet to be able to concentrate so effectively on the part of the coast south of Korčula was a measure not only of its success in the operations off the Illyrian coast but of his own failure to hold the allegiance of a province which he was supposed to have governed for ten years but had never visited because he had been so busy conquering Gaul. Admittedly there were one or two towns where colonies of Roman citizens whom he had established or benefited still maintained an active loyalty to him. When, for example, Pompey's admiral Octavius had besieged Salonae and reduced its inhabitants to near-starvation, they had suddenly counter-attacked with such desperate courage that they captured his camps and drove him into the sea. But while Caesar relates their exploit in terms as glowing as Homer's description of the Trojans driving the Greeks back to their ships – and in a sense they did even better since Octavius, unlike the Greeks, did actually give up and sail away – Salonae was no compensation for the naval victories of Octavius and Libo over the expeditionary force of Gaius Antonius and Caesar's combined Adriatic and Tyrrhenian fleets under Hortensius and Dolabella. The scale of those victories is measured by Caesar's failure to produce more than twelve warships to convoy his army across to Greece, by the loss of the fifteen cohorts which Libo had taken to join Pompey's land-forces, and by Octavius' subsequent operations on the Dalmatian coast when he had gone on 'to divert Issa from its friendship with Caesar and to stir up the Dalmatians and the rest of the barbarians'. For despite the setback at Salonae these operations had assured Pompey not only that Caesar would receive no effective help from his old province of Illyricum but that the land-route to Greece from Italy would be even more difficult and dangerous than before.

Pompey could therefore feel confident that there was nothing to fear from the province behind his back as he and Caesar watched each other like cats from their camps on either side of the Apsus. The only battle they fought was a brief propaganda skirmish which Caesar started by sending Cicero's old enemy Vatinius to use his smooth tongue among the troops fraternizing by the river, but though Vatinius seems to have organized something of a debating society, Labienus soon cut him short with some plain speaking followed by a hail of darts to drive his points home. Pompey's strategy was to rely on the fleet to keep Caesar without reinforcements, and he wondered how long it would be before his enemy either cracked or took desperate risks as the weeks turned into months of which the worst were yet to come, for Caesar had landed in January and the Roman calendar was two months ahead of the seasons. But the severe weather was hard on the navy too, and while even Caesar cannot help admiring the determination of his old enemy Bibulus who took no rest but 'remained at sea in the foulest weather and shirked no difficulties or duty if only he could get to grips with Caesar', Bibulus himself was not averse to playing Caesar at his own diplomatic game. Having ordered Libo to join him at Oricum, where they evidently still held the outer harbour, he began negotiating with the officer commanding the garrison which Caesar had left to hold the town. According to Caesar the two admirals 'requested the opportunity to confer with him personally on matters of the highest importance', and proposed an immediate truce. But Caesar was neither at Oricum nor in his camp on the Apsus, for he had taken a legion down to a place called Buthrotum some seventy miles south of Oricum 'to expedite the food-supply' – an incidental detail indicating how desperate his position must have become.

When Caesar received the message which had been sent post-haste from Oricum, he left his legion where it was, rode back as fast as he could, and was no doubt much relieved to find that the town had not changed its allegiance yet again. According to his own account he then conferred with Libo but not with Bibulus, whose absence Libo supposedly excused on the grounds of 'personal hatred of Caesar and a passionate temper', although it is possible that Caesar's conditions for a meeting made it prudent to risk only one admiral at a time in the lion's den, and it is always a good technique in negotiation to have an excuse for referring difficult questions to an absent colleague. At any event Caesar maintains that he demanded safe conduct for personal envoys to Pompey but that Libo put him off with the difficulty that 'the council' – as Caesar terms the exiled Senate – 'had given Pompey supreme command of the war and of everything else', and therefore he could not do more than report Caesar's request and leave the negotiations and the question of envoys to his commander-in-chief. The only thing that Libo seemed keen to talk about was the possibility of an immediate truce, says Caesar, 'for just as Bibulus was excluding Caesar from the sea and harbours, so Bibulus himself was being excluded from all landing in that district: the shores were occupied by Caesar with garrisons set at intervals, nor was any opportunity given him of procuring wood or water or of beaching his ships'. And when Caesar realized that 'everything Libo said was framed with a view to the present danger and the avoidance of want, he returned to the consideration of his further plan of campaign' – just as if his own interest in peace-negotiations had not ceased the moment he realized that he was not going to achieve the lifting of the blockade that might give Antony the opportunity to bring the reinforcements that would make further peace-initiatives superfluous.

But if Pompey's fleet was suffering, Caesar's army was suffering more, and though Caesar glosses over his own difficulties in his memoirs, his revelation that he had taken a legion over a hundred miles south of the Apsus to try to find supplies tells its own story, especially when combined with his increasingly desperate messages to Antony to sail from Brundisium at any cost. Indeed all the sources except Caesar himself maintain that he became so desperate that he set out one night in a small boat to fetch the legions in person but was driven back to land by a storm, despite the Canute-like confidence with which he had told the terrified skipper to 'brave the tempest with a stout heart: you carry Caesar and Caesar's fortunes!' And such is the tenacity of the story that there may be something in it despite Caesar's own very understandable silence on what Appian criticizes as a rash deed 'worthy of a soldier but not a general'. Caesar certainly sent a flurry of messengers across to Brundisium and finally his legate Postumius carrying separate letters to his various commanders there and one addressed to the whole army in case their commanders failed to respond. A few weeks ago he had been desperate to stop his reinforcements sailing to an almost certain disaster because the Pompeian blockade had already been so strong. Since then the blockade had not weakened but his army had, and his message to the legions at Brundisium was now 'to follow Postumius aboard and sail to any place where the wind might carry them regardless of what happened to the ships, for Caesar did not want ships but men'. But the order was easier to give than to obey, and for a long time it had been impossible for Antony even to leave Brundisium harbour however bold he might have been to run the gauntlet of the blockaded coast on the other side of the Adriatic.

The reason for this was the more aggressive blockading tactics adopted by Libo when Bibulus had succumbed to a disease 'brought on by cold and exhaustion', most probably pneumonia. According to Dio's account Libo had then succeeded Bibulus as commander-in-chief of Pompey's naval forces, and though Caesar's memoirs flatly contradict this statement, it is not unlikely that the father-in-law of Pompey's younger son came to hold that position informally if not formally in a war which was becoming more and more familial. Pompey may well not have wanted to refer the appointment of a new high admiral to the Senate in case it appointed someone else, or perhaps he wanted to avoid jealousy from Libo's peers or to keep control of naval strategy more closely in his own hands. All the same he will have needed a sea-borne co-ordinator of naval operations, and if he did not make Libo formally more than first among equals, the fact remains that Libo now appears to assume Bibulus' role while Pompey's elder son Gnaeus begins to feature more prominently in the Adriatic operations, just as Pompey's own father-in-law Scipio is most prominent among his commanders on land.

Libo had taken fifty warships across to Brundisium and occupied the islet which commands the harbour 'because he thought it better to guard the one and only place from which Caesar's reinforcements could set out than to keep all shores and harbours so closely blockaded'. According to Caesar he took Antony completely by surprise, seized and set fire to a number of merchant-ships, captured one that was full of corn, dislodged at least one of Antony's cavalry outposts by a landing of light-armed troops, and in general 'made such good use of the opportunities of his position that he sent a dispatch to Pompey to the effect that Pompey might now beach and repair all his other ships if he liked because Libo could keep off Caesar's reinforcements single-handed'. All the same Antony made a vigorous resistance to Libo. On one occasion he enticed five of the Pompeian quadriremes in pursuit of two of his own triremes and drew them to a point where they could be attacked by a large number of row-ing-boats packed with troops who managed to board and capture one of the giant warships. But while Caesar's memoirs make much of this episode, it was not the loss of one ship out of fifty or even the 'disgrace' of it that forced Libo to call off the blockade of Brundisium. Antony's more effective measures were less spectacular – the persistent harassing of Libo's landing-parties by cavalry patrols which made victualling and watering the fleet so difficult that Libo eventually had to recross the Adriatic for fresh supplies and revert to patrolling the eastern coast.

But Antony still failed to attempt a crossing, and Caesar's bland narra-tive disguises the desperation behind his 'feeling that some opportunities for crossing seemed to have been missed since steady winds had often blown by which, in his opinion, they should without fail have set their course'. It was now 'many months' since he had crossed on 4 January, and 'the more the time extended, the keener was the vigilance of the enemy fleet and the greater their confidence in stopping his reinforce-ments'. He intensified his messages ordering Antony to set sail at what-ever cost, and Pompey wrote just as often to his naval commanders to urge them not to relax their vigilance: the seasons were turning against Caesar, and with the likelihood of suitable sailing winds diminishing to the advantage of the oared battle-fleets, he expected Antony to make his attempt soon if at all. And Antony did not let Caesar down. He had lacked neither courage nor loyalty but ships, for it was only after Libo had been compelled to give up his close blockade of Brundisium that Antony could begin collecting sufficient vessels to tranship the four very full legions which he had been preparing. In early April he embarked twenty thousand men and eight hundred horse, and enjoyed the 'incredible good fortune' which Caesar did not attempt to disguise in his memoirs because he wished the world to know how strongly fortune favoured him.

There was no lack of vigilance from Pompey's fleet. The admiral Coponius commanding the Rhodian squadron at Dyrrachium put to sea the moment the enemy fleet came in sight sailing northwards up the coast with a following wind, and as the wind began to slacken, his sixteen first-raters and four smaller warships began to catch up the dawdling transports and would soon have had all Caesar's reinforcements at their mercy if the breeze had not suddenly freshened and carried the sailing-ships ahead again. But Coponius did not give up. Despite the increasing violence of the wind, his hundreds of oarsmen increased their rate until he saw the transports struggling into the doubtful shelter of a natural harbour called Nymphaeum, and since Nymphaeum was a safe haven from a south-westerly but not when the wind was blowing from due south as it was now, they obviously 'reckoned the danger from the storm less than that from Pompey's fleet'. But they were saved from both by the second instalment of Caesar's 'incredible good fortune'. The wind which had been strengthening southerly veered round to the south-west at the critical moment, the swell in the harbour subsided, and Caesar records with satisfaction how 'those who had so lately been in fear were now sheltered by a perfectly safe harbour while those who had been the cause of their peril were forced to fear for themselves'. After a chase of nearly forty miles the Pompeian crews were too exhausted to resist the gale which was now driving them on to the rocky coast. 'The same rough weather that now protected Caesar's ships shattered Pompey's vessels, so that all sixteen biggest were crushed and wrecked, and large numbers of rowers and troops were dashed onto the rocks and killed.' Antony's ships, on the other hand, were all miraculously safe except for two, which had been lost overnight and had run aground three miles to the south near Lissus where, if Caesar is to be believed, Pompey's garrison had put them to death after accepting their surrender. But the loss of two ships was nothing in the context of the whole operation. Antony had landed safely with four legions and eight hundred horse, and when he now advanced on Lissus, the Pompeian commander fled and the citizens opened the gates to his irresistible force.

When Caesar heard that Antony had landed safely and was on his way to join him he was scarcely less incredulous than Pompey, who heard simultaneously. Contrary to all expectation Pompey now had the enemy behind as well as in front of him, and he immediately set out to try to prevent Antony from joining forces with Caesar and to protect his own line of communication from Dyrrachium. Caesar of course was no less anxious to meet Antony first, but Pompey had a start in this new race because he was already on the north side of the Apsus whereas Caesar now found this natural line of defence a hindrance as he marched furiously upstream to find a place where he could cross. Pompey in the meantime was pushing his army northwards by forced marches, and when his scouts reported Antony's line of march, he set an ambush though not, as Caesar implies, because he was afraid to meet Antony in a fair fight. Nine legions were not afraid of fighting four but of finding four unwilling to fight nine, and that indeed is what happened. Although Pompey took elaborate precautions to keep his proximity secret by forbidding campfires and avoiding other tell-tale signs, his movements were betrayed to Antony by some Greeks, and Antony wisely kept his men in a fortified camp until Caesar's arrival caused Pompey to withdraw.

Exactly where Caesar and Antony met and Pompey retired to is disputed, but the principles on which Pompey acted seem clear enough. There was no possibility now that Pompey would let Caesar bring him to battle in the open field. With eleven legions totalling at least thirty-five thousand men Caesar's army was now close to numerical parity with Pompey's in terms of legionaries, and though he had far fewer reserves of light-armed and cavalry, Caesar was sufficiently confident in the superiority of his heavy infantry, nearly all veterans, to seek the pitched battle which Pompey was determined to avoid, though the means Pompey would take to avoid it would not include bombarding Caesar with specious peace-proposals. But Pompey was not entirely without consolation from the arrival of Caesar's reinforcements. If he was now militarily weaker than his enemy for pitched battle, he was organizationally far stronger. Whereas Caesar now had well over twice the number of mouths to feed and no additional means of feeding them, Pompey still enjoyed limitless supplies as long as Dyrrachium held firm and he remained close to the sea.

If, as seems most likely, the conjunction of Caesar and Antony took place somewhere near Tirana some twenty-five miles east of Dyrrachium, Pompey would clearly have retired to protect his lines of supply to his arsenal and possibly to give new instructions to his naval commanders there. If he had done anything else Caesar would almost certainly have advanced on Dyrrachium at once, but to attack Pompey and Dyrrachium together was of course inconceivable, and since he had probably brought few supplies with him in his haste to reach Antony, he was anxious to return to his old camp and his old bases at Apollonia and Oricum. What had happened to the baggage-trains of both armies is not certain. Pompey's had presumably followed him, either to Dyrrachium or at least as far as Asparagium to the north of the River Genusus where Pompey next encamped. If Caesar's followed its army it will no doubt have stayed well inland after crossing the Apsus in order to escape the attention of Pompey's cavalry, but it may well have been left behind under the protection of the garrisons which Caesar tells us that he had withdrawn from the coast. But Pompey himself had no intention of losing contact with Dyrrachium, and when he arrived at the town of Asparagium on the north bank of the Genusus, he advanced no further south but fortified a huge camp there and waited. Caesar in the meantime had recrossed the Genusus higher up, and after seeing to the security of his own supply-bases he came north again and confronted Pompey from the south bank of the Genusus. And once again two great armies sat in fortified camps to the north and south of a river with Pompey watching and waiting for the much enlarged but also much hungrier enemy to make a false move.

One cheering piece of news for Pompey at this time was the report of his elder son's naval attack on Oricum, which Caesar had left strongly garrisoned with three cohorts under the command of his legate Acilius Caninus. Gnaeus had taken advantage of Caesar's preoccupation with Antony's arrival and his withdrawal of the string of coastal garrisons which had made it difficult for the Pompeian naval patrols to beach their ships or to land watering and foraging parties. He had set out to capture or destroy all the merchant-shipping and their few naval escorts which had been helping to provide Caesar's army with the supplies which had been gathered so laboriously from the region to the south, for while Pompey's fleet had been concentrating on the blockade further north, it had been possible for supply-ships to creep up the coast from Buthrotum and bring in some corn at Oricum. Gnaeus took command of his father's Egyptian fleet, and when he arrived off Oricum to find that Caninus had removed all his vessels from the outer to the inner harbour and blocked the entrance, he enjoyed the challenge to his ingenuity. Caninus had sunk a large merchant-ship in the narrow channel and anchored alongside a floating tower full of troops and artillery ready to repel any attempt to clear the obstruction, but Gnaeus rapidly constructed similar towers on some of his own ships, rowed to the attack, fished for the sunken vessel with grappling-irons, and began pulling it clear with a windlass. At the same time the town came under attack from his landing-parties, and while the inhabitants were busy defending their walls, four of Gnaeus' biremes had turned amphibian and were being rolled across the natural break-water which protected the inner harbour. They resumed their natural element in the inner harbour and immediately created havoc among Caesar's warships and the merchant-vessels which had been moored there. They burnt most of them, but since the entrance channel had been cleared by the time the work of destruction was complete, they took the four best in tow and rowed triumphantly back with their prizes to the outer harbour. It was a good day's work. Gnaeus had not taken the town itself, but he had deprived the enemy not only of the ships but of the use of the port, which he now left a detachment of his own ships to keep under close blockade. With the rest he sailed north again to Lissus where Antony had left twenty of the merchant-ships which had brought his army from Brundisium, and again he destroyed all the ships although he failed to take the town.

While Pompey received encouraging dispatches from his son, Caesar maintains that he received envoys from the towns of Thessaly and Aetolia to say that they were ready to change sides if he would send them garrisons. What this means is that representatives of the less successful political factions of certain Thessalian and Aetolian towns sent envoys in the hope of securing assistance for revolution. They were acting in the worst tradition of Greek city-states whose whole history records the triumph of party-politics over patriotism. Rival parties looked to Pompey or Caesar for political self-aggrandizement now just as they once appealed to Athens or Sparta in the Peloponnesian War, and when Caesar responded by sending troops, it was a measure of his desperation over the food-supply that he was prepared to part with nearly a third of his heavy infantry and at least half his cavalry. He sent Cassius Longinus with one legion into Thessaly, admittedly the legion of recruits but a legion none the less, and it was accompanied by two hundred of his precious cavalry. He ordered the ex-consul Domitius Calvinus – the same who had been involved in the election-rigging in 54 – to take two veteran legions and five hundred horse into Macedonia to operate against Scipio who was approaching from Asia with the two legions from Syria. And he sent another five cohorts and a few more horsemen into Aetolia under Calvisius Sabinus, who, like Cassius in Thessaly, had special instructions to provide for the corn-supply. But even if these forces succeeded in occupying some towns and securing supplies, the transport of corn overland from such distances was a long and difficult business, and Caesar's eyes looked hungrily towards Dyrrachium which provided Pompey with immediate abundance. Dyrrachium was heavily fortified by natural as well as military defences and would be difficult to storm, but if only Pompey could be separated from his arsenal, he would be severely weakened even if Caesar could not secure it for himself. And there was always the chance that Pompey might be forced into a pitched battle, or even that treachery might capture Dyrrachium if Caesar was at hand to take advantage of it. At any rate there was no future for Caesar in staying where he was, and since he was not prepared to face the moral and military problems of a retreat further east, he now tried on Pompey himself the stratagem which he had used against Pompey's generals in Spain.

Knowing how desperate the enemy was for food, Pompey was not surprised when Caesar broke camp and began marching inland up the south bank of the Genusus as though on his way to Thessaly, but wisely he stayed where he was until he had more certain information of Caesar's movements. And it was as well that he did, for if his troops rejoiced to see Caesar apparently in retreat, they were just as mistaken as the Pompeian army in Spain: Caesar's plan was to double back through thickly wooded and mountainous terrain to come between Pompey and his source of supply. As soon as Pompey realized this he set out for Dyrrachium by the coastal route, but Caesar's stratagem had gained a day, and though Pompey's route was shorter and easier he arrived to find the enemy already fortifying a camp between him and the city. But he was not dismayed. He fortified a camp of his own on the impregnable crag of Petra some two miles south of Caesar's camp and nearly four from Dyrrachium, and waited for Caesar to make the next move. Caesar's own narrative presents the separation of Pompey from Dyrrachium as a strategical masterpiece, but he was not cutting a starving army from a line of retreat as he had done in Spain, and he had in fact achieved very little. If Caesar had hoped to reach Dyrrachium in time to terrify the town into surrender as he had done at Oricum and Apollonia, he had been frustrated by the speed of Pompey's appearance which had reassured the garrison against any false rumours of disaster. He could no more hope to storm Dyrrachium with Pompey behind him than if Pompey had been inside the walls, and if he had hoped to force Pompey to a pitched battle, he was similarly disappointed. Indeed he was little better off outside Dyrrachium than he had been at Asparagium, and Pompey was little worse. Pompey could no longer get supplies from Dyrrachium by land, it was true, but since he had wisely kept to the coast, his sea-borne supplies were actually facilitated by the shorter distance while his cavalry could still make foraging as difficult for Caesar in the hinterland as Caesar had made it for the Pompeian army in Spain.

Caesar describes his own problems and what he tried to do about them after a rueful reference to Pompey's instructions 'for some of his warships to come and meet him at Petra and for corn and stores to be brought in from Asia and all the regions that he held':

Caesar, thinking that the war was going to be a protracted one and despairing of receiving supplies from Italy because all the coasts were being guarded with such care by the Pompeians ... sent Q. Tillius and the legate L. Canuleius into Epirus in order to secure provisions, and because these regions were rather distant he established granaries in certain places and assigned the duty of transporting corn between the neighbouring territories. He also gave orders that all the corn that there was should be sought out and collected at Lissus and all other fortified posts. But this was a very small amount, partly from the nature of the land (for the terrain is rugged and mountainous and the local people generally use imported corn anyway), and partly because Pompey had foreseen this and had already used his cavalry to seek out and collect all the corn. When Caesar discovered this, he adopted a plan of campaign appropriate to the terrain, for around the camp of Pompey there were many high and rugged hills. First he occupied them with garrisons and built strong forts on them. Then, as happened to be suggested by the nature of each situation, he drew a continuous line of fortifications from stronghold to stronghold in order to lay siege to Pompey with three objects in view: first, since he had a shortage of provisions while Pompey had a large preponderance of cavalry, that he might be able to bring in corn and stores for his army from any direction with less risk; second, that he might prevent Pompey from foraging and make his cavalry useless for military operations; and third, that he might diminish the personal authority on which Pompey seemed to rely among the foreign nations as soon as the report had spread throughout the world that Pompey was being beleaguered by Caesar and did not dare to fight a pitched battle.

In other words Caesar was choosing what he considered the better of a difficult pair of possibilities. He had crossed the Adriatic to fight Pompey, but Pompey's preference for letting starvation fight for him had faced Caesar with the choice of staying near him or marching into the interior where supplies would be more plentiful. But to march eastwards had grave disadvantages. There might be more supplies in Thessaly or Macedonia, but every step in that direction would take him further from Italy, and Italy was insecure. News of a retreat from Pompey might precipitate a rebellion, and instead of following him Pompey might decide to recross the Adriatic. Or if Pompey did follow him, the superiority of the pursuing cavalry would give the retreating legions the same nightmarish experience which the Pompeian army had suffered in Spain as it had struggled to return to Ilerda. They would progress slowly and painfully, compelled to fight continuous rearguard actions, unable to forage on the way, and without even the encouragement of having a well-garrisoned Ilerda to march to. They would be free of Pompey's cavalry only if they kept to the mountainous country, but that was not where they would find the quantities of corn they needed, and Pompey also had the larger number of light-armed troops – archers, javelineers and slingers – who would be as troublesome to a retreating army in the mountains as cavalry on the plains. Nor did it seem likely that a pursuing Pompey could be ambushed or forced into a pitched battle in Thessaly any more easily than Caesar himself had been in Spain. In short, Caesar decided that to stay where he was would be bad but that to go east would be worse, and while he has to admit that it was 'rather unusual for the larger and better supplied army to be besieged by the smaller and hungrier one', his plan of building an enormous wall round Pompey's position seemed the only solution. It would hinder Pompey's cavalry from interrupting his foraging for what little food was available, neutralize its military effectiveness, and keep Caesar himself on the offensive in the hope of shaming Pompey into a pitched battle or at least of starving with honour.

Pompey could not but admire his old protégé's tenacity when he realized what Caesar was attempting, but as fast as Caesar worked to confine Pompey in the smallest possible area, Pompey constructed an inner line of fortifications that would not only make Caesar's lines as long and as weak as possible but give his own army the whole of the coastal plain in the bay south of Dyrrachium in which to manœuvre and forage. For while Pompey had unlimited supplies of grain from the sea, the coastal plain had better grazing and foraging possibilities than the more mountainous interior, and Pompey wanted to keep Caesar out of it as much as to have it for himself. Pompey's army also needed water, and since he was afraid that Caesar would try to dam or divert the smaller streams that entered the bay, he was doubly determined to prevent the enemy from closing the ring on the southern side short of a small river, the Lesnikia, which flowed into the sea about five miles south of Petra and would be extremely difficult to dam effectively. And it was probably Caesar's attempt to occupy a hill which would have enabled him to bring his circuit round to the coast only three miles south of Petra that caused the first major engagement in what Caesar calls 'this novel and unprecedented style of warfare'.

There had of course been constant skirmishes before this. The rival generals 'strove with the utmost energy to occupy positions' on what became a fifteen-mile front, and they found themselves experimenting with the problems of static warfare which were to perplex a different and possibly less versatile generation of generals in France between AD 1914 and 1918. Where the trenching-tool becomes blunted before the sword, numbers are more important than skill, and Pompey not only had more legionaries but very many more auxiliaries, who were just as good at digging and had a shorter line to fortify. Pompey also had less need to risk his own best troops against Caesar's legionaries because his large number of archers and javelineers, supported by artillery which he had shipped across from Dyrrachium, were as effective here as the auxiliaries of his Spanish army had been when Caesar had tried to occupy a hill outside Ilerda. For when Caesar now attempted to secure a hill from which he might have closed the ring two miles north of where Pompey was prepared to allow it, the result was much the same, and even involved the same legion.

That Caesar should have sent Antony and his crack ninth legion to seize that position suggests a very determined attempt to turn the flank of Pompey's inner lines of fortification which were already outstripping his own. Similarly the vigour of Pompey's reaction indicates the importance which he attached to stopping him, although he did not give Caesar the satisfaction of a pitched battle. Instead he lost no time in occupying a nearby hill connecting with Caesar's otherwise steep position by a saddle which offered an easier approach. He then threw a ring of archers and slingers round Caesar's hill, and while they kept the enemy from continuing the work of fortification, he brought up large forces of light-armed troops and sent them forward with the support of artillery which he moved along the saddle until he could bring it to bear on Caesar's struggling ninth. And Caesar admits that his position rapidly became untenable. 'The men found it difficult to defend themselves and fortify at the same time, and Caesar, seeing that his men were being wounded on all sides, ordered them to withdraw.' They were in the same predicament as the Spartans at Thermopylae who complained that the sky was so thick with Persian arrows that the sun was blotted out, but if Caesar admired Leonidas' famous retort that he preferred fighting in the shade, he did not want Antony and his best legion to share the Spartans' fate. But the retreat was easier to order than to carry out, and as Pompey sent in more and more men and missiles, he is said to have observed with satisfaction to his staff that he 'would not object to being called a useless general if Caesar's legions managed to get away without serious loss from that position to which they had so rashly advanced'.

Although Caesar explains that his legion's failure to retire at the first command was due only to a reluctance 'to appear to be abandoning the position through fear', his narrative makes it obvious that he was afraid of a complete rout since the only line of retreat was down a steep slope, and unless the descending forces could be supported in some way, they might easily be overwhelmed by the Pompeians attacking them in the rear with all the advantages of greater mobility and fire-power from higher ground. One possibility would be to leave a garrison on the hill to cover the retreat of the rest, but in the absence of fortifications an unacceptably large and suicidal garrison would be needed to withstand the Pompeians for even a short time. He therefore ordered the legion to dig a line of trenches to hinder the Pompeian pursuit across the saddle of land, and while they struggled to do this under the protection of the hurdles which had been prepared for the construction of a rampart but now served as a flimsy barrier against a hail of missiles, Caesar himself mustered all his available fire-power to try to cover the steep slope down which the retreat must take place. He seems to have had only slingers, but if the trenches failed, a few volleys of sling-bullets might retard Pompey's pursuit sufficiently to let the legion descend in good order to the protection of other heavy infantry. At any rate it was the best he could do in the circumstances, and when the slingers were in position, he sounded the retreat.

This time Antony obeyed, but the elated Pompeians scorned all obstacles in the excitement of having put one of Caesar's best regiments to flight. They threw the hurdles across the trenches, swarmed on to the hill, and began plunging down the other side, where the retreating legion apparently found so little protection from the slingers that Antony was compelled to take the same extreme measure which Caesar had used at Ilerda. Rather than let his cohorts break up into the sort of panic-stricken disorder that would leave them easy prey to the pursuers he ordered a counter-attack uphill, and as at Ilerda the Pompeians promptly disappeared back over the hill and gave the enemy the chance to get out of a mess. But Caesar did not of course continue the pursuit on either occasion. He was only too glad – or 'considered it sufficient' according to his own expression – to have gained a breathing-space in which to retreat without disaster. Although he claims to have killed 'several of the enemy for the loss of only five of his own men', he gives no figures for the killed and wounded in the earlier part of the engagement when 'his men were being wounded in every direction', and such selectivity in providing statistical information seems suspicious when he is clearly eager to prove that Pompey had failed to make good his battlefield boast. But whether Pompey had inflicted large casualties on the enemy or not, he had certainly achieved his tactical objective. He had not only compelled Caesar's best legion to retreat from a position which it had occupied. He had forced Caesar's siege-lines back inland, and as the rival ramparts now continued their race southwards more or less parallel to the coast, Pompey's greater speed of fortification kept Caesar from coming down to the sea until he reached the natural boundary of the River Lesnikia some five miles south of Petra. When they were completed Pompey's inner line was fifteen miles long, Caesar's outer one seventeen.

This massive work of fortification was the labour of many weeks, and though only the one serious engagement is recorded, the dreary work of digging was no doubt enlivened by the daily raids and skirmishes of trench-warfare. There were salients to establish, capture and recapture, prisoners to seize for intelligence purposes, weaknesses in the enemy lines to be probed and tested. Pompey's officers made a speciality of night-raids on Caesar's outposts. They pinpointed their objectives by the camp-fires, and having worked out a route which would take a raiding party through the thickest cover, they would creep up heavily camouflaged, pour a hail of arrows into the enemy position, and melt away into the darkness before the victims realized what had hit them. But while these raids were usefully destructive and demoralizing, it was not upon force but famine that Pompey relied to put Caesar to flight, and Caesar admits that his men were 'reduced to extremities' by want of food. He tells how they were first compelled to eat meat, and if that seems a small hardship in our century of carnivorous armies which win wars on bully-beef, the curious fact remains that the Roman soldier was a man who preferred to live on bread alone. In any case the local flocks and herds were soon exhausted. The troops even made an ersatz bread from some repellent root mashed with milk, and when the Pompeians taunted them with hunger, they threw a few of the loaves across to them in a gesture of defiance which supposedly prompted Pompey's remark that he was not fighting men but brutes. But even if it is true that Pompey forbade the loaves to be shown round his own army because they might indicate the toughness rather than the desperation of the enemy, not even brutes can live forever on the diet which Lucan describes, and Pompey could con-gratulate himself on the strength of his unseen ally in the enemy's camp:

> For though encamped on spacious heights and free to range
> The earth away from stifling air or stagnant pools,
> Yet Caesar's army suffered much from hunger's pinch
> As though they were themselves besieged. The ears of corn
> Were sprouting now but far from fat maturity,
> And Caesar saw his wretched men too weak to move,
> Or lying on the ground to eat the food of beasts,
> Or plucking bits of shrubs or tearing leaves from trees
> Or finding unknown roots from which to strip strange herbs
> That threatened death. They even fought their friends for food;
> Whatever fire could soften, teeth could break, or throats
> Could swallow down with rasping pain, they ate it all
> Including many things mankind had never tried before,
> And yet they still besieged a satiated foe.

On the other hand Pompey was not without problems of his own behind his fifteen-mile perimeter. If his men had all the corn they could eat, they were increasingly short of fresh water to wash it down, and this was the significance of Lucan's reference to stagnant pools. It had not, of course, been possible for Caesar to dam or divert all the streams which crossed Pompey's lines on their way to the sea, and he had probably found the Lesnikia too big even to attempt to stop; but that river was five miles from Pompey's camp at Petra, and it was rapidly becoming an organizational nightmare to ensure adequate supplies not only to Petra itself but to the forward positions and redoubts in the hills, especially as spring turned into early summer and the wells began to dry up. Nor was it only the men whom Pompey had to worry about. He had many thousands of animals, from thoroughbred chargers to humble beasts of burden, all of which needed enormous quantities of food and water. And while he had enough ships to bring in fodder as well as grain and to ensure adequate supplies at least for the cavalry horses, all the quadrupeds were pining for some fresh grass in their now barren and trampled plain, and many of the pack-animals had to be put down. But Pompey's biggest problem was neither food nor water but a disease which Lucan wrongly attributes to bad water. The symptoms which Lucan lists – constipation, flushed and bloated face with painfully congested eyes, a fiery rash that first appears on the abdomen before spreading upwards to the chest and shoulders, a terrific heaviness in the head leading to lethargy and the sort of coma which might resemble the 'divine disease' of epilepsy, and the unpleasant smell that may have accounted for his reference to 'foul air' – all identify the enemy within Pompey's camp as typhus, which is conveyed not by water but by lice. Admittedly drinking foul water will have produced all kinds of dysenteric complaints, but washing in clean water is the best defence against typhus, and if Pompey had only known the cause of the disease, he could have put to use the five miles of sea at his disposal. As it was, the lice and the epidemic thrived unchecked, and though there was probably quite a good recovery rate since his men were all well fed and the majority were under forty-five, the desire to get his army away from that unhealthy place must have been one of the two main factors which made him decide to break out of Caesar's siege-lines. The other was that the corn was now growing fast, and while there were still several weeks in which Caesar's troops would have to get weaker before they became stronger, their morale was improving as the prospect of a harvest assumed greater reality.

Unfortunately the accounts of the first set of battles which resulted from this decision are almost entirely missing from our texts of Caesar and Appian, Dio's is confused, and Lucan's poetic narrative degenerates into a ridiculous exaggeration of Horatian feats of arms by one of Caesar's centurions. From Caesar we learn that six engagements were fought in one day, three at Dyrrachium and three at the siege-lines, though Pompey also made subsidiary attacks on several other redoubts with the object of 'keeping Caesar's forces equally scattered so that there could be no assistance from the nearest garrisons'. Dio maintains that Caesar made an attack on Dyrrachium 'between the marshes of the lagoon and the sea in the expectation that the town would be betrayed by its defenders'; and since Appian has Caesar going to a secret nocturnal assignation with a supposed fifth-column outside the city-walls, we might suppose that it was Caesar who began the series of battles but for Lucan's insistence that the initiative was entirely Pompey's, and Dio's indication that Caesar was no sooner in 'the narrows' in front of Dyrrachium than he was attacked by a large force which Pompey had evidently put there to ambush him. It seems that Pompey decoyed Caesar and part of his army into an attack on Dyrrachium while himself making three major assaults on Caesar's lines of fortification. His objectives were probably limited. He can hardly have hoped to divide and conquer Caesar completely in this way, but he did hope to damage him as far as he could without running the risk of a pitched battle, and equally importantly he hoped to give his cavalry the opportunity of damaging the enemy even more in the future. Obviously Pompey was not seeking to march right away from his position as Lucan implies. He had no intention of leaving his arsenal at Dyrrachium to Caesar's mercy, and he was certainly not going to lose control of the coast from which he could import all his supplies. But if he could capture some of the commanding positions in Caesar's system of fortification, he would not only extend his own area and reopen the water-supply but free his cavalry to harry Caesar's future attempts at foraging and fortification. And that in turn might make Caesar's position so completely untenable that the starving besiegers would have to choose between surrender or retreat.

At first all went well. Decoyed by the vain hope of treachery Caesar marched obligingly to Dyrrachium only to find himself ambushed by large forces of Pompeians who had come up in boats. Pompey himself then launched his own attacks on various sections of Caesar's siege-lines. He gave his personal attention to one particular redoubt which could be approached under the cover of thick woods, and he achieved complete surprise with dramatic results:

> For all at once his eagles glittered into view
> And all his trumpets brayed. Surprise and fear combined
> To make the sword superfluous. The enemy
> Did all that valour could where duty bade them stand
> Until they fell, laid flat like corn in driving rain,

Smashed down by storms of missiles pouring now
To waste. Then torches flew with rolling, smoky fires,
And battered towers began to reel while ramparts rang
With savage blows from countless rams until there rose
Above the mounds of earth the eagles long confined
But gaining now for Pompey freedom of the world.

But if Pompey's legions succeeded in crossing Caesar's ramparts, they failed to capture the redoubt which was their principal objective. Thanks to the incredible bravery and leadership of a centurion named Scaeva, who ended the day with 120 arrows in his shield and every reward of valour that Caesar could bestow on his chest and in his pocket, the garrison managed to hold out until the legate whom Caesar had left in command of his main camp could arrive with reinforcements, which caught Pompey on unfavourable ground and forced him to retire to another defensible hill between the two lines. According to other Caesarian officers the legate could have ended the whole war if he had pressed home his advantage, but Caesar's own opinion, as recorded in his memoirs, was one of approval for a subordinate who did not presume to play the general, and he was clearly relieved that no rash attempt had been made. Caesar himself proved unable to take advantage of Pompey's need to retreat to his own lines from the hill which he was now occupying in no-man's land. Pompey could not supply his army where he was, but he did not attempt to move until he had secured his retreat against counter-attack by building fifteen-foot ramparts, huge towers and every kind of obstacle to pursuit. After five days he withdrew in good order on a moonless night and led the army back behind his old lines without loss.

But the success of the withdrawal, which is always one of the most difficult operations in warfare, was the only thing on which Pompey could congratulate himself. His troops had been driven back in all six engagements and he is said to have lost two thousand men and six standards, though these are Caesar's statistics and the disparity between the casualty-counts on each side is clearly exaggerated by Caesar's claim to have lost only twenty men. For even if Caesar's estimate of his own dead were credible – and it is certainly not the impression that Lucan gives, and Dio's expression 'great slaughter' is a flat contradiction unless Dio is confusing this battle with the next – Caesar himself admits that not one of his men remained unwounded of the garrison which had defended the redoubt into which Pompey had poured thirty thousand arrows. But even if Caesar's statistics are accurate, it was not the roll-call that worried Pompey, for whom two thousand represented perhaps four per cent of his force. It was far more worrying that he had failed in all his objectives. He was back behind his old lines with all the old problems of disease, foul water and lack of grazing, and far from inflicting significant damage on the enemy he had succeeded only in reinforcing the morale of Caesar's troops and giving them new courage to endure their deprivations for a few more weeks until the first corn would be ripe.

Caesar was certainly not euphoric by comparison. It was satisfying to have frustrated Pompey's attacks and driven them back at all points, but his own position was just as precarious. He would hardly have been so willing to believe the supposed fifth-column in Dyrrachium if he had not been so desperate for supplies, and while his memoirs maintain that his men 'enjoyed good health and abundant water', his picture of an army of robust ascetics is hard to square with their 'being driven to extremities by hunger', and Plutarch maintains that they suffered a disease 'brought on by the strangeness of their diet'. Caesar is evidently torn between his irreconcilable desires to emphasize the loyalty of his men despite deprivation and to clear his own memory of the charge of 'bad generalship' in putting his army in the ridiculous position of 'besiegers who were effectively themselves besieged by lack of provisions'. He made repeated efforts to make Pompey accept a pitched battle on level ground before elation at the recent successes evaporated leaving only the hard reality of hunger, but Pompey refused to be drawn. Every day Caesar advanced his army in battle-order towards Pompey's camp, but though Pompey drew out his own army 'to avoid losing face', he kept it within artillery cover of his ramparts, and made it clear that he would fight only at an advantage which the enemy could not afford to risk, for he had other plans.

His first concern was for his cavalry. Because he had failed to capture the redoubt and therefore maintain the breach which he had made in Caesar's lines, he now tried another way to provide the horses with fresh grazing and restore them to active service against Caesar's army by shipping them to the promontory behind Dyrrachium. But he was only partially successful. Caesar could do nothing to stop the landings or the grazing, but by throwing up some fortifications in the narrow entrances to the promontory on either side of the lagoon he was able to contain Pompey's cavalry, and when the grazing was finished Pompey had no alternative but to ship the horses back again behind his own lines, where he was planning another operation to get himself out of a rapidly deteriorating situation. His objectives were the same as before. He wanted to establish a permanent breach in Caesar's siege-lines but not to lose contact with the sea, and he chose for his new offensive the furthermost point of Caesar's seventeen-mile perimeter. And while he was making his plans, he had the good fortune to receive two prominent defectors from Caesar's army who were able to provide him with valuable intelligence.

According to Caesar's memoirs these men were the first deserters from his camp 'though men were deserting every day from Pompey', but it is hard to believe in this one-way traffic from ample provisions to ersatz loaves, and both Dio and Appian confirm what we should expect. But however many other desertions there had been from Caesar to Pompey, defectors of this importance were rare, for these two men were Gallic princes. They had served as cavalry-officers under Caesar throughout his Gallic Wars, and they had risen to positions of high command in his army and even to senatorial rank. Caesar maintains that they had taken to embezzling their troops' pay, and when they had been exposed they deserted to Pompey with some friends and a large number of horses after trying in vain to assassinate Caesar's senior cavalry commander as a further assurance of welcome. While this may be true, it is also possible that the defectors had been influenced by former service under Labienus or by the fact that they were Allobroges, the tribe with those leaders Domitius had hereditary ties of friendship. At any rate they were warmly welcomed by Pompey, who discovered from them 'anything incomplete in Caesar's fortifications or anything that seemed lacking to their experienced eyes after they had observed the times of things, the distance between points, and the varying vigilance of the outposts according to the ability or energy of the various commanders'. But already we can see Caesar the historian seeking to attribute the blame for what follows to anything or anyone but himself, and though he makes much of the valuable information which Pompey gleaned from these two apparently despicable defectors, he also lets slip that Pompey 'had already planned the next operation'.

Caesar's memoirs give the impression that he was taken by surprise by Pompey's next offensive in an area where nothing much had been happening, but a later reference in his narrative to a disused camp which he had constructed six hundred yards from the River Lesnikia and only three hundred from the sea, which he had abandoned 'for certain reasons', and which Pompey had enlarged for the accommodation of more than the single legion for which it had been intended, reveals that Pompey had in fact been active there. Caesar would hardly have transferred his crack ninth legion to an area he considered unimportant or put Antony in command of the nearest garrison. Clearly Pompey had succeeded in making that original camp near the sea untenable for the ninth legion. Probably by persistent harassment with his cavalry and the formidable archers who gave Caesar's troops 'so great a dread of arrows

that they nearly all made themselves jerkins out of felt, quilt, hide or anything that would give a measure of protection' he had forced the legion
to make another camp further inland, and thus not only retarded the
construction of Caesar's fortifications but removed a concentration of
enemy from the area in which he now proposed to break out. Caesar
must have been aware of the danger of a sea-borne attack from behind
his lines because he had proceeded to construct not one but two lines
of fortification down to the sea from the inland position which replaced
the abandoned camp. In other words he sealed off the southern end of
the coastal plain with a fortified corridor giving protection from attacks
from the south as well as from the area in which Pompey was besieged
to the north. The corridor itself was six hundred yards wide. The ditch
on the northward-facing side near the old camp was fifteen feet wide with
a rampart ten feet in height and depth, and though the south-facing fortifications were also formidable, the fact that the rampart was lower on
that side may indicate a more hurried entrenchment as well as a lower
estimate of the danger, and certainly the open end of the corridor near
the sea was still imperfectly sealed off at the time of Pompey's offensive.

Caesar seems to have had little excuse for being taken unawares by
Pompey's attack, and the fact that Pompey managed to achieve so great
a degree of surprise suggests either complacency on Caesar's part or some
skilful decoying tactics by Pompey who found only two cohorts on duty
at the lower end of the corridor when he launched his offensive. His preparations can hardly have gone unnoticed by the enemy. In order to be
able to fortify a new position without delay once he had achieved the
break-through he had prefabricated much of the foundation material for
ramparts, and having loaded it on to ships along with his artillery and
embarked large numbers of light-armed troops and archers in smaller
boats, he sent them down the coast by night while he advanced overland
with sixty cohorts of infantry. It was five miles from Petra to his objective,
but his men marched light because all their baggage was carried by sea,
and dawn broke to find the two cohorts of Caesarians struggling to
defend their fortified corridor against simultaneous attacks from north
and south. The air fairly sang with missiles as Pompey's men and artillery
directed a constant stream of arrows and javelins across the walls, and
while the defenders kept their heads down, Pompey's legionaries moved
up under cover of sheds and tortoises to fill in the ditches in readiness
for the escalade. The only missile-weapons available for retaliation by
Caesar's troops were slings, and Pompey had been so meticulous in planning this offensive that he had even equipped his men with wicker visors
to their helmets, which not only provided good camouflage for the night
march but saved many a head from concussion. The defenders fought

bravely and their fortifications were strong, but when Pompey observed that the transverse trenches were not complete at the seaward end of the corridor and sent a task-force in landing-craft to attack that third side too, they could resist no longer. The reinforcements that began pouring down the corridor from the new camp were no help. They served only to reinforce the confusion as they met their comrades in full flight, and the Pompeians pressed home their pursuit until they had laid a carpet of slain right up to the enemy camp. Pompey would even have captured one of Caesar's eagles if the standard-bearer had not either thrown it to a fleeing horseman or, according to a variation of the story, hurled it over the palisade before being cut down outside his camp. Only the arrival of Antony with twelve cohorts managed to check the Pompeian advance, and it was not until Caesar himself came on the scene with more reinforcements summoned by smoke-signals from other redoubts that the Pompeians finally withdrew under the cover of their cavalry. But Caesar was too late. Pompey's eagles had soared over the ramparts to gain the freedom of the world a second time, and now they meant to keep it.

As soon as his three-pronged offensive had driven the enemy back up the corridor, Pompey began destroying their fortifications and construct-ing a new camp of his own to the south near the sea. His ships had been landing all the building materials from the moment the rout of the enemy had begun, and by the time his own men were being hard pressed by the combined reinforcements of Antony and Caesar, he had a de-fensible camp ready to receive them as they withdrew. And Caesar had to recognize that this was not a position from which Pompey could be driven as from the inland hill which he had occupied in his previous attempt to breach the siege-lines. 'It was near the sea', writes Caesar, 'so that Pompey could not only forage freely but enjoy a safe approach for his ships.' In a few hours Pompey had destroyed the purpose of all Caesar's labour and suffering in constructing and maintaining seventeen miles of earthworks, and Caesar himself admits that 'he now had to change his tactics because he had failed to gain his purpose'.

Caesar constructed another camp as near as possible to Pompey's new position in the hope that he could force a pitched battle. For a time both armies were kept busy with the fortification of their new camps – the Caesarians hungrily, the Pompeians restored both in body and soul by abundant food, fresh water and the invigorating taste of success. But when Caesar's scouts reported that a Pompeian force of legion strength was moving under the cover of thick woods to the abandoned camp by the River Lesnikia, which was apparently not in use by either side at the time of the recent offensive though it was still intact, Caesar saw his oppor-tunity 'to crush the legion and repair the loss of that day'. He left two of the thirty-five cohorts which he had with him in the camp 'to give the appearance of fortifying' and set out with the rest 'including the ninth legion, which had suffered the loss of many centurions and a reduction of its rank and file'. Marching in two columns he reached his objective before Pompey became aware of his movements, and though the Pompeian legion was already there and the camp was intact, his attack with over three times the number of men drove the defenders from the ramparts. There was heavy fighting at the gates which were barred with great beams studded with spikes, but Antony's men eventually hacked them down and burst their way in only to find that they had to repeat the performance immediately. Because the position had been occupied originally by only a single legion before Pompey had taken it over and extended it, there was a camp within a camp, and the Pompeians promptly withdrew to this inner and more manageable set of defences. But even so the Caesarians broke through there too and 'killed the men who fought back'. This was all the work of the left wing of Caesar's army which had advanced seaward in two columns. The cohorts of his right had come up against a long rampart extending northwards, but what they took to be the outer wall of the camp was in fact only a single rampart connecting the camp to the River Lesnikia and designed to protect watering-parties from sudden attack from inland. When they discovered the truth after failing to find a gate, they soon filled up bits of the fosse, made gaps in the rampart, and poured through to attack the real walls of the camp from the north, and all Caesar's cavalry followed. But it was all too easy to last.

According to Caesar it was 'a fairly long time' before Pompey heard what had happened, but when he did he immediately led five legions to the rescue of the one which had been driven out of the old camp yet curiously remained intact, for it rallied and counter-attacked the Caesarians the moment Pompey appeared. Now Caesar found himself in difficulties. His right and left wings had become too far separated to recombine, and while the internal counter-attack by the Pompeians hit hardest at his right, his left panicked at being caught between two Pompeian forces within the fortifications, and in a short time the whole army was running for its life. His horsemen in particular were terrified at the prospect of being trapped by Pompey's cavalry within the fortification, and as they fought and jostled each other at the exits where the ramparts had been flattened and the ditches filled in, the equally terrified infantrymen struggled to climb back over the ramparts which were still standing and hurled themselves into the trenches below only to be crushed by others jumping on top of them. Caesar himself screamed at his men to stand firm and snatched standards with his own hands from the fleeing bearers, but all ran or galloped past him without heed. Some threw their colours away. One even thrust at him with the sharp point of his standard, and might have ended the war there and then if Caesar's bodyguards had not sliced off his arm in the nick of time. And when Caesar found that he could do nothing to stop the rout, he had for once in his life to follow in order to lead.

Caesar attributes his disaster more to bad luck than to bad management on his own part or to good management on Pompey's. But while it may well be true that many more reputations for generalship have been made or destroyed by luck than the writers of military history usually admit, there is something suspicious in Caesar's special pleading at certain critical points in his narrative. When, for example, his right wing was deflected along the rampart that led to the river so that it not only lost contact with the left but smashed its way through by the narrow gaps which were to prove so deadly in its retreat, it was all the fault of 'Fortune, which has great influence in affairs generally and especially in war, and produces important changes in human affairs by a slight disturbance of balance as on this occasion'. There is no suggestion of incompetence in all these platitudes, but surely it was remiss of Caesar to have been so ignorant of the layout and immediate surroundings of a camp so close to his own lines and recently occupied by Pompey. Similarly he blames 'the small number of his troops, the unfortunate conditions of the site, the narrow space, the twofold panic inside and outside the fortifications, the severance of the army into two parts, the common chances of warfare'. He actually says that 'the loss that had been sustained should be attributed to anyone rather than himself', and he is so sensitive about any criticism of his generalship that he even changes his mind about the conditions of the site and claims to have given his men 'a favourable situation for fighting'. If Caesar is so conveniently blind to his own failings, he may be equally blind to Pompey's excellence, and there are certain aspects of his narrative that suggest not only that Pompey made good use of Caesar's decision to attack the legion which he had sent to the old camp but that he had in fact engineered the whole affair.

One obvious question is why Pompey should have sent the legion to the old camp. Caesar offers no explanation, and while it is possible that Pompey was trying to ensure control of the fortified corridor which he had just captured (though it is much more likely that he had flattened it), it was obviously dangerous to separate one legion from the rest; and it is inconceivable that he was intending to move the whole army back to a position which both he and Caesar had found unsatisfactory in the past, especially when he was constructing a new camp in a site which had every advantage. Moreover it is strange that Pompey's legion was still sufficiently strong and coherent to mount a counter-attack of such devastating effect the moment Pompey himself appeared with reinforcements. And how had so coherent a legion been driven so easily from the camp in the first place? Admittedly Caesar had a superiority of over three to one when he attacked, but Caesar himself tells us that the fortifications of the camp were all intact, and there was a second camp built specially for one legion within the outer one 'like an inner citadel'. It should have been possible for the Pompeian cohorts to defend the walls for longer than they did, and if they had not been sure of rapid reinforcement they would surely not have withdrawn into open country, especially when the camp had no booty in it to delay the pursuit. An outnumbered army would have defended the walls to the last man unless it was very sure that help was coming, but by the time Pompey appeared his legion was in retreat through the decuman gate, and after drawing Caesar's pursuing infantry and cavalry into the entanglement of the fortifications where they would be easier prey for Pompey's horsemen coming up from the seaward side, it was able to counter-attack in good order. It is therefore hard not to suspect that Caesar deliberately suppressed the fact that he was decoyed into that position by Pompey, who far from making good use of an accident of fortune had planned the whole stratagem and won a second victory of the same 'great brilliance' which Appian attributes to the first.

But in assessing Pompey's generalship we must ask not only how far he was responsible for what he achieved, but whether he could have done more, as almost all the ancient sources suggest. Most of them attribute to Caesar an immediate observation to the effect that 'victory would have belonged to the enemy this day if only they had had a victor in command', and though Caesar himself does not mention this pithy condemnation of Pompey in his memoirs, he does say that his defeat was 'mitigated by two factors which prevented the destruction of his whole army', one of which was Pompey's fault, the other the converse of the bad luck which had 'interrupted the victory of Caesar'. The latter was the long earthwork joining the camp to the river. Caesar maintains that the narrowness of the passages which his men had made through the rampart 'hindered Pompey's pursuit as well as impeding his own retreat', but it is hard to see how any unimpeded pursuit could have been nearly as effective as the massacre of men struggling to climb ramparts and leaping on top of one another into the ditch. As for Pompey's alleged fear of ambush, the other factor mentioned by Caesar, it is hardly realistic to suppose that the counter-attack of a single and supposedly defeated legion against three apparently victorious ones could have been as effective as it was if Pompey had not rapidly committed some reinforcements to the battle, and

Pompey may have been right not to send in his whole force. The cavalry were obviously the best arm for pursuit, and within the complex of fortifications he might only have impeded their operations by sending in masses of infantry to increase the chaos, quite apart from the danger of losing control over his own legions which were not as well disciplined by experience as Caesar's veterans. And while it may be mistaken to overreact to Caesar's obviously biased memoirs and find excuses for a genuine failure by Pompey to press home his success, the ancient sources do suggest at least two more considerations that may have influenced him to be satisfied with what was happening without incurring what he considered to be unnecessary risks.

According to Lucan, Pompey had scruples:

> ...For when the civil war might now
> Have bled to death and left a legacy of peace,
> The general himself restrained his rabid swords.
> O Rome, how happy and how free you might have been
> If cruel Sulla could have taken Pompey's place
> In victory. Our sadness shall forever be
> That Caesar profited by vilest crime – his war
> Against a pious son-in-law.

Of course it is absurd to suppose that Pompey failed to follow up his victory out of filial piety towards a former father-in-law for whom he can have felt only bitter hatred now, but the idea that he might have preferred the least bloody victory may not be unreasonable, for all that Lucan idealizes Pompey and his cause as shamelessly as Caesar denigrates them. The fact that Pompey obtained his youthful greatness by shedding Roman blood need not mean that the elder statesman who had come to see himself as the guardian of Rome was anxious to shed more than was necessary, and Pompey's scrupulousness in this respect derives support from Caesar's own observation of his reaction when the victorious troops now saluted him *Imperator*. 'Pompey accepted the salutation,' says Caesar, 'but he neither used the title on dispatches nor displayed the insignia of laurel on his *fasces*.' But typically it is not Caesar but Dio who says 'that Pompey disliked to show exultation over the destruction of Roman citizens'. Caesar simply leaves the impression that Pompey did not really consider himself victorious despite the exaggerated dispatches which he now sent to Oriental kings, and mentions immediately afterwards that Pompey handed over his prisoners to Labienus, who 'brought them all out for the sake of display to increase his own credit as a traitor, and after addressing them as "comrades" and asking them with much insolence if veterans were in the habit of running away, put them all to death in public view'. Admittedly Caesar makes this public execution of prisoners of war the work of Labienus rather than Pompey, but that is less to free Pompey of responsibility than to impose the maximum odium on the 'traitor' Labienus, while at the same time strengthening the reader's impression that Pompey had no control over his subordinates and that his victory had been a lucky fluke. But the episode admits of a very different interpretation. It is inconceivable that Pompey would have allowed Labienus to put Roman citizens to death. Pompey had been only too delighted to incorporate in his own legions the Roman citizens who had surrendered under Gaius Antonius in Illyricum, and he would have been mad to give the demoralized but still formidable army of Caesar no hope of safety by surrender. But with non-citizens there were no such inhibitions, and just as Caesar's Transpadane Gauls from Opitergium had preferred mass-suicide to surrender in the Illyrian operations, so now the victims of public execution will almost certainly have been Gauls and Germans of Caesar's army, particularly cavalrymen. Labienus, after all, was primarily a cavalry commander, and those whom he sarcastically called his old comrades were very probably Gallic and German cavalry and auxiliaries whose execution would have carried a salutary message back to northern Italy and Gaul.

But if a worthy reluctance to shed more Roman blood than necessary may have influenced Pompey, the main reasons why he appears 'over-cautious' in not following up his victory more vigorously was that to take further military risks seemed unnecessary: 'for he expected', says Appian, 'that Caesar's army would come over directly'. And Plutarch says the same. He depicts Caesar's army as shattered both physically and morally, and since Caesar 'was neither strong in funds nor well supplied with food it was thought that within a short time his army would break up of itself'. And even Caesar cannot hide the fact that his position had become untenable, that he 'had been driven from his former plans, must alter his plan of campaign and abandon the siege', that he had 'insufficient confidence in his panic-stricken troops' to commit them to a pitched battle, and that he was 'in great anxiety for his corn-supply'. And was this all bad luck? His special pleading on that score – 'the loss that had been sustained should be attributed to anyone rather than Caesar' – serves only to confirm the realism of Plutarch's picture of Caesar 'returning into his tent after the battle and spending the night in great distress of mind because he was convinced that he had shown bad generalship'. And while Caesar's failure to admit deficiencies in his own generalship does not in itself prove that he was wrong to attribute no skill to Pompey, the fact remains that for Caesar to criticize Pompey for not pressing home a pursuit is to criticize the very policy for which he lavished so much praise on himself in his narrative of the Spanish campaign. Pompey had just as much reason to believe that he could compel Caesar's hungry and despondent army to surrender now in Epirus as Caesar had had for allowing hunger, thirst and demoralization to win him a bloodless conquest over the Pompeian army in Spain. With his control of the food-supply and his vast superiority in cavalry Pompey was in an exactly parallel situation, and if he turned out to be mistaken in his expectations, it is more a tribute to Caesar's generalship in keeping his army's loyalty after such a disaster than a condemnation of Pompey's, for when Caesar now abandoned his position and marched away by night it must have seemed that the war was as good as over. Caesar had wanted the whole world to see Pompey besieged. The world now saw a victorious Pompey pursuing a defeated Caesar, and when Cornelia received his 'joyful letters' brought by men who rushed to be the first to give her the news, she was being cruelly ill prepared for the reverse of fortune that would follow.

# 9
# PHARSALIA

Because of these men Rome was being forced to fight both in
her own defence and against herself, so that even in victory
she would be vanquished.
Dio Cassius, *History of Rome*, 41.57.4

Success was sweet for Pompey after six months of increasingly uncomfortable confrontation on the Adriatic coast. Being commander-in-
chief had the advantage that his orders were obeyed, but it also left his
subordinates free to criticize without responsibility, and Pompey will
have found it a welcome change to hear the cheers of a victorious army
saluting him *Imperator* after months of dreary carping from his peers.
Admittedly there will have been many who understood the strategy and
sympathized with his setbacks, but there will have been others besides
Cicero whose only contributions to the war-effort were gratuitous advice
and facetious remarks of the sort which Plutarch records. 'I hear that
Caesar's friends are depressed,' someone said. '"You mean they have
fallen out with Caesar,"' retorted Cicero, and not surprisingly Pompey
was soon wishing that Cicero would take himself, his snide remarks and
his ridiculous lictors across to Caesar's camp.

About May 48 Cicero received a letter from his son-in-law Dolabella,
formerly the undistinguished admiral of Caesar's Adriatic fleet in the unsuccessful operations of the previous year, now an officer in Caesar's
camp near Dyrrachium. Dolabella advised Cicero 'to be a friend to himself', and his letter gives us a rare glimpse of the propaganda battle which
must have been going on all the time:

You observe that neither the glory of his own name and achievements nor
that of the kings and nations over which he was always boasting of his
patronage has kept Pompey safe, and even that privilege which is available
to the very humblest of mortals – to escape without dishonour – is not available
to him after being expelled from Italy, losing both Spains, having a veteran
army captured, and finally being himself besieged – something which I believe
has never happened to any of our generals before. Apply your mind to the
question of what is left for either you or him to hope for. That is the way
you will most easily make the decision that will be to your best advantage.

Dolabella was preaching to the unhappy converted. If Cicero may not have gone so far as to spread gloom and despondency by correspondence, Plutarch tells us that he 'made no denial that he was sórry he had come, mocked Pompey's preparations, and showed a lurking displeasure in all his plans', that is until now. Two years later he would deny with convenient retrospect that he had ever had confidence in Pompey, but at the time he believed as firmly as anyone that the war was virtually over. 'You ask me for news of the war,' he wrote guardedly to Atticus just after Pompey's victory at Dyrrachium. 'You will be able to hear it from Isidorus. I shall just say that it looks as though what remains will not be too difficult.' And as always on military matters he was wrong.

Caesar was now in a very precarious position. His memoirs maintain that he gave his men such a stirring harangue that they were 'seized with eagerness to repair the disgrace' and demanded to be led out to battle, but when he adds immediately afterwards that he had 'insufficient confidence in his thoroughly shaken soldiery and thought that an interval should be allowed to restore their spirits', the incongruity of the two statements betrays his real fear. Perhaps he believed that Pompey would not accept a battle if he offered it. He himself, after all, had not accepted the last despairing challenge of the Pompeian army in Spain, but he was evidently not prepared to take the risk of being wrong. What he really feared was a possibility which he never acknowledges in his memoirs. He admits to being afraid to commit his troops to battle, and he confesses 'great fear for the corn-supply'. But what worried him most was the prospect of mass defection unless he made his men too busy to brood and got them away from Pompey's well-fed and victorious army. 'It was necessary,' he writes, 'for Caesar to go to Apollonia in order to deposit the wounded, pay the army, encourage the allies and leave garrisons for the towns.' However powerful his harangue, he evidently felt the need to reinforce rhetoric with financial inducements to continued loyalty, and it is hard not to believe that he shared what Appian states to have been Pompey's view, that Caesar's army would presently desert him'. He therefore withdrew all the garrisons from the redoubts which he had been holding for so many weeks, and after sending his baggage in advance by night with a legion to escort it and strict orders 'not to stop or rest until it reached Apollonia', he followed with the rest of his army at the fourth watch with only a valedictory trumpet blast from the rearguard to signal his departure to the enemy.

On his retreat to Apollonia Caesar suffered a nasty dose of the medicine which he had dispensed to Afranius and Petreius as they had struggled to convey their legions back to Ilerda. Pompey was after him at once. He sent his cavalry ahead to harass Caesar's rearguard and followed up with the legions as fast as he could, but Caesar, travelling light and fast, managed to keep his lead until he was over the Genusus and safely installed in his old camp at Asparagium. But Pompey was not far behind, and when he had settled into his old camp on the northern bank, the two armies were back to the positions which they had occupied over three months ago except that this time Caesar was the first to move, and in the opposite direction. His memoirs indicate that he used the same deception which Afranius had used in Spain to steal a march by pretending to settle into the camp but keeping his men ready to leave. Caesar sent his cavalry out very obviously as if to forage, but with orders to return by the rear gate; and when he saw Pompey organizing foraging parties of his own, he resumed his march south to Apollonia. What he does not mention is the advantage he had from the natural barrier of the River Genusus, and if we may suspect that Caesar suppresses Pompey's difficulties in continuing the pursuit (which might well have required a considerable march upstream), we may also doubt that Pompey was as incompetent as Caesar would like us to believe by suggesting that he let his legions drift back for their baggage 'after depositing their arms in camp'. Where Caesar had scored had been in reaching the Genusus first. The river, whose bridges Caesar will obviously have destroyed, gave him a much longer start this time, and by forcing the pace through country in which it was difficult for cavalry to operate, the chances of catching him up became so remote that Pompey gave up the pursuit on the fourth day.

The last thing Pompey wanted was to wear out his army with forced marches of the shattering severity to which he had subjected them six months ago when he had just heard of Caesar's landing on the Adriatic coast and was rushing to secure Dyrrachium. Then it had been necessary, but for Pompey to chase Caesar across difficult terrain without proper provision for his own food-supply would now seem counter-productive. Pompey could not be certain what Caesar would do, but he was equally able to assess the possibilities, and he was happy to let Caesar make the only realistic choice. Caesar was not likely to stay on the Adriatic coast. If Caesar were to try to establish himself in Apollonia, it would be too good to be true, for Pompey could soon come down with a siege-train from Dyrrachium and invest the town by land and sea. Nor could Caesar realistically hope that yet another relieving force would cross from Brundisium and land behind Pompey's back as Antony had done. He had been incredibly lucky twice, and to gamble on Fortune's favour a third time when she had already shown herself so fickle would be madness, even if he had had the food and morale to hold out for any length of time. What Caesar needed was not a trap but freedom. He needed time and food and the chance to bring a revived army into battle with Pompey on equal terms, and he therefore did what Plutarch says he now regretted not having done long before. But while it was undoubtedly the right decision now to go east 'to the fertile country and prosperous cities of Macedonia and Thessaly', it still had many of the disadvantages which had made Caesar reject it in April. He would be moving further from Italy and deeper into the Pompeian East. He would be in retreat. Pompey might not follow him, and if he did follow him, there would still be the problems of foraging on open ground against superior cavalry. But the corn would be ripe in a month, the cities were well supplied, and corn that has to be fought for is better than none at all. To have kept to the western side of northern Greece and gone into Acarnania and Aetolia would have brought him into possibly friendlier but more mountainous areas, and there seemed little future in going where there would be less to eat and nothing to fight for. If Caesar had any chance at all, it was by going to Thessaly in the hope that Pompey would follow him and that the light-weight contest which was already going on there between Scipio and Calvinus would develop into the heavyweight championship of the world, for which Caesar might yet deliver the knockout blow.

Caesar's memoirs express contingency plans in case Pompey did not follow him. If Pompey decided instead 'to besiege Apollonia and Oricum in order to exclude Caesar entirely from the Adriatic coast', he maintained that he would himself blockade Scipio in Thessaly and force Pompey to come to his father-in-law's assistance. But Pompey would have been mad to waste time besieging garrisons in a couple of Adriatic ports while Caesar recovered from his beating and rampaged through Thessaly and Macedonia. Moreover a blockade of Scipio was unrealistic. Pompey would not have left Scipio to face the combined armies of Caesar and Calvinus, and if he had not been going to follow Caesar, he would have ordered Scipio to retire into Asia or even arranged his evacuation by sea. But in that event Pompey would not have been wasting his time with Apollonia and Oricum. If he had decided not to follow Caesar into Thessaly, it would only have been because he was returning to Italy, and that was Caesar's greatest fear. 'If that happened', the memoirs boldly claim, 'Caesar would have joined forces with Calvinus and marched back to Italy through Illyricum', but it is doubtful if there would have been any memoirs from Caesar if he had had to face a march of several hundred miles through some of the most difficult and hostile country in Europe after Pompey's fleet had carried the enemy back across the Adriatic in a single day.

According to most of our sources a return to Italy at this point was favoured by a strong body of opinion in Pompey's camp, and Plutarch makes Afranius its leading spokesman. 'When a Senate had been convened,' he writes, 'Afranius gave the opinion that they should secure Italy, for Italy was the greatest prize of war and would at once put into the hands of her masters Sicily, Sardinia, Corsica, Spain and all of Gaul. The whole reason for the war was Pompey's native land, and when she was stretching out suppliant hands to him close by, it was not right to allow her to remain enslaved and insulted by the servants and flatterers of tyrants.' And there was a certain cogency behind this imaginative rhetoric, although it was only with hindsight that Appian called it 'the best possible advice'. That control of Italy would soon give control of the corn-producing islands of Sicily and Sardinia was true. It was also true that Spain was restive under the governor appointed by Caesar, and since many of the army units as well as the provincial towns were soon to rebel anyway, it would not have taken much to recover those provinces, and Afranius would no doubt have liked to try. While it is hard to know how Gaul would have reacted to a call by its governor for support against a Pompeian army of invasion, the shortage of Gallic cavalry in Caesar's battles of the next year may suggest a growing neutrality as far as the Civil War was concerned, and a rapid victory by a Pompeian army might well have won over the adherence of many tribes and cities of that fragmented nation, if only on the principle that men prefer to be on the winning side. But whether Pompey could have recovered the Western provinces quickly or not, he would certainly have been able to levy more Italian legions and to destroy the political legitimacy which Caesar enjoyed by controlling the centre of government. And it is unlikely that Pompey would have found great difficulty in regaining control of Italy itself. Italy may not have been so universally 'well disposed to him' or quite as 'free from hostile array' as Appian suggests, but Dio is undoubtedly right that 'the general sentiment over there was not opposed to him', and that 'even if it had been, there were no forces to match him in war'.

But cogent as these arguments were, there was a contrary set of which perhaps Appian gives the best summary:

Although this was the best possible advice, Pompey disregarded it and allowed himself to be persuaded by those who said that Caesar's army would presently desert him on account of hunger, or that there would not be much of it left anyway after the battles near Dyrrachium. They said it would be disgraceful to abandon the pursuit of Caesar when he was in flight and for the victors to flee as though vanquished. And Pompey sided with these advisers, partly out of regard for the opinions of the Eastern nations that were looking on, partly to prevent harm from befalling Scipio who was still in Macedonia, but most of all because he thought he ought to fight while his army was in good spirits.

Plutarch has Pompey influenced by some of the same considerations but in a different order of priority reflecting his own prejudices as a moral philosopher:

Pompey neither thought it good for his own reputation to run away a second time from Caesar and be pursued when Fortune had made him the pursuer, nor did he think it right before heaven to abandon Scipio and the men of consular rank in Thessaly and Greece who would at once fall into Caesar's power together with their funds and large forces. He said that the man who cared most for Rome was the man who fought for her at the greatest distance, in order that she might neither suffer war nor hear about any evil but quietly await her master.

And Lucan carries Pompey's concern for Rome's tranquillity to the very limits of his poetical rhetoric:

> 'Shall Pompey now return to precious Italy
> In Caesar's style? Rome never shall see my return
> Except with troops dismissed. When first this strife began
> I could have held our native land if I had wished
> To draw my battle-lines in temples, wage a war
> Inside the forum, make a battlefield of Rome.
> To keep the fighting far away I would transcend
> The furthest orb of Scythian cold or burning sands
> Of torrid zones. Shall I as victor steal Rome's peace
> Who fled from Rome to keep her free of war's distress?
> Nay, rather than you suffer anything, dear Rome,
> In this foul war, let Caesar think you still his own'.
> Thus Pompey spoke, and ordered then his army east
> To Thessaly, where destiny awaited him.

But while it is possible that Pompey said something on these lines when arguing against the proponents of a return to Italy – and it would have been particularly effective against men like Cicero who had complained so bitterly about his having left Rome in the first place – it is Appian who gets down to Pompey's more hard-headed reasons along with Plutarch's reference to 'funds and forces'. It was not a purely intangible loss of face before 'the Eastern nations looking on' that worried Pompey, nor even the danger to Scipio, who could have retired or been evacuated if necessary. It was also the loss of the wealth and power of the East where he had spent the better part of a year accumulating 'funds and forces' before Caesar had even arrived. He might take most of his troops and money to Italy (though the appearance of the Oriental archers and cavalry would hardly have been calculated to win the hearts and minds of Italians

even if they had been willing to go with him), but was he to hand over
the inexhaustible wealth of Asia to Caesar? Rome was virtually bankrupt
because he had severed her financial lifeline with the East, and though
he had command of the seas at present, for how much longer would
he be able to rely on the Eastern navies if he left their cities and principalities exposed to Caesar's legions? Moreover the considerations of personal
pride and power are inextricably combined. Pompey was as much the
champion of the East as of his own greatness. He had won victories in
Spain and Gaul too, but they were long ago. Caesar had since supplanted
him as the great conqueror in the West, and if he were now to desert
the East in preference for recovery of the West, it would be a tacit
admission of Caesar's superiority as an empire-builder.

And there was something else that worried Pompey. If he returned to
Rome, he might easily find that his peers became so deeply absorbed in
political warfare that they would not only lose interest in the real war
but resent the continuing supremacy of the one man who could win it.
Already they were arguing about consulships, praetorships and priest-
hoods, about the punishments to be meted out to their opponents, about
Caesar's own high priesthood of the state religion. Once these political
animals were back on familiar ground, would a Domitius still be content
to accept the orders of a Pompeius when he could raise troops of his
own instead of relying on Pompey's patronage of all the kings whom
he had made? If then Pompey indulged in the sort of rhetoric about his
love for Rome which Plutarch and Lucan attribute to him, it could well
have been a counterblast to the criticism of which he was to hear more
and more as the days went by – that he was simply 'trying to prolong
his authority over so many men of his own rank'. It was not long before
Domitius started calling him 'Agamemnon' and 'King of Kings', and Plutarch refers to accusations of 'directing his campaign not against Caesar
but against his own country and the Senate in order that he might always
be in office and never cease to have for his attendants and guards men
who claimed to rule the world'. But over and above all these things there
is one supreme reason why Pompey pursued Caesar into Thessaly instead
of returning to Italy, and though it is given by Appian, it is usually
swamped by the pervasive tradition that Pompey was reluctant to fight
a pitched battle. 'Most of all', says Appian, 'Pompey thought he should
fight while his army was in good spirits'. In other words, Pompey was
no longer thinking of long-term strategy but preparing for the great
formal battle which he believed he could and must now win.

Pompey wanted to fight soon, not only to make the most of his army's
high spirits before they evaporated but because there was only about
another month before the corn would be ripe, and after that any strategy

of attrition would be a strategy of diminishing returns. The corn ripens in Thessaly about the beginning of June, which was August by the old calendar which might have waited much longer for its reformation if Pompey's expectations had been fulfilled (and it would never had had months called July and August at all). But a month was ample time for Pompey's purposes. He saw no point in wearing out his own army by chasing Caesar over the difficult and poorly supplied country which he would cover on his way to Thessaly. He would organize himself properly with supplies from Dyrrachium, march comfortably into Macedonia along the Egnatian Way, destroy Calvinus' army if he came across it, join forces with Scipio, and then seek out an exhausted, hungry and demoralized Caesar in Thessaly. With luck he would win a bloodless victory as Caesar himself had done in Spain, but if he had to fight, he would do so with the confidence that the enemy was morally and physically at its weakest. And to make sure that his confidence would not be misplaced, he was already pursuing the enemy with his pen, the might of which Caesar soon began to appreciate once he had left his garrisons and wounded at Apollonia and Oricum and begun his long march up the valley of the Drino, through Athamania, and down into Thessaly, by the pass of Metsovo.

If Pompey had been unable to overtake Caesar with his army, Caesar was unable to outstrip the hundreds of messengers who had been galloping out of Pompey's camp every day since the victory as fast as his team of secretaries could write the dispatches. The seals all bore the impress of the lion which held a sword between its paws on Pompey's signet-ring, and every king and prince and civic magistrate who received one was promptly informed of Pompey's victory in the battles near Dyrrachium and his impending victory in the whole war. Only Rome was left officially uninformed, and when Dio wonders why, he can only see it as another example of Pompey's concern 'not to give the impression that Italy was the prize for which he was fighting or to cause any fear to Rome'. But Dio is naïve. If Pompey 'failed to send any dispatches about his success to the government in Rome', the reason was simply that there was no 'government in Rome' to which to write as far as he was concerned. The only government which Pompey recognized was the exiled Senate in his own camp, and far from giving reassurance to the Caesarian magistrates in the capital, he terrified them out of their wits by letting them hear at second hand what must have seemed like a sentence of destruction. But he wrote to everywhere else, and when Caesar sourly recorded that the dispatches were composed 'in a more exaggerated and inflated manner than the facts warranted', he was remembering their effectiveness. 'A report had spread that Caesar had been beaten and was

in flight after losing all his force,' he continues. 'It made the roads dangerous, turned many communities from their friendship with Caesar, and
made it impossible for Caesar's messengers to get through to Calvinus
or Calvinus' to him.' And that was potentially disastrous, for if Calvinus
had received Caesar's messages, he would have been on his way to meet
Caesar in Thessaly. As it was, he was near the western Macedonian town
of Heracleia, the modern Bitola, and dangerously unaware that he was
sitting in the path of Pompey's whole army as it marched eastwards along
the Egnatian Way.

It is impossible to reconstruct a complete picture of what had been
happening in the rest of northern Greece while Caesar and Pompey had
been confronting each other for nearly six months on the Adriatic coast.
Caesar had sent Calvinus and two legions into Macedonia shortly after
Antony had arrived with the reinforcements from Italy in April. Scipio
was then marching towards Macedonia from Asia, and Caesar's orders
to Calvinus were to keep Scipio occupied when he arrived and prevent
him from marching on down the Egnatian Way to relieve Pompey. At
the same time Caesar sent Cassius Longinus into Thessaly and Calvisius
Sabinus into Aetolia with orders to try to expedite the corn-supply. Longinus took the legion of recruits which Caesar could best afford to spare,
Calvisius five cohorts, but their success was inversely proportional to
the size of their armies. According to Caesar's account Calvisius was successful in using force or diplomacy to win control of important cities in
the mountainous areas of southern Epirus and the northern hinterland
of the Corinthian Gulf, though it is doubtful how much advantage this
was to Caesar's commissariat outside Dyrrachium. Caesar had been
struggling to get corn from as far south as Buthrotum opposite Corfu
before Antony arrived, and that had meant either running the Pompeian
blockade or carting it by land over a hundred miles when he had been
at the Apsus. When operations had moved to Dyrrachium this supply-
line had become longer still, and from Aetolia, where Calvisius was now
active, it was over two hundred miles. All the same Calvisius does seem
to have secured parts of southern Epirus, Acarnania and Aetolia for
Caesar, and to have recruited some useful javelineers and archers from
those mountainous regions to help repair a major deficiency in Caesar's
army. But Calvinus and Longinus were less effective in Macedonia
and Thessaly. In many Thessalian towns there were the usual rival political factions which looked to Pompey or Caesar to gain their supremacy,
and when they saw a Caesarian army beginning operations in their territories, the balance of allegiance began tipping against Pompey until Scipio
arrived and threw two crack legions on the other scale.

Even the most unimaginative reader of Caesar's memoirs feels the hatred that permeates almost every line which Pompey's former father-in-law writes about his present one, and we must therefore be even more than usually on our guard against falsification. 'After incurring some losses near Mount Amanus,' says Caesar sarcastically, 'Scipio had styled himself *Imperator*.' Scipio had evidently fought a campaign in the Amanus range that separated Syria from Cilicia, perhaps to teach the robber-tribes a salutary lesson that would keep the line of communication relatively safe for a while after his departure, perhaps because he was himself attacked on his way through the passes, perhaps to give his army some active service. Whether or not the gaining of a personal triumph was a cause as well as an effect of the campaign as Caesar alleges, it appears that Cicero's vaunted victory there had had no lasting result if it had to be repeated so soon, and whatever Scipio did to earn his salutation now was hardly likely to have been less than the fatuous *Imperator* who was annoying everyone with gratuitous military advice in Pompey's camp. But Caesar is merciless to Scipio's memory: Scipio had left his province undefended against the Parthians, spent the winter in Pergamum and the richest cities of Asia, and plundered that province with an apparently unlimited capacity for inventing methods of 'glutting his avarice' – poll-taxes, column-taxes, door-taxes, corn, soldiers, arms, rowers, engines, transport and 'any other form of contribution provided only that a specious name could be found for it'. He had even given orders for the removal of the sacred treasures from the Temple of Diana at Ephesus, and it was only the timely arrival of Pompey's urgent request for assistance – which in turn was due to Caesar's timely crossing of the Adriatic – that prevented him from carrying them out. Such is Caesar's humbug: to take credit for saving the wealth of Ephesian Diana when he had himself just ransacked the Temple of Roman Saturn. The fact is that Scipio was fighting a war and was highly efficient in raising the necessary 'forces and funds'. He was bringing two veteran legions from Syria together with cavalry and auxiliaries, the money to pay them and the corn to feed them, and when Pompey informed him that Caesar had landed, he marched up through Asia, across the Hellespont and so into Macedonia, where he was promptly met by a diplomatic counter-offensive of the type which Caesar always made when he wished to delay the enemy.

Caesar's peace-envoy carried letters written on the principle that flattery would get him everywhere. Caesar's previous peace-initiatives had failed because Pompey's intimates had been afraid to carry his proposals to their chief at a bad time, they said. Scipio on the contrary was a man of such great authority that he was not only able to express freely whatever he thought right but could to a significant extent drive and control a man who was going astray. Scipio also commanded an army in his own name, and therefore in addition to his authority he had the force to compel. Scipio need only use his influence to gain the sole credit for restoring tranquillity in Italy, peace in the provinces, safety throughout the empire. And so it went on. But Scipio was not the man to be seduced by such trowellings of flattery, and while Caesar attributes to Favonius stern reproaches that alone prevented Scipio from melting like butter in his hands, there was nothing soft or slow about Scipio's movements, which were full-speed in the direction of Calvinus. Caesar does not admit in so many words that Calvinus fled, but if not it is strange that Scipio should have swerved down into Thessaly to deal with Cassius Longinus, and 'have done this so swiftly that the news of his coming and his arrival were brought simultaneously'. For extra speed he left Favonius with eight cohorts to guard the baggage and establish a strong position on the River Aliacmon which forms the boundary between Macedonia and Thessaly, and with the help of a Thracian cavalry squadron sent by King Cotys he drove Longinus right out of Thessaly and down into Aetolia, though without bringing him to battle because he was recalled by frantic messages from Favonius who was under attack from Calvinus. Scipio then returned to the Aliacmon, Calvinus challenged him, and Scipio was afraid to fight a pitched battle. He tried instead to lure Calvinus into ambush, but his cowardice recoiled on him and he lost some cavalry in the attempt. Calvinus then returned the compliment, and Scipio lost more. But if Scipio had really been as ineffectual as Caesar makes out, what was Calvinus doing alone on the very edge of Macedonia many days march from the Aliacmon when Pompey marched up the Egnatian Way in July?

Caesar's account is typically selective if not downright false. Both Dio and Appian mention defeats. Dio maintains that Cassius Longinus had not only been driven out of Thessaly into Aetolia but 'severely defeated by Scipio and Sadalus', who was the son of King Cotys and commander of the cavalry which his father had sent to fight for Pompey. Dio also maintains that Calvinus had been driven out of Macedonia by Faustus Sulla, and when Caesar says that Scipio swerved south into Thessaly when only twenty miles from Calvinus in Macedonia, it could well be that Calvinus was not stationary but in full flight with Faustus still in pursuit. Then Appian speaks of a defeat of 'Calvisius' who 'lost a whole legion except eight hundred men', and the fact that Appian had access to statistics gives confidence in the reality of a defeat if not the detail. But the name of the defeated party is perplexing. Calvisius had been operating in Acarnania and Aetolia, and though he had probably recruited a considerable number of Aetolians, it is hard to imagine that he had converted his five cohorts into a legion. Perhaps the answer is that the victories of Scipio recorded by Dio and Appian are really the same one – the victory over Cassius Longinus in Thessaly. The legion that was all but destroyed will have been the legion of recruits which Caesar had sent with Cassius, and Appian's confusion of names could derive from the fact that Cassius now fled to join Calvisius in Aetolia. On the other hand Dio confirms Caesar's account of the subsequent encounter of Calvinus with Scipio. He explains that Calvinus received some Aetolian and Locrian reinforcements, presumably from Calvisius, and it was these light-armed troops who enabled him to recover sufficient composure to confront Scipio on the Aliacmon and play the game of ambushes in which Scipio suffered more than he did. But the fact remains that neither of them was at the Aliacmon when Pompey and Caesar arrived in Macedonia and Thessaly. We do not know what happened in the meantime, but their relative positions suggest that Calvinus had not stood up to Scipio for long. Scipio was stationed in the very centre of Thessaly at Larissa. Calvinus had retired to the very edge of western Macedonia, and if he was alarmed by the rumours of Caesar's defeat and the impossibility of communication, he was still unaware of the danger that was about to emerge through the mountains above him.

Pompey had left Cato at Dyrrachium with fifteen cohorts to guard the arsenal and the Adriatic coast, and had set out along the Egnatian Way with the eagles of nine legions and his several thousand cavalry. His route took him along what is today one of the most exciting and beautiful drives in southern Europe. The road climbs into the mountains from Elbasani up the valley of the Shkumbini (the ancient Genusus), crosses the present border between Albania and Yugoslavia on the western shore of Lake Ochrid, and skirts the top of the lake with its famous Byzantine churches. It then weaves up and down twice more until it emerges through the pass between the Plakenska and the Baba ranges just above Bitola, near the ancient Heracleia, which is about ten miles north of the present frontier between Yugoslavia and Greece. The distance from Durresi (Dyrrachium) to Bitola is all of 150 miles, but Pompey was only four miles from the unsuspecting Calvinus when some of his horsemen riding ahead came upon some of Calvinus' scouts and alerted them to the danger. According to Caesar the Pompeian horsemen were some of the Allobrogian Gauls who had defected with the two princely embezzlers, and since the horsemen they came upon were also Allobrogians, they did not silence them but 'told them all that had happened, that Caesar had been defeated and that Pompey was about to arrive'. They did this, says Caesar, 'either by reason of their former intimacy or because they were boastfully elated about their success', and it may be true, although

Caesar's vindictiveness towards the deserters leaves room for doubt. But however it happened, Calvinus was alerted to his danger in the nick of time, and if Pompey was disappointed to have missed the opportunity of crushing him, he was not going to exhaust his own army with the pursuit of a smaller enemy fleeing for dear life. Calvinus was no doubt helped on his way by Pompey's cavalry, and without time to make an orderly withdrawal he might be expected to reach Caesar suitably hungry and rattled. Pompey himself would continue marching steadily down to join forces with Scipio in the reasonable expectation that the combination of two well-fed and confident armies would be able to administer the *coup de grâce* to Caesar and Calvinus simultaneously.

But Caesar was no longer starving quite as seriously as he had been. As he had marched up the valley of the Drino from Apollonia and Oricum it had been more demoralizing than disastrous that towns previously friendly in the wake of Calvisius' operations now closed their gates, that 'no one would sell him corn', that 'everyone despised him because of his defeat'. But when two hundred arduous miles had brought him across the Pindus mountains through the pass of Metsovo from where he began the descent into Thessaly, the limited supplies which his men had been able to bring with them from Apollonia were exhausted, and he came to the conclusion that gates which would not open to persuasion must be forced. It would be difficult without a siege-train, but when the choice of death lay between starvation and fighting to avoid starvation, he did not hesitate, especially since Calvinus now joined him with more mouths to feed and swords to wield. When they came to the prosperous town of Gomphi, from which Caesar had received friendly approaches in the past, he still hoped that his arrival with the entire army might allow his former partisans to gain the upper hand in the city and persuade their fellow-citizens to receive him. But 'the exaggerated rumour of the battle near Dyrrachium had already outstripped him', and the gates were closed by order of a certain Androsthenes, 'who preferred to share the victory of Pompey than associate with Caesar in adversity'. Androsthenes sent messengers racing to Pompey and Scipio with requests for urgent assistance, and while he knew he could not withstand a long siege, he believed he could 'rely on the town's defences if help came quickly'. But the Greek had miscalculated. Caesar simply asked his starving army if they wanted food, wine and women, pointed to the walls, and added that if they made a real example of this town they would get what they wanted merely by asking at the next. It was not a case for siege but storm, and when Caesar's iron wave had broken over the walls, Gomphi suffered all that a town can suffer from an army in war, and its fate provided an object-lesson which was as effective as Caesar had hoped. For when the army advanced to the town of Metropolis and presented the miserable remnants of Gomphi's population before a second set of closed gates, the gates were opened without a fight, and Caesar 'carefully preserved this accommodating town from harm'. That he was able to do so is a great tribute to his own leadership and his army's discipline even after temporary satiation by the debauch at Gomphi, and the restraint was worthwhile. The contrast between the fates of the two towns was not lost on the rest of Thessaly, and as long as there was only Scipio's smaller army to encourage opposition, Caesar no doubt found it easier to gain supplies at least in southern Thessaly, although his picture of a wholesale change of allegiance throughout the whole of Thessaly except Larissa is an obvious exaggeration when Pompey's victorious army was about to descend from the north. For Caesar knew that he would not be left alone much longer, and 'having found a suitable place in the cornlands where the crops were nearly ripe, he decided to await the arrival of Pompey there'.

Pompey entered Thessaly 'a few days later' according to Caesar, possibly along much the same route as that taken by the modern road from Bitola to Larissa, a distance of some 150 miles. He would have crossed the Aliacmon into northern Thessaly after covering about half that distance, and with the exception of the climb from the valley of the Aliacmon to meet the headwaters of the Xinias, it would have been a relatively easy march from there to Larissa, where Scipio was sensibly guarding that central city and supply-base with his two legions. And when Pompey arrived and joined forces with Scipio, he was full of confidence in an early victory. 'He harangued the combined army, thanked his own men, and exhorted those of Scipio to consent to share the plunder and prizes once victory was won.' He then 'combined all the legions into one camp but shared the dignity of command with Scipio, for whom he ordered a separate headquarters to be established and the trumpet to be sounded before both of them'. He was not only honouring his father-in-law but making an effort to appear less autocratic by preserving the appearance, if not the reality, of proconsular equality, exactly indeed as he had done in 52 by taking Scipio as his partner to dualize the extraordinary 'sole consulship'. Pompey then led all eleven legions southwards to hunt Caesar down, and the great army felt such confidence in its massive array of strength 'that the interval which separated it from battle seemed merely the postponement of the return to Italy'. But Pompey would not hurry although it was an easy, fairly level march from Larissa down to Caesar's reported position in the Enipeus valley. He probably followed the route of the present-day railway-line south-westwards to about a mile beyond Doxara, then swung south-east to enter the northern side of the broad, flat

Enipeus plain through the gap between Mt Dogantzes on his right and the range of hills which includes Kastro Psychiko and ends with Kalogeros to his left. He found Caesar encamped about four miles up-river on the same side, for though the ancient town of Pharsalus which gave its name to the battle was probably on a hill to the south of the river, Caesar had no interest in having the Enipeus between him and his adversary. Nothing separated the two armies but four miles of level ground on which a pitched battle could be fought on even terms. Pompey selected a strong position on a hill-side, which was almost certainly the southeastern slopes of Mt Dogantzes, and having fortified a camp he settled down to wait and see how Caesar would react.

According to his own memoirs, Caesar was the first to offer battle 'after having arranged for his corn-supply, encouraged his troops and allowed sufficient time to elapse since the battles near Dyrrachium to feel confident again in the temper of his men'. He admits that when he first drew them out in battle-line it was in 'a position favourable to himself', but as the days went by and he advanced further and further from his own camp, Pompey still refused battle even when Caesar had 'moved his own lines right up to the Pompeian hills'. There were skirmishes between the rival horsemen and Caesar records feeling satisfaction at the performance of the mixed force of mounted and unmounted spearmen which he had developed to try to counteract Pompey's enormous superiority in cavalry. But this was hardly the reason why Pompey still kept refusing Caesar's daily challenges to a pitched battle. He drew out his army of course, but he kept it on the low slopes below his camp and seemed so reluctant to come down on to level ground that Caesar eventually despaired of fighting and gave the order to break camp and move to Scotussa, 'with a view to getting supplies more easily and wearing out Pompey's army, unaccustomed as it was to hard work, by daily marches'. But just as Caesar's vanguard was leaving camp before dawn on 9 August to march eastward, his scouts reported that Pompey's army was drawing up for battle in the open plain 'so that it now seemed possible for a battle to be fought in no disadvantageous position'. ' "We must put off our march for the present," ' he cried, ' "and think instead of giving the battle we have always demanded. Let us get ready to fight. We shall not easily get another opportunity after this." ' And he proceeded to lead his army against Pompey.

But what had prompted Pompey's apparently sudden decision to fight now? If he had been willing to fight a pitched battle all the time, why did he wait so many days? Or had he not wanted to fight a pitched battle after all but been forced into it by his army against his own better judgement? This last is the almost universal opinion of the ancient sources.

Plutarch, for example, maintains that Pompey was as fearful of victory as of defeat. 'He got wind of talk among the cavalry that as soon as they had routed Caesar they would have to put down Pompey too, and some also say that this was why Pompey left Cato without any service of importance but kept him at the coast in charge of the baggage, for he feared that if Caesar were removed, he might himself be forced to lay down his command by Cato.' Such talk was appropriate to the cavalry because that arm contained Rome's social élite, but however many may have suspected that Pompey would not be willing to relinquish supreme command once Caesar was out of the way, it is ridiculous to suppose that Pompey intended to spend the rest of his life in camp.

Appian gives a perfectly credible picture of Pompey 'surrounded by a great number of senators of equal rank with himself, by the most distinguished knights and numerous kings and princes all demanding battle, some by reason of inexperience, some because they were too highly elated by the victory at Dyrrachium, and some because they were tired of the war and preferred a quick decision to a sound one'. Even Caesar is almost sympathetic in his description of Pompey's predicament in the midst of so many senators who, 'when any action of Pompey showed a degree of slowness or deliberation, declared that a single day would finish the task and that he was simply enjoying his own *imperium* and treating men of consular and praetorian rank as his slaves'. And Pompey must have been sick and tired of the endless squabbling between Scipio, Domitius and Lentulus for Caesar's high priesthood, wearied by Domitius' obsession with the procedural problems of deciding gradations of punishment for neutrals and collaborators, bored by deputations of an absent envoy's friends seeking repeated reassurances that he would not be overlooked in the next elections, exasperated by the enormous amount of energy being given to using a victory which had yet to be won. But did Pompey allow all these people to influence him against his better military judgement?

Plutarch maintains that he did. 'They put pressure on Pompey, and because he was the sort of man who is too concerned with his good reputation and too respectful to his friends, they dragged him into following after their own hopes and impulses, abandoning the best of plans and acting in a way that would have been inappropriate for the captain of a ship, let alone a general in sole command of so many nations and armies.' Appian says much the same but also suggests that 'divine infatuation' was 'leading him astray', that he had become 'dilatory and sluggish contrary to his true nature', and that he now lacked the strength to keep to the strategy of 'driving Caesar from famine to pestilence'. Lucan invents a speech through which Cicero is made the chief opponent of delay, and when Pompey reluctantly agrees to fight, he groans at the realization that destiny is 'thwarting his attempts to secure a bloodless conquest'. But the flaw in these interpretations of Pompey's apparent reluctance to fight a pitched battle is Caesar's simple statement that 'the corn was nearly ripe', which means that the alternative strategy of attrition which Plutarch and Appian give as Pompey's real preference was no longer realistic. Interestingly Appian had seen that Pompey had marched from Dyrrachium with the intention of fighting a pitched battle 'while his army was still in high spirits', but if he had paid more attention to the time of year, he might have realized that it was no longer 'easier and safer to reduce Caesar by want'; and he might then have avoided being so caught up in the tradition of Pompey's passive reluctance to fight that he had to make him change his mind when he reached Pharsalus. But why then did Pompey delay in accepting Caesar's daily challenges to a set-piece battle on level ground? For exactly the same reason that Caesar had refused the last desperate challenge of the Pompeian army in Spain: he hoped that Caesar's army would be so desperate that it would either surrender or attack him on unfavourable ground. But the desperate bravery which had stormed Gomphi had combined with the wise restraint at Metropolis to relieve Caesar's army from utter deprivation, and though gates would no longer open so readily now that Pompey's larger army had arrived – Caesar after all was preparing to march eastwards to a hill-town over ten miles away for supplies – the corn was nearly ripe in the fields. And when Pompey realized that it was no use waiting any longer for a surrender or a suicidal attack by an army whose physical and moral health was now more likely to improve than deteriorate, he finally offered the pitched battle for which he had been ready ever since he left Dyrrachium but had nevertheless hoped to avoid, not so much from the idealistic humanity which Lucan attributes to him but simply because a bloodless victory would have been less risky. Admittedly the pressure from senators eager to seek office in Rome, princes to return to their principalities and Favonius to enjoy his Tusculan figs will have had an influence on him, but it was not against his better military judgement that he pleased them by deciding to fight Caesar before the corn ripened, even if Appian is right that he 'turned with concealed disgust' from the hubristic over-confidence of many of his peers who decked their tents with premature laurels and ordered their slaves to prepare the victory banquet in advance.

Plutarch gives another clue to Pompey's intentions, without realizing its full implications himself. He imagines Pompey's later self-recrimination 'for having been forced to do battle with his land forces while making no use of his navy, which was indisputedly superior, and for not having stationed it at a point where, if defeated, he might have had this powerful force nearby to make him a match for the enemy'. The very fact that Pompey had not stationed naval squadrons on the Aegean coast where they would have been needed in a war of attrition or for evacuation in the event of defeat shows that he was confident of a rapid victory, bloodless or otherwise. For he had not simply forgotten about his fleet, as Plutarch and Appian imply. Caesar's memoirs later reveal that the admiral Gaius Cassius had already taken the Syrian, Phoenician and Cilician fleets to attack Sicily, and that his colleague Laelius had taken the Adriatic fleet across to Brundisium and was blockading the rest of Caesar's forces there. These naval operations had almost certainly been ordered by Pompey when he had returned briefly to Dyrrachium before marching east in pursuit of Caesar, and they were not the orders of a man who was either reluctant to fight or doubtful about winning. As Dio rightly says, 'he had taken victory for granted', and far from taking any precautions against a protracted struggle or a defeat, he had sent his fleets to begin the reconquest of the West.

There is much speculation among the ancients on what Pompey and Caesar thought about before the great battle. The thought of 'Rome and its empire lying before them as the prize in one great contest of arms', should certainly have produced some sober reflection, and Dio may well be right that they sought reassurance from past glories: 'Pompey thought of Africa, Sertorius, Mithridates, Tigranes and the war at sea, Caesar of Gaul, Spain, the Rhine and Britain. They were wrought up to the highest pitch of excitement by the belief that these conquests too were at stake, and each was eager to acquire the other's glory; for the renown of the vanquished far more than his other possessions becomes the property of the victor, since the greater and more powerful the antagonist that a man defeats, the greater the height to which he himself is raised.' And if Dio was not the world's greatest historian, he was a sufficiently cynical student of the more depressing side of human nature to see through the humbug in which megalomania disguises itself in civil war. When he came to the obligatory speeches which the two generals made to their troops, he observed that both would have been saying the same thing. 'As they came from the same state and were talking about the same things, calling each other tyrants and themselves the liberators from tyranny of the men they were addressing, they had nothing different to say on either side but stated that it was the lot of one side to die, of the other to be saved, of one to become captives, of the other to enjoy mastery, to be deprived of everything or to possess everything, to suffer or to inflict a most horrible fate.' The Caesarians were told to rejoice that 'at last they were fighting men instead of hunger'. The Pompeians were told to rejoice 'now that they had the opportunity for fighting which they kept demanding'. Then over eighty thousand rejoicing men prepared to kill each other.

When I visited the area in 1979 it was full of shepherds with their flocks, and it must have been the sight of a lifetime for their ancestors on the morning of 9 August 48 BC by the old calendar, 6 June by ours, when two great armies commanded by the two greatest generals of the greatest nation in the world were deploying in long, undulating lines more or less perpendicular to the river. They might have counted the eagles of at least nineteen legions but not the hundreds of standards that bobbed about on the seas of burnished helmets gleaming in the sun. They would have recognized the uniform regiments of Italian troops weaving their way with practised ease through patterns of labyrinthine complexity, but it would have taken a Herodotus to identify the many thousands of non-Roman auxiliaries, particularly on Pompey's side. For while Caesar had a fairly cosmopolitan mixture with his Gallic and German horsemen and his light-armed Dolopians, Acarnanians and Aetolians, his army looked drab compared with Pompey's gorgeous array from all the nations of the East, wearing every sort of costume and carrying every sort of weapon imaginable.

From Greece had come the descendants of the old rivals of the Peloponnesian War, Athenians and Spartans now fighting on the same side, the latter marshalled under their own kings and accompanied by large numbers of Peloponnesians and Boeotians. There were Thracians, Hellespontines, Bithynians, Phrygians, Ionians, Lydians, Pamphylians, Pisidians and Paphlagonians. There were contingents from Cilicia, Syria, Phoenicia, the Arabs and the Jews. There were Cyprians, Rhodians, Cretan slingers and all the other islanders. There were kings and princes leading their own troops, Galatians, Cappadocians, Armenians and numerous lesser peoples unnamed. They came on foot and they came on horseback, the Oriental cavalrymen vying in magnificence with the flower of Roman chivalry which would have ridden alone but for Pompey's patronage. And as these thousands struggled to get into position alongside the legions, a watching shepherd might have wondered why there was now no skirmishing with the armies so close that only charging distance separated their front lines. He would not have understood that civilized men regarded this sort of warfare as a dangerous form of sport, and that they observed the rule of not starting the game until both sides were ready. And if the captain of the Thracian bowmen had suggested to Pompey that he might try to pick Caesar off as the enemy general rode along his lines, Pompey would undoubtedly have replied with the same horrified refusal of Wellington before Waterloo, that general officers have more to do than take pot shots at each other before a battle begins.

It is curious and disturbing to find that Caesar's account of so cataclysmal a battle differs in so many points from that of Plutarch and Appian, both of whom relied on Asinius Pollio who was himself at Pharsalus and fought on Caesar's side. But if there are loose ends that refuse to be tied up and many bare patches, the basic pattern is visible. Pompey seems to have placed his Cilician legion on the right wing, supported by some Spanish cohorts which Afranius had brought with him after the surrender. Who commanded there is not certain, but it was most probably Lentulus, the consul of the previous year who had been so resolute an opponent of any concessions to Caesar's political demands. Caesar hated him, but though it is true that Lentulus was enormously in debt and out to make a profit from the war, it would be easier to believe Caesar's claim that secret negotiations with Lentulus for the betrayal of Pompey at Dyrrachium had broken down only on the question of price if we could believe that there was any price which Caesar was not prepared to promise from the funds of the Roman people. At any rate Lentulus was now fighting to win the war which he had precipitated, and if he commanded Pompey's right wing, he was opposite Antony commanding the ninth and eighth legions of Caesar's left, the ninth 'so severely attenuated by the Dyrrachian battles that Caesar had added the eighth to it and virtually made the two legions into one'. In the centre Pompey had stationed the two veteran legions which Scipio had brought from Syria, and he had naturally put Scipio in command there against Calvinus. The left he commanded himself with the two legions which he had brought from Italy. They were the legions which had served with Caesar in Gaul – one of them Caesar's own, the other lent him by Pompey in 54 – until the Senate had recalled them to Italy against the danger of a Parthian invasion of Syria in the aftermath of Crassus' defeat. In 49 Pompey had doubted their reliability against their old commander's lightning invasion of Italy, but after a year and a half as the nucleus of Pompey's military build-up in Greece they were so utterly loyal that he could now put them in what was to be his strongest position. Curiously Plutarch and Appian say that Domitius commanded them whereas Caesar says Pompey, but it may be that both were there, Pompey as overall commander, Domitius commanding the wing exactly as Publius Sulla commanded Caesar's right in the shadow of Caesar himself, who took up his position opposite Pompey with his best legion, the tenth. But if we know the positions of only five Pompeian legions, they were not of course his only ones. Pompey almost certainly had eleven eagles in the battle, but the five mentioned were his strongest, and having placed them on the wings and in the centre he filled in with the rest together with some of the more disciplined Greek auxiliary infantry – the Macedonians, Peloponnesians, Boeotians, and Athenians 'since he approved the quiet behaviour of these contingents'. According to Caesar he made up a total of 110 cohorts consisting of forty-five thousand men, which Frontinus describes as being drawn up in three parallel lines each ten men deep. In fact he had at most eighty-eight cohorts containing a maximum of thirty-six thousand troops of the line, but even without Caesar's exaggerations Pompey had numerical superiority of one and a half times. And he had two thousand 'beneficiaries', veteran soldiers whom he had personally promoted for exceptional qualities of leadership and bravery in past campaigns. These men were as loyal as they were tough, and he dispersed them throughout the lines to give encouragement to the newer recruits by their leadership and example.

Caesar records that his own heavy infantry numbered twenty-two thousand men in a total of eighty cohorts, which must have been under half-strength if his figures are accurate. But it was not so much the disparity in infantry that worried Caesar but in cavalry, for even the most unmilitary of shepherds watching from the hills will have seen at once why Pompey was so confident of victory, and how he expected to win it. Because Pompey's right and Caesar's left were protected by the river and marshy ground, Pompey stationed only six hundred cavalry – his Cappadocian and Pontic squadrons – on the right wing, and all the rest on the left, together with all the archers and slingers. The numbers of archers and slingers are not recorded but they undoubtedly ran into several thousands, many times outnumbering the long-range troops on Caesar's side. But we can be fairly certain in putting the cavalry on Pompey's left flank at about six thousand, and if Pompey knew that man for man (or even two men for three) Caesar's average legionary was better than his own, he was confident that a six-fold superiority in cavalry would tip the balance decisively in his favour, though he was not perhaps as naïvely over-confident as Caesar makes out when imagining Pompey expounding his battle-plan to his staff on the previous day.

' "I know I am promising something almost incredible," ' Pompey is supposed to have begun. ' "But listen to the reasoning behind my plan so that you may go into battle with greater confidence. I have persuaded our cavalry – and they have confirmed that they will do it for me – to attack Caesar's right wing on the open flank as soon as the two armies have drawn near, and by surrounding his lines from the rear to drive his whole army in confused rout before even a single spear is thrown at the enemy by us. We shall thus finish the war without endangering the legions and almost without a wound. There is no difficulty because we are so strong in cavalry." ' But while the suggestion that Pompey expected to rout Caesar without engaging his legions is as ridiculous as the implication that he proposed to charge 'as soon as the armies had drawn near' (for Caesar's own account reveals that he had time for reorganizing his battle-lines after they had been drawn up), it is clear that the cavalry were to be the architects of victory. The infantry would obviously engage, but it would be enough for Pompey's legions to hold Caesar's advance in the centre and right until the cavalry on the left had swept away the horsemen protecting Caesar's right. Pompey's cavalry would then be able to outflank Caesar's right, whose cohesion, already loosened by the arrows and bullets of the massed bowmen and slingers, would be shattered by the simultaneous attack of Pompey's legions from the front and the cavalry, followed by the light-armed, moving in from the unshielded flank and rear. The whole of Caesar's line might then be rolled up from his right.

To protect his right (always the more vulnerable wing to flanking attacks in any case because the left arm carried the shield) Caesar had only about a thousand horsemen, and for all that he had given them the support of the young javelineers whom he had trained to fight among them on foot, he could not realistically expect them to withstand Pompey's six thousand or more cavalry and countless auxiliaries. He therefore withdrew three thousand of his best men from the third line of heavy infantry and created a fourth, which he drew up not frontally but obliquely behind the right wing so that it faced the direction from which Pompey's outflanking attack would come. For while a cavalry charge was devastating against infantry caught in the flank or rear or not properly formed up, a frontal attack against veteran legionaries tightly organized to receive them was a different matter altogether, and Caesar now ensured that when Pompey's cavalry outflanked one front line, it would find itself facing another. It meant weakening the centre and left, but it was the only thing to do, and Caesar gave these men instructions to use tactics which he evidently considered unsporting because he suppressed them in his memoirs. But if he wanted to disguise from posterity that he was a player rather than a gentleman, he reckoned without at least one other literary soldier who fought that day and provided the eye-witness account which was available to Plutarch and Appian, who both record the orders which Caesar gave. The men were not to throw their javelins as the best soldiers usually did in their eagerness to draw their swords. They were to use them as spears instead and thrust them up into the faces and eyes of the riders, ' "for these beautiful and blossoming war-dancers will not stand their ground for fear of having their youthful beauty marred, nor will they face the steel when it is right in their eyes" '. This sort of language has the ring of truth about it. It would appeal to

the tough, stinking, lousy legionaries who were about to face the social
élites not only of Oriental kingdoms but of Rome, and it combines with
several references in Lucan to suggest that Caesar was as willing to
mobilize class-antagonism in his interest on the battlefield as in the
Forum.

When all was ready Pompey and Caesar rode along their lines to give
the final exhortation to their men, though not the watery humbug about
past peace-initiatives which Caesar records as his own contribution. They
cried out their watchwords. 'Hercules the Invincible!' cried Pompey.
'Venus the Victorious!' yelled Caesar, ominously borrowing the deity
who presided over the monument to Pompey's greatness in Rome. And
the whole valley rang and re-echoed with the answering shouts from
more than eighty thousand men. Who first gave the signal for attack is
not clear. Appian says it was Pompey when he saw that some of his less
experienced and non-Italian troops were not keeping rank, but whichever
it was, the other responded immediately. The trumpets sang out, centurions barked their orders, standard-bearers encouraged their men. But
only one side charged. Pompey had ordered his legions to stand fast and
receive Caesar's charge with unbroken lines. He wanted the enemy to
become exhausted and disorganized by charging double the usual distance, and he thought that his own men would not only be able to aim
their own javelins more accurately but parry the enemy's more effectively
if they remained carefully shielded in disciplined ranks. The disadvantage
for which Caesar criticizes this order by Pompey is that a charge is essential to raise the men's courage which otherwise remains chilled, and perhaps if Pompey had had a whole line of veteran troops as Caesar did,
he might have been more conventional. On the other hand the British
lines were anything but disadvantaged by Wolfe's order to stand fast
against the French attack at Quebec, and if we are still tempted to fall
into Plutarch's error of assuming that all the military judgements of a
victorious general must be eternal verities, Montaigne's essay *On the Uncertainty of our Judgement* provides an elegantly cautionary parody setting out with great cogency the arguments which Plutarch would undoubtedly have used in admiration of Pompey's decision if the battle had
gone the other way. Admittedly Pompey did not have the satisfaction
of seeing Caesar's lines breaking up into exhausted chaos. Caesar's
veterans were experienced and disciplined enough to stop of their own
accord when they reached their usual charging distance: they re-formed,
counted ten, and charged again. But Caesar acknowledges that 'the Pompeians did not fail to meet this thing. They parried the shower of javelins,
withstood the attack of Caesar's legions without breaking their ranks,
and after throwing their own javelins they snatched out their swords.'

And if Pompey was gratified to see how well his infantry had stood up to Caesar's attack, he was delighted to observe his plan unfolding to perfection on the left wing where Caesar's cavalry was in headlong retreat.

'Those who fought at long range were less conscious of the horror of civil war as they shot their arrows, hurled their javelins and discharged their slings without knowing whom they hit.' This comment from Dio, ominously appropriate to the present century, referred to Pompey's thousands of archers and slingers who had poured a destructive hail of missiles on Caesar's right wing while Labienus had been driving its protective cavalry screen from the field. Labienus now redeployed the Pompeian squadrons for the next phase of the operations, and when they thundered forward again to take Caesar's legions in the flank, it seemed only a matter of time before Pompey would be signalling a general advance against rapidly disintegrating enemy lines. But things began to go wrong. Caesar ordered up his oblique fourth line to cover the threatened wing, and what was intended to be an irresistible erosion of the unshielded flank of cohorts preoccupied with the legions in front of them turned out to be a head-on crash into a fresh and unbroken line of Caesar's best infantry.

It is certainly not the case that Pompey's cavalry were all Oriental fops and Roman dandies who fled like startled rabbits at the thought of marring their good looks. The most valiant cavalry regiments in history have been among the most vain, and while the language in which Caesar conveyed his orders not to throw the javelins but thrust upwards with them at the riders was calculated to encourage the troops and appeal to their social prejudices, it would also have been the best advice for dealing with the basest and ugliest of horsemen. The fact is that the Romans did not have sufficiently heavy cavalry to be really effective in frontal attack on heavy infantry that was organized to receive them. If it could catch legionary units in the flank or rear or when manœuvring or on the march it could of course be devastating, and Pompey was justifiably confident of victory if his horsemen could encircle Caesar's right wing and thereby disorganize the advancing infantry. As it was, they rode into an advancing iron wall surmounted by spikes, their charge was disastrously broken, and they were driven from the field in utter chaos.

The next victims were the thousands of archers, slingers and javelineers. Deprived of the cavalry's protection they were now at the mercy of the cavalry's conquerors, and when all who failed to flee in time had been cut to pieces, the issue of the Civil War was left to be decided by the legions alone. Nor was it an equal struggle any longer. Pompey's right and centre were holding their own, but the cohorts which had kept Caesar's right from being outflanked were now themselves encircling

Pompey's left, and there was absolutely nothing that Pompey could do about it. The rest of his lines were too heavily engaged to be redeployed, and when Caesar now sent forward his own third line which he had previously kept back, the sudden reinforcement of his whole front by these fresh troops began to push the Pompeians back.

A general in the field recognizes the inevitability of success or defeat long before his men, who are concerned only with what is happening within a few feet of them. Many of Pompey's units were still advancing and feeling that things were going well, many more were conscious of holding their own, but Pompey could see that all their efforts were in vain, and he was helpless to do anything about it. He could either stay or flee – lose life, battle and war all at once, or preserve his life in the hope of losing only the battle. Caesar says that Pompey and all his officers and men had sworn not to leave the field except in victory, but it seemed more useful if less glorious now to ride back to the camp and try to organize its defence. There were seven fresh cohorts guarding it, and if they were ready to receive the fugitives who would soon come streaming back from the inevitable rout, there might yet be a chance of salvaging the nucleus of a future army from the mess.

According to Caesar's necessarily imaginative account Pompey called to the centurions at the gate to prepare to defend the camp 'if anything goes amiss', but after adding that he would ride round the rest of the garrison and encourage the men, he went instead to his headquarters – 'mistrusting his fortunes yet waiting to see the issue'. According to other accounts he was sunk in a daze like Ajax in the *Iliad* when Zeus had temporarily withdrawn his adrenalin, and since all the versions vie with each other to dramatize the state of fallen greatness, it is even more than usually difficult to discern any foundations of fact under so deep a layer of fiction. What is clear is that Pompey was mistaken if he now expected the enemy to be too exhausted to storm the camp immediately. Caesar's troops were certainly exhausted after fighting hand-to-hand all morning in the hot sun, but the prospect of the prize which awaited them in Pompey's camp soon dispelled their fatigue when Caesar urged them to drive home the pursuit.

The consciousness of failure sapped the spirit of the fugitives as effectively as success revitalized the victors. With a horror of further fighting many of the Pompeians ran straight past the camp and struggled up the heights behind it, and though the camp was bravely defended by those who remained, they were not enough to withstand the rush of so many more Caesarians all maddened with blood, greed and victory. The sight which met the victors' eyes defied the wildest imaginings of hunger. 'There were bowers constructed,' records Caesar, 'and a great quantity of silver plate laid out, pavilions laid with freshly cut turf and those of Lentulus and some others covered over with ivy and many other indications of excessive luxury and confidence of victory, so that it could easily be understood that they had felt no anxiety about the issue of the day.' But Pompey himself was not waiting among the ivied bowers for the ultimate indignity. As soon as the enemy had begun circulating within the ramparts and all hope of a successful defence had failed, he had ridden out of the rear gate with a bodyguard of thirty horsemen and made for Larissa, where he was one of the first to bring news of his own disaster.

For Caesar to be able to restrain his victorious troops from looting for long enough to deal with the Pompeians who had fled to the hills is another tribute to his authority and their discipline. The danger that the shattered army would try to counter-attack was negligible, but Caesar was determined to stop it from escaping, and he began by digging a line of earthworks that would keep the Pompeians on the waterless hill where they had taken refuge until they responded to his demands for their surrender. But they neither trusted him nor waited to be surrounded. Keeping to high ridges they marched off in the direction of Larissa and left Caesar with no alternative but to renew the pursuit. As Caesar could not leave either his own or Pompey's camp undefended, he divided his army into three parts and took his four best legions to try to intercept the fugitives. And the end of the Pompeian army in Thessaly in 48 was that of the Pompeian army in Spain in 49. When they had travelled a few miles in the direction of Larissa they found Caesar barring their path after marching more rapidly on a longer but easier route on more level ground – the way they had themselves come from Larissa with such confidence so short a time before. They then took up a position on a hill near a river, but Caesar's indefatigable excavators rapidly cut them off from the water-supply with more earthworks, and this time they had had enough. Deputations passed between the two armies, and though some senators made their escape by night, the rest of the fugitives surrendered *en masse* the next morning on the strength of a promise of safety for themselves and their property. Then at last Caesar was free to pursue Pompey to Larissa.

But Pompey was no longer there. According to Appian and Dio the citizens of Larissa had not shunned him in misfortune, but he had refused their invitation to enter the town and urged them to avoid the danger of reprisals by surrendering to Caesar. For there was no future for Pompey in Thessaly now. He had made no provision whatever for the possibility of defeat, mainly because he was confident of victory but also because a man of great power who stakes everything on one future event cannot conceive of surviving an unimaginable failure. But now the unthinkable had happened, and finding himself alive he found hope, and the hope seemed brightest in the East. With luck Caesar might give up the pursuit, return to Italy and give Pompey the time to rebuild his fortunes in the lands of his former successes. Or if Caesar pursued him, he would at least have the satisfaction of drawing him away from Dyrrachium where Cato's fifteen cohorts could be shipped to Africa or some other friendly land to form the nucleus of a new army. And who knew what else might happen? Caesar might have a heart-attack, or be assassinated, or catch pneumonia, and the whole situation might change overnight. But whatever destiny had in store for him, Pompey wanted to face it with Cornelia at his side and at all costs to keep her out of his enemy's clutches, as much for his own sake as for hers. From Larissa he fled rapidly through the Vale of Tempe to the sea. He avoided the towns in order to escape the attentions of the agents and bounty-hunters who were already scouring Thessaly for word of him, and when he reached the coast, he commandeered a merchant-ship to take him across to Lesbos.

# 10

# DEATH ON THE NILE

Such was the inconstancy of Pompey's fortune that this man
who had recently lacked more land to conquer found none to
give him burial.
Velleius Paterculus, *History of Rome*, 2.53.3

If Pompey had harboured any doubts that Cornelia's love and loyalty
would be proof against disaster, they were soon dispelled when he
reached Mytilene, if Lucan and Plutarch may be believed. Both authors
dramatize the meeting with great emotion. Plutarch tells how Pompey's
messenger could not bear to salute Cornelia, but 'indicating the greatness
of her misfortunes more by tears than words he bade her hasten to the
harbour if she wished to see Pompey with only one ship, and that not
his own. She fainted and lay a long time bereft of sense and speech,
but when she at last recovered consciousness, she ran through the city
to the shore where Pompey caught her in his arms.' Lucan pictures Cornelia already waiting on the shore to see what news the approaching ship
would bring. Until then her worst fear had been bad news and ominous
reports, but now the messenger was Pompey himself, bringing word and
proof of his own disaster. When she recovered from the initial shock and
found herself in Pompey's arms, her paroxysm of grief was cut short by
words which seem to us inappropriate for a man who loved his wife as
much as Pompey is supposed to have done but are worth quoting if only
to help us understand the alien mentality of the Roman aristocracy to
which Lucan himself belonged:

> 'A woman graced with such ancestral fame as you
> Should not let fortune break her strong nobility
> With but a single blow. Before you lies a road
> That leads to everlasting glory for your sex,
> Which has no scope for praise in government or war
> But only in a husband's grief. Arouse your heart,
> And let your love do battle now with destiny!
> Love even my defeat which brings you pride and joy.
> For now the magistrates, devoted senators

And retinue of kings are scattered far and wide
And you henceforth are Pompey's sole companion.
Such grief, incapable of increase, scarce becomes a wife
Whose husband lives. It was not Pompey who succumbed
But only Pompey's fortunes. Mourning ought to be
Affection's ultimate display and kept for tombs,
Unless the thing you weep is what you really loved.'

These are not the sentiments that could have been addressed to any but
the most devoted of wives, and when Lucan imagines Cornelia's reply,
he evidently follows the same source as Plutarch in making her blame
herself for bringing ill luck on both her husbands. She recalls the death
of Publius Crassus in his father's disastrous invasion of Parthia in 53,
and wishes she had brought her luckless dowry to Caesar's marriage-
bed instead of turning heaven's face against the better cause. But Pompey
had more to do than comfort Cornelia or bemoan his own fate, for he
almost certainly knew that Caesar was pursuing him. According to
Caesar's memoirs Pompey had not in fact sailed direct from Thessaly
to Lesbos but first coasted northwards to Amphipolis where a proclamation had been made in his name for a general conscription throughout
Macedonia, though Caesar was unable to say whether Pompey had seriously intended to try to hold Macedon or published the edict 'as a blind
to keep his plans for distant flight concealed'. Caesar also has him calling
friends to a meeting in Amphipolis and collecting money for travelling
expenses, but 'when he heard the news of Caesar's approach', he sailed
on to Mytilene 'after only one night tied up in Amphipolis harbour'.

In the face of Caesar's assertion it is hard not to believe that Pompey
visited Amphipolis despite the silence of the other sources, but it is even
harder to see why he did so. If he seriously intended to try to hold Macedonia it could only have been in the hope that Caesar would have
marched back to the Adriatic after Pharsalus, but it remains odd that
he should have risked the long and dangerous circumnavigation of the
Chalcidic promontories and Mt Athos before getting that essential piece
of intelligence which must have been readily available much nearer. The
edict moreover would surely have been more effective in throwing Caesar
off the scent and giving Pompey a start in his 'more distant flight' if Pompey had not wasted time by going there himself, especially since Amphipolis was on Caesar's direct line of march from Thessaly to the Hellespont
and this was the only way that Caesar could pursue Pompey to the East
without a fleet. At any rate, if Pompey did go to Amphipolis first – and
it is not impossible that Caesar was falsely told that Pompey had called
there by the same friends who had issued the edict in order to confuse

the pursuit – he would hardly have reached Lesbos with only the one merchant-ship which he had picked up by chance off the Thessalian coast. If he still had the authority to issue edicts and collect money at Amphipolis, he could also collect a few more ships. If, on the other hand, our admittedly dramatizing sources are right that he arrived with only one ship, they are also likely to be right that he sailed direct to Mytilene. But whether he took a detour or not, he certainly had no forces to coerce that island-city against its will, and the fact that he could recover Cornelia and sail away unharmed shows how fully Mytilene deserved his trust and repaid the benefactions of happier days. For as Lucan observed, the Mytilenaeans 'had already earned Caesar's anger by keeping Cornelia safe, and yet Pompey had not feared to sail into their harbour and put into their hands the one certain means of gaining Caesar's forgiveness'. But Pompey would not put them to unnecessary risk. He refused to enter the city itself in order not to incriminate them further in Caesar's eyes, and when he left, he urged them to surrender at once to the pursuer.

According to Appian he had four triremes from Rhodes and Tyre at Mytilene, and after only two days there – which Caesar says would have been even less but for bad weather – he sailed southwards down the present-day Turkish coast. If he sailed far and fast enough he might yet shrug off Caesar's more ponderous pursuit by land, or at least gain time to recover something of his lost fortunes. To keep his progress as secret as possible and to avoid the danger of being seized by bounty-hunters from cities less devoted than Mytilene, he put in at harbours only when necessary to take on board food and water until he was safely past Rhodes, out of the Aegean, and sailing east along the southern coast of Asia Minor. 'How could Pompey have believed when he gave peace to the sea that he would profit by it himself one day?' asks Lucan, observing that Pompey was now fleeing unharmed along the coast which had been infested with pirates until his great campaign of 67 had swept them from the seas and rehabilitated them in less anti-social employment. But that investment in enlightened humanity now paid him bigger dividends than mere security from attack on the high seas. His bloodless victory at Coracesium and the wisdom with which he had used it had made the Cilicians 'the most loyal of nations to Rome', and Pompey was still their personification of benign imperialism.

When he reached the coast of Pamphylia which formed the western end of his enlarged Cilician province, Pompey entered his first city since Pharsalus. Lucan says it was Phaselis, Plutarch Attaleia, but the discrepancy serves only to show the widespread loyalty of this region where he now began to rebuild his shattered forces. According to Caesar he had picked up 'a few small craft' on the way to add to the four triremes

with which Appian says he had sailed from Mytilene, but it was not until
he reached Pamphylia that he received his first significant accession of
strength. 'At Attaleia,' says Plutarch, 'some triremes from Cilicia met him,
soldiers were assembled for him, and he was again surrounded by senators, not less than sixty of them. ... He sent messengers round to the
other cities and sailed to some in person, requesting money and manning
ships.' Pompey was heartened to learn that Cato had safely conveyed
the forces which had been left at Dyrrachium and Corcyra to Africa. It
should be possible to organize a combined resistance there with King
Juba, and while Pompey laboured under no illusions about the difficulties
of recovering from Pharsalus, he had nothing to lose by heartening his
peers with the sort of encouragement which Lucan puts into his mouth
at the Cilician city of Syedra:

> 'At Pharsalus I fell but not so heavily
> That I can never raise my head and shake defeat
> From shoulders still unbowed. If Marius could rise
> From ruined Carthage, climb again to consulship
> And make the calendar still fuller of his name,
> Shall Fortune keep great Pompey crushed by lighter blows?'

And whether or not the real Pompey ever drew this parallel between himself and Marius, there is a fine irony in Lucan's suggestion that the man
who had won his early greatness as Sulla's pupil now sought to become
the pupil of Sulla's arch-enemy in recovering it.

From Syedra Pompey seems to have travelled no further east along the
Cilician coast but to have crossed to Cyprus, an island which had evidently remained more loyal to him than the goddess whose birthplace
it was. According to Caesar he raised two thousand troops there from
the households of the Roman business community, but that need not
mean that he was no longer recruiting elsewhere. He probably saw
Cyprus as the safest and most central headquarters from which to organize a general mobilization of troops, ships and money throughout the
eastern Mediterranean and particularly from Cilicia and Syria, the two
great provinces which in their present forms had been his own creations.
But if Cilicia remembered its benefactor and received his envoys in all
its coastal cities from Phaselis to the reconstructed Pompeiopolis, Caesar
records with satisfaction how Antioch closed its gates against Pompey's
friends and warned those who came to neighbouring towns that they
would approach the Syrian capital at their peril. Nor was it only the news
of Caesar's victory that shut Pompey out of Syria and closed the harbours
of Rhodes to Lentulus who tried to come ashore there on his way to join
Pompey. Caesar himself was rapidly approaching through Asia with a

flying column made up of two slim legions and eight hundred cavalry. He had experienced some nasty moments at the Hellespont when one of Pompey's naval squadrons had appeared while he was struggling to ferry his forces across, but the Pompeian commander was in no mood to fight the victor of Pharsalus, and Caesar not only crossed safely but received the surrender of the warships, which presumably formed the nucleus of a much-needed fleet of his own. After that it had been a matter of marching as fast as possible through Asia Minor and no doubt sending officers ahead to requisition transports and triremes from the maritime cities on the way, but it was probably not until he reached the south-west corner of Asia Minor that he had sufficient merchant-vessels and protecting warships – 'a few from Asia and ten from Rhodes' – to continue the pursuit by sea. And by then it was not Cyprus to which he sailed but Alexandria, for Pompey had moved on.

'Fearing the speed of his enemy who might catch him up and seize him before he was ready to defend himself,' says Plutarch, 'Pompey began to look about for a temporary refuge and retreat', though surely not in the direction which Plutarch, Appian and Lucan suggest. All three authors, two of them generally sympathetic to Pompey, make the incredible claim that Pompey now seriously proposed fleeing to Parthia. Plutarch and Lucan maintain that it was a last-minute decision, Appian that he had planned it at Lesbos but only now dared to reveal it to his companions, but Dio rightly rejects the whole story on the grounds of common sense:

I have heard that Pompey even thought of fleeing to the Parthians but I cannot credit the report. For that nation so hated the Romans in general since Crassus' expedition against them, and Pompey in particular since he was related to Crassus, that they even imprisoned his envoy, a senator no less, who had come to ask for aid in the Civil War. And Pompey would never have endured in his misfortune to have become a suppliant to his bitterest foe for what he had failed to obtain while still successful.

Why Plutarch, Appian and Lucan should have accepted so transparent a piece of character-assassination is a mystery. Their source must have been more vindictively Caesarian than Caesar himself, who makes no such allegation in his memoirs though he does mention Pompey's envoy to the Parthian court, and this is obviously the slender thread of fact on which the whole fabrication hangs. Caesar mentions the envoy, Lucilius Hirrus, only to illustrate the over-confidence in victory which prevailed in Pompey's camp before Pharsalus, when deputations of Hirrus' friends kept seeking assurances that Pompey would keep his promise to ensure that the absent ambassador would not be excluded from the elections that would take place immediately after the expected victory. Caesar does not say why Hirrus had been sent to Parthia, either because he did not know or preferred not to say, and his silence leaves room for doubt that Dio was right in suggesting that the mission had been designed to seek military help for Pompey in the Civil War. If that had been the case, or even if Caesar had thought that anyone would have believed it, he would hardly have omitted so damaging a reference to his enemy who is always being blamed for using Orientals in a Roman civil war. As it is, we are tempted to assume that Pompey's embassy to Parthia was more to his credit than discredit. It would be easier to believe that Hirrus was seeking help from Parthia if Pompey had felt that he needed it, and since Caesar's mention of the embassy is only in the context of over-confidence in victory, it is singularly improbable that he did. The far more likely reason for Hirrus' mission was to protect Syria by diplomacy once Scipio's forces had been withdrawn, but since Caesar's hatred of Scipio forbade any mitigation of the criticism that 'he had left his province undefended against the Parthian enemy which had a little before slain the *Imperator* Marcus Crassus and had kept Marcus Bibulus closely invested in Antioch', Caesar would not have mentioned any diplomatic threats of retaliation which Pompey could well have made to warn off the 'King of Kings'. He may even have demanded the return of Crassus' eagles, and if his expectations had been fulfilled at Pharsalus it is unlikely that he would have stopped short at diplomacy to get them back and wipe out the disgrace which Rome was destined to suffer for nearly three more decades.

Geography alone ought to have been enough to warn Plutarch, Appian and Lucan against their gullibility. When Pompey had discovered in Cilicia that 'his fleet still held together and that Cato had taken many soldiers aboard and was crossing to Africa', it would have been madness to leave the Mediterranean to take a caravan many hundreds of miles to an alien capital, and it was neither the remonstrations of his colleagues nor his fear of seeing Cornelia consigned to the harem that dissuaded him from a proposal which he never made. What Pompey wanted was a ready-made army and navy with which he could turn on his pursuer and defeat him, and there were only two possible sources: Egypt and Africa. Cato probably had at least two legions in Africa already, and Pompey could count on the powerful support of King Juba whose defeat of Curio and the annihilation of his army had put him beyond the scope of Caesar's mercy. On the other hand the very security of Africa was a disincentive, though not merely because Pompey was too proud or fearful to beg the assistance of King Juba as the less realistic sources suggest. He would not have relished the prospect of supplicating Juba, or facing Cato for that matter, without bringing a bigger contribution to the war-effort, but there were sounder reasons than pride or fear which now made him chose a more risky and, initially at least, more humiliating course. To have joined Cato in Africa would have been to put all his eggs in one basket, lose contact with the eastern Mediterranean, and miss the best chance of turning and catching his pursuer at his weakest. Indeed the advantages of Egypt were so obvious to Caesar himself that he records how he was still in Asia when he 'heard that Pompey had been seen in Cyprus, and guessed at once that Pompey was on his way to Egypt on account of his close personal ties with that kingdom and the other advantages of the place'.

What these advantages were – too obvious to Caesar to be worth mentioning – is explained most succinctly by Appian: 'Egypt was near, a great kingdom still prosperous and powerful in ships, provisions and money, and ruled by children who were allied to Pompey through their father's friendship.' Nine years ago, when the exiled King Ptolemy Auletes had come to Rome to seek his restoration by the greatest citizen of the most powerful nation in the world, it would never have crossed his mind to suggest that one day his kingdom might be able to do the same for Pompey. Pompey's patronage had replaced him so securely on the throne of Egypt that he had not only died a king but been able to hand on his kingdom to the two children who had succeeded him as his joint-heirs three years ago. Since then Pompey had received contributions of ships and a few troops from Egypt for the Civil War, but it remained to be seen if the old king had handed down anything more than a fair-weather friendship to Ptolemy XIII and Cleopatra who were now fighting each other with anything but the fraternal affection which might have been expected from that incestuous dynasty. The young Ptolemy, a boy of about thirteen, had expelled his older sister a few months ago, and while he waited in camp at Mount Casius near the Pelusian mouth of the Nile to repel Cleopatra's expected reinvasion, he received the disturbing news that Pompey the Great had anchored a small fleet offshore and was sending envoys to seek an audience under a guarantee of safe conduct.

Pompey was taking a desperate risk. The Numidian Juba had forfeited any hope of keeping his kingdom under a victorious Caesar, but the boy-king of Egypt might find that his father's friendship with Pompey weighed light against the defeat at Pharsalus on the scale of political expediency. Clearly Pompey would have to convince him that there was mutual advantage in opposing Caesar, and though it is nowhere recorded what he planned to say to the king, it is not hard to imagine. He would point out that Caesar was pursuing him with only a small force, not more than four thousand men and a small fleet. The Egyptian navy could easily overwhelm them before they reached the shore, and even if Caesar managed to land his troops, the royal army would be a match for them (as indeed it would soon prove even without Pompey in command). The risk was small compared with the rewards. What could Ptolemy expect from Caesar, who did not need him, that could compare with his expectations from Pompey and the senatorial government whose eternal gratitude he now had the chance to secure? And could he be sure that the Pompeian cause would not triumph in the end even without his help? Would it not be sound statesmanship to strike now to win a certain victory for Pompey that would guarantee the safety of his throne against internal dangers or the recurring demands for Egypt's annexation which had been heard in Rome in recent years? Would he not like to see his kingdom recovering some of its ancient territory? The status of Friend and Ally of the Roman People would be no empty name if he restored the fortunes of its legitimate government.

'It was a dreadful thing that the fate of Pompey the Great had to be decided by such a tribunal,' says Plutarch, referring to the three close advisers who were now closeted with the young king while Pompey waited anxiously on his trireme to hear if his request for an audience had been granted. They were Theodotus, the boy's Greek tutor, Achillas, his commander-in-chief, and his treasurer Potheinus, and all three were unenthusiastic at the prospect of Pompey's arrival, which they considered as much a threat to their own influence with Ptolemy as to the safety of his kingdom. If Pompey were admitted to an audience, the impressionable young man might fall under his influence, and if not the king, then the king's Roman troops who were even now being subverted by Pompey's envoys. Gabinius had left a considerable Roman garrison in Egypt when he had reimposed the old king on his reluctant subjects 'as a favour to Pompey' in 55, and since many of these men were veterans of Pompey's Eastern campaigns they might not have needed much persuading 'to show their duty to Pompey and not despise his fortunes'. But if it was dangerous to receive Pompey, there were also dangers in sending him away, and Plutarch makes the rhetorician Theodotus demonstrate his art of making the worse argument appear the better by expounding a course of action worthy of Machiavellian *Realpolitik*. If they received Pompey, they would have Caesar for an enemy and Pompey for a master. If they rejected him, Pompey would blame them for casting him out, Caesar for making him continue his pursuit. The best course therefore was to send for the man and put him to death, for by so doing they would at once gratify Caesar and have nothing to fear from Pompey.

Lucan gives the decisive speech to the eunuch Potheinus instead, and it seethes with his own hatred of the Neronian absolutism under which

he lived dangerously and died young, and from which he believed that
Rome might have been saved if Pompey had won the Civil War:

'Your Majesty, divine and human laws bring guilt
To many. Loyalty is praised but pays the price
When foolishly supporting those whom Fortune spurns.
Take you the side of destiny and heaven's will,
Avoid unfortunates and cultivate success.
As stars from earth or fire from water, doing right
Is distant from expedience. A sceptre's might
Will perish utterly if justice weighs it down,
For virtue overthrows the citadels of power.
Unbounded wickedness protects the hated king
Who sets the sword no limits. Cruel deeds are safe
Until they cease. A court must shun the pious man,
Since goodness cannot coexist with regal power,
And he who feels ashamed will always be afraid.
Shall Pompey with impunity despise your youth,
A beaten man who thinks you cannot shield our shores?
Let not a stranger steal our throne. Restore the Nile
To her whom you condemned, your father's flesh and blood,
If you despise your crown. Keep Egypt free of Rome!
We owed our throne to Pompey, true, and therefore prayed
For his success. The sword which fate now bids me use
I sharpened not for Pompey but whoever lost.
I hoped to thrust it through the heart of Caesar, but
I must strike Pompey after all. We have no choice.'

Pompey's spirits rose when his envoys returned to report the 'generous
reply' which they had been given in public and the king's 'warm invitation
to visit him' which they had been asked to convey. He then waited for
the king to send an appropriate vessel to take him ashore, but though
the small boat which eventually put out seemed disturbingly incongruous
with the warmth of the royal reception which he had been led to expect,
he refused to listen to his companions who begged him to beware of a
trap and put to sea while there was still time. When the boat came alongside, it was reassuring to hear a Roman voice hailing him as *Imperator*.
The voice belonged to a Roman named Septimius, who had been one
of Pompey's junior officers in the Pirate War of 67 and now held high
rank in the king's Roman guard. Then Pompey was addressed in Greek
by Achillas, the commander-in-chief, and after receiving profuse expressions of regret that dangerous sandbanks had compelled the use of so
small a vessel, he embraced Cornelia and his son for the last time and

stepped down into the little boat with a few companions. To Cornelia and the rest who had been left behind it seemed a hopeful sign that the whole army began drawing up on the shore and the king himself could be distinguished among them by his purple robe. They saw the boat safely beached and Pompey rising to his feet with Achillas and Septimius apparently helping him ashore, but the next moment their hopes froze in horror as Pompey suddenly reeled and fell back. He was dead, and the speech which Theophanes had written for him to deliver to the king was covered in blood.

The cries of horror from Pompey's ships were heard on the shore, but there was no time for lamentation if they were to escape the Ptolemaic fleet which was already putting out to intercept them or chase them away. And it was as well that Cornelia did not see what followed. Septimius hacked off Pompey's head and carried it in grizzly triumph to the king along with his sword, seal-ring and other marks of identification that were to be the guarantees of Caesar's friendship. The naked trunk was left bleeding on the sand. 'So died in his fifty-eighth year', says Velleius, 'on the very eve of his birthday, that most august and illustrious man who had held three consulships, celebrated three triumphs, conquered the whole world and climbed to that pinnacle of fame beyond which it is impossible to rise.' Exactly thirteen years ago, on the eve of his forty-fifth birthday, Pompey had been driving in triumph through the imperial capital and treating his fellow-citizens to the most glittering display of conquered Oriental power and wealth that they had ever seen. Now this same man 'who had recently lacked more land to conquer found none to give him burial'. There was no state funeral for the corpse of fallen greatness. The head, embalmed, awaited the pleasure of his enemy. The trunk was washed, wept over and hurriedly cremated on the beach by a faithful servant, and though some remains were later sent by Caesar to Cornelia for burial at his villa in the Alban Hills, Pompey's first grave-stone was a little cairn on the Egyptian shore.

* * *

Pompey's death was not the end of the Civil War as Caesar's might have been if Pharsalus had gone the other way. The Pompeians were rapidly regrouping in Africa. Scipio had now joined Cato and assumed the supreme command which had belonged to his son-in-law. Pompey's own sons were there too, Gnaeus and Sextus, together with Labienus, Afranius, Petreius and Faustus Sulla. Lentulus and Cicero were not, the former unavoidably, the latter by miserable choice. Lentulus had arrived in Egypt the day after Pompey and suffered the same fate. Cicero, as the senior ex-consul on the spot, had been offered command of all Cato's forces at Corcyra after the news of Pharsalus had arrived, but he had refused, preferring to creep back to Italy and write grovelling letters that might reingratiate him with the winning side. Gnaeus Pompeius had wanted to kill that womanly *Imperator* and all the rest who now deserted his father's cause, but Cato had contrived to restrain him, and Cicero lasted another five years until he made his last and fatal miscalculation of the strength and direction of a political wind. As for Cornelia, she left her step-sons in Africa to avenge Pompey's memory and returned to mourn him in Italy at the villa in the Alban Hills where they had known their greatest happiness.

The Pompeians in Africa had over a year to recover their strength because Caesar became preoccupied in the East. He had arrived in Egypt a few days after Pompey's death, and after weeping crocodile tears over the embalmed head he had favoured Cleopatra, with the result that the royal army made belated war on him. Caesar won in the end, but he endured many anxious weeks before the final defeat and death of Ptolemy left him free to take Cleopatra on a cruise up the Nile and recover his energies for what he believed would be one last effort against the Pompeians in Africa. But he had reckoned without the imperial ambitions of Mithridates' son, reawakened by Pompey's failure and the chaos of the Civil War. Pharnaces had safeguarded his Crimean principality by sending Pompey his father's embalmed corpse in 63, but now he disdained to follow the example of other client-kings hastening to ingratiate themselves with the unknown victor of Pharsalus who was soon reported to be fighting for his life in Alexandria. He swept the Romans from his ancestral kingdom of Pontus like dry leaves before a gale, defeated the legions of Calvinus whom Caesar had sent to secure the provinces and principalities of Asia Minor, and began threatening not only Armenia but Roman Asia itself. Unless he was stopped quickly before his power grew to match that of his father he might endanger the whole imperial structure which Pompey had created in the East, and when the campaigning season opened in 47, it was ironic that Caesar had to postpone his pursuit of the Pompeians in Africa in order to defend Pompey's greatest achievement. And by the time Pharnaces had been defeated and Caesar had returned in September to a troubled Italy, the Pompeians and King Juba in Africa could field between them an army that was probably as big as that which Pompey had had at Pharsalus, and Gnaeus was already recovering Spain.

It was Caesar who had become Sulla's pupil in the end. He had had himself appointed dictator immediately after Pharsalus, but with no such limited objectives as Sulla whom he considered 'an innocent' for laying down his autocracy. He now held elections of tame consuls in a capital which had been without magistrates for the first nine months of 47, and then proceeded to do for himself what the young Pompey had done for Sulla by following his enemies to Africa and Spain. In Africa he struggled for four months to recover victory from near defeat, but the pattern of Dyrrachium and Pharsalus was repeated in Africa, and the Pompeians were eventually shattered at Thapsus. Scipio, King Juba, Cato and Petreius all committed suicide. Afranius and Faustus Sulla were captured and executed. Sextus and Labienus escaped to join Gnaeus, who was already in Spain and preparing to play the Sertorius to Caesar's Pompey. And history repeated itself. Although Gnaeus raised an enormous army of thirteen legions and six thousand cavalry and Munda was perhaps the nearest run thing that Caesar had ever experienced in his life, the Pompeians lost again. Labienus died fighting, Gnaeus was hunted down and beheaded three weeks later, and only Sextus survived to show that a Pompey was still a force to be reckoned with for another decade in which he earned the surname Pius that he added to the Magnus inherited from his father.

But Caesar did not long survive the victories of 46 which left him temporarily unchallenged as master of the Roman world. On the Ides of March 44, on the eve of his departure for a campaign against Parthia which Pompey would almost certainly have undertaken if he had won Pharsalus, the daggers of a group of disgruntled senators accomplished in a few seconds what all the Pompeian armies and navies had failed to do in nearly four years of war. Caesar was stabbed to death in the Senate House at the foot of Pompey's statue. It was a drastic attempt to save the Republic from a terminal disease, but four years of autocracy and vested interest were not so easily eradicated. Antony seized the initiative in the weeks that followed, and though he had no love for Caesar's great-nephew Octavian whom the dictator had made his heir and adopted son under the terms of a dynastic will, the two men came to see more in common with each other than with the republicans whom they combined to defeat at Philippi in 42. But though they divided the provinces between them and Antony went to the East, absence did not make the hearts of Caesar's pupils grow fonder of each other. Actium decided the issue between the champions of East and West in 31 as surely as Pharsalus had done seventeen years earlier. But this time there were no more fundamental issues at stake than the identity of the monarch. Antony's long infatuation with Cleopatra and the life of Oriental courts may have made him less reluctant to wear a crown in Rome, but his victorious rival who had taken Caesar's name as the adopted son of a god was no less determined to keep and hand down to an heir of his own the *insociable regnum* which was a monarchy in all but name.

In the perspective of history it is Pharsalus which condemned the

Republic to die. Thapsus, Munda, Philippi and Actium are like the
stations of its cross marking the painful progress to Octavian's permanent
institutionalization of Caesar's absolutism from which there would be
no resurrection. The assassination of Caesar was four years too late. Pompey might not have been the ideal guardian of the ideal republic envisaged
by Cicero, but if a guardian was needed for the very imperfect republic
in which Cicero lived, Pompey's ambitions were more compatible with
its preservation than Caesar's. Pompey had been exposed to the seduction
of Oriental absolutism for five years when he returned to Rome in 62,
but he had disbanded his army the moment he set foot on Italian soil.
Caesar had needed only a few weeks of dalliance in Egypt to toy with
the crown, bring Cleopatra and their son to Rome, and establish so complete an autocracy that government had been paralysed by his absence
in Africa and Spain. It is hard to imagine that the machinery of the Roman
Republic would have ceased to function if Pompey had carried victorious
arms from Pharsalus into Parthia, or that he would have wanted it so.
He wanted to be first citizen no less than Caesar, but primacy in the state
meant different things to the two men, as Dio explains:

> Pompey desired to be second to no man, Caesar to be first of all, but whereas
> the former was anxious to be honoured by a willing people and to preside
> over and be loved by men who fully consent to his primacy, the latter did not
> care if he ruled over an unwilling people, issued orders to men who hated him,
> and bestowed their honours upon himself with his own hand. Unfortunately
> the deeds by which they sought to realize their different ambitions were neces-
> sarily common to both, for it was impossible for anyone to gain such ends
> without fighting against his fellow-citizens, leading foreigners against fellow-
> countrymen, plundering unjustly vast sums of money and killing unlawfully
> many of the men most dear to him.

Pompey must not be judged by the standards of Utopia but against
the background of his own violent lifetime which had seen the character
of Roman political life assume the new dimensions of violence explained
by Appian in the quotation which began the first chapter of the first
volume of this book. Before the Civil War between Sulla and the Marians
'the political murders and seditions in Rome had been intermittent
domestic affairs on a relatively small scale, but from now on the leaders
of the factions began to assail each other with great armies according
to the laws of war, and looked upon their country as the prize in a contest
of arms'. Pompey may not have deserved his virtual canonization by
future generations of rose-tinted republicans reacting against the rule of
endless Caesars, but even Cicero, writing to tell Atticus after the event
how he had never doubted it, 'could not help feeling sorry for Pompey's
fate, for I knew him as a man of integrity, honour and principle'.

But the best obituary of Pompey the Great is that which Lucan puts into the mouth of Cato when Pompey's companions had carried the news of his death to Africa. There they lit a great funeral pyre in his honour as they would have done if they had had a body to cremate, and Cato's speech is the very best sort of obituary in which affection is not so blind to imperfection that the man of flesh and blood becomes a mere icon in the hagiography of lost causes:

'The citizen who died, though far from equalling
Our ancestors in knowing Law's restraints, yet served
An age which had no reverence for what is right.
Our liberty was not endangered by his power
And he alone, when people wished to be his slaves,
Remained in private life. He ruled the Senate House,
But still it was a house of kings. He based no claims
On force of arms, and when he sought a thing, he left
The possibility of having it denied.
He gained immodest wealth, but gave much more to Rome
Than he retained. He seized the sword but also knew
To lay it down. He much preferred a soldier's dress
To robes of peace, but still loved peace when armed for war.
It pleased him both to take and to resign commands,
His home was chaste and free of luxury's excess,
His household stayed unspoilt despite its master's wealth.
His name is great, revered throughout the world
But most of all at Rome for benefits conferred.
Sincere belief in liberty died long ago
When Marius and Sulla thrust themselves on Rome,
But Pompey's death destroys the fiction that remained.'

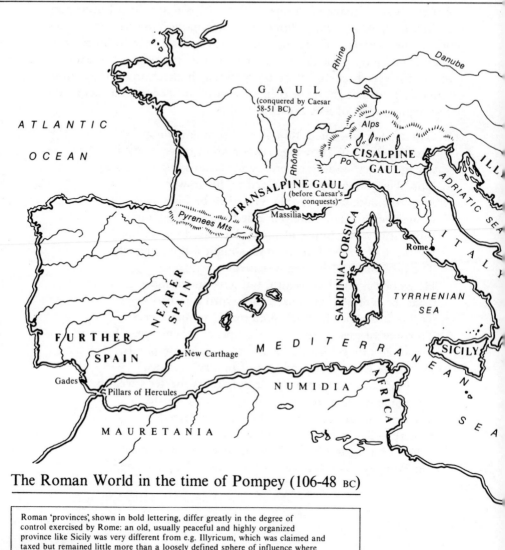

# The Roman World in the time of Pompey (106-48 BC)

Roman 'provinces', shown in bold lettering, differ greatly in the degree of
control exercised by Rome: an old, usually peaceful and highly organized
province like Sicily was very different from e.g. Illyricum, which was claimed and
taxed but remained little more than a loosely defined sphere of influence where
irregularly appointed governors fought sporadic campaigns. Provinces acquired
(or, in the case of Cilicia, extended and properly organized for the first time) by
Pompey are underlined.

RICUM

Dyrrachium

Brundisium

Danube

THRACE

MACEDONIA

Thracian
Bosporus

Hellespont

AEGEAN SEA

Athens

ASIA

RHODES

Coracesium

CRETE

CYPRUS

CYRENE

Alexandria

Pelusium

Mt Casius

Nile

EGYPT

Crimea

SEA OF
AZOV

BOSPORAN
KINGDOM

Cimmerian Bosporus

BLACK    SEA

Caucasus Mts

COLCHIS

BITHYNIA—PONTUS

GALATIA

CAPPADOCIA

CILICIA

Pompeiopolis

ARMENIA

COMMAGENE

OSROENE

PARTHIAN

EMPIRE

Mesopotamia

Tigris

Euphrates

Antioch

SYRIA

NABATAEA

0    100    500
miles

100    700 km

Italy

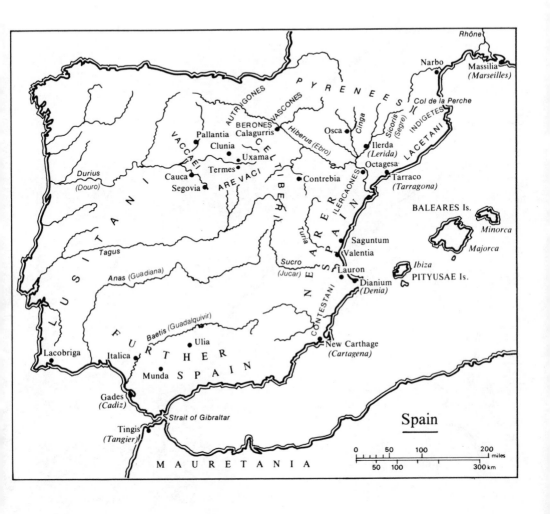

Rhône

Narbo

Massilia
(Marseilles)

PYRENEES

Col de la Perche

AUTRIGONES

VASCONES

Osca

Cinga

Sicoris (Segre)

INDIGETES

BERONES

Calagurris

Pallantia

VACCAEI

Clunia

Uxama

CELTIBERI

Ilerda
(Lerida)

LACETANI

Termes

Octagesa

Cauca

AREVACI

Contrebia

Tarraco
(Tarragona)

Segovia

Durius
(Douro)

LUSITANI

Hiberus (Ebro)

BALEARES Is.

Minorca

ILERCAONES

Majorca

Tagus

CELTIBERI

NEARER

SPAIN

Turia

Saguntum

Valentia

Anas (Guadiana)

Sucro
(Jucar)

Ibiza

Lauron

PITYUSAE Is.

Dianium
(Denia)

CONTESTANI

Baetis (Guadalquivir)

FURTHER

Ulia

New Carthage
(Cartagena)

Lacobriga

Italica

SPAIN

Munda

Gades
(Cadiz)

Strait of Gibraltar

Tingis
(Tangier)

MAURETANIA

Spain

0    50    100    200
                   miles
50  100      300 km

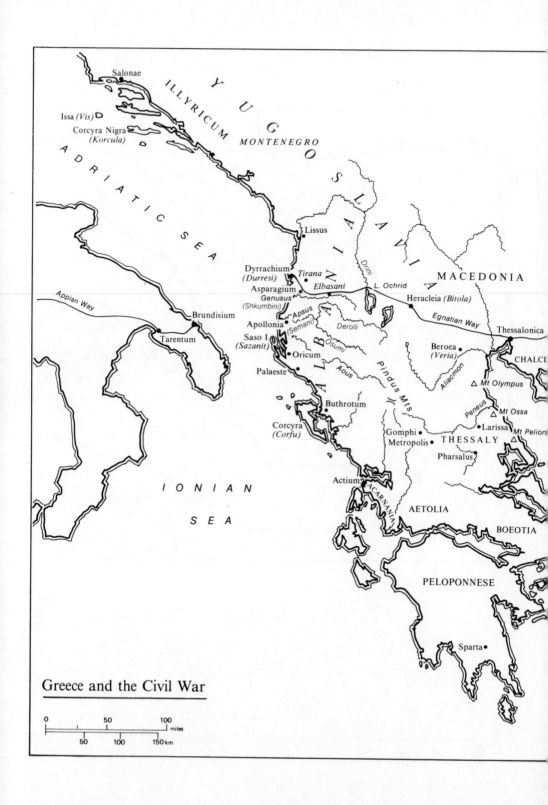

Greece and the Civil War

| 0 | 50 | 100 | miles |

| 50 | 100 | 150 km |

Salonae

Issa *(Vis)*

Corcyra Nigra
*(Korcula)*

ILLYRICUM

Y U G O S L A V I A

MONTENEGRO

A D R I A T I C   S E A

Lissus

Dyrrachium
*(Durresi)*          *Tirana*

Asparagium         *Elbasani*

Genusus          L. Ochrid
*(Shkumbini)*

Appian Way

Brundisium

Tarentum

Apollonia        Apsus
*(Semani)*

Saso I.          Derolli
*(Sazanit)*

Oricum

Palaeste

Corcyra
*(Corfu)*

Buthrotum

I O N I A N

S E A

Actium

Drini

MACEDONIA

Heracleia *(Bitola)*

Egnatian Way        Thessalonica

Beroea
*(Veria)*          CHALCI

Osumi

Aous

Pindus Mts

Aliacmon

△ Mt Olympus

Peneus          △ Mt Ossa

Larissa   Mt Pelion

Gomphi           △

Metropolis     THESSALY

Pharsalus

ACARNANIA

AETOLIA

BOEOTIA

PELOPONNESE

Sparta

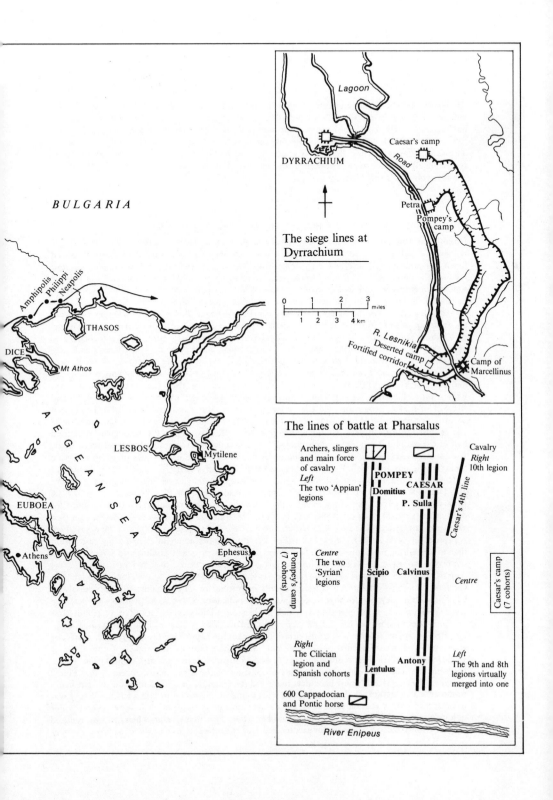

BULGARIA

Amphipolis
Philippi
Neapolis
DICE
THASOS
Mt Athos

A E G E A N   S E A

LESBOS
Mytilene

EUBOEA

Athens
Ephesus

The siege lines at
Dyrrachium

Lagoon

DYRRACHIUM

Caesar's camp
Road

Petra
Pompey's
camp

Camp of
Marcellinus

R. Lesnikia
Deserted camp
Fortified corridor

0   1   2   3
        miles
1   2   3   4 km

The lines of battle at Pharsalus

Archers, slingers
and main force
of cavalry
Left
The two 'Appian'
legions

Cavalry
Right
10th legion

POMPEY          CAESAR
Domitius
            P. Sulla

Caesar's 4th line

Centre
The two
'Syrian'
legions

Scipio   Calvinus          Centre

Right
The Cilician
legion and
Spanish cohorts

Left
The 9th and 8th
legions virtually
merged into one

Lentulus   Antony

600 Cappadocian
and Pontic horse

River Enipeus

Pompey's camp
(7 cohorts)

Caesar's camp
(7 cohorts)

# NOTES

*Abbreviations:* The abbreviated references to ancient literary sources and collections of inscriptions will be recognized by the specialists who will use them. Modern works are cited by the authors' names, occasionally with an abbreviated title but usually with the date of publication of their works, full details of which will be found in the Bibliography. The only idiosyncratic abbreviations are TP and SB, referring to the collections of Cicero's correspondence by Tyrrell & Purser and Shackleton Bailey. References to an otherwise unspecified 'vol I' are to *Pompey: The Roman Alexander*, the first volume of this biography.

## CHAPTER ONE (pp. 1–27): CLODIUS, CICERO AND CORN

**Domitius and Memmius**: see Suet *J* 23; *Schol Bob* 89 Hild (on *Sest* 40), 116 (on *Vat* 15; Caesar's replies); Cic *QF* 1.2 (D and M his intimates; n.b. also *Att* 2.24 for D's name on Vettius' revised list of conspirators against P). **Clodius**: for power-base see Dio 38.12–14 (n.b. for dating first four laws see Cic *Pis* 9 + Asc 8C; for *collegia* suppressed in 66: *ib* 7); Cic *Sest* 55 (contrast Cic's attitude to Cato's measure in 62: Plut *Cat Min* 26.1; *Caes* 8.4); *Pis* 9; *post red ad Q* 13 ('Catiline's veteran bands'; cf. *in Sen* 33); Plut *Cic* 30; *P* 48; see further Lintott 1968, esp. 77ff, 193ff; Yavetz 1958 (= Seager 1969, 162–79) on living conditions of urban plebs (cf. Boren 1957–8 = Seager 1969, 54–66, on urban side of Gracchan economic crisis); Gruen 1974, 228, 445–6; for different assessments of Clodius' political role 58–56 see e.g. Lacour-Gayet 1889; Marsh 1927, 1932); Pocock 1924, 1925, 1927; Seager 1965; Gruen 1966, 1974; Lintott 1967; Ward 1977, 231–58. **Cicero's exile**: see Dio 38.14–17 (cf. 38.30.1); Vell 2.45; Cic *QF* 1.4; *Att* 8.3; *Sest* esp. 15, 24, 39–41; *Pis* 75ff; *post red ad Q* esp. 13; *post red in Sen* 16; Plut *Cic* 30–1; App 2.15. **Cato's Cyprus commission**: see Dio 38.30.5; Vell 2.45; Cic *Sest* 57–64; Plut *Cato Min* 34ff; see also on annexation Oost 1955; Badian 1965. **Tigranes**: see esp. Dio 38.30.1–2; Asc 47C; Cic *Att* 3.8 (incident forgotten by end May); Plut *P* 48.6. **Brogitarus**: see Cic *de har resp* 28–9; *Sest* 56; also Magie *RRAM* 1235–6 n 40, also for restoration of Byzantine exiles; for a view that Clodius' interference in East not originally against P but to increase Claudian *clientelae* see E. Rawson 1973. **P's 'retirement' in second half of 58**: see Plut *P* 49 (confused chronology); Cic *Sest* 69 (assassination plot dated to 11 Aug); Asc 46–7C; *Pis* 28; *de domo sua* 40 (Clodius 'fetters himself to Caesar's laws of 59 by attacking them on religious grounds'). **P's political nexus for 57**: see esp. Cic *Att* 3.22 (Spinther as Pompeian as Nepos, cf. *QF* 2.1; for change in Nepos' attitude compare *Att* 3.12 of July 58 with 3.23 of Nov; also Dio 39.8.2: 'under pressure from P'). **Cicero's restoration**: for P's role see esp. Cic *Att* 3.9 (13.6.58); *QF* 1.3 (13.6.58); *Att* 3.10 (17.6.58: '*discordia istorum*', presumably Gabinius and Clodius); 3.12 (17.7.58); 3.14 (21.7.58); 3.13 (5.8.58); *QF* 1.4 (Aug 58); *Att* 3.15 (17.8.58); 3.18 (Sep 58); *Fam* 14.2 (5.10.58); 14.1 (25.11.58); cf. Dio 39.6.2); *Att* 3.23 (29.11.58); 3.26 (Jan 57); *Fam* 5.4 (prob July 57); *Att* 4.1 (Sep 57); 8.3 (Feb 49: 'P was more active in effecting my restoration than in preventing my banishment'); *Sest* 67–77, 89 (Nepos, Appius Claudius and Serranus); *post red in Sen* esp. 24–9, 31–2; *post red ad Q* esp. 14, 16–18; Dio 38.30; 39.6–8; Plut *P* 49.3; *Cic* 33; App *BC* 2.16 (n.b. hopeless chronology); for Crassus' attitude see Dio 39.10; Plut *Cic* 30 (cf. 33); Cic *Fam* 14.2 (5.10.58); *QF* 2.3 (Clodius openly operating for Crass against P; Crass supplying Clodius with money, not for first time). **Caesar's 'supplicationes'** (15 days, probably in Oct): see Cic *de prov cons* 25–7 (proposed by Cic with P's blessing); Dio 39.5.1; Caes *BG* 2.35.4; Plut *Caes* 21. **Corn-commission**: see Cic *Att* 4.1 (Sep 57); 4.2; Dio 39.9; 39.24.1–2; Plut *P* 50, 51.6; Cic *QF* 2.5; *Fam* 13.75; on sources and transportation of grain for capital see Frank 1933–40, 5.218–20; also 1.328–31 for cost calculations of dole but n.b. Frank's false assumptions, e.g. that Cic *Sest* 55 means not that Clodius' remission of the 6⅓ asses consumed nearly one fifth of *vectigalia* (meaning?) but that the total dole then cost this proportion of the total annual revenue; that Plut *P* 45 does not mean that P's new provinces increased the revenues *by* 85m denarii but *to* that figure (impossible translation; cf. Jones 1974, 115 n 8); that 40m HS voted to P in 56 (Cic *QF* 2.5) was to be spread over 5 years instead of being a single emergency subvention (one of several?). For dole-takers the only reliable indication of number is Suet *J* 41 (that Caesar, when dictator, reduced number from 320,000 to 150,000; for amount received the reference to 5 modii (c. 44 litres; presumably monthly?) in Macer's speech at Sall *Hist* (M) 3.48.19) is evidence for 73, not for 57 by when dole was hardly still at level of 'prison rations': even on 'prison ration' basis some 300,000 citizens would consume 18m modii or 157m litres (approaching 4¾m. bushels); on corn-dole under Empire see Berchem 1939; on quaestor at Ostia see also Chandler 1978; on number of recipients in Late Republic see also Rowland 1965.

CHAPTER TWO (pp. 28–53): THE MONSTER REVIVES

**Main source**: Cic's contemporary correspondence, esp. *QF* 2.1 (mid-Dec 57); *Fam* 1.1 (13.1.56); 1.2 (15.1.56); 1.4 (events of 15.1.56); *QF* 2.2 (17.1.56); *Fam* 1.5A (2–6.2.56); 1.5B (after 8.2.56; for background to Milo/Clodius vendetta see esp. *Att* 4.3, re Nov 57); *QF* 2.3 (12–15.2.56; cf. Plut *P* 48.7; Dio 39.18–19 ('nominally Milo was the defendant but in reality P'); Clodius first openly names Crassus for Egyptian command; P arms against Crassus' nexus, n.b. not against Caesar as Dio 39.26.3); *QF* 2.4 (late Mar; cf. *in Vatinium*, criticizing V's role as agent of P and Caesar in 59; see also *Fam* 1.9.7; n.b. evidence of realignment of Crassus' nexus with P-Caesar nexus: C. Cato makes 'outrageous proposals' in interest of Caesar with acquiescence of *all* the tribunes, i.e. including the Pompeian Caninius who now lets his Egyptian Bill drop; but this realignment does not deter Monster's old opponents of 59, now led by Marcellinus; Appius Claudius visits Caesar, presumably as part of realignment: intervention with P's principal protégé on behalf of his brother Clodius); *QF* 2.5 (11.4.56; n.b. nothing obviously suspicious about P's route: for Etruria as important source of corn see e.g. Columella 2.6.3; Pliny *NH* 18.66; *CIL* 14.2852 for dealer in Etrurian and Umbrian wheat '*notus in urbe sacra*'); *Att* 4.5 (late Apr/early May 56); for palinode's addressee see esp. Holmes 2.292ff); *QF* 2.6 (after 15.5.56); *Fam* 1.7 (prob July, certainly before consular elections usually held in second half July: ineffectiveness of opposition to Pompeian interest); *de prov cons* (n.b. Caesar's conquests as extensions of P's); *pro Balbo*; *de har resp* 50–1 (evidence of Clodius' political volte-face: his eulogies of P called 'insults' by Cic; cf. Dio 39.29.1). **Late consular candidature of P and Crassus**: see Dio 39.27.3; Cic *Fam* 16.12 (explains prescribed interval); Sall *Cat* 18 (parallel example); see also Greenidge 1901, esp. 187 for procedure. This invalidates usual assumption that decision was made at the so-called 'Conference of Luca' in Apr (as Plut *P* 51; *Crass* 14; *Caes* 21; Suet *J* 24; cf. App *BC* 2.17, who does not name Luca but assigns decision to a meeting in Po valley; Dio 39.27.1, who mentions no meeting at all, only an agreement). Elections were usually held in latter half of July (never before 10 because 1–9 non-comitial): see e.g. Cic *Verr* 1.17–18, 30 (elections for 69 held few days before date of speech, 5 Aug 70; *Att* 3.14) (21.7.58: P promises to bring Cic's case forward after elections); 3.13 (5.8.58: 'elections must have been held by now'); *Fam* 8.4 (1.8.51: consuls already elected despite adjournments); n.b. Nov polling-date indicated by Cic *Att* 4.8B surely not the consuls' first attempt to hold elections in 56. **Domitius' candidature**: see Cic *Att* 4.8B (c. 17 Nov; see also SB *Att* 82 and vol 2, App III, against TP 118 based on misunderstanding of Licinian law); Suet *J* 24.1 (D's open threat; cf. 23.1: so does this mean to challenge *all* the legislation of 59?). **Electoral saga**: see esp. Dio 39.27–32 (detailed but garbled); Plut *P* 51–2; *Crass* 15; *Cato Min* 41–2 (also 39–40 for Cato's return from Cyprus: cf. Vell 2.45.5; n.b. Domitius married to M. Cato's sister); App *BC* 2.17–18; Livy *Ep* 105; Cic *Att* 4.8B (c. 17.11.56); *Fam* 1.8 (prob early 55); *QF* 2.7 (Feb 55). **Proconsular commands** (*lex Trebonia* for P and Crassus; *lex Pompeia Licinia* for Caesar: see App I): Plut *P* 52 (P lends two of his four legions to Caesar, supplemented by a third raised by P in 55 (*Caes* 25.2); but P surely lent only the one referred to in Caes *BG* 6.1; Hirt *BG* 8.54; Cic *Fam* 8.4.4 etc. Plut's confusion could derive from ambiguity of *BG* 6.1, where Caes records his request to P to order the recruits from Cisalpine Gaul sworn in by him as consul to join the colours and start for Caesar's headquarters: P 'made this concession to public service and private friendship', and during that winter (54/53) Caes acquired over three new legions. Plut could have assumed that all 3 legions were formed from P's levies, not just the one which P had raised from Cisalpine Gaul in 55 but had not yet put into service. The other two were almost certainly levied by Caesar: '*per suos*'; see further App II); *Cato Min* 43 (Cato warns P against strengthening Caesar but P trusts Caesar and his own good fortune and power); *Crass* 15; *Caes* 21; Dio 39.33–6; Cic *Att* 4.9 (27.4.55: '*iactans*' taken in sense of '*iactor*' of *Att* 11.16.3, not as 'boasting' which seems inconsistent with '*sibi displiciens*'); 7.7; 7.9; 8.3; *Fam* 8.8; 8.9; Vell 2.46.2. **Ptolemy restored by Gabinius**: see Cic *Att* 4.10 (22.4.55); Livy *Ep* 105; Dio 39.55–9 (P's orders; P and Crassus both benefit financially); for G's supposed preparations for Parthian campaign before diversion to Egypt see Jos *JA* 14.98, 102; *JW* 1.175–6; Strabo 12.3.34; 17.1.11. **Julia's miscarriage**: Plut *P* 53.3–4; Dio 39.32.2. **Modern**

278

works: on Egyptian Question see further Bouché-Leclercq 1904 and Bevan 1927 (histories of Ptolemaic dynasty); TP vol 2 (1906) xxix–l; Shatzman 1971; Ward 1977, 249–53; also vol I ch 11; vol II ch 4; for Cic's growing independence stifled by recognition of his political miscalculation see e.g. Cary 1923 ('asinus germanus'); also (for different view of attack on Vatinius) Albini 1959; and on Campanian debate Balsdon 1957A; Stockton 1962; Dorey 1959; Mitchell 1969; Ward 1977, 259–61; for different interpretations of 'Conference of Luca' see also Lazenby 1959; Gruen 1969A; Luibheid 1970; Ward 1977, 262ff.

CHAPTER THREE (pp. 54–80): PRINCE OF CITIZENS

**Theatre, Portico, Senate House and Mansion**: Plut P 40.9 ('famous and beautiful house'); 42.4 (Theatre plans from Mytilene); Pliny NH 36.114–15 (example of temporary theatre (Scaurus'); P's theatre seats 40,000); 36.41 (Coponius' statues of 14 Nations); 35.59 (Polygnotus); 35.126 (Pausias' 'Sacrifice of Oxen'); 35.132 (Nicias' 'Alexander'); 35.114 (Antiphilus' 'Cadmus and Europa'; see further Lippold 1953–4); 33.54 (Nero gilds Theatre); 34.57 (Heracles statue by Myron); 7.34 (images of marvels); Cic Att 4.9 (Att asked to arrange statues); Suet Aug 31.5 (P's statue moved to regia; cf. J 88); Claud 21.1 (rededication by Claudius); Dio 39.38.6 (story that Demetrius erected Theatre); Livy Ep 48 (Cassius Longinus and Valerius Messalla, censors in 154, prevented from building a stone theatre: cf. Vell 1.15.3; App BC 1.28; Val Max 2.4.2); Ovid Ars Amat 3.387 ('Pompeian shade'); Propertius 2.32.11–16 (delights of Portico; cf. 4.8.75); Tertullian de spect 10 (Theatre protected by Temple); Gellius 10.1.7 (suggests dedication of Temple in 52 rather than 55; improbable in view of Pliny NH 8.20; P would naturally erect more inscriptions recording third consulship); Tacitus Ann 14.2 (alleged censure of P for building first permanent theatre); see also Platner and Ashby 1929, 428–9 (Portico), 515–17 (Theatre), 555 (Temple), 146 (Curia); Bieber 1939, 333, 343–6 (with plans of Theatre, figs 449–50), 335 (fig 437: Pan statues from Theatre); Nash 1968, 423–8 (with bibliography for Theatre; also ill. 1216–23; see alongside Ooteghem 1954, 404 fig 33 for Via di Grotta Pinta; 408 fig 35 for reconstruction of Theatre); D.K. Hill 1944 (Temple criticized as architectural eyesore); for significance of Venus Victrix as presiding deity see Gagé 1936; Weinstock 1957; Crawford RRC 2.733–4; see also ch 9 on 'Hercules Invictus'. **Dedication of Theatre**: Cic Pis 65 (cf. Asc 1C); Fam 7.1 (jaundiced account to M. Marius, described in QF 2.8); Dio 39.38 (music, gymnastics, horse-racing and beast-hunts, including 500 lions in 5 days, also 18 elephants; elephant episode; overall popularity of games); Pliny NH 8.53 (numbers of lions: P has 600, of which 315 maned; Caesar as dictator shows 400); 8.64 (female leopards: Scaurus showed 150 in one pack, P 410, Augustus 420); 8.70 (lynx and baboons); 8.72 (rhinoceros); 8.84 (cervarius; ? = chama of 8.70); 8.20–1 (elephant episode); Plut P 52 (500 lions; P's great popularity from games). **Crassus**: Plut Crass 16 (contrast P 53); Dio 39.39; Vell 2.46.2; App BC 2.18; Cic Att 4.13; Fam 1.9.20 (cf. Plut Cic 26); 5.8 (Cic's letter to Crass, Jan 54); for campaign and disaster see esp. Plut Cras 17–33; Dio 40.12–30; CAH 9.602–12; for difficulties on leaving Rome see also Simpson 1938 (unconvincingly sceptical; criticized by Ward 1977, 285–6). **Gabinius**: see Cic Fam 1.9.20 (Crassus' volte-face in autumn 55); QF 2.11 (13) (publicani before Senate Feb/Mar 54; cf. Dio 39.60–2, though n.b. Tiber flood not till autumn: Cic QF 3.7, after G's acquittal in Oct); QF 3.1 (Sep 54); 3.2 (11.10.54); 3.3 (21.10.54); 3.4 (24.10.54); Att 4.18; QF 3.5–7, 9; Dio 39.55–63 (G's restoration of Ptolemy and subsequent trials); Cic frags (Müller), p. 291 (notes from Cic's speech for G; cf. Rab Post 32 for claim to be 'of a forgiving nature'!); Val Max 4.2.4; see also references collected by Gruen 1974, 322–31; also R.S. Williams' political biography of Gabinius (1973). **Other trials of 55 and 54**: on Caninius see Cic Fam 7.1 (Sep/Oct 55); on C. Cato (acquitted on charges under Junian and Licinian law and Fufian law, re postponing elections in 56) see Att 4.16 and 15 (July 54); Asc 18C (Scaurus spoke in defence: Pompeian nexus: acquittal 4.7.54); on Vatinius see Fam 1.9.19; QF 2.15 (16) (end Aug 54; contrast in Vatinium of 56; cf. Fam 1.9.7); on Scaurus see Att 4.15 (July 54); 4.17 (18) (1.10.54: Scaurus recently acquitted; tribune Scaevola postponed elections by announcing ill omens in meantime); Asc 19C (Scaurus relies on connection with P: he had married Mucia after P's divorce, and his son and P's were step-brothers; 20 and 28 laudationes given by P and staunch Pompeians like Metellus Nepos and Volcatius; acquittal 2 Sep); Cic pro Scauro (extant but mutilated); see also Gruen 1974, 331–7 with bibliography. **Julia's death**: see Plut P 53; Livy Ep 106; Dio 39.64; Cic QF 3.1 (Caesar wrote to Cic re Britain on 1 Sep, but Cic did not reply out of respect for mourning; death datable to Aug or July?); Vell 2.47.2 (n.b. 'son' also in Suet J 26 and Livy Ep 106; 'daughter' in Dio, more likely right because less significant). **Tiber floods and corn-supply**: Dio 39.61 (description of flood-damage but see Cic

*QF* 3.7 for correct dating; n.b. seriousness of grain losses after harvest and just before winter);
39.63 (P away organizing corn-supply but back in time for Gabinius' second trial in Dec; cf. Cic
*QF* 3.9); 40.45–6 (protracted absence of P in 53 until July may be connected with corn-commission).
**Elections for 54:** Cic *Att* 4.13 (mid-Nov 55: 'some expectation of elections'); Dio 39.60 (Domitius
Ahenobarbus and Appius Claudius evidently elected before year-end because ready to take over
from P and Crassus); for D's impotence as consul see Cic *QF* 2.13 (15a): daily joke that he had
not even the appointment of a military tribune in his gift; for Appius Claudius' marriage-connection
with P see *Fam* 3.10, cf. 8.6, 2.13 and 3.4 (giving *terminus ante quem* June 51); but Appius' swing
to Pompeian interest in 56, consular election in 55, Cicero's morbid fear of Clodius (against whom
he no longer considers P reliable and thus courts Caesar: e.g. *QF* 2.11 (13), 2.13 (15), 2.14 (15b),
3.5–6) combine to make 55 most probable year for marriage; n.b. also *QF* 3.8: P tells Milo not
to expect help from him or Caesar in proposed candidature for consulship of 52; on Cato see
also Afzelius 1941. **Electoral campaigns for 53:** Cic *QF* 2.13 (15a) (June 54); *Att* 4.16 (c. 1.7.54;
though see TP 144 and SB *Att* 89 for possible reading 'P's Gaul'); 4.15 and *QF* 2.14 (15b) (both
27.7.54); *QF* 2.15 (16); 3.1; *Att* 4.17 (18) (1.10.54: scandal breaks); 3.2 (11.10.54); 3.3. (21.10.54:
continual *obnuntiationes*); 3.4 (24.10.54); *Att* 4.18 (24.10.54 and 2.11.54); 4.19 (end-Nov 54); *QF*
3.8 (end-Nov; '*ineptus*' etc. surely refers to P; though Cic admits P's intercession over Vinicianus,
on whom see *Fam* 8.4.3; Plut *P* 54.2–3); 3.9 (Dec 54); Dio 40.45 (n.b. '*chiliarchoi*': consular tribunes?; also misplaced imprisonment of Pompeius Rufus, who was tribune in following year);
Plut *P* 54 (n.b. Hirrus' proposal, foreshadowed by Cic in Nov 54, unlikely to have been made
until well into 53; surely not in Dec since P back in Rome at time of Gabinius' second trial; presumably P went away again in 53, and during this absence Hirrus and Vinicianus formalized a proposal
as anarchy developed: see also Cic *Fam* 8.4); App *BC* 2.19; see also Neuendorff 1913, 56–65; Meyer
1919, 191–211; Gruen 1969B. **Elections for 52:** see Cic *QF* 3.8 (end-Nov 54); 3.9 (Dec 54; n.b.
Milo's debts; games costing 1m HS; but consulship 'will end his financial problems'); Dio 40.46
(on garment-changing see Lintott 1968, 16–21; on anarchy in new year 52 cf. Plut *P* 54.3; App
*BC* 2.20); 40.48–50 (n.b. inverted order of events, corrected by Asc: Dio presumably confuses
appointment of *interrex* with the much later *S.C.U.*: Asc 43 and 34); Asc (*in Mil*, Clark) 30–6
(detailed narrative of events leading to P's sole consulship 4 days before 1 Mar in intercalary
month); also 43, 50–2; Caes *BG* 7.1 and 6–7 (supplementary levy on strength of Senate's decree
authorizing conscription of all young men of military age throughout Italy; anarchy at Rome en-
courages Vercingetorix's 'rebellion'; Caesar takes troops with him); App *BC* 2.21–3 (from Clodius'
murder to sole consulship); Plut *P* 54.3–4; n.b. not only was sole consulship unprecedented but
for P to become consul at all this time contravened the 10-year rule; for further references and different interpretations see e.g. Neuendorff 1913, 66–73; Gruen 1974, 150–5. **Tribunician elections:**
only tribunes, elected by *plebs* (not whole *populus*), were available to take office at the end of
54 and 53: the inability to elect consuls in 54 for 53 and in 53 for 52 meant that no other 'magistrats
proper' could be elected as their elections followed that of the consuls in order of seniority: for
Cato's role in holding forfeits to ensure a clean tribunician election in his praetorship in 54 see
Cic *Att* 4.15 (elections 28 July). **P's relations with Caesar:** n.b. Caesar desires to recreate a marriage-
alliance after Julia's death (Suet *J* 27.1); complies with P's attempt to control Cic by appointing
him to his staff in 54 (*QF* 3.1; *Att* 4.19); gives up planned support for Memmius in 54 (*QF* 3.8);
P speaks for Caesar too in warning Milo that they will not support his candidature for 52 (*ib*);
P lends Caesar a legion in winter 54/53 (Caes *BG* 6.1; Plut *Caes* 25.1). **Caesar's campaigns:** see
Caes *BG* 4 (55), 5 (54: second invasion of Britain truncated by serious risings in northern Gaul
in autumn), 6 (53: occupied in re-subjugating northern Gaul and second demonstration in force
across Rhine); 7 (52: preoccupied by revolt of Vercingetorix); Dio 39.47–53; 40. 1–12, 17, 31–
41; see further e.g. Holmes 1923, vol 2; *CAH* 9.537–73; and biographies.

CHAPTER FOUR (pp. 81–108): STATE PHYSICIAN

**Judicial legislation in 52 and ensuing litigation:** Asc (Clark) 36–42 (four- or five-day trials? Problems
aired by Holmes, 2.315–16, but conclusions unconvincing. Cic spoke on 8 Apr (MS unjustifiably
emended by Clark at 26.1); Milo summoned before both *quaesitores* on 4 Apr; but narrative indicates four-day trial, and *quarta die* surely same as *postera die* in 39 (sortition proceedings on last
day). Clearly 4 Apr was not first day of trial but preliminary: Milo could be summoned by both
on same day but not 360 jurors; also Marcellus speaks before Torquatus on 4 Apr *and* interrogates
witnesses on first day of trial, i.e. 5 Apr), 53–4 (n.b. Milo's indebtedness: property sold for $\frac{1}{24}$th

value); Dio 40.52–5; Cic *pro Milone* (speech he would have given; n.b. tactful re P at 79); *Att* 9.7B.2 + *Fam* 3.10 (P gives Cic bodyguard); *Att* 8.16 (probably X dropped out of *CCCLX*; P's 'special admirers'); Plut *P* 55; *Cato* 48 ('*sent* encomium', as Dio 40.55); App *BC* 2.23–5; Tac *Ann* 3.28 ('maker and breaker of his own laws'); for M. Marcellus see Asc 39–40 (in 52); Cic *QF* 2.3 (had defended Milo in 56 against Clodius' charge of *vis*); *Brut* 249–50 (oratory; cf. Dio 40.58.3); TP (1894) vol 4, lxxiv–lxxv (brief sketch); for Caelius see Asc 36 (opposes P's laws; P's threat); Quintilian 8.6.53 (*quadrantariam Clytaemnestram*; cf. Cic *Cael* 62, also e.g. 35, 49 for Clodia's debauched life; see also Mainzer 1931 on Clodia's society; McDermott 1970 on her sisters; Dorey 1958 on *pro Caelio*); Cic *Mil* 91 (public meeting addressed by Caelius broken up); TP (1914) vol 3, xxxvii–lx (sketch of Caelius); for other helpers of Milo see Asc 34 (Hortensius, Calidius, M. Cato, Faustus Sulla). **Marriage-alliance and shared consulship** with Q. Caecilius Metellus Pius Scipio Nasica: Plut *P* 55; Dio 40.51, 57 (Scipio's law restoring censorship powers removed by Clodius' plebiscite of 58); Asc 31 ('*Pompeius, gener Scipionis*' is no evidence that P was already married to Cornelia at beginning of 52: such an identification need have no chronological significance, even if correct; Plut *P* 55 puts marriage after P's entry to city as consul); Suet *J* 26–7 (anachronistic); App *BC* 2.25. **Lex P de provinciis** (five-year gap): Dio 40.46 (proposed in 53 but evidently vetoed and left as *auctoritas*), 56 (enacted in 52); Caes *BC* 1.85 (not evidence for his attitude in 52); see further Greenidge 1901, 323 (accepts Dio's motive); SB *Att* 94 (genuine reform, probably part of Cato's *politeuma*, on which see also 115.4; A.J. Marshall 1972); for anti-Caesarian interpretations see e.g. L.R. Taylor 1949, 151; Gelzer 1968, 152; 1959, 179; Cuff 1958, 464–6. On basis of Caesar's retrospective complaint (*BC* 1.85 in 49; cf. 1.6: '*provinciae privatis decernuntur*') Cuff observed democratic objections to which the new system was open, that if consuls did not take up provincial governorships immediately after year of office their *imperium* lapsed (i.e. they were *privati*) and was invalid unless recreated by another *lex* (and the vestigial *lex curiata* was not enough: see Greenidge 251). But there is no record of 'democratic' agitation or attempted veto of P's law at the time, and it is unlikely that such considerations had worried Caesar in 52 when P was looking after his interests both politically and militarily (and, as Stockton 1975 observed, even if Caesar had been a prophet, he would have realized that enemies would be appointed to provinces against him in 49 whether they were the consuls of 50 or other allottees of the Senate). Cuff also argued that P's law deliberately set out to make 1 Mar 50 a day for 'supersession' rather than 'succession' of Caesar's command, i.e. the date which had formerly been a procedural date for the allotment of provinces under the old *lex Sempronia* now became in effect a terminal date. But even ignoring the forced arguments for fine meanings of '*succedere*' and the problem that the Sempronian system would have been allotting in 50 for 48 (not 49 as Cuff indicates), there are fatal objections to seeing the anti-Caesarian aspect as a motive rather than an unintentional result. If P had been anti-Caesar in 52, why did he not incorporate the Sempronian prohibition of tribunician veto against the allotment of provinces under his new system? He was all-powerful in 52, and could have preempted the vetoes of 50 and 49 without innovation and on Gracchus' impeccably 'popularis' precedent. P's law is far less undemocratic than Cuff realized: the restorer of tribunes' rights in 70 was restoring another in 52, and it was only when the tribunes' vetoes were eventually overborne by the Senate in 49 that there was any basis for Caesar's complaints in *BC* 1.85. Note also the basic improbability that the omnipotent P was scheming so pettily for an unforeseeable situation two years ahead. **P's proconsulship extended**: see Dio 40.56 (five years); Plut *P* 55 ('four years' improbable; P also voted 1,000 talents annually for army maintenance); *Caes* 28.8 ('Africa' mentioned (wrongly) besides Spain and 1,000 talents); App *BC* 2.24 (2 more legions and extension of provincial command); cf. Cael *Fam* 8.4 (senatorial vote for payment of P's troops scheduled for 22.7.51: perhaps 'annual' vote of 52 was annually renewable). n.b. Caesar neither wanted, nor believed that he needed, an extension in 52: he was looking forward to getting back to Rome for a triumph and another consulship, for which P made arrangements to his advantage. The politically self-protective aspect of P's extended proconsulship does not make it specifically anti-Caesarian. Caesar would have his *clientelae* among his veteran troops to be settled on farms (which he could arrange as consul for himself as he had done for P in 59), also Cisalpine Gauls etc. P was boosting his own *clientelae* through the armies in Spain; their combined *clientelae* would complement each other. **Ten Tribunes' Bill**: for P's backing see Cic *Att* 7.1, 7.3 ('a struggle'), 7.6 (Cic claims to have disapproved), 8.3 (P 'fought' to get it through; 'confirmed it by a law of his own': presumably special exemption clause inserted in general law mentioned by Dio 40.56); *Phil* 2.24 (Cic claims in 44 to have urged P against it, but n.b. *Att* 7.1 of Oct 50 admitting he had put pressure on Caelius to drop opposition to fellow-tribunes at request of Caesar and P in 52); *Fam*

6.6 ('the people insisted on it at the urgent insistence of the consul himself'); Caes *BC* 1.32 ('If P disapproved, why did he allow it to be carried?'); Dio 40.51 (P 'arranged it through the tribunes'); for candidature *in absentia* see also Balsdon 1962, 140–1. It was only when Caesar wanted to retain command beyond expiration of *lex Pomp Lic* that he began to claim that the right to stand *in absentia* implied the right to keep his provinces and armies (not merely the residual *imperium*) until he became consul (*BC* 1.9, 32 etc.; n.b. Cic *Att* 7.7 is not accepting the *legal* validity of this view: it is a despairing shrug of the shoulders: we have been conceding all Caesar's wishes for the last ten years so why stop now?). Caesar further stretched the implication (*BC* 1.32) to argue that under Sulla's law requiring a ten-year gap between magistracies, he could not legally stand until 49 for 48, and since the Law of the Ten Tribunes had guaranteed his 'command' at least until election as consul, he was entitled to keep his provinces and armies until after the elections of 49. But this was only a retrospective self-justification after he had started the Civil War. There is no mention of the 10-year law in all the discussions in our sources for 51 and 50. The question of a year for a second consulship was probably not even considered in 55 when Caesar was simply given another five years to get on with his Gallic wars secure from replacement, and when he did begin planning for it in 52 and P secured him the Law of the Ten Tribunes it was clear that the 10-year gap was a dead letter for P's friends as for P himself, whose consulship had just broken it and set the precedent; n.b. Adcock 1932, 22: all Caes *BC* 1.32 ('*legitimo tempore consulatus*' etc.) proves is that Caesar did not in fact apply for dispensation. **Law on magistracies**: see Dio 40.56; Suet *J* 28; Cic *Att* 8.3 (suggests formal rather than informal re-enactment): for heavy anti-Caesarian weather made of this by modern historians see Gruen 1974, 456–7, though he does little better in following Balsdon (1962, 141) in rejecting an 'oversight'. Obviously P was not trying to annul surreptitiously what he had just granted Caesar by the Ten Tribunes' Law and hoping that this other law would pass unnoticed, but it is not 'absentmindedness' or 'colossal ineptitude' not to have pre-empted a contradiction which was picked up by men with an interest in driving a wedge between P and Caesar – the sort of men who had suffered from P's clean-up campaign and flocked to Caesar (App *BC* 2.25), whom they tried to turn from P. The law would have been a long, formal document setting out general regulations and obviously not applying to legalized exemptions. It would not have occurred to P (even if he read it, let alone drafted it), or to its legal draftsmen, that anyone would seek a contradiction; and the point was evidently not picked up immediately because the inscription had already been made: it was probably weeks or months after the passing of the law. Even Roman lawyers were not perfect. **Supplicationes** for Caesar's victory over Vercingetorix: see Caes *BG* 7.90; Dio 48.50. Caesar's previous *supplicatio*, also of 20 days, was decreed in P's previous consulship in 55 (Caes *BG* 4.38) unless the unspecified *supplicatio* mentioned by Cic *QF* 3.8 of Nov 54 was also for Caesar (so long a postponement of those decreed in 55 surely unlikely). Not surprisingly Caesar 'spoke well of P' (App *BC* 2.25; Caes *BG* 7.6). **Consular elections for 51**: see esp. Dio 40.58 (Cato's abortive candidature, cf. Plut *Cato* 49; popularity-seeking of Marcellus and Sulpicius, on whom see Saunders 1923; Meloni 1946; TP 1894, vol. 4, lxxvii–ix). **Caesar's financial/political power of corruption**: e.g. Plut *Caes* 29 (n.b. re Curio and Paullus, on whom see also Cic *Att* 4.17 (18) of 1.10.54; cf. Cael *Fam* 8.4: Caelius dying to hear what Paullus will say to proposals for Caesar's recall in 51); Lucan 4.818–20; Cic *Att* 5.1 and 5.4 (May 51: Cic anxious to repay loan of 800,000 HS from Caesar; cf. 4.17 (18): 'we friends of Caesar, myself and Oppius'); Suet *J* 8 (largess to 'princes and provinces all over the world', also loans of troops, adornment of cities in Italy, Gaul, Spain, Asia and Greece – already happening before 51), 29 (buys Paullus and Curio), 30 (P used to declare that Caesar had insufficient means to complete all the public works he had begun or do all he had promised the people: he needed civil war); Dio 40.60–1 (Caesar buys Curio in 50; cf. Vell 2.48; 10m HS). **Transpadane Question**: see vol I ch 12 for previous attempts to extend *clientelae* by this means; for P's father's law confirming full Roman citizenship on Cispadanes and giving Latin rights to Transpadanes see Asc 3; Pliny *NH* 3.138; Strabo 5.1.6, 213 (presumably all the 5,000 made citizens, not just the Greeks); for the flogging see Cic *Att* 5.11 (6.7.51: reference to P's likely anger (reading '*nostro*') indicates P's inherited patronal relationship to Transpadanes); App *BC* 2.26; Plut *Caes* 29 (consuls of 49 confused with those of 51); Suet *J* 29 (cf. Cic *Att* 5.2 of 10.5.51: rumour that Transpadanes are electing *quattuorviri*; n.b. the mention of an evidently vetoed resolution of Senate, presumably on the Transpadane question and probably the one referred to by Suet as opposing full citizenship for Novum Comum; cf. Cael *Fam* 8.8); Cael *Fam* 8.1 (late May 51: rumour of *comitia* of Transpadanes: cf. *Att* 5.2). The most probable reconstruction is that Caesar had been authorized to set up a colony of Roman citizens (able to vote in Roman elections and serve in legions) by *lex Vatinia* of 59, possibly 5,000 strong. This was as much in P's interest as his protégé's at the time: an extension of P's electoral and military *clientelae*, as was the settlement of his own veterans as colonists in Campania and the regeneration of Capua (i.e. Suet's '*per ambitionem*'). It was probably a refoundation of the existing Comum (Como), now greatly enlarged by addition of 5,000 colonists and renamed New Comum. Perhaps Caesar's inclusion of existing Latin population in the Roman colony explains '*ultra praescriptum*'. Marcellus used this as his excuse to propose disenfranchisement of Comum in the Senate. Presumably his resolution was passed but vetoed, but he showed that he did not recognize the citizenship (and therefore voting power) of the inhabitants of Novum Comum by the flogging. This would also have been illegal if the man had been a magistrate of this 'Latin' town – a point which had not been confirmed. But even if the man 'turns out not to have been a magistrate' and therefore not entitled to citizenship *ex officio* (keeping MS '*gesserit*' of *Att* 5.11) Cic indicates that the long Latin status of the Transpadanes made this treatment outrageous and highly provocative. P was likely to be angry with Marcellus, clearly because of inherited patronage of Transpadanes but also perhaps because he still regarded Caesar as his political protégé. Rumours that Caesar was organizing elections of the magistrates appropriate to Roman municipalities in all Transpadane Latin towns turned out to be false (Cic *Att* 5.2; Cael *Fam* 8.1). Perhaps P had helped to restrain Caesar. But in 49 Caesar had recruited large numbers of Transpadanes for service in the Civil War (possibly as legionaries), hence the preference of Transpadane Opitergians for mass-suicide to surrender: see ch 7. See further on Transpadane Question Holmes 2.317–20; Badian 1958, esp. 268; SB *Att* 95.3, 104.2; Sherwin-White 1939, 105, 176; and on Caesar's legionary recruitment in general see Parker 1928, 57. **Attempts in 51 to recall Caesar:** see Dio 40.59; App *BC* 2.25–6; Suet *J* 28 (cf. Hirt *BG* 8.53; Cic *Att* 8.3); Cic *Att* 5.2 (10.5.51: 'Senate's opinion written down' is presumably on Transpadane question next mentioned, not on succession to Caesar's command since Caelius says that Marcellus has not brought that up yet: *Fam* 8.1 on or after 24 May); 5.6 (18/19.5.51); 5.7 (22.5.51: 'dangers feared': presumably of Marcellus' pushing Caesar into a corner, Caesar's provocative moves on Transpadane enfranchisement, etc.: no need to assume fear of military action yet; n.b. Cic regards P as moderator to both sides, hence worried that P will go to Spain; cf. *Att* 5.11 of 6.7.51 and *Fam* 3.8 of 8.10.51 in reply to Appius' letter of late Aug; also *Att* 5.7 and *Fam* 2.8); Cael *Fam* 8.1 (late May 51: suggestion that Marcellus had been bought; Caelius anxious to know P's attitude; rumours of Caesar in difficulties in Gaul and Cicero murdered by Rufus!); Cic *Att* 5.11 (6.7.51 from Athens: flogging incident); Cael *Fam* 8.4 (1.8.51); 8.5 'more than 2 years' not evidence that Caesar's term did not expire until 49: could simply be an expression of a long time for Cic (e.g. 'you hoped for only one year' (*Att* 5.2) 'but it will be two at this rate'); on dating see SB *Fam* 83 for arguments. Marginally more likely to have been after 8.9 than before 8.4, i.e. mid-Sep rather than early Aug, but if so it is strange that the supplementary tribunician elections at which Curio was elected in place of the condemned Servaeus were so late: Servaeus had been condemned and Curio was canvassing before *Fam* 8.4 of 1.8.51); 8.9 (early Sep; '*aperte ⟨non vult⟩*': n.b. this is Caelius' opinion, not statement by P; Lambinus' '*consul ⟨em esse⟩*' or SB's '*⟨-em fieri⟩*' are shorthand for 'consul-designate' as in 8.8 ('*consulem esse*'); for the full expression see 8.11: (M) '*consulem desig.*'); *Att* 5.19 (letter took 46 days from Rome to Cicero); *Fam* 3.8 (8.10.51); Cael *Fam* 8.8 (Oct 51; gives text of decree and vetoed resolutions (for different discussion of which see Bruwaene 1953); '*sine iniuria*': no need to assume technical sense, as Mommsen; '*negotium*': 'trouble' rather than 'business'?; '*hoc anno*': clearly 'this [electoral] year', i.e. 50; Senate's decree of late Sep postponing debate to 1.3.50 surely the result of the vote against, referred to in Hirt *BG* 8.53: Marcellus had brought forward the proposal '*ante tempus*' in that there were still some 5 months of Caesar's legal command to run: Marcellus had wanted to send successors to Caesar at once, which would certainly have been '*contra legem Pompei et Crassi*'; cf. Suet *J* 28.2 and see App I for compatibility of these references; Cael *Fam* 8.16 (17.11.51; suggestions in Rome re Parthia; consul Paullus agitating for provincial governorship, i.e. against P's law; Curio's plans for Campania: clearly further distributions, not attack on Campanian law of 59: Caes relaxed but P disturbed, presumably because he does not now want Caes to return and find that evictions have produced a lot of tenantless farms available for his veterans: *clientelae* of P and Caes now diverge); Cic *Att* 5.20 (19 and 26.12.51: Cic has received *Fam* 8.8 from Caelius on the decree which Caelius says he had already sent). **Parthian menace:** see Cic *Att* 5.16, 18, 20, 21 (13.2.50; doubtless Deiotarus and other kings had also been in direct communication with P, their patron); 6.6 (20.2.50; n.b. indication of P's vast wealth: satisfied with interest on enormous personal loans to King Ariobarzanes of Cappadocia which cannot be repaid: see further Magie *RRAM* 1249 n 41: 3,300 talents); 7.2 (n.b. Cato supports triumph for his son-in-law but not for Cic); *Fam* 2.10; 15.1, 2 (Cic's formal dispatches), 3, 4; Cael *Fam* 8.10, 16; Dio 40.28–30. See further Dobias 1931; Ziegler 1964; Magie *RRAM* 396–7, 401.

### CHAPTER FIVE (pp. 109–132): 'ARES ALIKE TO ALL'

**Curio**: see vol I ch 12 re 59; for candidature in 51, tribunate of 50 and anti-Caesarian attitude see Cael *Fam* 8.4 (1.8.51), 8.8 (Oct 51); for legislative programme see Cael *Fam* 8.10 (Campanian land-bill); 8.6 (road-building scheme under own five-year supervision, cf. App *BC* 2.27; grain law; demand for intercalary month, cf. 8.11 and Dio 40.62.1); Cic *Att* 6.1 (restoration of Memmius; sumptuary law); Caes *BC* 2.25 (annexation of Juba's kingdom; cf. Dio 41.41.3; Lucan 4.689–92: 'to take Africa from its rightful king and set up a king in Rome'); for Rullus' comparable schemes of 63 see vol I ch 11; for Curio's transfer to Caesar see Dio 40.60–2; Vell 2.48.3–5 (on size of bribe see Holmes 2.321); Cael *Fam* 8.16 (17.11.51); 8.6 (Feb 50: n.b. Caelius' failure to specify bribery as reason for Curio's volte-face in the few surviving letters does not discredit evidence of later sources;? sarcastic attribution to pique over intercalation); Cic *Fam* 2.13 (early May 50: reply to *Fam* 8.6 of Feb); *Att* 6.3 (between 7.5.50 and 5.6.50: 'hateful things have reached me about Curio and Paullus', on whom n.b. the supposed feud with P inherited from Lepidus affair (e.g. Gruen 1974) can be overdone: even Brutus fought as Pompeian in Civil War; on Paullus see also *Fam* 8.4); App *BC* 2.26; Plut *P* 58.1; Caes 29.2–3; Suet *J* 29.1; Val Max 9.1.6; Lucan 4.816–24; Pliny *NH* 36.116–20 (extravagance; 'his principal financial asset was the feud between the leading citizens'; cf. Vell 2.48.3 and Cael *Fam* 8.11.3); for weak arguments against bribery of Curio see Lacey 1961 and Gruen 1974, 470–83. Note widespread personal debt as incentive to political extremism, e.g. Catiline, Milo, Caelius, and see in general Cic *Att* 7.3 ('all the debt-ridden, whom I perceive to be richer than I thought, flocking to Caesar'); on debt problem in general see also Royer 1967; for possible influence of Fulvia, Clodius' widow, see Babcock 1965. **Curio's first attack on P** (presumably in Senate's debate on 19 Feb in accordance with decree of previous Sep: Cael *Fam* 8.8; Cic informed about Curio's volte-face by *Fam* 8.6 in Feb, to which he replied by *Att* 6.12 of Apr/May) see App *BC* 2.27 (cf. Dio 40.62). **P's first compromise proposal after 1 Mar**: see Cael *Fam* 8.11 (Apr 50: n.b. Ides Nov obviously 50 and not 49 as e.g. Frank 1919, Holmes 2.303, Elton 1946; against SB *Fam* 91.4 I read and punctuate '*Caesar defendetur* [M]: *intercessorem si, quod videntur, reformidarint, Caesar quoad volet manebit*'. SB's 'Caesar will defend the intercessor' suggests premature threat of military action. M's better reading 'Caesar will be protected by tribunician veto and will stay in command of province and armies as long as he likes if the Senate shy away from a confrontation with the intercessor' is exactly what does happen: they refuse to 'treat with the tribunes': *Fam* 8.13; *Att* 7.7). **P's illness, recovery and second compromise proposal**: see App 2.28; Cic *Att* 6.3 (datable May/June 50; '*valeat modo*' seems to refer to P's illness, of which Cic will have been informed in Apr since letters took at least a month to reach Cilicia; this letter also replies to news of 'nasty things about Curio and Paullus' which became clear in late Feb/Mar; it is therefore uncertain that Cael *Fam* 8.13 of June is still referring to P's illness, at least as a continuing one, by '*stomacho languenti* etc.', which could be simply metaphorical like our 'fed up' despite SB on Celsus and symptoms of *cardiacus morbus*: *Fam* 94.2); see also Ciaceri 1931 on P's illness; and Plut *P* 57 on his recovery and its effect. **Legions recalled against Parthian threat to Syria**: see App *BC* 2.29; Plut *P* 56.3; 57.4 (on 'Appius' see SB on *Att* 140.3); Caes 29; Hirt *BG* 8.54 (n.b. these partisan, retrospective complaints are not necessarily either Senate's real intentions or what Caesar believed them to have been at the time); Caes *BC* 1.9 (similar; cf. Calidius' supposed remarks on 1 Jan 49 at 1.2); Cic *Att* 7.13.2 (retrospective of 23.1.49; recalled legions kept in Italy '*invidiose*'); *Fam* 2.17 (c. 18.7.50); for dating of Parthian withdrawal from Syria between 26 June and mid-July see Magie *RRAM* 1255 n 73; F.W. Sanford 329; Holmes 2.323: Senate's decree therefore in May at latest since Cic knew about it by July; possibly in Apr (also App *BC* 2.28 puts decree at time of Curio's demand that P should resign his command first; also Apr/early May fits likely date of P's recovery from illness). **P's move to hard line**: see Cael *Fam* 8.13 (June 50; cf. *Fam* 8.11; *Att* 7.7; n.b. in TP 271 and SB *Fam* 94.2 '*aut armis resistat*' is only Wesenberg's guess for filling gap in text); *Fam* 8.14 (5–10.8.50: n.b. first surviving letter in which Cael specifically fears civil war: we cannot be sure that 'repeated' mentions in a lost spate of correspondence go back as far as 8.13 of June; on cynical weighing of forces cf. Vell 2.49.3; on Appius' censorship cf. Dio 40.63). **Summer elections of 50 for 49**: see Hirt *BG* 8.50–2; Suet *J* 29; for families and affiliations of C. Claudius Marcellus and L. Cornelius Lentulus Crus see e.g. Syme 1939, 43–4; Gruen 1974, 102–5, 157–8; but beware obsession with interpreting politics in terms of family loyalty and feud among the pragmatic Roman aristocracy. **Cold war in autumn 50**: see Cic *Att* 6.8 (1.10.50; cf. *Att* 5.11 and 7.9 for constant fear of P's going to Spain); 6.9 (15.10.50; alarmist rumour (cf. 7.1): evident confusion with Caesar's military review at Nemetocenna mentioned in Hirt *BG* 8.52); 7.1 (16.10.50; evidence of propaganda war between P and Caes in simultaneous letters; cf. 7.2 for P's buttering of Cic to Att at Naples); n.b. the burning questions are (a) prevention of candidature *in absentia* and (b) making him give up army: there is no mention of trying to annul his provincial command (cf. 7.7) as there surely would have been if the command had not expired by now; cf. Caesar's failure to claim infraction of *lex Pompeia Licinia* in his self-justification in *BC* 1.9; for Marcellus' frustrated attempt to secure appointment of successors to Caesar and his reaction in late Nov/early Dec (for which we lack Cic's letters) see App *BC* 2.30–1 (n.b. 370–22 vote is surely the '*sc. per discessionem*' of Hirt *BG* 8.52); Dio 40.64–6 (puts Marcellus' appeal to P after his failure to secure condemnation of Curio for assaulting Appius Claudius in the Senate, and at 66 associates this with arrival of two legions from Caesar; but discrepancies from Appian's version are undermined by chronological confusion: he puts the episode 'at the end of the year' whereas arrival of legions and Appius' censorial attack on Curio were much earlier; Dio's addition, that Marcellus caused consuls-elect to issue the same commands, is convincing; n.b. 'P needed troops so badly that he did not scruple about the source or means but took them gratefully'); Plut *P* 58–9 (cf. *Caes* 30). To Dio's rough 'at the end of the year' and App's 'as Curio's tribunate was expiring' (i.e. before 10 Dec) F.W. Sanford (310–19) adds computations based on estimates of couriers' and legions' speed, and argues that if Caesar reacted by summoning legions VIII and XII from Transalpine Gaul, the arrival of the latter before Caesar reached Firmum on 2.2.49 indicates that P was commissioned 'before 2 December, possibly as early as 25 November': see also Holmes 2.324–6; TP (1914) vol 3, lxxxix–xciii (though unconvincing on alternation of *fasces* and in agreeing with Bardt that Marcellus's action was 'a mere theatrical display' with 'no constitutional validity'). n.b. also that the absence of so striking an incident from Cic's correspondence, beginning again on 9 Dec (*Att* 7.3) after gap from 26 Nov (7.2), suggests it had taken place in first day or two of Dec at latest, and probably in last week of Nov: *Att* 7.3 and 7.4 bewail personal power-struggle and the virtual certainty of war in a way which indicates a major development, doubtless reported to Cic by Att and commented on in lost letters before 9 Dec. Schmidt's 13 Dec (1893, 94, 100) is clearly impossible. **Month's run-up to S.C.U. on 7.1.49**: see Cic *Att* 7.3–9; *Fam* 16.11; Caes *BC* 1.1–7; App *BC* 2.32–4; Dio 41.1–3; Plut *Caes* 30–1 (n.b. confusion of aspects of debate on 1 Jan with episode of late Nov/early Dec involving Curio's (then) popular proposal for bilateral disarmament and Marcellus' reaction; confusion of Marcellus and Curio with Lentulus and Antony); *P* 58–9; Vell 2.49; Suet *J* 29; Livy *Ep* 109. On Caesar's compromise proposals: (1) Were residual legion(s) and provinces to be retained (only) until Caesar had been *elected* consul, as App and Plut specify? Suet's '*quoad consul fieret*' is ambiguous. Vell does not specify. Holmes (2.331 n 7) argued that App and Plut were mistaken and that Suet meant 'until he becomes consul', i.e. enters office. But while this would clearly give Caesar greater security (and Cael had seen that he wanted this and P was determined to refuse it in *Fam* 8.14 of Aug), Holmes was blind to see 'no advantage' to Caesar in keeping them only until he had been elected: they were his guarantee of being elected. (2) Were these proposals made (if at all) in the period 1–7 Jan? App's careful account places them between Curio's popular proposal of late Nov/early Dec (which led Marcellus to commission P on his own authority as consul) and the meeting of 1 Jan when Curio brought Caesar's ultimatum letter: bilateral disarmament or war (i.e. Curio's proposal revived). Plut maintains that the compromises were made after this and in 'letters' from Caesar. Cic indicates that he made hopeless (unspecified) attempts at peacemaking when he arrived at Rome on 4 Jan, and Plut associates these with the proposals for reduced forces and provinces until election. Perhaps such suggestions were still bandied around, but there was certainly no second formal 'letter' from Caesar conveying them to Senate on 6 or 7 Jan (as Nissen, TP, etc.). Caesar would surely have mentioned them; and Cic specifies that there was only the one letter, the 'threatening and sharp' one delivered by Curio on 1 Jan (*Fam* 16.11 of 12 Jan). (3) Did P agree to such compromises (whether before or after 1 Jan) only to be overborne by Lentulus and the hard-liners, as maintained by Plut and App followed by Nissen, TP, Raaflaub etc.? Surely not in the face of Cic's references to P's activities and uncompromising attitude through Dec (*Att* 7.3–9, esp 7.8 of 25/26 Dec: 'P's view is that if Caesar is made consul even after giving up his army it will mean the subversion of the constitution'; 'there is not even the desire for peace') and Caesar's account of 1–7 Jan (in which Scipio was clearly P's mouthpiece for the hard-line proposal), also P's filling the city with troops (cf. Plut, App), summoning Senate to suburbs to encourage them for the S.C.U., and his immediate acceptance of the formal commission afterwards: P was the leader, not the led. (Also Vell, for what he is worth, contradicts Plut and App: 'P rejected all proposals'). (4) Was there another vote on Curio's old proposal for bilateral disarmament on 1 Jan, as Dio? Very unlikely, for though Caesar does not specify what his letter contained, Dio himself maintains it was this ultimatum, and Caesar says it was impossible to get a motion presented on the subject of his letter. (Calidius as second best proposed that P should go to Spain, but this too was refused.) The only motion allowed to be put was Scipio's, that Caesar should dismiss his army before a fixed day or be considered a public enemy (n.b. attempts to associate 'fixed day' of Caes *BC* 1.2 and Plut *Caes* 30 with the *'legis dies'* under the *lex Pomp Lic* of 55, which would not therefore have expired, are totally unwarranted). Dio's description of the division on the proposal in Caesar's letter is evidently a confusion with the division on Scipio's proposal (the only one to be put). (5) 'Expulsion' of tribunes Antony and Cassius? Dio says Lentulus 'advised them to leave', Plut (*Caes*) that he 'drove them from the Senate' (and they fled dressed as slaves in hired carts), Appian that both consuls 'ordered Antony and his friends out of the Senate before they should suffer harm'; but significantly Caesar's own mention of 'decrees being made of the severest and harshest character concerning the command of Caesar and those most important men, the tribunes of the people' (*BC* 1.5; cf. 1.7, 32) may imply but does not specify that violence was threatened or used against them, and Cic is emphatic that it was not (*Fam* 16.11.2). Admittedly the presence of P's troops will hardly have been conducive to their comfort in Rome, but their flight could well have been a voluntary act to give Caesar 'the cause' – the overriding of the tribunes' rights – which was the only thing that Cic had said he lacked (*Att* 7.3; cf. Plut *Caes* 31), and Caesar made full use of it (*BC* 1.5, 7, 32 etc.). But n.b. when Plut (*Caes* 31) speaks of expulsion of 'Antony and Curio' from the Senate as 'giving Caesar the most specious of his pretexts for war', the outrage which he stressed was not to the political rights or personal sacrosanctity of tribunes (and Curio of course was no longer a tribune) but to their status as 'men of high repute'. They were distinguished representatives of Caesar himself and of Caesar's army (of which Antony had been a popular officer). An insult to these men was an indirect insult to Caesar's army, which would also depend for retirement gratuities, farms and honour on Caesar's political success (cf. App *BC* 2.33: Caesar's army was declared a public enemy, P's army the protector of Rome); note also Caesar's appeal to the dignity of the army and its commander as indissoluble (*BC* 1.7). The development of the more 'professional' Roman armies since Marius' reforms, their reliance on their commanders for rewards and the development of an intense, almost separatist *esprit de corps* from years of fighting together in one part of the world are important factors in the Civil Wars, the last factor becoming increasingly prominent under the Empire when troops serve the greater part of their careers in one frontier camp: on this factor of the rivalry and 'separatism' of regionally based army-groups in the Civil Wars of AD 69 see e.g. Greenhalgh 1975. On the significance of the increasing 'professionalism' of Roman armies from Marius' reforms see e.g. Gabba 1973, 1–69. The Pompeian veterans immediately available in Italy (as distinct from the legions in Spain) are unlikely to have felt the same *esprit de corps* after ten years' farming in Campania as Caesar's active army which had been fighting together for ten years, nor were they still waiting for the rewards of long service. **Sociological aspects of the conflict**: see e.g. Cael *Fam* 8.14 ('P will have on his side the Senate and all who settle cases at law; all who live with fear or despair will join Caesar, for his army is altogether beyond comparison'; augural elections fought on 'party lines'; n.b. the more egalitarian democratic nature of the election of augurs and tribunes than of magistrates with *imperium*: see Greenidge 252–5); Cic *Att* 7.3 (Caesar has 'all convicted criminals and those stained with disgrace [cf. 7.8: Antony's *'querela de damnatis'*], all who deserve conviction or disgrace, nearly all the younger generation, all the abandoned city rabble, the powerful tribunes including C. Cassius, and all those who are overwhelmed with debt'); App *BC* 2.27 (P unpopular with urban plebs 'on account of his prosecutions for bribery', i.e. the reduction of electoral largess; n.b. corn-supply and glories of 52 now forgotten (cf. 2.24–5), but contrast P's undiminished popularity among rural and municipal rather than urban plebs as evidenced on recovery from illness); Dio 40.60 (Caesar's efforts to build up urban *clientelae*); Cic *Att* 7.7 (Caesar has Transpadanes, urban plebs, and Rome's 'abandoned youth'); *Fam* 16.11 (*'improbi cives'* have never had a readier leader; i.e. all elements inimical to Cic's settled aristocratic ideal, from the *perdita plebs* as a class to those nobles who should know better).

CHAPTER SIX (pp. 133–164): GOVERNMENT IN EXILE

**Main literary sources**: Caes *BC* 1–28; App *BC* 2.34–40; Dio 41.1–13; Plut *P* 60–2; *Caes* 32–5; *Cic* 37; *Cato Min* 51–3; Lucan 1–2 (esp. 2.319–728); Vell 2.49–50; Cic *Fam* 16.11–12; 14.18; *Att* 7.10–21, 23, 26; 8.1–4, 6–16; 9.1–4, 6–7, 9–14; for P's letters preserved by Cic see *Att* 8.11A and 11C (to Cic), 6 and 12A (to consuls), 12B and 12C (to Domitius). **Bias of Caesar's memoirs**: see also (briefly) Balsdon 1957B and (detailed) Rambaud 1953, Barwick 1951; for partisan defence of his veracity see Holmes e.g. 2.329–31, 334–7; 3.383; for more balanced discussion of Caesar's factual accuracy and propaganda see J.H. Collins 1972 with bibliography; on purposes of peace-negotiations of Jan 49 Fritz 1941 is closer to my own view; see *contra* Raaflaub 1975. **Caesar's invasion of Italy**: see also Binder 1928, Mueller 1973. **Political factions**: see Fuchs 1920, Shackleton Bailey 1960B (warning against obsessive prosopography). **Domitius**: on family connection with Transalpine Gaul see Münzer 333 (family-tree); for grandfather's wars against Salluvii, Allobroges and Averni in 122–20 see Livy *Ep* 61; Vell 2.10.2; Florus 1.37.4–6; Suet *Nero* 2; Degrassi 82, 560 (triumph over Averni); for Domitian Way see Cic *Font* 18; for Narbo and D's father's role in foundation see Crawford *RRC* no. 281 and pp. 71ff (supports the surely incontrovertible date of 118 given by Vell 1.15.5 and 2.7.8); Ebel 1975, 358–9; for spread of name 'Domitius' see e.g. ILS 6976 from Nemausus; for P's role in organizing Transalpine Gaul as separate province see Ebel and notes to vol I ch 4. **North African kingdoms** since P's victory over Marians (vol I ch 2): see Gsell 7.289–95; 8.1–5 (early 49). **Mission of L. Caesar**, son of one of Caesar's legates but only very distantly related to Caesar, and praetor L. Roscius: see Caes *BC* 1.7.10; Cic *Att* 7.13 (Cic sees L. Caesar at Minturnae on 23.1.49 'bearing a ridiculous message': Caesar must be 'making fun of us'), 14, 15, 17 (on Sestius' frigid style see also Catullus 44); *Fam* 16.12 (27.1.48: contrast Caesar's version, *BC* 1.9); Dio 41.5 (L. Caesar and Roscius sent by P; n.b. Dio's indication that they went twice goes against Caes, Cic and chronological probabilities, despite Holzapfel). Evidently not an official embassy from Senate: see Shackleton Bailey 1960A, reprinted in *Att* vol 4, 441–7; on purpose of mission see conflicting views of e.g. Raaflaub 1975 (genuine desire for peaceful settlement by P and Caes); Fritz 1941 (no real desire for peace by Caesar); Adcock *CAH* 9.639 (P probably offered Caes 'something more seductive' than we are told; intention to delay Caesar's advance); Shackleton Bailey 1960A (follows Dio in suggesting general fear among P's supporters that he would make private deal with Caesar). **Labienus**: see also W.B. Tyrrell 1972, Syme 1938, L.R. Taylor 1921 (connection with Cingulum). **Corfinium**: for different interpretations of Domitius' stand and P's strategy see Fritz 1942, Burns 1966, Shackleton Bailey 1956 (in modified form, *Att* vol 4, 448–59); Veith 1913. **Military strength of P and Caesar at outbreak of war**: see Appendix II.

CHAPTER SEVEN (pp. 165–196): 'WAR THROUGHOUT THE WORLD'

**Affairs in Italy** from P's evacuation to Caesar's invasion of Spain: Caes *BC* 1.29–33; App *BC* 2. 40–1; Dio 41.15–17; Lucan 3. 71–168; Cic *Att* 9.15 (25 Mar), 15A, 18–19; 10.1, 1A, 4, 6–10, 12, 12A, 16 (14 May). **P's strategy** belatedly appreciated by Cic: *Att* 9.9 (17 Mar), cf. 9.7 (13 Mar), 9.4 (12 Mar), 8.11 (27 Feb); and for later letters e.g. 10.8 (2 May); but n.b. his claim in 9.9 to have known about the grand strategy all along is contradicted by e.g. 8.8 (23 Feb); cf. 7.7. SB (*Att* vol 4, 450 n 2) makes heavy weather of these contradictions. Cic simply hated being excluded from decision-making and bitterly resented that his advice was neither asked nor taken. When he finally understood P's strategy, he claimed to have known about it all the time: his convenient '*me oblivisci*' is equally apparent in his change of tune over P himself (contrast e.g. 8.3, 7, 8 with 9.12, 13). **Corn-weapon**: Cic *Att* 9.4; 9.9; cf. 8.1 (Cic had formerly appreciated need to secure corn-supply but only in the context of maintaining control of Campanian coast); 7.7 (P had wanted Cic to take control of Sicily as early as mid-Dec); 7.15 (26 Jan: Cato, assigned to Sicily *pro praetore*, refused to go, as did Postumius; n.b. Caesar's bogus peace-initiative did help him to secure Sicily; for Cato's belated efforts see also 10.12, 16); for Caesar's immediate moves to secure Sicily and Sardinia see Caes *BC* 1.30–1; App *BC* 2.40–1; Dio 41.18; Florus 2.13; Lucan 3.52; n.b. also Dio 41.15 (Caesar sends for corn immediately after returning from Brundisium); App *BC* 2.48 (emergency distribution to 'the starving people' after return from Spain: important sweetener before elections); 54 (Caesar's few warships are used to guard Sicily and Sardinia). **Spanish campaign**: Cic *Att* 9.15a (25.3.49: Caesar's immediate decision after failing to stop P's evacuation), 18 (Cic threatens to disapprove publicly); 10.8 (Spain in context of P's total strategy), 12 (5.5.49: expecting news from

Spain), 12A (6.5.49: boldness of Massilians suggests that things go well in Spain); Caes *BC* 1.30 (decision), 37–55, 59–87; App *BC* 2.42–3; Dio 41.18–24; Lucan 4.1–401; Livy *Ep* 110; Plut *Caes* 36; on Varro see Boissier. **Massilia:** Caes *BC*1.34–6, 56–9; 2.1–16; Dio 41.19, 21, 25; Lucan 3. 298–762; Livy *Ep* 110; Cic *Att* 10.12A; for city's history see Clerc; for siege see also Holmes 3.409–21. **African campaign and Curio:** Caes *BC* 2.23–44; App *BC* 2.44–6; Dio 41.41–2; Lucan 4.582–824; Livy *Ep* 110; see further Ferrabino; Holmes 3.421–9; Gsell 8.5–24; Bouchenaki. **Adriatic and Illyrian campaigns:** App *BC* 2.47; Dio 41.40; Livy *Ep* 110; Florus 2.13.30–3; Lucan 4.402–581; Orosius 6.15.8–10; Caes *BC* 3.10 (n.b. MSS have Corcyra, not Curicta, and Lucan places Antonius' defeat near Salonae. The island was obviously Corcyra Nigra, now Korčula, formerly Curzola. 'Currictico litore' of one MS of Florus is hardly evidence for Krk near Rijeka right at the top of the Adriatic when Florus also says that Dolabella and Antonius had been ordered to defend the *fauces*). **P's build-up of forces in 49:** Caes *BC* 3.3–5; Plut *P* 64; App *BC* 2.49; Dio 41.52. **Caesar's preparations and crossing:** Caes *BC* 3.2, 6–7; Lucan 5.374–80, 403–60; App *BC* 2.52–4 (n.b. con-trast role of P's naval squadron at Oricum with Caesar's version); Plut *Caes* 37; Dio 41.44. n.b. Caesar's enormous superiority of cavalry in Spain would be reversed in Greece; his war-fleet was negligible compared with P's: the Adriatic campaign had been a disaster, and what ships he had, except for an escort of 12 warships, were deployed to guard the corn-supply from Sicily and Sardinia (Appian). **Military statistics:** see Appendix II. **Constitutional battle:** P scored heavily by evacuating consuls and large part of Senate (200: Dio 41.43) to Greece. Before leaving Rome the Senate had out-lawed Caesar, and the consuls had proclaimed a *iustitium* (Lucan 5.32), involving sealing Treasury and suspending all public business (which could technically be remitted only by decree of the magis-trate who had enjoined it: see further Greenidge 175). After failing to prevent evacuation, Caesar evidently sought to legalize his position by holding elections, but the absence of the consuls made it constitutionally impossible, and when he canvassed Cicero (and no doubt many others) for sup-port, Cicero baulked at the illegal suggestion that a praetor (the highest available magistrate) could hold even praetorian, let alone consular, elections, or nominate a dictator (*Att* 9.9.3 and 9.15.2, cf. Gellius 13.15.4; Greenidge 147, 195). The elective *'populus'* as distinct from the *'plebs'* could not legally meet except under the higher *imperium* or *auspicia* of the consuls or dictator, who was correctly nominated only by one of the consuls (Greenidge 191–3, but even the dictator lacked authority to take money from the Treasury without senatorial decree: Zonaras 7.13). The other possibility was appointment by *interrex* (as Sulla had been: Cic *Att* 9.15.2), but Cicero observed that 'it was of the greatest concern to Caesar to avoid an *interregnum*' (*Att* 9.9.3). A prerequisite of *interregnum* was the non-existence of consuls, and Cicero's sarcastic remark at *Att* 9.15.2 ('why cannot Caesar arrange to do what Sulla did and get himself nominated by an *interrex*?') points the contrast between Sulla's position, when both consuls were dead, and Caesar's, when both are not only alive but presiding over the more respectable part of the Senate in exile. Moreover the declaration of an *interregnum* would automatically end the legal existence of the elective *populus* and return the auspices (representing the divine sanction of the *imperium* conferred by the 'people' whose legal existence depended upon the life of its supreme magistrates) to 'the fathers', from whose patrician members the *interrex* would then be chosen. That in turn would give the Senate in exile the better right to appoint the *interrex* and remove from Caesar his chief constitutional support, the existence of the *'populus'* which it was less easy for the government in exile to pretend to have with it. An *interregnum* also required the resignation of the lesser so-called 'patrician' magistrates, which meant that Caesar would lose the legally elected praetors who were with him, and that it would be for a tribune of the *plebs* (whose existence was not affected) to put the question of the appointment of an *interrex* to the Senate (which would then suggest that the *patricii* should meet for the purpose), and another tribune could veto the suggestion (as the tribunes Pompeius Rufus and Munatius Plancus did in 52: Asconius 31; see further Greenidge 148). And at least one tribune, L. Metellus, was ready to do that. For Metellus' opposition to Caesar's breaking into the inner treasury locked by the consuls see Cic *Att* 10.4.9 (Caesar was so angry that he wanted to kill Metellus); App *BC* 2.41; Dio 41.17; Lucan 114–68; Plut *P* 62; *Caes* 35; Florus 2.13.21 (refers to 'tribunes': perhaps Metellus not alone in opposition? cf. 'vetos' in Cic *Att* 10.9A, though this could refer to more than one veto by Metellus alone; and n.b. Caesar's careful suppression of the fact that Metellus was objecting to his removing money from the Treasury (*BC* 1.33). That a tribune actually suggested to Caesar's senate the appointment of an *interrex* is unlikely, and to what extent it was formally discussed is unknown; but the result is clear, that Caesar decided not to try to force elections at this stage. His constitutional position was a shambles, and he decided to keep to the least of the evils by doing nothing to jeopardize the legal *imperium* of those magistrates like the praetor Lepidus who were on his side. Moreover the senators whom Caesar gathered with difficulty in Rome ('a synod of senators, for I cannot call it the Senate': Cic *Att* 10.1 (though n.b. Cic's annoyance that his peace-making role has been usurped by someone else, probably Volcatius Tullus: see 9.19.2); Lucan 3.104–9) were not all collaborators to judge from his own indications of disappointment at their 'unhelpfulness' (*BC* 1.33), confirmed by e.g. Caelius (*Att* 10.9A); and Atticus told Cicero of anti-Caesarian demonstrations in the theatres after Caesar had left for Spain (*Att* 10.12A; cf. 10.4.8: 'even the plebs had not liked his behaviour over the Treasury'). Evidently Caesar found enough senatorial collaborators to confer grants of propraetorian rank (at least) on Antony (*Att* 10.8A: letter heading) and Curio (*Att* 10.4.8–11; Caes *BC* 1.30: 'propraetor') and probably *imperium* in view of Cicero's remarks on Curio's *fasces* (*Att* 10.4.9): their number (six) indicated *imperium* granted by the Senate *pro praetore* but the laurels indicated that he was a *legatus* of the *Imperator* Caesar and derived his *imperium* from him (cf. Suet *J* 36: '*legatos*'). Curio laughed about having desired 'to get them by a snatched decree of the Senate,' (*Att* 10.4.9), possibly by a meeting rigged to avoid the presence of Caesar's enemies, especially the tribune(s). By his treatment of the tribune Metellus and the quasi-legal senate's grants of *imperium* (however much disguised in Curio's case by laurelled *fasces*) Caesar had trampled the two constitutional principles whose defence was his justification for making war: the rights of the tribunes (*BC* 1.7, 32) and the Senate's usurpation of the popular right to grant *imperium* as a result of the five-year gap instituted under the Pompeian law of 52 ('*privati*' appointed to provinces: *BC* 1.6; cf. 1.85 where the argument has subtly shifted from illegality to cliquery; see also notes to ch 4 on *lex Pompeia de provinciis*). For careful attention to constitutional forms by government in exile see esp. Dio 41.18.4–6; 41.43 (some 200 senators; appropriated a piece of land for auguries; 'regarded the people and the whole city as present there'); Plut *P* 64–5 (n.b. story of P's respect for the lame Tidius Sextius (? the same who had found Clodius' corpse: Asc 32); Senate's first meeting in Greece; passed decree on Cato's motion that no Roman to be killed except in battle and no subject city plundered). For the great meeting just before year-end see App *BC* 2.50–2; Lucan 5.7–65. But Caesar's position, strengthened by a year's control of Rome and Italy and victory in Spain, appeared less illegitimate after his elections. His nomination as dictator by the praetor, though still technically illegal, was sanctioned by a popular *lex*, and the creation of a *dictator comitiorum habendorum causa* was at least precedented (e.g. Livy 8.24, when consuls were ill; 8.26, when they were absent in the field; 30.39, the most recent precedent in 202; cf. *Fast Capit*, Degrassi, 48, 121, 452): for full references to his legislative and electoral activities see Broughton *MRR* 2.256–7 (n.b. Lucan 5.381–402 for indications that elections had practical as well as legal problems). Dio (41.43) was unusually stupid to say that the Pompeians held no elections simply because the *lex curiata* had not been passed before they left Rome. He may have picked up the point which Caesar made (*BC* 1.6), when searching for an unconstitutional mote in his enemy's eye: that the new governors appointed by the Senate in Rome in Jan 49 after the S.C.U. had left the city without bothering about the vestigial sanction of the *lex curiata* (which in any case was a doubtful requirement now even theoretically: contrast Cic *Rull* 2.30; *Fam* 1.9.25). It will have been the thirty lictors representing the long defunct *comitia curiata* (Cic *Rull* 2.31) who helped to represent the '*populus*' in Greece, and while they could obviously not presume to hold elections, their very *inactivity* will have helped to stress the invalidity of Caesar's elections and provincial appointments which, even if they had been valid in other respects, would not be complete. But the Pompeians' constitutional position was that absolutely nothing which had been done in Rome since they had left was valid, and their care not to assign any fresh *imperium* themselves would help them to claim that the *populus* had legally ceased to exist with the expiry of the consular year, that the auspices had returned to the fathers, and thus the Senate was more than ever the sole authority, though they did not of course try to appoint an *interrex* to make P dictator: that would have been not only constitutionally counter-productive against Caesar's claim to be a legally elected consul but un-acceptable to many of P's peers already afraid of monarchy.

CHAPTER EIGHT (pp. 197–228): UNLAURELLED IMPERATOR

**Main literary sources:** Caes *BC* 3.6–73 (on whose general reliability see Barwick 1951, J.H. Collins 1972, Knoche 1951, Rambaud 1953); App *BC* 2.54–64; Dio 41.44–51; Plut *P* 65–6; Caes 37–40; *Cato Min* 54–5; *Ant* 7–8; *Cic* 38; Lucan 5.425–6.332; Florus 2.13; Vell 2.51; Livy *Ep* 101; for military studies see also Heuzey 1886; Stoffel 1887; Veith 1920; Holmes 1923; and the Kromayer – Veith atlas 1924. **Illyricum** and difficulties of land-route to Greece for Caesarian forces: see App

*Ill* 12 (a 'large army' sent by Caesar into Illyricum during his governorship (probably in 50) was 'annihilated'; though on timing of Gabinius' disaster n.b. that App *BC* 2.59 is corrected by *Bell Alex* 42–3 (winter of 48/7) and cf. Cic *Fam* 11.16); see further Veith 1924 on Caesarian campaigns in Illyricum, also Zippel 1877. **Antony's crossing:** n.b. *'multi menses'* (Caes *BC* 3.25) must involve entry into a third month, i.e. early April, which agrees with *'hiems praecipitaverat'* (since spring could hardly be before early Apr by unreformed calendar, i.e. early Feb by ours); this cannot be challenged by Suet *J* 35: Suet is weak on chronology; and since P probably did not break out until early July, the siege did at least span 4 months even if its duration is unlikely to have been 'nearly four months'. n.b. the only certain dates are Caesar's sailing from Brundisium (4 Jan 48 = 5 Nov 49 reformed: *BC* 1.6) and Battle of Pharsalus (9 Aug 48 = 6 June reformed: *CIL* 1.324, 328). **Movements of P, Caesar and Antony** after Antony's landing at Nymphaeum: Holmes (3.441–2) follows Göler, Heuzey and Veith against Stoffel's argument that Caesar and Antony met north of the Genusus. Stoffel suggests the vicinity of Tirana some 20 miles east of Dyrrachium (Durresi). Holmes and others object that P, when marching to intercept Antony, 'did not cross any river, and that Antony had crossed the Genusus when Caesar joined him'. But this is an unwarranted assumption from Caes *BC* 2.30, which is not concerned with the crossing of any rivers other than the Apsus, on opposite sides of which P and Caesar were encamped. Caesar's point is solely that P had a start over him because he was already on the north side of the Apsus and 'did not have to cross the river' whereas Caesar had to march a long way upstream to find a ford. River crossings are only worth mentioning if some difficulty is attached to them. P would have no difficulty in crossing the Genusus because he controlled the crossing points, and Caesar, having marched inland across the Apsus, might similarly have no trouble in crossing the Genusus so much higher up (and, if we are to use arguments from silence, Caesar says nothing about Antony's crossing of the Genusus if Antony had crossed it). The objections to supposing that Antony had already come as far south as the Genusus before P tried to intercept him are overwhelming: (a) Caesar admits that he and P learnt of Antony's landing and the size of his army simultaneously (3.30), whatever the difficulties of the corrupt sentence which follows. Antony's fleet had been seen going by Apollonia and Dyrrachium, Coponius had pursued it vigorously from Dyrrachium, and P's cavalry will have been active up the coast to bring him immediate news of the landing and the fate of Coponius' squadron (e.g. P's garrison commander at Lissus had 400 horsemen acting as coastal patrols in that area). If then Antony had crossed the Genusus by the time P came up with him, we must suppose that Antony (despite the delay at Lissus) had marched over 70 miles (the Genusus is over 50 miles south of Lissus as the crow flies) while P had marched only a tiny fraction of that distance (the Apsus, now the Semani-Derolli, and the Genusus, now the Shkumbini, are only between 5 and 20 miles apart). (b) If P did wait until Antony had crossed the Genusus, he had left Dyrrachium exposed to a much larger army than Caesar had with him at the Apsus. (c) If Antony had crossed the Genusus, Caesar's having to march up the Apsus to find a ford would be more of an advantage than the disadvantage that he maintains, because the two rivers become closer inland (until they diverge again east of Elbasani, but neither Holmes nor anyone else suggests that Caesar and Antony met farther inland than that): Pompey would never have gained well over a day's advantage over Caesar if Antony was south of the Genusus in the area suggested by Veith and followed by Holmes. (d) Even allowing for the storming of a town on the way it is incredible that it took Caesar rather longer to reach Asparagium from a point of junction with Antony south of the Genusus (3.41: 'on the third day') than it took him to march all the way to Dyrrachium from Asparagium by a 'great circuit along a narrow and difficult route' (*ib*: Caesar leaves Asparagium camp on one day, P moves camp on the next day, and Caesar reaches Dyrrachium on the third morning). If then Antony was not south of the Genusus when P tried to intercept him – if in fact they were somewhere near Tirana as Stoffel suggested – Holmes objected that Caesar's account has P marching south again to Asparagium and leaving Dyrrachium exposed to the combined armies of Caesar and Antony – the very situation which Caesar tries to achieve after confronting P at Asparagium: 'P left that position [where he had been hoping to intercept Antony] to avoid being shut in between two armies, and with all his forces arrived near Asparagium, a town of the Dyrrachians, and pitched his camp there in a suitable position.' But there is no difficulty in Stoffel's suggestion that P retired towards Dyrrachium first before going south to Asparagium. Caesar, with over double the numbers to feed now, will have returned for his baggage-train and supplies which he no doubt left behind in his haste to reach Antony before P could destroy him. The baggage-train may have been left under guard or have been following more slowly: in any event it is hardly likely to have crossed the Genusus even if it had crossed the Apsus. As Caesar retraced his steps, P will have followed on a more or less parallel course down the coastal plain along the Egnatian Way, following the course of the present-day road from Durresi to Rogozhina while Caesar followed the inland road from Tirana (the town of the Parthini stormed?) to cross the Shkumbini somewhere near Elbasani, collect his baggage-train from south of the river, resecure his own lines of communication with Apollonia, meet the legion which he had withdrawn from Oricum 'after joining forces with Antony's army': compare 3.39–40 with 3.34), and come up to confront P from the southern side of the river (since 3.76 shows that Caesar's camp was on the south side, and P's was surely on the northern (Dyrrachian) side as Holmes, not on the southern side as Stoffel). Caesar's failure to mention P's falling back towards Dyrrachium before advancing again to Asparagium is hardly a fatal objection in view of his frequent suppression of information (and even Holmes admits that his claim to have offered battle to P at Asparagium was 'a sham') and the curiously placed digression at this point (between 3.30 and 41): Caesar likes the reader to think that he kept the initiative all the time. **Military statistics**: see Appendix II.

### CHAPTER NINE (pp. 229–255): PHARSALIA

**Main literary sources**: Caes BC 3.31–8, 73–101; App BC 2.64–82; Plut P 66–73; Caes 40–7; Cic 38–9; Cato Min 55; Dio 41.51–62; 42.1–2; Lucan 6.333–8.43 (on whom as source for Civil War, Pharsalus in particular and picture of P, see also Lounsbury 1976, Lintott 1971, Rutz 1968, Rambaud 1955A); Oros 6.15–27, 419–20; Florus 2.13; Vell 2.52; Eutrop 8.20–1; Frontinus Strat 2.3.22; Cic Fam 9.9 (Dolabella's letter; contrast picture of Caesarian Italy by Caelius Fam 8.17); Att 11.3, 4, on dating of which see SB Att 214, Holmes 3.478–80, Drumann-Groebe 3.749–50, but n.b.: while agreeing that SB 215 is datable by content to c. 15 July as Fam 14.6, I put 214 only a few days earlier as referring to Dyrrachium fought c. 8 July. First sentence of 215 need only be informing A that his letter had been received in case 215 arrived before Isidorus and 214; and if so, 215 and 214 will be closer in date that SB believes. 214 cannot be dated by reference to the vague expectation of some new development in 213 (possibly only an excuse for belated reply, or, if specific, more likely to refer to P's first attempt to break out of completed siege-lines than the earlier battle to dislodge Caesar from the hill, which was a sudden reaction to a move by Caesar not a planned development by P). The terminology of 215 is appropriate only to Dyrrachium. Bardt's and Holmes' objection, that Cic would never have contemplated following P to Thessaly alone, is futile: P could still have been in his new camp near the Lesnikia or pursuing Caesar towards Apollonia. **King Burebista's embassy**: meeting with P 'Imperator' (recorded on SIG². 1.342, 32ff) was surely not a response to letters sent out by P after Dyrrachium: too little time for P's messengers to reach west coast of Black Sea and for envoy to return from there to Heracleia. If in 48, the embassy must have been on its way to P before Dyrrachium (P need not have been 'Imp' when the envoy set out, only when he arrived); but it could belong to 62 when P was returning from Eastern victories (more appropriate to ambassador's pride in the value of his mission). On the Getae and Burebista's empire-building see Strabo 7.3.1–14 (esp. 11, 13), 304–5. **Mixed cavalry and light infantry units**: compare Caes BC 3.84 with Frontinus Strat 2.5.33; for earlier examples see Thuc 5.57 (418 BC), 2.79 (429 BC); Greenhalgh 1973, 135–6; also 78–80 (for cavalry against regular infantry, Parthian cataphract cavalry, stirrups etc.). **Watchwords at Pharsalus** (App BC 2.76): see also B. Rawson 1970 on republican generals who honoured Hercules, particularly Eastern victors: Mummius after Achaean War (ILS 20); Scipio Aemilianus, who might have brought the famous statue from Carthage and whose career was quoted by Cic (pro lege Man 60) as a precedent for P; and Sulla, who similarly favoured Hercules and Venus (Plut Sulla 35); also Pliny NH 7.95; 34.57 (Myron's Hercules in P's house); Weinstock 1957 on 'Victor and invictus'; Gagé 1936; Crawford RRC no. 426.3 and 4a (coins of 56 minted by Faustus Sulla associate P's three triumphs with Venus on 3 and Hercules on 4a). **Site of Pharsalus**: Pelling 1973 demonstrates the impossibilities of Béquignon's 1960 revival of his 1928 theory that the battlefield was south of the Enipeus (cf. Heuzey 1886, 104–35; Stoffel 1887, 17–27; Kromayer 1907, 401–25; Kromayer–Veith 1924, pl 20), which should have been stillborn after the work of Holmes (3.452–67) and Lucas 1919–21. Clearly the battle-lines were drawn perpendicular to the Enipeus with P's right and Caesar's left close to the river somewhere in the seven-mile plain between Mt Dogantzes to the west and the modern main road from Larissa to modern Farsala, but I am not convinced by Pelling's arguments for a position as far east as the modern main road against Lucas' case for a site below Mt Dogantzes. Pelling's position for P's camp requires a half-turn of P's lines, and while he can argue that this would not have been a perilous movement with Caesar still in camp and with 600 cavalry to protect the right wing as the lines pivoted on the left, the fact that a movement need not have been perilous does not prove that it took place. Admittedly Caesar's account is bare of details (suspiciously so for Rambaud 1955B, though the lack of names of small villages in a fairly remote area is not surprising in memoirs designed for general consumption at Rome, and he does mention the important topographical details: river, mountains, etc.). But Caesar's expression of the position of P's lines in relation to his camp at *BC* 3.85 and esp. in the first sentence of 88 fails to support such a reorientation as distinct from a mere advance in distance from the camp. Moreover the *'altissimi montes'* required for *BC* 3.95 (cf. 3.93) are too far from Pelling's site; a retreat from a position east of Krini to Lucas' hill of surrender, which Pelling accepts, would be initially north-westwards and much less convincingly *'Larisam versus'* than the direct line north-eastwards from Dogantzes; and the case against Ktouri hill as Palaeopharsalus is feeble. My own visit to the area convinced me that Dogantzes is the outstanding candidate for P's camp, and there is ample room for the battle in the plain between the river and the modern village of Avra. The retreat will have been from Dogantzes along the range of hills running more or less north-east to the plain by the little river Kapakli, from which Caesar prevented the Pompeians from getting water after pursuing them for six miles along the level route by which they had first approached the Enipeus valley: between Dogantzes and Kastro Psychiko, then swinging north-east along the line of the modern railway. **Military statistics**: see Appendix II.

CHAPTER TEN (pp. 256–269): DEATH ON THE NILE

**P's flight and death**: see esp. Plut *P* 74–80; *Caes* 48; Lucan 8.33–872; App *BC* 2.83–6; Dio 42.2–5; Caes *BC* 3.102–4; Vell 2.53. **Date of death**: Velleius (day before 58th birthday, i.e. 28 Sep 48 = 25 July reformed; cf. Dio 42.5.5: anniversary of triumph over Mithr) is unassailable by Plut *p* 79.4 or by Bayet 1940 and Bonneau 1961, who propose 16 Aug on basis of astronomical data in Lucan and data about the Nile flood in *Bell Alex*, Lucan and Pliny. **Site and nature of burial**: see Strabo 16.2.33, 760 (description of Mt Casius, Ras el Kasaroun); Pliny *NH* 5.68; Dio 42.5.6; for contrasts between P's greatness and his wretched tomb see e.g. Lucan 8.712–872; Vell 2.53.3; Val Max 5.1.10; Dio 42.5.5–6; App *BC* 2.86 (epigram 'How slight a tomb for one so rich in temples' inscribed on monument; enlarged and decorated with bronze statues later by P's relatives; eventually neglected and covered with sand until restored by Hadrian). **Fate of remains**: see App 2.90 (Caesar had P's head buried near Alexandria in a small plot dedicated to Nemesis, later ruined by the Jews when Trajan was holding a pogrom); Plut *P* 80.6 ('remains taken to Cornelia who buried them at the Alban villa': reconcilable with Appian? but see Lucan 8.834ff). **Caesar's crocodile tears**: see Dio 42.8 against unbelievable sentimentality of e.g. Plut *P* 80.5; *Caes* 48.2; Val Max 5.1.10; and n.b. Cic *Phil* 2.64 (cf. 4.9, 13.10–11) for Caesar subsequently auctioning P's property in Sullan fashion. **Remainder of Civil War**: see esp. Caes *BC*3.105–12 (pursuit of P, arrival in Alexandria and trouble there), followed by the three books written by unknown officers on the campaigns in Egypt, Africa and Spain: *De Bello Alexandrino*, *De Bello Africo* and *De Bello Hispaniensi*; Plut *Caes* 48–56; *Cato Min* 55–73; App *BC* 2.87–106; Dio 42.6–9 (pursuit to Egypt), 33–44 (Egypt), 45–8 (Pharnaces), 49–55 (return to Rome), 56–8 (Africa); 43.1–13 (African war continued), 28–41 (Spain); Lucan 9–10 (Cornelia charges Sextus to carry on his father's war; Cato and army in Africa; Caesar attacked in Alexandria: book 10 breaks off abruptly). **Tributes to P's memory**: see Lucan 9.190–214 (Cato's funeral speech); Cic *Att* 11.6 (Nov 48; contrast shabby letters of reingratiation with victors, e.g. *Fam* 7.3; and compare his ultimate regrets, e.g. *Phil* 2.54 *'imperii populi Romani decus ac lumen'*, cf. 5.39, a bad political miscalculation!). **Modern biographies and evaluations**: see e.g. E. Meyer 1919 (dared to attack Mommsen); Gelzer 1949; Miltner 1952; Ooteghem 1954; Mansuelli 1959; Leach 1978; Seager (political only) 1979; more briefly Oman 1903, H.P. Collins 1953, Caldwell 1953, MacKendrick 1966; also John Masefield's disappointing play *The Tragedy of Pompey the Great*. **Other relevant biographies**: see e.g. *Caesar*: Ferrero 1962, Balsdon 1967, Carcopino 1968, Gelzer (Eng trans) 1968, Grant 1969; *Cicero*: Smith 1966, Gelzer 1969, Shackleton Bailey 1971, Stockton 1971, E. Rawson 1975, Lacey 1978; *Cato*: Gelzer 1934; *Sextus Pompeius*: Hadas 1930.

# APPENDIX I
## The *lex Pompeia Licinia* of 55

The terminal date of Caesar's command is critical to any evaluation of P's relations with his protégé in 51 and 50. That a date was specified in the law is not only *a priori* likely but certain from '*legis dies*' of Cic *Att* 7.7 (cf. App *BC* 2.28; Dio 40.59.1: 'the appointed time'). The fact that no source tells us plainly what the date was is not evidence that no date was specified or that it was variable according to circumstances or ambiguous (as e.g. Balsdon 1939) but that it was so well known that it was taken for granted. Even the Gauls knew it (Hirt *BG* 8.39).

A date in 50 is clear from App *BC* 2.26 (in 51 Marcellus proposed sending successors to Caesar 'before the end of his command'; P objected to insulting him 'merely on account of *a short interval of time*, but he made it plain that Caesar's command must end immediately on its expiry. *For this reason* enemies of Caesar were elected consuls for the next year', i.e. 50); 27 (consul C. Marcellus early in 50 proposes sending successors to Caesar 'for his term was expiring': this comes immediately after discussion of Curio's legislative programme at the beginning of his tribunate; C. Marcellus' proposal was probably made on 19.2.50 in accordance with Senate's resolution of previous Sep: Cael *Fam* 8.8); 28 (at time of P's illness in Naples about May 50 he was supposedly pretending fairness but really exciting prejudice against Caesar 'for not giving up his command even at the appointed time'; n.b. also that P's letter to the Senate referred to his willingness to give up his own command 'without waiting for the appointed time', i.e. his own command prolonged by the Senate in 52: if this had a terminal date, surely the law of 55 also had one, whether or not Cic *de prov cons* 36–8 proves that the Vatinian law of 59 specified 1.3.54: see Cuff (1958, 455), Stockton (1975, 233) for detailed argument that it does); Dio 40.59 (P objected to M. Marcellus' proposal in 51 to remove Caesar 'even before his appointed time' but 'arranged matters so that when Caesar's command expired in the following year', i.e. 50, 'he should lay down his arms and return to private life'); Cic *Att* 7.11 (19 or 21.1.49: 'Is it good to have an army without the public authority?', i.e. Caesar's command must have expired by then; cf. 7.7 of 19(?).12.50 'Should a commander who retains his army after the expiry of the term legally assigned to him be allowed to stand for office?', though admittedly this could be hypothetical). Mommsen's arguments for 28.2.49 (defended by Holmes 2.299–310) were demolished by e.g. Adcock 1932 and Stockton 1975: it is incredible that Caesar would have based his justification for invading Italy on the law of the ten tribunes rather than the *lex Licinia Pompeia* if the terminal date under the latter had not expired (Caes *BC* 1.9; n.b. the 6 months referred to here are clearly from context the period from the appointment of successors under Scipio's resolution of Jan to the July elections, at which Caesar claims that the plebiscite granting him the right to stand *in absentia* remained valid and implied the right to keep his provincial command until he had been elected. Note also Cic *Att* 7.1 of 16.10.50: the argument is over candidature *in absentia* and making Caesar give up his army – there is no indication that the *lex P. L.* is still operative; cf. 7.7: the argument that the concession over the candidature *in absentia* implies permission to keep the governorship until elected would be meaningless if the *legis dies* had not expired). Arguments based on Cic's loose and often rhetorical references to a ten-year command (which would give a terminal date in 49 or 48 reckoning from Caesar's consulship in 59 when the Vatinian law was passed or from the start of his taking up command in Gaul in 58), e.g. *Att* 7.7 ('Do we approve of the ten-year command?') are confounded by *Att* 7.5 (Dec 50: 'It is late in the day for us to resist a force which we have been nurturing [perfect tense] against ourselves *for ten years*'). The 'ten-year command' derives from the two quinquennial but overlapping commands. Caesar's first quinquennium had not expired in 55 when he was given a second by the *lex P. L.*, and it is incredible that the second quinquennium was not supposed to begin until the first had expired, esp. since Caesar was surely anxious to have his Transalpine governorship (previously added by senatorial decree) confirmed by popular legislation, and the five-year commands of P, Crassus and Caesar were most likely co-terminous. Dio insists in his narrative of 55 (39.33.3) that Caesar's command was extended 'for three years as will be found to be the truth': clearly it did not occur to Dio that the second quinquennial command could have started before the first one expired, and since Caesar had taken up his first command in Gaul in 58, Dio maintained that the second could only have been for three years because he knew that it expired in 50: Dio 40.59.3). Dio is decisive that the combination of the *lex V.* and *lex P.L.* gave Caesar *de facto* 8 years to command in Gaul. On Caesar's claim (*BC* 1.32) that 48 was the first year for which he was legally entitled to stand, i.e. at elections of 49, see notes to ch 4 on Ten Tribunes' Bill.

For 1 Mar 50 as the date n.b. (a) Senate's resolution of Sep 51 postpones debate on the appointment of proconsular governors until 19.2.50 and does not allow any other business to take precedence after 1.3.50 (Cael *Fam* 8.8). (b) Cael *Fam* 8.13 of June 50 indicates that Caesar's command had already expired: 'The view they had come round to is that the candidature of one who was handing over neither his army nor provinces should be admitted.' Also the drastic proposal to treat with the tribunes is hardly likely to have been made before the expiration of the term. App *BC* 2.28 also indicates that at the time of P's illness (not later than May 50) Caesar's appointed time had expired and he was 'not giving up his command'. (c) Adcock 1932 maintained rightly that 13 Nov 50 must have had some significance but wrongly that it was the '*legis dies*'. He rightly observed that the commands of P, Crassus and Caesar were most likely co-terminous in 55; but the fact that Crassus left Rome about Ides Nov need not mean that the command formally began then. Co-terminous commands support a much earlier date in the year: P had sent his legates to Spain 'at once' (Dio 39.39), i.e. when the Bill had been passed. Crassus had also sent legates ahead (Dio 39.60.4: the reluctance of Gabinius to accept them is hardly surprising since he was being ousted prematurely from his proconsular command), and troops were being levied. And there was no reason to postpone implementing Caesar's command. Admittedly commands need not start on the day the laws are passed – and the laws (which were passed on the same unspecified day according to Dio 39.36) may or may not have been passed on 1 Mar 55 – but it remains more likely that a commencement date which is not that of the law's passage would be a date which had some constitutional significance either as the old date for the commencement of proconsular commands (Mommsen's 'Imperienjahr' theory, though whether this had more than archaic significance now is highly doubtful: for criticism see Cuff, 453–4, 456; Balsdon 1939, 64ff) or the procedural significance which Baldson or Cuff attributes to it as the date on which the Senate usually dealt with the allocation of provinces to the consuls about to be elected in the summer: this could have become the conventional date ever since the *lex Sempronia* of 123 had instituted the system of allotting the consular provinces in advance of the election of their future incumbents (Cic *de domo sua* 24; *de prov cons* 3, 17; *Balb* 61; *Fam* 1.7.10; Sall *Jug* 27.3; though n.b. *de prov cons* itself was given long after 1 Mar: late June or early July); and possibly when a provincial governorship was for the first time secured by a special law for 5 years to a consul leaving office (i.e. to Caesar by the *lex Vatinia* of 59 when the *lex Sempronia* was still in full force) the law took as its formal starting and concluding date the then established 1 Mar date for provincial allotments by the Senate; then similarly the five-year commands of 55 by precedent. (d) Cuff 1958, while possibly helping to explain why

1 Mar was chosen as the inaugural/terminal date of a five-year law which was probably not enacted on that day (esp. as 1 Mar seems not to have been a *dies comitialis*: see Macrobius *Sat* 1.16; Greenidge 255) does not prove that the terminal date (whether the period of the command was expressed as being granted 'for five years from 1 March 55' or 'to expire on 1 March in the fifth year from the second consulship of P and Crassus' regardless of a starting-date) was only a procedural date, i.e. the first date on which the provinces could be considered for reallotment and not the date on which the command formally expired. Cuff's interpretation of '*succedere*' is unconvincing; a consul might formally 'succeed' to a command in Mar (or any other month) but not be able to take it up actively until 1 Jan when his year in Rome would be over: that, after all, is exactly what Caesar did in 59. Cuff's reliance on procedure under *lex Sempronia* means that in 55 Caesar would have felt himself securely in command of his provinces and armies not only until 49 as Cuff argues but until 48 since the allotment on 1 Mar 50 (if that was the first day on which 'allotment' was possible as he argues) would be to the consuls who were to be elected in the summer of 50 to hold office in Rome in 49 and would therefore be free to take up proconsular governorships actively only on 1 Jan 48. On this basis the *lex P. L.* of 55 offered Caesar not a five-year command but nearly a seven-year one. It would also ruin Cic's arguments in *de prov cons* of 56 against allotment of Caesar's provinces to the consuls to be elected for 55 if the *lex V*'s terminal date had this significance. Cuff could only circumvent this difficulty by inventing a clause in the *lex V.* containing an imaginary ambiguity that was corrected by another invented clause in the *lex P. L.* (460–4); but even then we are left with Cic supporting an ambiguity *against* Caesar's interest in 56! Conversely, if Caesar claimed security only until 49, the 1 Mar date before which reallotment was illegal according to Cuff would have been 1 Mar 51, not 50: the supersession of the *lex Sempronia* in 52 could not have been foreseen in 55. That the terminal date of the command granted by law in 55 would ever become significant was hardly foreseen in 55, or even in 52. Half a decade was simply a good, long period to choose. No one in 55, least of all Caesar, would have expected to want to stay on to the bitter end, and if he needed more time, it could be done by another *lex* (as in 55 itself). Caesar was keen to return to glory and political power at Rome as soon as he had completed his conquests, which he did not expect to take all of another five years (and would not have done but for Vercingetorix). Similarly in 52 P was not being anti-Caesarian in taking another five years' command in Spain: he was looking after himself, while giving Caesar what *he* wanted, which was the right to stand for the consulship *in absentia*. The terminal date only became an issue when in 51 Caesar began to confront the reality of handing over his provinces and armies and realized that his political security against his enemies would depend on P's good will and patronage, on which he was no longer prepared to rely (not least for reasons of personal '*dignitas*'). The *lex Pompeia* of 52 (neither anti-democratic nor anti-Caesarian in concept) had the following relevance to the termination of Caesar's command: (i) the allotment of Caesar's provinces by the Senate, if Caesar was to be removed as soon as possible after the expiry of his command in 1.3.50 (without another law to give someone else an extraordinary command, or their change to praetorian status) need no longer be before the elections in 51 of the consuls of 50 because ex-consuls were available to take up governorships immediately, and while there is no reason to suppose that the *lex Pompeia* envisaged that new governors would start taking over provinces in mid-year rather than at the beginning of a year as usual, the possibility of mid-year appointments with immediate practical effect was now available; and (ii) the allocation of proconsular provinces now became subject to tribunician veto. Marcellus began to capitalize on (i) in 51 with his demand to have Caesar's provinces transferred to successors (who would formally take over immediately) before the *legis dies*. This was illegal, and P resisted it; he refused even to countenance discussion of a reallocation until the expiry-date, and even after that he was prepared to concede that Marcellus' faction was manipu-

lating his law of 52 beyond its intentions by seeking to appoint governors to go and take over immediately instead of waiting until the new year: this was not illegal, of course, but unnecessarily provocative in P's view, esp. since Caesar's provinces had been brought into line with the others, and though Caesar's command expired on 1 Mar, it was inequitable to say that governors allocated to Caesar's provinces should take over at once when everyone knew that any other provinces would have stayed in the hands of their present occupants until the year-end. That was why he backed a resolution safeguarding Caesar until Ides Nov (a 'morsel' deliberately ignored by Cuff: 471). Hirtius *BG* 8.53, where '*ante tempus*' clearly qualifies '*retulerat*', does not contradict Suet *J* 28.2 where '*ante tempus*' qualifies '*succederetur*'. The motion, if passed and not vetoed, would be followed by an immediate decree appointing the new successors who would now be ex-consuls available to succeed Caesar at once and would be sent out immediately to do so; cf. 'to *send* successors': Appian's expression for C. Marcellus' proposal in Feb 50 (*BC* 2.27.) In so far as the proposing of a motion would, if successful, have led to the appointment of successors with immediate *imperium* before the expiry-date of Caesar's command, it had been '*contra legem Pompei et Crassi*'. An accurate translation is: 'Contrary to the law of P and Crassus he had proposed a motion prematurely to the Senate concerning Caesar's provinces.' Hirtius gives no support to Cuff's view that the '*legis dies*' of the *lex P. L.* was a mere procedural date any more than he supports Mommsen's extraordinary but still current invention of a clause in *lex P. L.* forbidding discussion of reallocation until 1 Mar 50 (which ignores the plain fact that so much discussion did in fact take place, all presumably illegally!).

For a spectrum of views on dating (and even existence) of the *legis dies* see Mommsen 1857; Holzapfel 1903, 1904; Hirschfeld 1904, 1905; Judeich 1913; Holmes 2.299–310; Stone 1928; Adcock 1932; Stevens 1938; Balsdon 1939; Elton 1946; Cuff 1958; Stocker 1961; Jameson 1970; Stockton 1975.

# APPENDIX II
## Military statistics in the Civil War

*Legions at outbreak of war*: Caesar had had eleven legions in 51, apparently numbered I and VI–XV, one of which had been loaned to him by P. In 50 he had returned two to Italy for the Parthian emergency (ch 5), i.e. P's legion and one of his own. Hirtius (*BG* 8.54) explains the disposition of the remaining nine in the winter of 50/49, that eight were beyond the Alps and one (XIII) in Cisalpine Gaul; but all other sources give Caesar either ten or eleven legions at the outbreak of war. Cicero (*Att* 7.7 of Dec 50) speaks of 'our now having to deal with eleven legions, all the cavalry he wants, the Transpadanes' etc. Florus (2.13.5) also gives eleven on Caesar's side, but his vague account does not specify that this was the position at outbreak of war, and his attribution of eighteen to P was clearly not valid in Jan 49. Suetonius (*J* 29.2) indicates that Caesar's compromise suggestions for keeping a reduced army for a limited period were based on a total of ten legions. Plutarch (*P* 58) has Marcellus refusing 'to sit listening to speeches when he saw 10 legions looming up over the Alps'. There are two main possibilities for reconciling the discrepancies (if indeed Cicero is not simply wrong, or the 10 of other sources is not just a round number): (a) Caesar had raised another legion not mentioned by Hirtius. Dio certainly indicates further recruitment (40.65.4: 'Caesar complied with the demand [to return two legions to Italy] because he did not wish to be accused of disobedience and especially because he could use this as an excuse to collect many more troops in place of these'). Holmes and Parker postulate the recruitment of a new legion of Roman citizens subsequently numbered XVI but kept unofficial until after the outbreak of war, but they have no evidence except the desire to turn Hirtius' nine into Suetonius' and Plutarch's ten. There is also the Gallic legion '*Alaudae*' referred to in Suetonius (*J* 24) as having been conscripted by Caesar at his own cost from the 'Transalpini': 'he trained and equipped it in the Roman tactics and arms and later bestowed Roman citizenship on the whole of it'. Suetonius places its conscription among the conscription of other (Roman citizen) legions after the grant of his second quinquennium in 55 (by the *lex P. L.* ) had given him the 'confidence' to do so (cf. Caesar *BG* 7.1: Caesar's recruitment under the authority of the S.C.U. of 52). For such a legion to have remained unofficial until after the war had begun – it is almost certainly this legion which fights in Africa under the number V in 47 (see Holmes 3.355–6) – is more likely than for the Roman legion hypothesized by Holmes and Parker to have been raised: the Senate's extreme sensitivity about the enfranchisement of Transpadanes expressed in the Novum Comum affair (ch 4) would have made the formal constitution of a legion of Transalpines, mostly if not entirely non-citizens, extremely provocative, and Hirtius' partisan account could well have ignored it (*BG* 8.54): it might conceivably have drilled and fought as a legion but not have been given a standard, number or citizenship. The case for the unofficial existence of a Gallic legion is therefore stronger than for that of a Roman one, but if Holmes and Parker are right that both existed unofficially, the discrepancies between ten and eleven in the other sources are explicable by the inclusion of both or only the Roman one with Hirtius' official nine. (b) Cicero in an excited outburst may simply have been thinking of Caesar's legionary strength before the two legions were sent to Italy in 50, or he may have been consciously including them to indicate that they were still Caesar's in all but name after fighting for him for so many years (n.b. the constant doubts about their loyalty in the first months of 49, e.g. Cic *Att*

8.12A; see also *Att* 7.13.2 for their having been kept in Italy *'invidiose'*: cf. Caesar's complaints, *BC* 1.4, 1.9; also Hirtius *BG* 8.54: P's legion had itself been raised in Caesar's
(Cisalpine) province). Similarly it is possible that the sources for ten legions are including
Caesar's but not P's out of the two which Caesar sent to Italy, but it is less probable:
in the case of Suetonius, his having mentioned the formation of the Gallic legion at *J* 24.2
suggests that he would have included it in the ten of *J* 29.4; in the case of Plutarch, because
he makes Marcellus (*P* 58) talk of ten legions 'looming across the Alps' (i.e. evidently not
including two in Italy already, although round numbers in Plutarch's rhetorical passages
are not eternal verities), and unless we accept the inclusion of two unofficial legions
beyond the Alps (i.e. a Roman as well as a Gallic), there is the problem that one of Hirtius'
official nine was already in Cisalpine Gaul. But the specific legions included need not be
the same for each source. That Cicero's eleven were all the official ones (i.e. the two in
Italy plus Hirtius' nine) seems most plausible, but Suetonius (and Plutarch?) seems more
likely to have been including *'Alaudae'* with Hirtius' nine. I believe that Caesar had nine
plus the still unofficial Gallic *'Alaudae'*. But the number of legions is a poor guide to the
strength of an army: legions at theoretical full complement number 6,000 men but often
they are far below strength, sometimes below half strength; a battle-hardened veteran
legion might be a match for two of recruits; Caesar's recruitment may have strengthened
existing legions as well as creating new units; cohorts not yet enrolled in legions, native
auxiliaries and cavalry must also be taken into account. At the outbreak of war there is
no doubt that Caesar was stronger in terms of experienced legions, but P was potentially
stronger not only world-wide but by being in Italy, which was the inexhaustible recruiting-
ground of legionaries if only he had time to raise them.

Pompey's statement to the Senate in early Jan that he had ten legions 'ready' (*'paratas'*)
is recorded only by Caesar (*BC* 1.6) and is therefore even more suspect than a round number
would normally be. If accurate, it obviously includes some or all of the Spanish legions:
Mommsen's assumption that P had the equivalent of ten legions ready in Italy is untenable
in the light of the events of the next few months (as Holmes 3.357; Adcock *CAH* 9.638–
9, though Adcock overemphasizes his point that P must have been talking about legions
'available for the defence of Italy since that was the first concern of his hearers'. Not all
Caesar's nine or ten legions were 'available for the invasion of Italy'. Only one was on
the Italian side of the Alps, and while two others had been summoned, Gaul could not
be left completely ungarrisoned any more than Spain). *'Legiones paratae'* need mean no
more than 'battle-ready legions', i.e. legions fully formed, trained and equipped with the
legionary eagle. P had only two of these in Italy: the two recalled from Caesar in 50 for
the Parthian war which failed to materialize. He had an unknown number of cohorts
dotted about in Italy or near Rome – raised either for the Spanish armies or under the
emergency authorization of 52 or since Marcellus' consular authorization to recruit troops
in late Nov/early Dec 50, although P had probably not relied too heavily on that dubious
legal authority in order not to alienate the Senate from which he wanted the formal authorization by S.C.U. He had seven legions 'battle-ready' in Spain (Caes *BC* 1.38). The tenth
may represent the odd extra cohorts which were not a *'parata legio'* but were nevertheless
included to make up the round number of 10 which Caesar attributes to P, partly to tell
posterity that P was at least as strong, and partly because he himself was said by his enemies
to have ten instead of nine: if Caesar's enemies were going to include the unofficial Gallic
legion among his forces, he would include P's odd cohorts. Florus (2.13.5), evidently not
talking about the situation at the outbreak of war, speaks of P's eighteen against Caesar's
eleven. To reach eighteen for P it is necessary to add to the nine fully formed legions available to P at the outbreak (i.e. the two in Italy and seven in Spain) those later raised or
gathered for Pharsalus, as detailed by Caesar *BC* 3.4: the five which he took from Italy
with him, the two from Syria, two from Asia, and one from Crete and Macedonia, and
even that involves double-counting the two 'Appian' legions (unless perhaps Florus begins

with the ten attributed to P by Caesar *BC* 1.6 and counts the Cilician 'Twin' legion as two, or counts loose cohorts as legions, or is simply wrong).

*Government forces recruited, lost and evacuated to Greece*: According to Caesar (*BC* 3.4), P took five legions from Italy, i.e. 50 cohorts of uncertain numerical strength. Excluding the two 'Appian' legions he therefore had three legions or thirty cohorts of recruits, mainly from Campania (P asks consuls to bring them, (?)18.2.49; Cic *Att* 8.12A, SB 162A). Domitius had lost over thirty to Caesar from the surrender of Corfinium and Sulmo. Caesar (*BC* 1.15–18) says thirty-three, of which thirteen had been brought in by Vibullius (who had taken over Hirrus' six fleeing from Camerinum) and Domitius had raised 'about twenty' from Alba, the Marsi, Paeligni and nearby districts. Pompey (Cic *Att* 11A, 12A), who was more likely to be accurate about his own forces, says thirty-one, of which only twelve were Domitius' own and the rest had been on their way from Picenum to join P himself under Vibullius (14) and Hirrus (5). It is unclear whether D's twelve included the four thousand men (about eight cohorts?) with which Appian says that D had set out for Gaul (*BC* 2.32): perhaps he was to raise them on the way. Assuming that D's four thousand were also conscripted after the outbreak of war the total of new recruits lost at Corfinium and evacuated by P is sixty-one cohorts, to which must be added nine lost subsequently on their way to join P from Alba and Tarracina under Manlius and Rutilius Lupus (Caes *BC* 1.24), plus 'several cohorts' and 'others' unspecified, plus some of the cohorts mentioned as having deserted government officers in the face of Caesar's advance to Corfinium, not all of which will have been recovered by Vibullius for inclusion in those surrendered by Domitius. (n.b. According to Caesar *BC* 1.12–13, five cohorts deserted Thermus; an unspecified number were lost to defeat or desertion under Varus; Spinther was deserted by ten, etc.: surely these were not all recovered by Vibullius and Hirrus, who will also have taken some from other towns.) Caesar later maintains (*BC* 3.10) that 'P' lost 130 cohorts altogether in Italy and Spain. Deducting seventy for the seven legions in Spain gives sixty for Italy, which requires unspecified or doubtful numbers in the above analysis to total twenty, which is not impossible (though Caesar's figure of 130 cohorts is evidently a round number). On this basis, if P had, say, ten cohorts (the unofficial tenth legion attributed to him by Caesar at *BC* 1.6 at the outbreak of war), the government succeeded in raising some eighty new cohorts in Italy between early January and early March, or one third of the Senate's authorization according to Appian *BC* 2.34 (taking the 130,000 men to represent twenty-six legions at an average strength of five thousand men, as indicated by Appian's use of this figure in 2.32 and 34). The number of men represented by these units is doubtful, but it is likely that cohorts of the five legions which P took to Greece were much closer to full strength than Holmes (3.371) maintains. Cicero (*Att* 9.6) reports on a letter from Clodia saying that P's first transhipment was of thirty thousand troops, which Cicero corrected after receiving further information in 9.9 where he explains that Clodia's figure was double the correct one (see SB *Att* 9.9.2 on the meaning of '*dimidio plus*'). Plutarch (*P* 62) says the consuls took thirty cohorts, agreeing with Caesar's statement that twenty cohorts (*BC* 1.25) remained with P in Brundisium of the total of five legions (3.4). If therefore thirty cohorts represented fifteen thousand men, the cohorts were of five hundred men and the legions of five thousand men, i.e. only one thousand men short of theoretical full complement and very much stronger than is usually supposed. This squares with Appian's equation of five thousand men with a legion, and it is unlikely that the fifteen thousand (if all foot-soldiers) included any non-legionaries since P had been recruiting in Italy and legionaries were what he wanted: he would find plenty of auxiliaries in the East. The total number of legionaries transhipped was probably therefore approaching twenty-five thousand (less the troops captured by Caesar because their two ships fouled his pontoons in the harbour mouth: *BC* 1.28). Cavalry transhipped may have included the eight hundred 'raised from his own slaves and herdsmen' (3.4: presumably brought from Italy rather than from estates in

Greece?) plus 'the flower of Rome and Italy', for which say, perhaps, between a thousand and fifteen hundred(?).

*Forces of P and Caesar in Northern Greece*: Caesar (*BC* 3.6) had shipped seven legions totalling fifteen thousand men (i.e. 215 men per cohort) plus five hundred horse (or six hundred: Appian *BC* 2.54; perhaps 'C' dropped out of the Caesar MSS?) on 4 January. As shipping was tight and feeding the troops would be a problem when he arrived, he no doubt selected only his very best men in the various units. P had taken five legions the previous March, possibly approaching a total of twenty-five thousand men plus an uncertain number of cavalry. The discrepancy in numerical strength between P's legions and Caesar's need not be doubted. Caesar's were all veteran legions, no doubt attenuated by their long campaigns but with a camaraderie in their constituent units which may have made Caesar reluctant to tamper with them by filling up numerically weak units even if he had had the ships to take more men (*BC* 3.6: much baggage had to be left behind). On the contrary, Caesar is more likely to have discarded weaker men from the existing units and taken only the best. P in contrast had taken only two veteran legions and three newly recruited ones, which had not been reduced by fighting, had no experience or *esprit de corps* as battle-hardened units, and were probably at or near full numerical strength. (Indeed the three new 'legions' may not have existed formally except as three legions' worth of cohorts, which would be formed and trained as legions and equipped with eagles only after reaching Greece.) As for P's two veteran legions, their long experience as fighting units under Caesar in Gaul had made their camaraderie and *esprit de corps* not a reason for leaving them alone but for filling up their constituent units with levies of loyal troops from Picenum (see e.g. P's letter to Domitius: Cic *Att* 8. 12D). By Jan 48 P had nine legions, the other four having been gathered or raised from veterans in the East (Caes *BC* 3.4: one of veterans from Cilicia formed from the two skeletal legions there; one from veterans who had settled in Crete and Macedonia; two from Asia levied by the consul Lentulus). The numerical strength of these four additional legions is unknown. If it was the same as for the five which had been taken from Italy, P could have had as many as forty-five thousand legionaries in Greece and still be expecting Scipio's legions from Syria, but this should be regarded as an absolute maximum. (The fifteen Caesarian cohorts captured from G. Antonius and the recruits from Boeotia, Thessaly, Achaea and Epirus were evidently included in the nine legions: *BC* 3.4; cf. ch 7.) How many of these troops P had with him when he heard of Caesar's landing is unknown. Macedonia and Thessaly cannot have been left ungarrisoned, and there was no doubt a sizeable garrison in Dyrrachium at least. Perhaps thirty-five/forty thousand is a reasonable guesstimate for the Roman legionary strength of the army with P at the time of Caesar's landing, plus an unknown number of native auxiliary units (especially light-armed troops: *BC* 3.4 gives only partial numbers) and several thousand cavalry, though probably not the seven thousand which Caesar curiously gives as the size of P's cavalry both at the end of 49 (*BC* 3.4) and seven months later at Pharsalus (3.84).

The numerical strength of the four legions which Antony took across in early April (?) is not recorded, but the average numbers were evidently much greater than in Caesar's original seven: they were probably as numerous as the five which P took just over a year earlier, i.e. about five thousand men per legion or twenty thousand in all, giving Caesar a reinforced total of thirty-five thousand or near parity with the legions accompanying P in April 48. Working back from the twenty-two thousand which Caesar claimed to have in eighty cohorts (eight legions) in the Battle of Pharsalus we find (*a*) the average cohort strength of 275 to be greater than the average of 215 for the cohorts of Caesar's original seven; (*b*) Caesar's oblique fourth line composed of three thousand men (*BC* 3.89) may have been made up of eight cohorts, i.e. an average of 375 men per cohort (Holmes 3.469 is probably right that Plutarch (*Caesar*) says 'six' cohorts because he habitually reckons five hundred men to a cohort); (*c*) thirty cohorts (three legions' worth out of the eleven legions which had been transhipped from Italy) were absent from the battle, and it is not the case that they had been scrapped or merged through losses because Caesar tells us where most of them were (eight had been left as garrisons at Apollonia, Oricum and Lissus (BC 3.78) and fifteen were in Achaea (3.34, 56): that leaves seven to be accounted for, which were probably guarding Caesar's camp: the MSS of BC 3.89 have '*II*' left at the camp but '*V*' could easily have dropped out and is 'restored' by most edd.: in any event not more than five are unaccounted for). Applying the average strength of the eighty cohorts in battle at Pharsalus to all eleven legions gives a numerical strength of over thirty thousand men (and even if the other cohorts were not as strong as those in battle and down to, say, one third strength, i.e. two hundred men, the total Caesarian legionaries at the time of Pharsalus would be at least twenty-eight thousand). Moreover this was after *recorded* losses in battles of 1,205 killed (Caes BC 3.19, 28, 37, 44–6, 53, 50, 71), plus a vastly greater number of sick and wounded (e.g. Caesar claimed only twenty killed in P's first attempt to break out of the siege-lines at Dyrrachium but 'not one of the men in [Caesar's] redoubt was unwounded, and four centurions of one cohort lost their eyes (3.53)'; the Caesarians' terror of arrows (3.44); the unrecorded numbers of wounded at the great Battle of Dyrrachium in which Caesar records nearly a thousand killed (3.71); the wounded deposited in Apollonia, Lissus and Oricum; the unknown effects of disease, Caesar's denial of which (BC 3.49) is contradicted by Plutarch (*Caes* 40), speaking of disease brought on by the strange and inadequate diet which Caesar himself admits (BC 3.47–8; cf. Lucan 6.106–17, and certainly malnutrition will hardly have been conducive to a low mortality rate among the wounded). Holmes (3.475) would add to the toll of Caesarians the captives executed after Dyrrachium (Caes BC 3.71), but it is questionable whether these were legionaries rather than auxiliaries (see ch 8). He would also deduct 'almost daily' desertions to Caesar from P claimed by Caesar (BC 3.61), but in view of Caesar's special sensitivity over his generalship, the *a priori* improbability of one-way traffic from a well-fed army to a starving one, the evidence of a movement in the other direction in Dio (41.51.1) and Appian (2.61) and Caesar's own admission that most of the desertions to him were of 'troops levied in Epirus, Aetolia and all regions in Caesar's occupation' (who were not legionaries but auxiliaries), the question of desertions is best ignored in a computation of purely legionary strengths. If then Caesar had some thirty thousand legionaries at the time of Pharsalus after recorded (by himself) deaths in battles of some twelve hundred and wastage from wounds and illness that will surely have run into several thousands, the four legions which Antony brought over in April to add to Caesar's original fifteen thousand men must have been very near full strength, numbering at least five thousand each (like the five Pompeian legions transhipped a year earlier). The reasons suggested above for Caesar's having taken seven veteran legions of barely over one third strength rather than having merged them no longer applied. Antony had only three veteran legions left, one of which was probably the Gallic '*Alaudae*' despite Caesar's understandable failure to specify it (and he fails to specify the Seventh either). He no doubt brought these up to near full strength with drafts of recruits and formed the best of his remaining recruits into a fourth legion (the only new legion of recruits which Caesar had out of his total eleven in Greece after Antony's crossing: BC 3.29). The legionary strengths of P and Caesar after Antony's junction with Caesar can thus be estimated as follows: Pompey with nine legions totalling perhaps thirty-five/forty thousand men; Caesar with eleven legions totalling thirty-five thousand men (less whatever garrisons he left at Apollonia and Oricum, and Antony had left at Lissus).

Numbers of auxiliaries are less easy to guess, but it is unlikely that Caesar had any to speak of until he had enough legions to send expeditions down into Aetolia, and in the skirmishes and battles near Dyrrachium he is constantly having to use legionaries against P's light-armed troops, and he seems to have little fire-power save a few slingers (e.g. Caes BC 3.46: possibly legionaries here too?) and the slings carried by the legionaries (e.g. 3.63: 'stones, the only missiles our men had'). P on the other hand has very large numbers of archers and javelineers: he makes Caesar's legionaries 'terrified' of arrows (3.44), can pump thirty thousand arrows into a single redoubt during an engagement covering many positions simultaneously (3.53), engages in constant night-attacks against Caesar's pickets (3.52), uses them to soften up Caesar's defences in the big attacks (3.63: 'a great multitude of archers streaming round on every side'), and often seems to use them in serious engagements without committing the legions at all (3.45: '*levis armaturae multitudine missa*'), which he carefully conserves. A figure less than fifteen/twenty thousand would seem inadequate for all this, and it may have been much higher.

For cavalry, Caesar had transhipped five/six hundred, Antony eight hundred, giving some thirteen hundred in all. P had seven thousand at the end of 49 according to Caesar (*BC* 3.4), and while the fact that the contingents which Caesar specifies add up only to 3,600 need not in itself indicate exaggeration since he specifies only 4,200 archers and slingers among P's light-armed troops which evidently numbered many times more (and he would be naturally reluctant to detail 'the flower of Rome and Italy' which preferred to fight against him), it is suspicious that the same figure of seven thousand is given for P's cavalry strength at Pharsalus (*BC* 3.4; 3.84), as Holmes observed (3.476). Admittedly Scipio brought some cavalry from Syria (3.81) which may have helped to make good losses (which must have been considerable in the months at Dyrrachium and the battles), but Holmes was right to 'suspect that Caesar did not allow for wastage'.

Unfortunately Holmes did not apply the same sound suspicion to Caesar's estimates of P's infantry. He went to great lengths to refute Delbrück's arguments that Caesar habitually minimized his own forces and exaggerated those of his opponents, but his refutation of the latter is less convincing than that of the former, just as the latter is *a priori* much more likely to have occurred than the former (see below). After the combination of the armies of Caesar and Antony near Dyrrachium and Caesar's inability to bring P to a pitched battle or to feed so large an army he dispatched Calvinus to Macedonia with two legions and five hundred horse, Cassius Longinus into Thessaly with the legion of recruits and two hundred horse, and Calvisius Sabinus with five cohorts and a few horsemen. On the basis that Calvinus' two legions were two of those numerically low ones which Caesar had shipped (215 men per cohort) they would account for 4,300 men. The legion of recruits brought by Antony will have been at least five thousand strong. Assuming a round four hundred for the other five cohorts the total comes to 11,300, representing nearly one third of Caesar's legionary strength. The cavalry (over seven hundred) represent at least half of his cavalry strength, a very large proportion which we may suggest that a considerable portion of P's total cavalry strength of seven thousand was operating in Macedonia and Thessaly and not all were therefore with P: that P had a 'multitude of cavalry' (*BC* 3.43) is undoubted, but it would not take all seven thousand to give P massive superiority in that arm over the mere six hundred which Caesar retained. P's losses during the Dyrrachium campaign are hard to estimate. Caesar mentions vaguely '*compluribus interfectis*' in P's side against five men on his own (*BC* 3.46), but these seem to have been light-armed rather than legionaries anyway, as were perhaps the two thousand recorded as killed in P's first attempt to break out of the siege-lines. P's losses in skirmishing or in the ultimate breakout are unknown, as are losses from disease, which were probably very much more serious, particularly among the legions. At some stage P was reinforced by Afranius and 'cohorts' brought from Spain, though when or how many is not clear. Caesar mentions them specifically only at Pharsalus (3.88), although he had evidently mentioned their coming to P in an earlier passage, presumably lost. Caesar says they were 'united with the Cilician legion', which may mean integration rather than mere proximity. They were almost certainly few in number, perhaps not more than several hundred men. And how had they reached Greece from Spain: through occupied Italy, or by ship all the way? And were they with P all through 48, or did they arrive at Dyrrachium during the campaigning? P's only substantial reinforcements for Pharsalus were Scipio's two legions from Syria, of unknown strength – perhaps eight/ten thousand men at the very most. Let us assume then that P's nine legions at the beginning of 48 had totalled the very maximum of forty-five thousand suggested above. Wastage of eight/ten thousand would not be unlikely over the campaign of the first half of 48, and if Scipio's two legions made up P's losses, Caesar's evidently vague figure of 110 cohorts making up forty-five thousand men for P's total legionary strength at the time of Pharsalus may be about right (3.88: or forty-seven thousand if the two thousand *beneficiarii* are not included), though they were not all in the battle as he implies in his self-congratulatory account.

*Battle of Pharsalus*: Plutarch reveals that P had left fifteen cohorts at Dyrrachium (which Cato subsequently took to Africa: *Cato Min* 55), and Caesar himself says later that P left seven more guarding his camp. Evidently then P had at the most eighty-eight cohorts actually in the battle (the number which Orosius gives: 6.15.23). If then 110 cohorts gave forty-five thousand men, 88 would give thirty-six thousand, though even that is probably on the very top side with an average of 410 men per cohort, which looks high after so many months of campaigning. P's numerical superiority over Caesar in terms of legionaries was therefore of the order of 3:2 (a ratio given incidentally by some authorities available to Appian: *BC* 2.70) rather than the 2:1 which Caesar implies, and Caesar's very vagueness in estimating P's losses (3.99) only confirms his unreliability over P's figures. Caesar gives no cavalry figures for Pharsalus but merely indicates P's undoubted superiority. About a thousand (App *BC* 2.70; Plut *Caes* 42) seems reasonable for Caesar in view of the numbers transhipped. (Orosius and Eutropius also say a thousand for Caesar, but they are obviously wrong in attributing only 1,100 to P.) It is questionable whether P had all the seven thousand mentioned by Appian and Plutarch, i.e. the total figure attributed to him by Caesar in the catalogue of P's forces raised by the end of 49 (*BC* 3.4), in view of Caesar's attribution of the whole of P's legionary forces (110 cohorts comprising 45,000 men) to the battle-lines: a comparable scaling down would give P about 5,500 cavalry at Pharsalus. Appian and Plutarch could similarly be following maximum figures for the Pompeian side, to which Appian gives 'more than double' the number of Caesar's (legionary) troops and seven thousand cavalry (though he is surely wrong to include Caesar's cavalry in the twenty-two thousand which Caesar specifies for his legionary infantry, and the cavalry were not of course all Italian or citizen: n.b. Appian's perplexity at the vast discrepancies in the large number of sources available to him). Figures for auxiliaries – archers, slingers, javelineers etc. – must be guesstimates. Caesar had an unquantified number of 'light-armed Greeks consisting of Dolopians, Acarnanians and Aetolians' (*ib*), and P had a great many contingents from almost every people east of the Adriatic (see for catalogues e.g. Caesar *BC* 3.3–4; Appian *BC* 2.70–1). Caesar put P's archers at the end of 49 at three thousand (from Crete, Lacedaemon, Pontus, Syria and other states), his slingers at twelve hundred. P also had numerous javelineers. Perhaps the total number of combatants at Pharsalus was about fifty-eight thousand legionary infantry (P 36,000; Caesar 22,000), a maximum of eight thousand cavalry but probably only six thousand, plus auxiliaries (say, fifteen/twenty thousand), giving a grand total of the order of eighty/eighty-five thousand men. Caesar (*BC* 3.99) gives twenty-four thousand Pompeians surrendered (including the cohorts 'left on garrison duty in the forts') and fifteen thousand fallen, but the latter is very vague ('*videbantur*'): Caesar was too busy after the battle to bother about the casualty figures, and he says only 'of the Pompeian army', not that they were all legionaries. Appian quotes Pollio (*BC* 2.82), 'one of Caesar's officers in the battle', as having recorded the number of Pompeians found dead at six thousand (which, added to Caesar's probably more reliable twenty-four thousand surrendered, suggests a much lower figure than Caesar's forty-five thousand for the Pompeian legionaries in battle and makes even thirty-six thousand appear on the high side: a scattering of six thousand Italian legionaries from the battlefield is possible but the evaporation of fifteen thousand is hard to believe); and

Caesar habitually seems to record his own losses in terms only of killed but the enemy's in terms of wounded and killed. Appian says that ten senators were lost on P's side (including Domitius) and about forty distinguished knights. He also observed that none of his authorities had bothered to record losses of auxiliaries 'either because of their multitude or because they were despised'. Caesar does not quantify his own losses, which is inconsistent with his careful record of the losses at Dyrrachium (BC 3.71). But in the one case he was anxious to minimize a severe defeat, and the number of dead given for Dyrrachium probably excluded even the most badly wounded who died afterwards. In the case of his victory his losses did not matter so much, though his failure to record them could mean that they were heavier than he would have cared to admit. Appian's sources provided him with the figures of thirty centurions and between two hundred and twelve hundred legionaries (BC 2.82) killed on Caesar's side.

# BIBLIOGRAPHY

(The names of journals are abbreviated according to the conventions of *L'Année Philologique*)

ADCOCK, F.E., 'The legal term of Caesar's governorship in Gaul', *CQ*, 26 (1932), 14–26.

ADCOCK, F.E., 'From the Conference of Luca to the Rubicon' and 'The Civil War', *Cambridge Ancient History* (1962), vol 9, chapters 15 and 16.

ADCOCK, F.E., *Marcus Crassus, Millionaire* (Cambridge, 1966).

AFZELIUS, A., 'Die politische Bedeutung des jüngeren Cato', *C&M*, 4 (1941), 100–203.

ALBINI, U., 'L'orazio contro Vatinio', *PP*, 14 (1959), 172–84.

ANDERSON, W.S., 'Pompey, his friends and the literature of the first century B.C.', *Univ. of California Publications in Classical Philology*, 19.1 (Berkeley and Los Angeles, 1963), 1–88.

ASTBURY, R., 'Varro and Pompey', *CQ*, 17 (1967), 403–7.

BABCOCK, C.L., 'The early career of Fulvia', *AJP*, 86 (1965), 1–32.

BADIAN, E., *Foreign Clientelae, 264–70 B.C.* (Oxford, 1958).

BADIAN, E., 'M. Porcius Cato and the annexation and early administration of Cyprus', *JRS*, 55 (1965), 110–21.

BALSDON, J.P.V.D., 'Consular Provinces under the late Republic', *JRS*, 29 (1939), 57–73, 167–83.

BALSDON, J.P.V.D., 'Roman history 58–56 B.C.: three Ciceronian problems', *JRS*, 47 (1957A), 15–20.

BALSDON, J.P.V.D., 'The veracity of Caesar', *G&R*, 4 (1957B), 19–28.

BALSDON, J.P.V.D., 'Roman history 65–50 B.C.: five problems', *JRS*, 52 (1962), 134–41.

BALSDON, J.P.V.D., *Julius Caesar. A political biography* (New York, 1967).

BARDT, C., 'Die Uebergabe des Schwertes an Pompeius im Dezember 50 v. Chr.', *Hermes*, 45 (1910), 337–46.

BARWICK, K., *Caesars Bellum Civile: Tendenz, Abfassungzeit und Stil* (Leipzig, 1951).

BAYET, J., '16 août 48: la date de la mort de Pompée d'après Lucain', *Mélanges Ernout* (Paris, 1940), 5–10.

BENEDETTI, G. de, 'L'esilio di Cicerone e la sua importanza storico-politica', *Historia*, 3 (1929), 331–63, 539–68, 761–89.

BEQUIGNON, Y., 'Études thessaliennes. Le champ de bataille de Pharsale', *BCH*, 52 (1928), 9–44.

BÉQUIGNON, Y., 'Études thessaliennes, X: Nouvelles observations sur le champ de bataille de Pharsale', *BCH*, 84 (1960), 176–88.

BÉRANGER, J., 'Dans la tempête: Cicéron entre Pompée et César (50–44 av. J.-C.)', *Cahiers de la Renaissance vaudoise*, 29 (1946), 41–54.

BERCHEM, J. van, *Les distributions de blé et d'argent à la plèbe romaine sous l'empire* (Geneva, 1939).

BEVAN, E.R., *A History of Egypt under the Ptolemaic Dynasty* (London, 1927).

BIEBER, M., *The History of the Greek and Roman Theatre* (Princeton, 1939).

BINDER, M., *Studien zur Geschichte des zweiten Bürgerkrieges, besonders zum Verlauf des Januars und Februars 49 v. Chr.* (Diss. Freiburg, 1928).

BOISSIER, G., *Étude sur la vie et les ouvrages de M.T. Varro* (Paris, 1861).

BONNEAU, D., 'Nouvelles données sur la crue du Nil et la date de la mort de Pompée', *REL*, 39 (1961), 105–11.

BOREN, H.C., 'The urban side of the Gracchan economic crisis', *AHR*, 63 (1957/8), 890–902. Reprinted in Seager (1969), 54–66.

BORLE, J.P., 'Pompée et la dictature, 56–50 av. J.C.', *LEC*, 20 (1952), 168–80.

BOUCHÉ-LECLERCQ, A., *Histoire des Lagides* (Paris, 1904), vol 2 (181–30 B.C.).

BOUCHENAKI, M., 'Relations entre le royaume de Numidie et la république romaine au Ier s. av. J.C.' *RHCM*, 7 (1969), 7–9.

BROUGHTON, T.R.S., *The Magistrates of the Roman Republic* (New York, 1951–2) and *Supplement* (New York, 1960): MRR.

BRUWAENE, M. van den, 'Précisions sur la teneur et l'importance du senatusconsulte d'octobre 51 av. J.C.', *LEC*, 21 (1953), 19–27.

BURNS, A., 'Pompey's strategy and Domitius' stand at Corfinium', *Historia*, 15 (1966), 74–95.

CALDWELL, W.E., 'An estimate of Pompey', *Studies presented to D.M. Robinson* (ed. G.E. Mylonas and D. Raymond, Saint-Louis, Mo, 1953), vol 2, 954–61.

CARCOPINO, J., *Jules César* (Paris, 1968).

CARY, M., ' " Asinus germanus" ', *CQ*, 17 (1923), 103–7.

CHANDLER, D.C., 'Quaestor Ostiensis', *Historia*, 27 (1978), 328–35.

CIACERI, E., 'Le febbri di Pompeo', *Mondo Classico* (May–June 1931), 39–45.

CLERC, M., *Massilia, Histoire de Marseille dans l'antiquité*, vol 2 (Marseille, 1919).

COLLINS, H.P., 'Decline and fall of Pompey the Great', *G&R*, 22 (1952), 98–106.

COLLINS, J.H., 'Caesar as a political propagandist', *Aufstieg und Niedergang der Römischen Welt* (ed. H. Temporini, Berlin and New York, 1972), I.1.922–66.

CRAWFORD, M.H., *Roman Republican Coinage* (Cambridge, 1974): RRC.

CUFF, P.J., 'The terminal date of Caesar's Gallic command', *Historia*, 7 (1958), 445–71.

DEGRASSI, A., 'Fasti Consulares et Triumphales', *Inscriptiones Italiae*, 13.1 (Rome, 1947).

DELBRUECK, H., *Geschichte der Kriegskunst* (Berlin, 1920).

DOBIAS, J., 'Les premiers rapports des Romains avec les Parthes et l'occupation de la Syrie', *ArchOrient*, 3 (1931), 215–56.

DOREY, T.A., 'Cicero, Clodia and the *Pro Caelio*', *G&R*, 27 (1953), 175–80.

DOREY, T.A., 'Cicero and the *lex Campana*', *CR* 9 (1959), 13.

DRAGSTEDT, A., *'Cato's Politeuma'*, *Agon*, 3 (1969), 69–96.

DRUMANN, W., *Geschichte Roms in seinem Uebergange von der republikanischen zur monarchischen Verfassung* (2nd edition, revised by P. Groebe, Berlin and Leipzig, 1899–1929).

EBEL, C., 'Pompey's organization of Transalpina', *Phoenix*, 29 (1975), 358–73.

ELTON, G.R., 'The terminal date of Caesar's Gallic proconsulate', *JRS*, 36 (1946), 18–42.

FERRABINO, A., 'Curione in Africa', *Atti R. Accad. Scienze Torino*, 48 (1912–13), 157–71.

FERRERO, G., *The Life of Caesar* (New York, 1962).

FRANK, T., 'Pompey's compromise, *ad Fam.*, 8.11(3).68', *CR*, 33 (1919), 68–9.

FRANK, T., *Economic Survey of the Roman Empire*, vols 1 (Baltimore, 1933); 5 (*ib* 1940).

FRITZ, K. von, 'The mission of L. Caesar and L. Roscius in January 49 B.C.', *TAPhA*, 72 (1941), 125–56.

FRITZ, K. von, 'Pompey's policy before and after the outbreak of the civil war of 49 B.C.', *TAPhA*, 73 (1942), 145–80.

FUCHS, B., *Die Parteigruppierung im Bürgerkriege zwischen Caesar und Pompeius* (Diss. Bonn, 1920).

GABBA, E., *Republican Rome, the Army and the Allies* (translated by P.J. Cuff, Oxford, 1973).

GAGÉ, J., 'Sylla, Pompée et la théologie de la victoire', *RH*, 177 (1936), 279–342.

GELZER, M., 'Cato Uticensis', *Die Antike*, 10 (1934), 59–91.

GELZER, M., *Pompeius* (Munich, 1959; first published 1949).

GELZER, M., *Caesar: Politician and Statesman* (trans. P. Needham, Cambridge, Mass., 1968).

GELZER, M., *Cicero: Ein biographischer Versuch* (Wiesbaden, 1969).

GOELER. A., von, *Caesars gallischer Krieg und Teil seines Bürgerkrieges* (Tübingen, 1880).

GRANT, M., *Julius Caesar* (London, 1969).

GREENHALGH, P.A.L., *Early Greek Warfare* (Cambridge, 1973).

GREENHALGH, P.A.L., *The Year of the Four Emperors* (London, 1975).

GREENIDGE, A.H.J., *Roman Public Life* (London, 1901).

GRUEN, E.S., 'P. Clodius: instrument or independent agent?', *Phoenix*, 20 (1966), 120–30.

GRUEN, E.S., 'Pompey, the Roman aristocracy and the Conference of Luca', *Historia*, 18 (1969A), 71–108.

GRUEN, E.S., 'The consular elections for 53 B.C.', *Hommages à Marcel Renard* (1969B), vol 2, 311–21.

GRUEN, E.S., *The Last Generation of the Roman Republic* (Berkeley and Los Angeles, 1974).

GSELL, S., *Histoire ancienne de l'Afrique du Nord* (Paris, 1928, reprinted Osnabrück, 1972).

GWATKIN, W.E., 'Some reflections on the battle of Pharsalus', *TAPhA*, 87 (1956), 109–24.

GWATKIN, W.E., 'Pompey on the eve of Pharsalus', *CB*, 33 (1957), 39–41.

HADAS, M., *Sextus Pompey* (Columbia, 1930).

HARMAND, J., *L'armée et le soldat à Rome de 107 à 50 avant notre ère* (Paris, 1967).

HAYNE, L., 'L. Paullus and his attitude to Pompey', *AC*, 41 (1972), 148–55.

HAYNE, L., 'Who went to Luca', *CP*, 69 (1974), 217–20.

HEUZEY, L., *Les opérations militaires de J. César* (Paris, 1886).

HILL, D.K., 'The Temple above Pompey's theater', *CJ*, (1944), 360–65.

HIRSCHFELD, O., 'Der Endtermin der gallischen Statthalterschaft Caesars', *Klio*, 4 (1904), 77–88; 'Nochmals ...', 5 (1905), 236–40.

HOLMES, T. RICE, *The Roman Republic* (Oxford, 1923).

HOLZAPFEL, 'Die Anfänge des Bürgerkrieges zwischen Cäsar und Pompeius', *Klio*, 3 (1903), 213–34; 4 (1904), 327–82.

JAL, P., 'Le rôle des barbares dans les guerres civiles de Rome, de Sylla à Vespasien', *Latomus*, 21 (1962), 8–48.

JAMESON, S., 'The intended date of Caesar's return from Gaul', *Latomus*, 29 (1970), 638–60.

JONES, A.H.M., *The Roman Economy* (Oxford, 1974).

JUDEICH, W., 'Das Ende von Caesars Gallischer Statthalterschaft und der Ausbruch des Bürgerkrieges', *RhM*, 68 (1913), 1–10.

KNIGHT, D.W., 'Pompey's concern for pre-eminence after 60 B.C.', *Latomus*, 27 (1968), 878–83.

KNOCHE, U., 'Caesars *Commentarii*, ihr Gegenstand und ihre Absicht', *Gymnasium*, 58 (1951), 139–60.

KRAFT, K., 'Taten des Pompeius auf den Münzen', *JNG*, 18 (1968), 7–24.

KROMAYER, J. and VEITH, G., *Antike Schlachtfelder* (Berlin, 1903–12).

KROMAYER, J. and VEITH, G., *Schlachten-Atlas zur antiken Kriegsgeschichte* (Leipzig, 1922–9).

LACEY, W.K., 'The tribunate of Curio', *Historia*, 10 (1961), 318–29.

LACEY, W.K., *Cicero and the end of the Roman Republic* (London, 1978).

LACOUR-GAYET, G., 'P. Clodius Pulcher', *RH*, 41 (1889), 1–37.

LAZENBY, J.F., 'The Conference of Luca and the Gallic War', *Latomus*, 18 (1959), 67–76.

LEACH, J., *Pompey the Great* (London, 1978).

LEPORE, E., *Il Princeps ciceroniano e gli ideali politici della tarda repubblica* (Naples, 1954).

LINTOTT, A.W., 'P. Clodius Pulcher – Felix Catilina?', *G&R*, 14 (1967), 157–69.

LINTOTT, A.W., *Violence in Republican Rome* (Oxford, 1968).

LINTOTT, A.W., 'Lucan and the history of the Civil War', *CQ*, 21 (1971), 488–505.

LIPPOLD, G., 'Antiphilos', *MDAI(R)*, 60–1 (1953–4), 126–32.

LOUNSBURY, R.C., 'History and motive in Book Seven of Lucan's *Pharsalia*', *Hermes*, 104 (1976), 210–39.

LUCAS, F.L., 'The battlefield of Pharsalos', *ABSA*, 24 (1919–21), 34–53.

LUGLI, G., 'Albano Laziale, Scavo dell' "Albanum Pompei"', *MAL*, 7 (1946), 60–83.

LUIBHEID, C., 'The Luca Conference', *CP*, 65 (1970), 88–94.

MACKENDRICK, P.L., 'Old guard general, Pompey "the Great"', *N&C*, 9 (1966), 1–11.

MAGDELAIN, A., *Recherches sur l'imperium. La loi curiate et les auspices d'investiture* (Paris, 1968).

MAGIE, D., *Roman Rule in Asia Minor* (Princeton, 1950; reprinted New York, 1975): *RRAM*.

MAINZER, F., *Clodia: Vie de la société à la fin de la République romaine* (Paris, 1931).

MANSUELLI, G.A., *La politica di Cneo Pompeo Magno* (ed. E. Pettorelli, Bologna, 1959).

MARSH, F.B., 'The policy of Clodius from 58 to 56', *CQ*, 21 (1927), 30–6.

MARSH, F.B., 'The gangster in Roman politics', *CJ*, 28 (1932), 168–78.

MARSHALL, A.J., 'The *lex Pompeia de provinciis* (52 B.C.) and Cicero's *imperium* in 51–50 B.C.: Constitutional aspects', *Aufstieg und Niedergang der römischen Welt* (ed. H. Temporini, Berlin and New York, 1972), 1.1.887–921.

MARSHALL, B.A., 'Pompeius' temple of Hercules', *Antichthon*, 8 (1974), 80–84.

MASEFIELD, J., *The Tragedy of Pompey the Great* (1910).

McDERMOTT, W.C., 'The sisters of P. Clodius', *Phoenix*, 24 (1970), 39–47.

MEIER, C., *Res Publica Amissa* (Wiesbaden, 1966).

MELONI, P., 'Servio Sulpicio Rufo', *AFLC*, 13 (1946), 67–245.

MEYER, E., *Caesars Monarchie und das Principat des Pompeius* (Stuttgart and Berlin, 1919).

MILTNER, F., 'Cn. Pompeius Magnus', *RE*, Erste Reihe, 21.2 (1952), 2062–2211 and 2549–52; sons (2211–13; 2213–50); father (2254–62).

MITCHELL, T.N., 'Cicero before Luca', *TAPhA*, 100 (1969), 295–320.

MOMMSEN, T., 'Die Rechtsfrage zwischen Caesar und dem Senat', *Abh. der hist.-phil. Ges. in Breslau*, 1 (1857), 1–58.

MOMMSEN, T., *Römische Geschichte* (Berlin, 1888–94).

MUELLER, A.C., *Untersuchungen zu Caesars italischem Feldzug 49 v. Chr.: Chronologie und Quellen* (Diss. München, 1973).

MÜNZER, F., *Römische Adelsparteien und Adelsfamilien* (Stuttgart, 1920; reprinted 1963).

NAPOLEON III, *Vie de César* (Paris, 1865).

NASH, E., *Pictorial Dictionary of Ancient Rome* (London, 1968).

NEUENDORFF, A., *Die römischen Konsulwahlen von 78–49 v. Chr.* (Breslau, 1913).

NIMTZ, H., *Römische Innenpolitik vom Beginn des Konflikts zwischen Caesar und Pompeius bis zur Schlacht von Mutina* (Diss. Heidelberg, 1954).

NISSEN, H., 'Der Ausbruch des Bürgerkriegs 49 v. Chr.', *HZ*, 44 (1880), 409–45; 46 (1881), 48–105.

OMAN, C.W.C., *Seven Roman Statesmen of the Later Republic* (London, 1903).

OOST, S.I., 'Cato Uticensis and the annexation of Cyprus', *CP*, 50 (1955), 98–112.

OOTEGHEM, J. van, *Pompée le Grand, bâtisseur d'empire* (Brussels, 1954).

PARKER, H.M.D., *The Roman Legions* (Oxford, 1928; revised Cambridge, 1958).

PELLING, C.B.R., 'Pharsalus', *Historia*, 22 (1973), 249–59.

PLATNER, S.B., and ASHBY, T., *A Topographical Dictionary of Ancient Rome* (Oxford, 1929).

POCOCK, L.G., 'Publius Clodius and the Acts of Caesar', *CQ*, 18 (1924), 59–65.

POCOCK, L.G., 'A note on the policy of P. Clodius', *CQ*, 19 (1925), 182–4.

POCOCK, L.G., '*Pompeiusve parem*', *CP*, 22 (1927), 301–6.

POCOCK, L.G., 'What made Pompeius fight in 49 B.C. ?', *G&R*, 6 (1959), 68–81.

RAAFLAUB, K., *Dignitatis Contentio: Studien zur Motivation und politischen Taktik im Bürgerkrieg zwischen Caesar und Pompeius* (Munich, 1974).

RAAFLAUB, K., 'Caesar und die Friedensverhandlungen zu Beginn des Bürgerkrieges von 49 v. Chr.', *Chiron*, 5 (1975), 247–300.

RAMBAUD, M., *L'art de la déformation historique dans les Commentaires de César* (*Ann. de l'Univ. de Lyon*, 3rd series, fasc. 3. Paris, 1953).

RAMBAUD, M., 'L'apologie de Pompée par Lucain au livre VII de la Pharsale', *REL*, 33 (1955A), 258–96.

RAMBAUD, M., 'Le soleil de Pharsale', *Historia*, 3 (1955B), 346–78.

RAWSON, B., 'Pompey and Hercules', *Antichthon*, 4 (1970), 30–37.

RAWSON, E., 'The eastern clientelae of Clodius and the Claudii', *Historia*, 22 (1973), 219–39.

RAWSON, E., *Cicero* (London, 1975).

ROWLAND, R.J., 'The number of grain recipients in the late Republic', *Acta Antiqua*, 13 (1965), 81–3.

ROYER, J.P., 'Le problème des dettes à la fin de la république romaine', *RD*, 45 (1967), 191–240 and 407–50.

RUTZ, W., 'Lucans Pompeius', *AU*, 9 (1968), 1, 5–22.

SANFORD, E.M., 'The career of Aulus Gabinius', *TAPhA*, 70 (1939), 64–92.

SANFORD, F.W., 'The narrative in the eighth book of the "Gallic War", chapters 50–55: a study in chronology', *University Studies* (Lincoln, Nebraska), 11 (1911), no. 4.

SAUNDERS, C., 'The political sympathies of Servius Sulpicius Rufus', *CR*, 37 (1923), 55–68.

SCHMIDT, O.E., 'Der Ausbruch des Bürgerkriegs im J. 49 v. Chr.', *RhM*, 47 (1892), 241–68.

SCHMIDT, O.E., *Der Briefwechsel des M. Tullius Cicero* (Leipzig, 1893).

SEAGER, R., 'Clodius, Pompey and the exile of Cicero', *Latomus*, 24 (1965), 519–31.

SEAGER, R. (ed.), *The Crisis of the Roman Republic* (Cambridge, 1969).

SEAGER, R., *Pompey: A Political Biography* (Oxford, 1979).

SHACKLETON BAILEY, D.R., 'Exspectatio Corfiniensis', *JRS*, 46 (1956), 57–63. Reprinted (modified) in *Cicero's Letters to Atticus*, vol. 4, Appendix 4, 448–59.

SHACKLETON BAILEY, D.R., 'The credentials of L. Caesar and L. Roscius', *JRS*, 50 (1960A), 80–83. Reprinted in *Cicero's Letters to Atticus*, vol 4, Appendix 3, 441–7.

SHACKLETON BAILEY, D.R., 'The Roman nobility in the Second Civil War', *CQ*, 10 (1960B), 253–67.

SHACKLETON BAILEY, D.R., *Cicero's Letters to Atticus* (Cambridge, 1965–8): SB, *Att.*

SHACKLETON BAILEY, D.R., 'The prosecution of Roman magistrates-elect', *Phoenix*, 24 (1970), 162–5.

SHACKLETON BAILEY, D.R., *Cicero* (London, 1971).

SHACKLETON BAILEY, D.R., *Cicero: Epistulae ad Familiares* (vol 1, Cambridge, 1977): SB, *Fam.*

SHATZMAN, I., 'The Egyptian Questions in Roman politics (59–54 B.C.)', *Latomus*, 30 (1971), 363–9.

SHERWIN-WHITE, A.N., *The Roman Citizenship* (Oxford, 1939).

SIMPSON, A.D., 'The departure of Crassus for Parthia', *TAPhA*, 49 (1938), 532–41.

SMITH, R.E., *Cicero the Statesman* (Cambridge, 1966).

STEVENS, C.E., 'The terminal date of Caesar's command', *AJPh* (1938), 169–208.

STOCKER, A.F., 'The *legis dies* of Caesar's command in Gaul', *CJ*, 56 (1961), 242–8.

STOCKTON, D., 'Cicero and the *Ager Campanus*', *TAPhA*, 93 (1962), 471–89.

STOCKTON, D., *Cicero, A Political Biography* (London, 1971).

STOCKTON, D., '*Quis iustius induit arma?*', *Historia*, 24 (1975), 232–59.

STOFFEL, E.G.H.C., *Histoire de Jules César, Guerre civile* (Paris, 1887).

STONE, C.G., 'March 1, 50 B.C.', *CQ*, 22 (1928), 193–201.

SYME, R., 'The allegiance of Labienus', *JRS*, 28 (1938), 113–25.

SYME, R., *The Roman Revolution* (Oxford, 1939).

TAYLOR, L.R., 'Labienus and the status of the Picene town Cingulum', *CR*, 35 (1921), 158–9.

TAYLOR, L.R., *Party Politics in the Age of Caesar* (Berkeley, 1949; reprinted 1975).

TYRRELL, R.Y. and PURSER, L.C., *The Correspondence of M. Tullius Cicero* (Dublin and London, 1904–33): T-P.

TYRRELL, W.B., *Military and Political Career of T. Labienus* (Diss. Washington, 1970).

TYRRELL, W.B., 'Labienus' departure from Caesar in January 49 B.C., *Historia*, 21 (1972), 424–40.

VEITH, G., 'Corfinium, eine kriegsgeschichtliche Studie', *Klio*, 13 (1913), 1–26.

VEITH, G., *Der Feldzug von Dyrrhachium zwischen Caesar und Pompejus* (Vienna, 1920).

VEITH, G.,'Zu den Kämpfen der Caesarianer in Illyrien', *Strena Buliciana* (Zagreb, 1924), 267–74.

VOLPONI, M., 'M. Celio Rufo ingeniose nequam', *Mem. Ist. Lombardo Cl. di Lett.*, 31, 3 (1970), 197–280.

WARD, A.M., *Marcus Crassus and the Late Republic* (Columbia and London, 1977).

WEINRIB, E.J.,'The prosecution of magistrates-designate', *Phoenix*, 25 (1971), 149–50.

WEINSTOCK, S., 'Victor and invictus', *HThR*, 50 (1957), 211–47.

WILLIAMS, R.S., *Aulus Gabinius: a political biography* (Diss. Michigan State University, East Lansing, 1973: microfilm).

YAVETZ, Z., 'The living conditions of the urban plebs in republican Rome', *Latomus*, 17 (1958), 500–17. Reprinted in Seager (1969), 162–79.

ZIEGLER, K.H., *Die Beziehungen zwischen Rom und dem Partherreich* (Wiesbaden, 1964).

ZIPPEL, G., *Die römische Herrschaft in Illyrien bis auf Augustus* (Leipzig, 1877).

# LIST OF QUOTATIONS

The following list gives the sources page by page of all direct quotations (whether the author's name is specified or not) and all citations of authors by name in the text. (Readers who are not familiar with the literary sources for this period will find a brief introduction to them in the first volume of this biography, *Pompey: The Roman Alexander*.)

60  Plut *Cras* 16.3–4
    Vell 2.46.2
    App *BC* 2.18
61  Plut *Cras* 16.1–5
    Dio 39.39.5
62  *ib.* 39.53.1
    Plut *P* 53.1
    *id. Cras* 16.1
    Dio 39.39.2
63  *ib.* 39.29.1
    Cic *Fam* 7.1
    *id. Att* 4.13
    *id. Fam* 5.8
    *id. QF* 2.11 (13), 13
    (15A), 14 (15B)
64  *ib.* 14 (15B), 13 (15A)
    *id. Att* 4.16
    *id. Fam* 1.9.21
    *id. Att* 4.15
65  Plut *P* 53.4–5
    Dio 39.64
66  *ib.*
    Cic *Att* 4.17 (18)
67  *id. Fam* 1.9.19
    *id. QF* 3.2
    *ib.* 3.9
    *id. Att* 4.18
    *ib.* + *QF* 3.4
68  *ib.*
    *id. QF* 2.13 (15A)
    *ib.* 3.7
    Dio 39.61.2
    Cic *Att* 4.19
69  *id. QF* 3.8
    *ib.* 3.9
    *ib.* 3.1
    *ib.* 3.4
    *ib.* 3.9 (quoting Homer
    *Iliad* 4.182)
    Müller *Frags Cic* 291
70  Dio 39.63.5
    Cic *QF* 3.1 *ib.* 3.4
    *id. Fam* 1.9.19
    *id. Att* 4.18
    (*cf. QF* 3.4)
71  Dio 40.45.4–5
72  App *BC* 2.20
    Plut *P* 54.2–3
    Dio 40. 46.1
73  *ib.* 40.46.2
    Asc 30 (Clark)
    Plut *P* 54.1–2
    App *BC* 2.19
74  Plut *Solon* 14
75  Asc 31 (Clark)
    Dio 40.48.2
76  Asc 32 (Clark)
    Dio 40.49.1, 3
77  Asc 33 (Clark)
    *ib.* 43
78  Cic *Mil* 95
    (*cf. QF* 3.9)

78  Asc 35 (Clark)
    *ib.* 51
    App *BC* 2.22
79  *ib.*
    Asc 34 (Clark)
    Caes *BG* 7.1, 6
80  Cic *Mil* 67–8
    Plut *P* 54.3–4
    App *BC* 2.23
82  Dio 40.52.2
    Asc 38 (Clark)
83  Dio 40.52.3
    Asc 38 (Clark)
    Catullus 43.7
    (*cf.* 86.5–6)
    *ib.* 3; 68.70
    Quint 8.6.53
    (*cf.* Cic *Cael* 63)
84  Asc 36 (Clark)
85  *ib.* 40
86  *ib.* 40–2
    Dio 40.54.2
    *ib.* 40.53.2–3
    Cic *Mil* 79
87  App *BC* 2.23
    Dio 40.52.3–4
    App *BC* 2.25
    Plut *P* 55.4, 6
    Tac *Ann* 3.28
88  Plut *P* 55.4; 55.1–3
    Dio 40.51.1
89  Cic *Att* 8.3
90  *id. Phil* 2.24
    (*cf. Att* 7.6)
    *id. Att* 7.3
    *ib.* 7.1
    App *BC* 2.23
    Dio 40.56
91  *ib.*
    Caes *BC* 1.85
92  App *BC* 2.25, 28
    Dio 40.46.2
93  Cic *Att* 8.9
    *id. Rep* 5.5, 8–9; 6.1, 12
    App *BC* 2.25
95  *ib.* 25–6
    Suet *J* 28
    Dio 40.59.1
96  Hirt *BG* 8.53
    Cael *Fam* 8.1
    Cic *Att* 5.2
97  *ib.* 5.6
    Cael *Fam* 8.1
    Cic *Fam* 2.8
    *id. Att* 5.7
    *ib.* 5.11
98  *ib.*
    App *BC* 2.26
    (*cf.* Plut *Caes* 29)
99  Cael *Fam* 8.1
    *ib.* 8.4
    Dio 40.59.2

100  Cael *Fam* 8.4
     App *BC* 2.26
     Dio 40.59.4
101  Hirt *BG* 8.44, 46
     Cael *Fam* 8.9
103  *ib.* 8.9
     *ib.* 8.5
     *ib.* 8.8
104  *ib.*
106  *ib.*
     Cic *Fam* 3.8
     Cael *Fam* 8.8
107  *ib.*
108  Cic *Fam* 2.10
     Cael *Fam* 8.16
     Cic *Att* 6.6
     *ib.* 5.2
     Lucan 1.9–12
109  Homer *Iliad* 18.309
     (quoted Cic *Att* 7.8)
     Vell 2.48.3
     Cael *Fam* 8.4
110  *ib.* 8.6
     Dio 40.60–2
     App *BC* 2.26
     Cic *Fam* 2.13
     Lucan 4.814–15
     Pliny *NH* 36.116–20
111  Lucan 4.816–24
     App *BC* 2.27
112  *ib.*
     Cic *Att* 6.3
     Cael *Fam* 8.11
113  *ib.*
114  *ib.*
     Cic *Att* 6.3
     Vell 2.48
     Plut *P* 57.1–3
115  App *BC* 2.28
116  *ib.*
     Cic *Att* 8.9
     Suet *J* 29
     App *BC* 2.28–9
117  *ib.* 2.29
     Cael *Fam* 8.13
     *ib.* 8.8
     *ib.* 8.11
118  Cic *Att* 7.7
     Cael *Fam* 8.13
     *ib.* 8.14
     *ib.* 8.8
119  *ib.* 8.14
     Cic *Att* 7.2
     Dio 40.30.2
     Cic *Att* 7.1
     Caes *BC* 1.9
120  Plut *P* 57.4–5
121  Cael *Fam* 8.14
122  Cic *Att* 7.3
     Cael *Fam* 8.14
     Dio 40.63–4
123  Cic *Att* 7.1

187 Lucan 4.572-3, 462, 549-
    50
189 ib. 4.716-17, 799-803
    Caes BC 2.38, 44
190 ib. 3.3-4
    App BC 2.49
    Plut P 64.1
191 Lucan 3.287-90
    Caes BC 3.4
    App BC 2.49
    Plut P 64.1-2
192 Lucan 5.17-34 (abr.)
193 Dio 41.43.1-5
    Lucan 5.13-14, 45-9
194 App BC 2.50-2
    Caes BC 3.5
195 App BC 2.52, 48
    Dio 41.44.1
    Caes BC 3.5
197 Lucan 5.727-47
198 ib. 5.808-15
    Caes BC 3.10-11, 13
199 ib. 3.11-12
    App BC 2.54-5
200 Caes BC 3.13, 10
    Dio 41.47.2
    Plut P 65.4
201 Caes BC 3.8, 73, 14
    Dio 41.44.4
202 Caes BC 3.14, 9
203 ib. 3.8, 15-17
204 ib. 3.17-18
    App BC 2.57-8
    Dio 41.48.1
205 Caes BC 3.23-5
206 ib. 3.26-7
209 ib. 3.34
210-11 ib. 3.42
212 ib. 3.47, 45
213 ib. 3.45
214 ib. 3.46, 45
215 ib. 3.47
    Lucan 6.106-17
216 ib. 6.94-7
217 Caes BC 3.52
    Dio 41.50.3
    App BC 2.60
    Lucan 6.129-39
218 Caes BC 3.53
    Lucan 6.132, 154, 170-2
    Dio 41.50.4
219 Caes BC 3.49
    (cf. 3.47)
    Plut Caes 40.2, 39.6
    Caes BC 3.55
220 ib. 3.61, 44
    Dio 41.51.1
    App BC 2.61
222 Caes BC 3.65, 67
223 ib. 3.67, 69

224 ib. 3.68, 72-3
225 ib. 3.66, 70, 73
    App BC 2.61
    Plut Caes 39.5
    (cf. P 65.5; App BC 2.62)
226 Lucan 6.299-305
    Caes BC 3.71
    Dio 41.52.1
227 Plut Caes 39.5, 40.2, 39.6
    App BC 2.63 (cf. 2.65)
    Caes BC 3.73-4
228 Plut P 74.1
229 id. Cic 38.5
    Cic Fam 9.9
230 Plut Cic 38.2
    Cic Att 11.4A
    Caes BC 3.74, 78, 75
    App BC 2.65
231 Caes BC 3.76
232 Plut Caes 39.9
    Caes BC 3.78
233 Plut P 66.4
    App BC 2.65
    Dio 41.52.2
234 Plut P 66.5
    Lucan 6.319-22
    App BC 2.65
235 Plut P 66.5, 67.2-3
    Lucan 6.319-29
    App BC 2.67, 65
    Plut Caes 41.2
236 Dio 41.52.3
    Caes BC 3.79
238 ib. 3.31-2
    Plut P 66.5
239-40 Caes BC 3.57, 36
    Dio 41.51.2-3
    App BC 2.60
241 Caes BC 3.79-80
    Plut Caes 41.6
242 Caes BC 3.81-2
243 ib. 3.84-6
244 Plut P 67.1, 67.4
    App BC 2.67
    Caes BC 3.82
    Lucan 7.123-7
245 ib. 7.86 + 93
    Caes BC 3.81
    App BC 2.65-6, 69
    Plut P 76.2
246 Caes BC 3.101
    Dio 42.1.2
    ib. 41.56.1-57.2
    Plut P 68.4
247 Lucan 7.251
    App 2.70-1
248 Caes BC 3.89, 88
    Plut P 69.1
249 App BC 2.75
    Caes BC 3.88, 86

249 Front Strat 2.3.22
250 Caes BC 3.86
    Plut P 69.2-3
    id. Caes 45.2-3
    App BC 2.76
    (cf. Florus 2.13.50)
251 Caes BC 3.90
    App BC 2.76, 78
    Caes BC 3.92
    (cf. Plut Caes 44.8; P
    69.5)
    Montaigne, Essays &
    Letters (ed. Hazlitt,
    London, 1923) 2.170-2
    Caes BC 3.93
252 Dio 41.59.1
253 Caes BC 3.94
    (cf. Plut P 72.1-2; App
    BC 2.81)
    Homer Iliad 11.544-6
254 Caes BC 3.96
    Dio 42.2.3
    (cf. App BC 2.81
256 Plut P 174.2-3
    Lucan 8.72-85
257 ib. 8.88-105
    Caes BC 3.102
258 Lucan 8.134-7, 256-7,
    251
    App BC 2.83
    Caes BC 3.102
    Florus 1.41.14
    Plut P 76.1
259 ib. 76.1, 3
    Lucan 8.266-71
    Caes BC 3.102
260 ib. 3.106
    Plut P 76.3-6
    App BC 2.83
    Lucan 8.279-327
    (cf. Florus 2.13.52; Vell
    2.53)
    Dio 42.2.5-6
261 Caes BC 3.82, 31
    Dio 42.2.5
    (cf. 41.55.3-4)
    Plut P 76.2
262 Caes BC 3.106
    App BC 2.83
263 Plut P 77.2, 4
    Dio 42.5.4
    Caes BC 3.103
264 Lucan 8.484-501, 519-24
    Caes BC 3.104
    (cf. Dio 42.4.1)
265 Vell 2.53.3
268 Dio 41.54.1-2
    App BC 1.55
    Cic Att 11.6
269 Lucan 9.190-206

# INDEX

*Note:* After locating a reference in the text through this index the reader should also consult the detailed notes to the appropriate chapter.